UNIQUELY GIFTED:

D1235634

Identifying and Meeting the Needs of Twice-Exceptional Students

DISCARDED

edited by
Keisa Kay

UNIQUELY GIFTED
IDENTIFYING AND MEETING THE NEEDS
OF TWICE-EXCEPTIONAL CHILDREN

Published by: Avocus Publishing Inc.
4 White Brook Rd.
Gilsum, NH 03448
Telephone: 800-345-6665
Fax: 603-357-2073
email: pbs@pathwaybook.com
www. avocus.com

All rights reserved. No part of this book may be reproduced or transmitted in any form or by any means, electronic or mechanical, including photocopying, recording or by any information storage and retrieval system without the permission of the authors or editors and Avocus Publishing, except for brief quotations.

Disclaimer:
Nothing in this book is intended in any way to be libelous in nature. Neither is it the intent of Avocus Publishing, Inc. to publish any accusatory statement, direct or implied, of improper motives or illegal actions by any individual or educational institution. Any other interpretation of our printing is erroneous and therefore misunderstood. We believe that the public interest in general, and education in particular, will be better served by the publication of the authors' experiences and opinions.

Copyright © 2000 by Avocus Publishing, Inc.

Printed in the United States of America

ISBN 1-890765-04-X: 34.95 Softcover

Dedication
For Benjamin and Ameli,
with love and admiration
I would not change a thing about you—not a single thing.

ACKNOWLEDGMENTS

This book began with hope, as my family sought resources for our two brilliant, creative children. Thanks go to Clark Cyr, Benjamin Cyr, and Ameli Cyr for their unrelenting love. Dr. Linda Kreger Silverman has been of incredible value to my family through every step of the educational process. Her writing, research, and personal commitment to giftedness have been inspirational. Thanks to her and to the staff of the Gifted Development Center, 1452 Marion Street, Denver, Colorado. Annette Revel Sheely, Harriet Austin, Cindy Kalman, Sheryl Shafer, Denitta Ward, Stephanie Tolan, and Kris King have provided insight and perspective at crucial junctures. Thanks also to Leila Levi, Suzy Stevenson Ryan, Darrell Preston, Vic Contoski, the Ray Family, the Ward Family, Marlo Payne Rice, Joan Graham, Carol Heimann, Barbara Gilman, Chris Perkins, Kathy Miles, Brian Daldorph, Rebecca Hein, Michelle Bierstadt, the Boulder Parents of Gifted Offspring group, the PG-List, and the GT-Special online group. Sue Ellen Webber Turscak, Kathleen Larkin Britt-Wilburn, Sachiko Imamura, Carol Hammon, and Judy Defelice provided support before this work began. Chris Turnbull-Grimes, Karen Petterson, Caroline Evans, Kathy Littlejohn, Barry Hoonan, Darrow Chan, Jeffrey Anker, Dr. H. Richard Winn, Holly Daley, and Portia Hinshaw have illuminated pathways for my family.

This book blossomed from my first month as guest editor for *Highly Gifted Children*, the newsletter of the Hollingworth Center for Highly Gifted Children. Kathi Kearney and Jill Howard's editorial insights influenced the earliest stages. Open Space Communications, Inc., also offered early encouragement. Craig Thorn, editor in chief at Avocus Publishing, provided superb suggestions and support throughout the process of bringing ideas to fruition.

TABLE OF CONTENTS

FOREWORD:

TOGETHER WE CAN CREATE PROGRESS!

by Kiesa Kay

She can think, but she can't write. He can write, but he can't sit still. Gifted children who think differently sometimes have big trouble in class, especially as middle school and high school approach. Lists of brilliant, creative thinkers who haven't made the grades in school abound, and many of these thinkers have disabilities of one kind or another. These disabilities, while frustrating in the school setting, can become the pathways to original, creative thought and intuitive leaps that lead to excellence well beyond the boundaries of the schoolhouse walls. Working together, we can find ways to help these students flourish in schools that more often than not are a hindrance and not a help.

Schools traditionally do not address twice exceptionality successfully for reasons that can vary as much as individual students do. Identifying these students can be problematic, as their strengths often mask their areas of lesser ability. A highly gifted or profoundly gifted learner often looks about average in overall skills when other factors restrict the expression of what that child really knows. Even students who obtain identification often find that no programs exist for their unique constellations of learning needs.

Parents, teachers, and administrators sometimes squabble about the learning plans of brilliant children who have special needs. When Dr. Galen Alessi informally surveyed several groups of psychologists, he learned that in 5,000 cases, the professionals identified children's learning problems as existing solely within the child and family, in ways that could not be resolved by school change ("Diagnosis Diagnosed: A Systemic Reaction," *Professional School Psychology* 3(2):145–151). Not one of the psychologists would admit that any existing problems were due to school-related factors. Since they wanted to keep their jobs, they blamed the children instead of looking for administrative or teaching problems (Wright, 1999).

Alessi maintains that a child may have trouble because the child has been misplaced in the curriculum; the teacher may not be implementing effective practices; the administrators may not be effective; the parents might not be effective; or the child may have physical and/or psychological problems. However, all psychologists in the informal survey placed the blame on the children, implying that no need existed anywhere to improve teaching, administration, or management. Pamela Darr Wright, in "Educational Problems: It's the Kid's Fault" (www.ldonline.org), suggests that every parent obtain outside assessment for children, because the school systems can't be trusted to monitor their own efficacy.

The existing assessment model has been to decry the intelligence, excellence, and learning capacity of the child, in order to protect the status quo of the schoolroom learning environment. In a democracy, majority rules. Geniuses are a definite minority. When intellectual genius blends with specialized learning needs, the chances of real help and learning for the child tend to disappear. Even with adequate outside testing, though, parents often spend their own money to discover their child's learning needs, only to find that the system remains unresponsive to those needs.

Even students who obtain identification often find that no programs exist for their unique constellations of learning needs. Parents, teachers, and administrators sometimes squabble about the learning plans of brilliant children who have special needs. One serious problem is the lack of training on how to teach special-needs students. "Does it matter what learning style Max has, if the teachers only know one way to teach?" asked Dana Lear, parent of a gifted child. In addition, the curricular program frequently does not match the kinesthetic learner because it focuses on the student's passive relationship to a lecture style and abbreviated exposure to topics that are not connected. The kinesthetic learners have little chance in the traditional lecture class.

Some minority groups of gifted learners, including African American, Hispanic American, and Native American, have been underrepresented in gifted programs. The twice-exceptional gifted learner from a minority group is not likely to receive any identification or services. Students of lower socioeconomic status frequently receive encouragement to find jobs rather than continue education. Profoundly gifted children also receive discouraging, disparaging comments when they strive to reach their fullest potential.

Twice-exceptional children thrive with special attention that requires energy and imagination. "Extremely high intelligence often comes with quirks that require great tolerance from the supervising teacher; these tend to diminish as the child matures into young adulthood, especially when those around the child respond calmly," say Mary Anna Thornton and Marilyn Wallace, "The Total Teacher for the Total Child," *UOG*, vol. 11, no. 1, Fall 1998. Sometimes those quirks reflect asynchrony, with below age-level skills in some areas, and skills at double the age in other areas. Although the Children's Defense Fund estimates that one in every twelve children has a disability, anecdotal evidence points to a different blend among profoundly gifted children. In a group of twenty-seven families with profoundly gifted children, one-third of the children had been identified with a disability, most typically sensory integration dysfunction, visual processing deficits, or attention deficit disorder.

Unfortunately, as long as schools continue to blame children for their own learning differences instead of accommodating and celebrating those differences, education will stagnate in this country. The problems intensify in the middle and high school years. At that age, making friends sometimes becomes more important than making the grades, anyway.

". . . peer conformity with anti-learning friends can be a terrible waste of educational opportunity," says Dr. James Alvino, *Parenting for High Potential,* National Association for Gifted Children, March 1997, p. 13.

Leta Stetter Hollingworth has estimated that gifted children waste a large percentage of their time learning nothing in the regular classroom. For the child with twice-exceptional needs, wasting all that lifetime becomes excruciating. Yet the system blames the child, identifies the child as the culprit, and emphasizes methods of making that child fit into an inappropriate structure for that child's learning needs. It's time to recognize that the child need not fit into an unrelentingly destructive structure for that child's own mind and imagination.

"When teachers or parents fail to understand highly creative individuals, refusal to learn or withdrawal may be a consequence," says E. Paul Torrance in "Are There Tops in Our Cages?" *American Vocational Journal,* vol. 38, no. 3, pp. 20–22. "The highly creative person has an unusually strong urge to explore and to create. When he or she thinks up ideas, or tests them and modifies them, he or she has an unusually strong desire to communicate these ideas and to tell others what they have discovered. Yet both peers and teachers named some of the most creative students in our studies as ones who do not speak out their ideas; there is little wonder they are reluctant to communicate their ideas. Frequently, their ideas are so far ahead of those of their classmates and even their teachers that they have given up hopes of communicating" (Torrance, *AVJ*).

Referring a 2E (twice-exceptional) child into a program for children with disabilities often makes no sense. They learn so fast. Referring that child into a program for gifted children without individualized support can be inadequate. A new revolution must occur in education, a revolution that celebrates the individual and differences.

Mentor relationships work. Individual education plans that figure out how to make the child miserable and make the child turn in meaningless assignments in a way that fits the teacher's needs for conformity—those things don't work. Are we teaching standards or children here? Standards-based education has become another cruel hoax for children who actually love learning.

Yet what is a teacher supposed to do? In the current public school system, one teacher has twenty-five or thirty students to teach for an hour, before she gets a whole new group and begins again—and again—five or six times a day. How is that single teacher supposed to adjust the classroom curriculum to meet the individual learning needs of all those children? She's doing well if she knows their names, let alone their learning styles.

Many children just don't learn in fifty- or sixty-minute bursts. By the time they settle into the material, by the time their minds begin to make those enormous leaps of logic and intuition that facilitate understanding, it's time for the class hour to change. Then, they go into a completely different class, with new material, new rules. When did school begin to take on the traits of television viewing? Why do we tolerate it? It's because it's easy for the administrators to organize full coverage of standards that way, and it's the way things have been done in the past. Change can create too much trouble, too much work for teachers and political risk for administrators who struggle to keep their own programs going.

This book brings together some of the most recent thought on how to create what's needed for these students. Section One offers some real-time stories from parents, siblings, and students. Section Two offers teaching insights. Section Three addresses the latest research into these matters, and Section Four discusses how school administrators approach the task at hand.

By blending these diverse views, I hope to motivate an upsurge of understanding for twice-exceptional learners. The learners themselves are not the problem. They are not to blame. They deserve an education—a free, appropriate education—that takes diverse learning styles into consideration. Before it can happen, teachers have to learn to teach differently, in order to reach learners who learn differently. Administrators must finance and support mentorships and programs that will allow the finest minds to blossom. Parents must allow their children to learn in their own ways, and recognize when a struggle comes not from laziness, but from a real difference in learning style and needs. Students must survive whatever educational experiences befall them, until they reach that point where they're allowed to learn and grow in their own ways.

Adolescents, especially, crave peer support and a place to call home in the classroom. The twice-exceptional learner often would prefer to fit in with the gang than to be known for any special trait or ability. As they establish identity, being different can mean being ostracized from social settings.

For many 2E learners, the fitting finally happens in college. They find peer groups with like interests, mentors with the same concerns, and educational excellence. Too many of them, though, don't make it that far. We can do better. We must. We need the intuitive, brilliant minds of our 2E children to survive the doldrums and missteps of our current educational system. We must find ways to bring in the dawn for the next generation of geniuses.

Dr. Linda Kreger Silverman, in her 1989 article, "Invisible Gifts, Invisible Handicaps," suggested that entrance IQ criteria for gifted students with learning disabilities be dropped 10 points, and that scores where abilities are not affected by disabilities should be given more weight in the evaluations. Doors would open to more twice-exceptional students then. Even so, more work remains. These doors must open onto new vistas, not closed rooms. I would like for this book to open and intensify the dialogue among teachers, administrators, researchers, parents, and students on what works and what doesn't for those brilliant, beautiful children who color outside the lines. Parents of gifted children often don't know how the school system works or what to expect from hardworking, overextended teachers. Many parents have not heard of the laws that protect children with disabilities, like Section 504 of the Rehabilitation Act or the Individuals with Disabilities in Education Act. At the same time, parents of gifted children often are gifted themselves. They care about their children, and they learn very quickly.

If parental love and support could combine with teaching excellence, administrative discourse, and the best of research available, we could find answers for our 2E children. First, we must admit that the system that predominates has not worked for twice-exceptional students. We must work together to create a new paradigm, a pedagogical approach that celebrates brilliance, creativity, and the minds that think in patterns beyond the pale.

FAMILY MATTERS:
PERSPECTIVES FROM FAMILY MEMBERS

Before the diagnosis, before the teaching, before kindergarten, twice-exceptional students are born into families. Often, the family members, too, have both giftedness and disabilities. Many of the strongest advocates for children are single mothers, running in all directions to meet the needs of their children. In my family, each disability brings its own gift. One family member has epilepsy and arteriovenous malformation; he's also a profoundly gifted genius. Dealing with the seizures and the brain surgery exhausts everybody. We've become really tired of the inside of the emergency room. Yet, in some cultures, people with epilepsy are considered to be more spiritually powerful than other people, more in tune with the unseen magic in the world. A student of mine once told me that having epilepsy meant that she couldn't be shallow. She knew what it meant to survive and to value life, because things could change so suddenly.

The same characteristics that give flight to an ADD diagnosis also imbue one of my children with an intuitive, creative depth that's fascinating. Sensory integration disorder, which is rare in the general population, is surprisingly common among highly gifted children. These family members share their personal journeys.

LIGHTS IN THE FOG:
LIVING IN A TWICE-EXCEPTIONAL FAMILY

by Benjamin Cyr

I had just entered my fourth-grade classroom, smiling oddly as I felt face upon face turn and steal a glance at me, the new kid. I felt my cheeks burning hot, like a freshly melded black-smith's tool, but proceeded to my seat. It had been two weeks since the beginning of the school year, and one day following my decision to skip third grade after multiple hours of lethally monotonous work in the classroom.

My new teacher walked up to me. I remember the first conversation we had:

"Ben, you know why you were moved up, don't you?"

I looked at her vacantly. "Because I'm smart."

"But why were you moved up instead of all the other kids in your previous class?"

In short, this question had me stumped. Though I raced mental fingers across the rough fabric of my well-baled tapestry of a brain, I could not, for the life of me, find out why I had moved up.

These days, however, it's next to impossible to avoid the reasons why I moved up, and why, even to this day, quick insights and a strange wit I carry in conversation garnish my life. These qualities are true with many a person with my malady, however. I have ADD, a disorder that feeds creativity and draws from analytical reasoning. I also was identified as a gifted learner, long before anyone suspected that I had ADD. The traits are intertwined for me. I can't stand to be bored, and I rarely think in straight lines.

My family has influenced me the most—intellectually as well as emotionally—more than any other group of people I've known. This idea makes obvious sense, but the fact that each member of my family is wildly smart yet saddled with a different disability makes my situation unique.

Blessed with a twice-exceptional family, I have gained a better sense of compassion as well as intelligence, as one cannot usually adorn themselves with the ability to understand, endure, and love wide ranges of both furious intellect and certain mental challenges at such an early stage in life as I have. By sharing my life with a twice-exceptional family, I have gained a keener perception of forbearance alongside a heightened appreciation of intellect in any given person I meet.

For instance, my sister and I share a link between both our intellectual capabilities as well as our learning differences. While my beautiful eight-year-old genius of a sibling provides a home for sensory integration disorder—a condition that affects even the simple physical realms of writing, playing an instrument, or throwing a ball, a disability that differs drastically from my own ADD—we both stumble our ways across the spectrum of organization and neatness. Though we both attempt to contain this annoying habitual nuisance, it's extremely difficult to do so, and time and again, I grow closer to her as a brother when we clean together, do homework together, and get ready for school in the morning as a pair. In this way, our sibling relationship will forever reside in an unbreakable bond.

Likewise, though our types of brilliance differ quite a bit from each other—she's the poster analytical child, a squire to subjects in the areas of math and science, and I am more the creative type—we combine to create a fiercely passionate problem-solving team. Her critical reasoning is, at times, unmatched for someone her age, and my insights can add undercurrents to our simplest conversations.

These academic life skills would not have been recognized and nourished, though, had not my loving parents brought attention to some special needs that our thinking styles require. My attention deficit disorder makes it easy for me to forget little, trivial things that quickly begin to add up and hurt me in the scholastic world. ADD, as it is commonly called, is a renegade-type disorder, in that if I am bored or don't want to discuss or go over certain topics, my brain simply shuts out whoever or whatever wishes for me to participate in them. I'll look out windows during lectures, for example, or find myself playing solitaire during unorganized class periods where homework or other long-term assignments are to be worked on in class.

It was instances like those that brought my family to the conclusion that my life needed structure and reassurance if I were to succeed. This idea led to the formation of the 504 Plan, an academic ordinance of sorts that allows people with ADD and other disabilities some small but invaluable privileges, like a textbook for each of my classes both to take home as well as to leave in school, and extra teacher care and assistance. I thrive on the opportunity to delve into meaningful projects.

Extra care and assistance also are the main ingredients that my sister requires for success with her sensory integration disorder, dubbed "SI." SI gives my sister Ameli a strange form of claustrophobia, since she is extremely sensitive to physical touch and can literally feel contacted by someone who is just standing near her. This fact unfortunately leads to some components of highly sensitive behavior, so those around her must commit themselves to emitting something of a pleasant aura around her.

My parents radiate with the care and helpfulness both Ameli and I need to survive; though they, themselves, are also affected with disabilities.

Though stricken with treatable but vicious epilepsy, my father constantly helps me understand academic subjects that are important to him. With his background as a physics major at a prestigious university, my dad makes sure that I fully understand the subjects that I, at times, don't comprehend. Along with my father's bearish compassion and will to use time with me comes his sharp brilliance, which also leads to poignant conversation.

Dad is a gentle man who can sit down with me and discuss anything from the decision to drop the bomb in World War II to geometry to aspiring dreamily and talking about my future. In this way, I know my father is gifted, both emotionally as well as analytically. Many times, he has driven himself to his own personal limit emotionally in order to console or advocate for me in my most painful hours or times of greatest accomplishments. I tend to take this stretch for granted, but I know that it takes a smart man to work so successfully and fiercely at prospering in the areas that he knows are weak points within himself. Change is often a very difficult concept to conceive and almost always a hard obstacle to overcome. Through showing me in many ways that he can accept this idea and work his best in order to consolidate his diverse traits, my father has proven his brilliance to me. He is an award-winning software design engineer, but what means most to me is that he cares, he loves, and he listens.

My mother has been the driving emotional counterpart for me all my life, and her deep, understanding ways make it possible to work through rough times. Her disorder doesn't affect me much, and she contains any component of it very, very well.

Added to the great deal of compassion I've gained through living with my family comes the freedom of not expecting conformity in my day-to-day lifestyle. I can confront odd situations with relative ease because of the support my family has given me. Since my family and I have learned to deal with each other's limitations, a sense of irregularity and nonconformity has spread throughout my life; thus I can handle situations that require a nontraditional way of learning.

Stress can be the by-product as we all attempt to deal with our disabilities, but with that comes a solid ability to understand and appreciate people who have differences. I have experienced an immense amount of emotional growth as well as mental toughness and durability just by having knowledge of my family's struggles and endurance.

Being with my father when he has a seizure doesn't damage my respect for him. In some ways, sharing those times is like playing catch with my sister. Even though she drops the ball, Ameli is no more or less of a fine person than when she's doing complicated math problems—just as my dad maintains his internal dignity throughout his disability's effects on him. A person's challenges do not contort their strengths. Moreover, I find that I can admire my family members to a greater extent after they have confronted their weaknesses, as a showing of toughness and dedication to success shines through even the hardest ordeals. I can accept myself as I am, focusing on my strengths, because they've shown me how to do it.

Through merely living amongst these three twice-exceptional beings, I have been able to deal with my own personal problems better so I can be more of a connected participant in the lives of other people. I utilize the compassion that comes from knowing differences from the inside out.

In times of trouble, my family has been a group of welcoming lights through the gray fog. I've learned from loving them how to weave my radiance through the vapor that sometimes threatens to keep me from shining.

DYSGRAPHIA: HIDING IN PLAIN SIGHT

by Kevin Kearney

From reading his first words at ten months of age to entering Montessori kindergarten at three, Michael performed well in numerous intellectual domains with unusual focus, drive, and commitment. Although Michael never developed clear flowing handwriting, he was able to zip through any type of academic material. Cassidy and I assumed that his fine motor skills were normal for his age and that he would catch up over the years. His gross motor skills and intellectual skills were enormous so we didn't worry or think too much about fine motor coordination. Our hands were already full in any event.

What concerned us more than handwriting skills was Michael's hyperactivity and need for stimulation. He didn't like to learn as much as he *needed* to learn. He had some kind of inner spring that drove him. At times it was as if he was on fire. When he wasn't engaged in some learning-related activity he was in constant motion, challenging us, trying to find out how things worked or operated and generally pushing the limits of being a child. He was so dynamic that I began to call him our "Tasmanian devil." Michael had a self-driven "rage to learn" and nothing we could do would stop it. We were essentially in a constant disciplinary mode in order to live with him. I used to joke that he must think his name is "No-no!"

Michael displayed unusual early development in a variety of areas. He began speaking at four months and began reading single words on signs at ten months. As a toddler, before he learned to walk, Michael enjoyed moving our furniture. We would find him under the dining-room table, slowly pushing it across the room. Every day we would have to replace the sofa and chairs to their original positions. I took him to work one day and he entertained himself by moving my desk across the office floor, much to the amazement of my coworkers. We thought perhaps all the activity would tire him out and he would go to sleep early but hardly anything tired him out. He was up at 5:30 and went the entire day, without naps, until 11:30 or 12:00 at night.

I placed childproof caps on all the electric outlets but they were only for show. We would find them pulled out and left lying in Michael's daily trail of mischief. He quickly learned the secrets of "childproof" medicine caps and "childproof" door latches. We responded by slowly moving all of our possessions higher and higher. He then learned to pull out drawers in the kitchen to make himself a ladder up to the countertop where the interesting things were. We were never so alarmed as when it was quiet. Then he learned to pull himself up and unlock and open the front door. We began to think seriously about nailing our windows and doors shut.

I began to doubt whether he would live into adulthood. We felt it was essential for all of us that we find some means to distract, entertain, and contain him. That's how we began to introduce activity books, workbooks, and primers into his day. It was all designed to divert him from his other increasingly dangerous activities.

To a large extent our plan worked. We discovered through an expensive series of trials and errors what would work and what wouldn't. We quickly discovered that a few quality hours of activity books seemed to tap his drive for new experiences and sensory input. By upping his rate of intellectual input we achieved a calming effect which lasted through the day. This level of appropriate distraction lasted for only a few months when without warning he would surge to a new level. His ability to learn and retain complex information would increase so that the workbooks, which he had loved, were suddenly inadequate. He would take a book meant for several weeks of activity and finish it in a half hour.

We also encouraged him to begin using our typewriter as he could not clearly or easily write out the words and phrases that he knew. His handwriting was lagging but that didn't seem dangerous. I also thought at the time that his requiring long periods of effort to write in his books was a good thing, given our circumstances. It served to keep him busy and extended the use of his increasingly expensive materials. We had found by then that we had to regularly increase both the quality and the quantity of material if we were to achieve the calming effect in him that we so desired. By the age of three we had expended our teacher's bookstore's material and I was beginning to make up lesson plans on my own to keep up with him. We decided to try him out in kindergarten as a means of distracting or weaning him from his workbooks.

Unfortunately, kindergarten didn't contain his "rage to learn." He would come home after four hours of school and demand his "work." I began to prepare additional lesson plans for six months at a time, as I was the executive officer of a Navy ship and had to leave home port for weeks or months at a time. Michael would surge and obtain a higher level of raw intellectual ability and speed of absorption, consuming my carefully prepared lessons in only a month. We finally introduced Michael to formal home-schooling packages, at the age of three years, because we had depleted our own resources.

As a teaching methodology, we essentially used curriculum compression with the removal of repetitive material. Michael's retention was nearly 100 percent and excessive repetition would drive him into a frenzy. He could finish an entire grade in only four months, which for us was a pretty good compromise. At age three he finished Montessori kindergarten and first grade in home school. His handwriting wasn't improving and when we thought about it we ascribed this to his not having the regular drill that an ordinary student gets in grade school. Besides, he was still only three years old.

Michael was soon able to master four grades per year and enrolled in high school at the age of five. He was used to typing his work and already had learned to use WordPerfect on our computer. His handwriting was still that of a three-year-old. High school took him only one year to complete, much to our chagrin. He still was extremely hyperactive if left to his own devices. He still challenged our authority and pushed the limits of childhood. We needed school of some type in order to live with him. We had expended the teacher's bookstores, the library, and the home-school curriculum and the public school curriculum of both California and Iowa. We therefore approached Santa Rosa Junior College, in Santa Rosa, California, and proceeded to negotiate Michael's admittance as a full-time college student at the age of six years.

It turned out that note taking was the single area that required the most support when Michael went to college. Cassidy or I were required to be in close proximity to Michael while he was on campus at Santa Rosa Junior College. Cassidy actually had to enroll in the same classes he did for insurance reasons. She took the notes for Michael in the class and then got a withdrawal at the end of the semester.

Our young college student still had to use wide-ruled paper and usually didn't have enough room to write his answers on the minimal space provided on exam papers. He took a freshman English course, which required writing in the computer lab on a Macintosh computer. When required, he had to write out his essays laboriously, and his hands would be cramped and painful afterward. Some professors accommodated him with extra time, some didn't. We thought of it as part of the price he had to pay for being allowed to be in college.

At the age of eight Michael transferred to the University of South Alabama in Mobile. Here we were trying to extract ourselves from having to be with him constantly. Sometimes we would find another student in the class who took great notes, which we would then copy. These students were fairly rare, we found. Some of his professors were downright obstinate that Michael receive no advantages that the other students didn't receive, such as extra time or use of a typewriter or computer. Some professors would accommodate Michael by allowing him to take their exams on the computer in his adviser's office. It was a case by case situation and always caused us some stress because we were placed in the position of "trying to get away with something" each time. There were many professors who simply could not accept that a child could master their course work and indeed be the top student. They used their not giving consent to a modest accommodation for Michael as a test of the prodigy. They rarely understood that we didn't have Michael in college for grades or to get a degree. He was there to keep him busy and to quench his "rage to learn." We would ask ourselves through the years, "Why must Michael always be held to a higher standard?" We took what we could get, however, and moved on.

We occasionally obtained permission from a professor for Michael to bring in a tape recorder instead of Cassidy providing note-taking services. Cassidy would then review the tape and make up notes for him. This would take several hours of her time each day and often lasted into the night. I then obtained a scanner and optical character recognition software and began to scan his textbooks into word-processing files. Michael could then edit the text for his own notes and Cassidy could include whatever else was covered in the taped lecture. The time it took to support Michael in college went down by a factor of ten. We were compensating without thinking about it for Michael's inability to write clearly, quickly, and for long periods. We never made the connection.

When he was a junior in college and nine years old, a professor of special education happened to notice Michael writing. She warned us that Michael might have a learning disability called dysgraphia, the inability to write in cursive. She asked us to bring him into her office for a formal evaluation. It was quite a shock to us. It took us several days to come around because we didn't want to think that our child had a disability. His inability to write was something that we always took in stride and went on. It had not held him back. After the professor's diagnosis, however, we made the connection between all our compensation strategies and Michael's writing disability.

Cassidy and I had never even heard of dysgraphia. I had bad handwriting myself and the fact that Michael did also was probably to be expected. The signs to look for were:

- cramped fingers on any writing tool;
- odd wrist, body, and paper positions;
- excessive erasures, mixture of upper- and lowercase letters;
- mixture of printed and cursive letters;
- inconsistent letter formations and slant;
- irregular letter sizes and shapes;
- unfinished cursive letters, misuse of line and margin;
- poor organization on the page, inefficient speed in copying;

- general illegibility;
- decreased speed of writing;
- decreased speed of copying;
- inattentiveness about details when writing;
- frequent need for verbal cues;
- heavy reliance on vision to monitor what the hand is doing during writing; and
- slow implementation of verbal directions that involve sequencing and planning.

Michael was evaluated and subsequently listed with the campus disability office. It made quite a difference right away. If he wanted to tape a professor's lecture, suddenly there was no longer resistance. He was entitled to a note taker provided by the college instead of Cassidy's filling in. Professors actually began to hand him prepared class notes. He also was entitled to write his essays on a word processor in the learning disability office. He was given extra or unlimited time on tests that he did by hand. The presumption that the only way the "kid" could be in college and doing so well was by cheating somehow disappeared. It was as if a great weight was lifted from our shoulders.

Our association with the disability office revealed several parallels between severely gifted children in college and disabled adult college students. Generally the environment is not built for children or people with physical disabilities. Doors are too heavy, water fountains too high, desks the wrong size, countertops too high, and the like. There is also a need to provide an accommodation of some type in the typical classroom for these students to be able to perform up to their levels of excellence. The blind student can't physically see the chalkboard, for instance. The student in a wheelchair can't reach the lab countertop or open doors and fit though all doors. Some students need assistance to get between classes in the five minutes or so allowed on most campuses. It's a matter of accessibility to achieve excellence.

For Michael, accessibility meant much more than simply obtaining support for his dysgraphia. Accessibility also meant having support for learning at his own extremely rapid cognitive level and pace. We were primarily concerned that his potential for academic success shouldn't be summarily dismissed just because Michael was the first six-year-old to attempt college full time, or later, the first eleven-year-old to attempt graduate school. Michael earned a master's degree in biochemistry at the age of fourteen years and is currently enrolled in a second master's degree program in computer science. Removing attitudinal obstacles cleared the way for him to progress. It required a suspension of disbelief.

INFORMATION ON DYSGRAPHIA:

Books

Richards, Regina G. 1998. *The Writing Dilemma: Understanding Dysgraphia.* RET Center Press.

Olsen, Jan Z. *Handwriting Without Tears.* www.hwtears.com.

MacArthur, Charles A., Ph.D. *From Illegible to Understandable: How Word Prediction and Speech Synthesis Can Help—1998.* New software helps writers by predicting the word the student wants to type and reading what s/he has written.

Rozmiarek, Daniel J. 1998. *Speech Recognition Software.* University of Delaware. A review of the new continuous speech recognition software now available.

EDUCATING THOMAS

by Harriet B. Austin

When I was a child, I loved going to school. Although I don't remember many of the specifics of what I learned there, I do remember learning how important it was to follow directions. One assignment in particular brings this lesson to mind. My third-grade teacher had given us the task of creating a leaf notebook. We were to collect various sorts of leaves, identify them, and paste them into a notebook. We were given very specific directions on how this was to be done, but when I began working on the project at home, my parents intervened with suggestions on how I could improve my notebook by using colored paper and by covering each page with a protective sheet of plastic. With their help, I created a notebook that was probably the loveliest in the class, but my teacher gave it only a "C" and wrote on the bottom of the first page that I had failed to follow the directions for how it was to be made. Apparently we were not supposed to be creative with the assignment. I also don't remember having learned anything from the project other than the importance of following the teacher's directions. As an adult, I can identify some of the more common trees based on the shapes of their leaves, but it's something I learned later in childhood while walking through the woods with my father. I learned them when I was ready and had an interest in knowing them. These minor events in my own education didn't seem particularly important to me until some time after the birth of our first child, Thomas.

Thomas arrived when we were in our early thirties because we had delayed having children until I was out of graduate school and my career seemed safely launched. Despite being older, we went into parenthood with many of the usual assumptions that new parents hold. One of those assumptions was that Thomas would happily attend one of the local schools. We also assumed that he would be an average child in most ways. Instead, his arrival sent shock waves through our lives that have forever changed us.

The first surprise was that Thomas was bright. Of course we had hoped that he would be, but when he began sight-reading half a dozen words before his second birthday, we suspected that his abilities were unusual. At two, he began asking us to spell everything. Walking into his bedroom each day, we would say "Good morning, Thomas," and he would grin and ask us "How do you spell it?" It seemed like a harmless enough game, and we humored him whenever he asked us to spell something. He continued to ask the question endlessly each day for several months until one day he cracked the code. I remember we had gone to the grocery store that day, and when he realized that the sea of words greeting him made sense, he became jubilant, shouting them out as he read them. We felt a strange mix of pride, embarrassment, and uneasiness. Obviously a two-year-old wasn't supposed to be doing this. Shortly after that, when a colleague asked me how my children were doing, I replied that Thomas had learned to read. His smile turned acid, and he remarked that we must have pushed him to do that. His reaction caught me completely off guard. It was our introduction to a number of unpleasant experiences related to other people's misconceptions of exceptionally gifted children.

In fact, after Thomas turned three and was ready for preschool, most of our encounters with educators and caregivers were negative. Many of the teachers we met were not interested in the unusual child. They preferred to have the easy child in their classroom, and Thomas was anything but that. They wanted children who were good at following directions and staying out of trouble, just as I had been as a child. Thomas was far too inquisitive, too loud, too active, and too intense. He was, and still is, too strong-willed and resistant to instruction. It's as though he has always considered himself an adult and expects to be treated as one. In addition, he is a perfectionist to the extreme so that even minor errors on his part can send him into a fit of frustration and anger.

Although it was hard to blame some teachers for finding him to be more than they wanted to handle, it also was hard to understand the extent of their hostility. I remember one incident when Thomas was three and a half. He had been enrolled in a part-time preschool for about two weeks and wasn't adjusting well, though we weren't sure why. When I picked him up, I found that he had fallen asleep during circle time. He awoke disoriented, and as we left the classroom, the teacher said, "Good-bye, Thomas," at which point he turned around and said back to her, "Good-bye, Thomas." It wasn't meant to be disrespectful, but it made her furious, and she stopped him and demanded that he tell her who she was. He hesitated, unable to say or remember her name. She finally had to tell him and then insisted that he say good-bye again using her name. I was too stunned to react at the time, but when Thomas refused to return there, we honored his request.

It was a year later before we learned that Thomas has a nonverbal learning disability called prosopagnosia. It is the inability to recognize faces. In the meantime, Thomas was tested using the Stanford-Binet L-M, and we were not surprised that his IQ measured in the profoundly gifted range of 180+. He'd been doing too many unusual things for too long for us not to know. At that point we began to address the question of how best to educate Thomas. At first the solution seemed simple enough. There were several schools for the gifted in the area, and we would just choose the most suitable among them. We didn't doubt that they would know how to educate Thomas since that was the reason for their existence, to educate gifted children. What we failed to recognize was that they were designed to accommodate children in the moderately gifted IQ range of 125–155, what Leta Hollingworth (1942) considered the optimal range for success in school, but as Miraca Gross (1993) reported, "In terms of intellectual capacity alone, the profoundly gifted child of 190 differs from moderately gifted classmates of 130 to the same degree that the latter differ from intellectually handicapped children of IQ 70." We began to discover this when we visited the schools. Usually each class consisted of children within a two-year span, and the samples of work that we saw were fairly consistent across the class. In other words, there was less individualization than we had hoped, and the curricula we saw often resembled what you would expect to find at any good private school, except that the work was a bit more advanced. In addition, grade advancement was uniformly discouraged, and several administrators seemed openly unenthusiastic about enrolling a child who might require special attention. To make matters more complicated still, it was around this time that we discovered Thomas's prosopagnosia.

If Thomas hadn't been our first child, we might have picked up on the oddity of his misrecognitions earlier, but instead we passed them off as his being overly involved in the thoughts going on inside his own head much of the time. When Thomas was four, though, we discovered that he was unable to recognize me in a photo on the refrigerator. With a growing sense of alarm, we showed him other family photos, all of which elicited the same response. He was unable to identify any of the people in the pictures, not even himself. It was a frightening moment.

The following day at work, I launched an Internet search under "face recognition" and was surprised to find a number of articles. Prosopagnosia results from the malfunction of a very specific region of the brain. Most cases are those of people who have experienced damage to that region as the result of a stroke. Developmental cases where the person is born with the condition are very rare.

Although it was devastating to begin to realize the implications of Thomas's handicap, at least there was a fair amount written about prosopagnosia in the literature, and we read as much as we could find. Also during this time, we set about tracking down someone who could make the diagnosis official. Unfortunately, the developmental psychologist we finally found was unable to do any more than that. We knew from our reading, however, that prosopagnosics frequently have other associated visual processing anomalies that can vary widely from person to person. We desperately wanted to know as much as possible about what these other visual deficits might be in Thomas and how he was seeing the world. Fortunately, by going back to the literature, we were able to find a group of experts at the University of Iowa Medical Center. When I sent an e-mail message to the principal investigator, he invited us to come to Iowa City, and said they would be very interested in testing Thomas. It was a rare opportunity for them since they had never before examined a child with prosopagnosia.

At the University of Iowa, we found caring, compassionate researchers who could more accurately define Thomas's abilities and disabilities. We spent a week there during which time Thomas thoroughly enjoyed being the center of attention. Various aspects of his face recognition and visual processing were assessed, and they also administered achievement testing to determine Thomas's strengths in reading, spelling, and math. At five years and two months, Thomas was reading beyond the high school level, spelling at the eighth-grade level, and his math was at third-grade level. His lack of face recognition was profound, and his inability to read faces and the vast amount of information they impart made it difficult for him to interpret social situations accurately. He also had trouble recognizing people's gender and age, and the testing indicated that his spatial and topographical perception were abnormal in some ways. Certainly we had already noticed that he gets lost easily. Considering the gap between what he was capable of intellectually and the normal things he found difficult, it seemed to us that our son must be one of the most asynchronous people on the planet.

It's no wonder that we had great misgivings about Thomas entering school in a few short months. We had finally decided to try the local public school where the principal had an advanced degree in gifted education. She had assured us that she knew how best to educate a profoundly gifted child like Thomas, and unlike some of the other schools we had visited, she seemed eager to accept the challenge. She decided to advance him into first grade, and she placed Thomas with the teacher she thought would be most suitable. We had told her about Thomas' prosopagnosia, but I was never certain she either believed it or had fully considered the difficulties it might pose for Thomas in school even after she received the report from Iowa in late September. No special accommodations were made except to discuss with Thomas's teacher certain issues that might arise and how best to handle them.

When we took Thomas to school the first day, the scene was like a parade. Many parents were walking their children to school, and the atmosphere was one of joy and celebration. Parents had brought their video cameras to record the momentous event, the first day of first grade. It brought home to us the tremendous discrepancy between our hopes and expectations and those of the other families. These parents had every reason to assume that their children were embarking on a relatively smooth twelve-year journey through school, at the end of which they would emerge as educated adults ready for college or career. Although the parents would need to add their support and encouragement, little else would be required. For us, this was an event filled with enormous anxiety and trepidation. Even with the best of intentions by everyone involved, we were skeptical that the school would be able to meet Thomas's intellectual needs or that school would be a positive experience for him. I couldn't help but feel grief that this pleasant normalcy was not to be ours.

The first week went fairly smoothly. At first Thomas loved the routine, the regularity of doing certain things at certain times. It was novel and fun, but as the newness of the schedule wore off, Thomas became physically and emotionally worn out by the long days. He had less reserve with which to handle what must have been sensory overload. After all, he was in a classroom with twenty-two other children, during recess several classes crowded onto the playground at once, and almost a hundred children at a time shared the cafeteria during lunch. Adding to this sea of changing faces were those of his teachers for art, music, P.E., and library. I suppose we should have foreseen that the average public school would provide numerous scenarios that could be potentially overwhelming for Thomas, but then we were woefully ignorant of what a typical day in elementary school looked like until Thomas started going to school. In fact, it wasn't just the number of people that disturbed us. We were surprised at the rigidity of the schedule, and that controlling the children seemed to be such an important issue. Almost every moment of their time was dictated. The children were expected to be entirely compliant in following the teacher's directions at all times, learning exactly what was taught at the "right" time and in the "right" manner. Thomas, on the other hand, likes to pace when he's thinking; he usually has his own ideas about what he wants to learn, and it usually involves immersion in the topic. Without even considering the appropriateness of the material he would be presented with, we didn't see how the rigid schedule of the classroom would allow him the flexibility we thought he would need to thrive.

During the second week of school, I received the first of what were to be a number of calls to come and pick Thomas up early. He had initially gotten into trouble on the playground because someone had interfered with the complex game he had devised, and as his frustration level had mounted, he had continued to misbehave in each of his successive classes. That incident resulted in his being sent to the office for "problem solving," where he went on a rampage and kicked the secretary. I took him home, and we had a long talk, not the first, about how to handle potentially frustrating situations.

The same thing happened again the following week, but when I arrived, I found Thomas being held by the assistant principal as he tried to hit and kick her. His eyes were blank as though he wasn't there, and his mouth was in a strange sort of smile. I had to call his name repeatedly before he began to come out of his trance, and I was finally able to take him home. Apparently it had started with a minor infraction, his protest to not being excused by the gym teacher to get a drink of water. The injustice of that set him off, and it escalated when he refused to accept his punishment. A conference with the principal was scheduled, and we were able to convince her that full days were too much for Thomas.

Once Thomas dropped back to half days, things improved considerably. He could make it to lunch most days without difficulty. Now our focus turned to what he was learning in the classroom. Unfortunately, no accommodations had yet been made for him other than twice weekly trips to the library and more difficult math problems for him to work on by himself. He was still sitting through the regular first-grade lecture material and assignments that included such things as learning the meaning of the "+" symbol in preparation for adding, beginning reading, and learning the months of the year. Although he tolerated the work, in part because he idolized his teacher and wanted desperately to please him, he wasn't learning anything new. We were reminded of what Leta Hollingworth has said about gifted children in the regular classroom. "In the ordinary elementary school situation children of 140 IQ waste half their time. Those above 170 IQ waste practically all of their time." Consistent with this, Thomas's normally strong spirit seemed dampened somehow, and for the first time, we saw him acquiescing to peer pressure. He had lost some of his self-confidence, and we worried about what this experience was doing to his self-esteem.

In all, we began to ask ourselves what exactly Thomas was getting out of school. He certainly wasn't advancing academically, and though he was learning how to sit still in class and follow directions most of the time, he seemed to be paying a price for that. He was losing his ability to think independently, and he was less interested in initiating learning experiences. For example, he didn't want to read a book or undertake a science experiment if it wasn't assigned for class.

It caused us to consider more deeply what we wanted his education to be. Should we leave it to the school to decide what he should learn and when he should learn it? Should they dictate the pace and manner of his learning, or had we done a fairly good job already by following his lead and facilitating the process as much as possible? After all, how had he arrived in first grade at the age of five already able to read as well as most adults, able to multiply and divide, already knowledgeable about a wide variety of topics and with a thirst to learn more?

What about the socialization that school can provide? We were beginning to think that it was vastly overrated. Thomas had made no meaningful friendships during his several months in school. In fact, he instead saw his differences reflected back to him as a negative thing, and he was much less sure of himself as a result. We had always tried to emphasize to Thomas that he was unique and that his uniqueness was a positive attribute. According to Winner (1996), "Gifted children are well aware of being different: they report feeling different, and they report that others see them as different. Most, however, say they are proud of being different." Unfortunately, in school, Thomas's uniqueness, his interests, his play at recess, his abilities and disabilities, and his behavior made it hard for other children to relate to him. Burks, Jensen, and Terman (1930) have said "the child of 180 IQ has one of the most difficult problems of social adjustment that any human being is ever called upon to meet." Certainly children in that IQ range who also have learning disabilities must face an even greater adjustment problem. Being unable to change who he was, which we would not have wanted anyway, meant that he was unlikely ever to relate well to his classmates. This is what Miraca Gross (1993) found in her study of exceptional children in Australia. "The difficulties in socialization which arose out of the academic discrepancies were intensified by the sophistication of the reading interests, hobbies and play preferences of the exceptionally gifted children. As a result, the majority experienced extreme difficulty, from their earliest days at school, in establishing positive social relationships with their classmates."

In November, we took Thomas out of school. In our final meeting with the principal she asked what had led us to this decision. We didn't mention that with rare exception Thomas had not been provided with appropriate academic material, we didn't mention the negative changes we had observed. Instead we told her that we felt he was too different for this to be a good fit for him. She took it as a personal affront to the school that we lacked faith in their ability to normalize and accommodate Thomas. She went on to question our parenting methods, our sincerity, and our understanding of our own son. It was obvious to us that we had indeed made the right decision.

Although we might have been able to find a suitable private school with more flexibility and a much smaller student:teacher ratio, we decided to try home schooling first. We've been home schooling for three years now, and Thomas is a generally happy, self-confident, and self-motivated learner. One of the biggest advantages to home schooling is that he is able to learn at his own pace. In academic matters he can be lightning fast, like the two days he spent learning to read music using the computer program "Music Ace." In social matters, which come more slowly for him, we can pick and choose the situations, and because the pace is more relaxed, there is plenty of time for us to discuss what is and isn't appropriate behavior for a variety of circumstances. In public school there were too many social interactions for him to successfully process them all, and it became overwhelming. Then, when he responded inappropriately, the consequences were more punitive than instructive.

In addition, we no longer have to worry about acceleration. In the school setting, he probably would have needed additional acceleration in order to remain adequately challenged, but I doubt that it would have been suitable for him emotionally. Once we took him out of school, those concerns vanished. As it is, Thomas can continue to learn at his own pace without going to high school or college early, unless, of course, that is what he wants to do. Finally, he's learning to be an independent thinker, responsible for his own education. He has the time and freedom to explore any topic he chooses as deeply as he chooses, and he has the time to develop and explore topics of a more profound nature, such as who he is and what is his place in the world.

Although we have no plans other than to continue home schooling until Thomas is ready for college, we're also aware that things can change at any time. These children seem to require constant reevaluation, and it's impossible to be certain what their needs will be next year, let alone five years from now. In addition, home schooling isn't possible or even desirable for everyone, but under the right circumstances, it can enable twice-exceptional children to develop at their own rate, however asynchronous. Regardless of the particular educational setting one chooses, we, as parents of such special and unique individuals, owe it to our children to protect them from those who don't understand them, to provide them an environment in which they are safe to develop their particular talents so that they can grow up whole. In order to do that, we must listen to our hearts and trust our instincts, even when the expert advice is otherwise. Although the world may not appreciate them now, it is their special talents that, if fostered, have the potential to make the greatest contributions to the world.

REFERENCES

Burks, B. S., D. W. Jensen, and L. M. Terman. 1930. Genetic Studies of Genius (vol. 3), in *The Promise of Youth*. Palo Alto, Calif.: Stanford University Press.

Gross, M. U. M. 1993. *Exceptionally Gifted Children*. Routledge Press.

Hollingworth, L. S. 1942. *Children Above 180 IQ*. New York: World Books.

Winner, E. 1996. *Gifted Children: Myths and Realities*. New York: BasicBooks.

OPTIMISM BEYOND REASON

by Deborah Robson

most of all, this is for Teague and Bekah

Over the past half dozen years, my daughter, Bekah, and I have lived something more akin to a siege than a life. This is a success story. Neither of us is dead nor over-the-edge crazy. Bekah will graduate from high school. There may be a life after education, although I am so tired that I question my ability to find or enjoy it. "This, too, shall pass" has been our mantra.

I've spent years practicing what environmental advocate Betsy Rieke calls "optimism beyond reason." Often this has tightened down to "optimism despite reason." At the worst times, it torqued toward "persistence with flagrant disregard for common sense." Now that this part of the journey is almost over, I keep collapsing inwardly. My rational mind knows the worst is past. My emotions haven't caught up.

The greatest casualty has been my ability to trust either "the system" or other people. Small memories—a few extended hands, raised eyebrows, helpful or honest comments (often spoken with a glance over the shoulder)—keep the confusion and doublespeak from over-whelming me.

The siege is almost over.

It's Saturday evening and I have a choice about how to use the next few hours. This isn't normal, if normal describes our lives since Bekah started school more than twelve years ago. Bekah is at boarding school in New York; this is her second and final year there, after four years of being out of school entirely. I'm slowly adjusting to life without constant need for argument, defense, soul-searching, uncertainty, saying "no" to experts who take years to get past "it's just the mother."

We're not home free, but I'm not cramming for the next showdown. We didn't "win," but Bekah is safe and doing well.

I'm afraid to start a project I might care about. I listen with every cell for the next internal siren. I have trouble believing the silence. I don't trust that I can now choose activities based on criteria other than emergency response.

* * *

Dark falls on this evening in late February. I decide I will put fresh sheets on the bed. First I have to find the bed. The half where I don't sleep is still drowned in debris from my desperate scramble for information. I close the books, stack the papers, untangle the covers. I never found the answers, but clues seem to have been sufficient. Bekah's safe now. I pull off the flannel sheets, then billow clean, rose-colored percale across the futon.

You make your bed and you lie in it.

Sometimes you don't even have time to make your bed, after the first time.

Changing the sheets feels like a luxury.

Shift five years back and to the adjacent bedroom. Bekah, twelve, has slammed its door, retreating again in panic and fury. Her school problems, which began to poke into our lives when she was in kindergarten, have since grown into demons. She's been in weekly therapy for about two years. Bekah heaves things against the wall. I worry most when she raises red welts on her arms or legs, or bangs her head against the wall until the pounding produces a headache.

There's nothing I can do until the maelstrom subsides. I remember to breathe. I try to work while I'm waiting. Fortunately, I work at home so I can work at all hours.

After a while, Bekah shoves a note under the door. It says, "I'm sorry, Mom. I don't know what's happening." Her writing is tiny, contrite.

I scribble back: "I don't know either, but we'll work on it together. I love you."

Later she responds to my knock and says she's ready for a hug.

I don't want to think about this any more. I am exhausted. In the end, the school district officials were right. Finally, finally, we did go away. They never said that was their goal (they couldn't, of course, legally). It took longer for us than for most. I don't believe the people who run the schools are evil, as individuals.

I'm trying to make what Bekah and I have been through have a shape, make sense. I also want to leave it behind.

I can't yet. She's not securely launched, although we have good news. Not only will Bekah graduate from high school, she has been accepted at two colleges so far. One will interview her for a merit scholarship. When I called a friend long-distance, she said, "Would it be too much to call this a miracle?"

I've learned not to count on anything. I wake up tired every morning and put one foot down, then the other.

I'm writing for Austin, fourteen, veteran of two trips to the adolescent psych unit for depression. He has begun to write down his own stories.

My cousin has begun the battle. Her tenth-grade daughter has been losing ground for three years. If she fails her courses this year—extremely likely—she will repeat the same program next year.

I'm writing for A., fifteen. She has newly diagnosed attention deficit disorder. Sex, her other new discovery, probably gives her a fleeting sense of success.

I recognize the pattern too well. The problem is the child's inadequacy, not the system's. In the airport during the recent holidays, I waited for Bekah's overdue plane next to a woman who's trying to find answers for her son.

I'm writing for Colin, fifteen, who dropped out last year. He's started coursework at a public school that operates on the Internet. He works alone.

I keep running into kids who are intelligent, sometimes extraordinarily intelligent, but can't learn successfully within the public schools. Often they have identifiable learning disabilities. Because many perform "at grade level," they keep succeeding enough not to trigger availability of the help they need. They scream for attention in different ways, depending on their personalities.

I'm writing for Benjamin, whose desperate parents tried a private school where he was beaten up for being "different." The administration said "Boys will be boys," and his parents brought him home again.

The problems look familiar, regardless of state, city or town, family or community. The kids' reactions also follow patterns: depression, anger, rebellion, vague illness, self-sabotage, even suicide.

I'm writing for Ozzy, who died at seventeen. His parents published his book of poetry posthumously.

I'm writing because I want to say to other parents and to their children that it's possible to get an appropriate education and you'll need other people to do it, but you'll have to put together your own puzzle and it will be harder than you can imagine and it will go on for what seems like forever. And although other people will be able to offer you crumbs, you won't be able to count on anyone else to do more than that. Ever.

You have to trust only yourself, being aware that you might be conning yourself. You'll never know enough to make decisions. You'll have to make decisions anyway.

You have to trust only your child, who is manipulative but is fighting for survival with kid tools, with kid perspective. Your child reflects reality through an unformed mirror, but it's *that* mirror and *that* reality which matter.

You need to learn mirror writing, sign language, legal hieroglyphics, the difference between *should be* and *is,* the bureaucrat's waltz.

You need to invest more time, money, intelligence, soul, and courage than you ever imagined you could muster.

You probably won't win, but you might survive. Both of you.

A free, appropriate public education.

My daughter didn't get one.

The phrase is abbreviated as FAPE by those in the know, and you will become one of those in the know, whether you want to or not. It refers to what every public school system in the United States is legally required to provide to every child within its boundaries. An accompanying principle called "zero reject" means that no child can be denied this.

This is the law. That doesn't mean you, a parent, can enforce the law unless you have both time and money. Even if you win the legal battle—a case similar to my daughter's, heard by the U.S. Supreme Court, was decided in favor of the student—your child will be an adult by the time it ends. You will be more exhausted than I am, and your child will not have been educated unless you also took charge of that. Few lawyers take special education cases. They don't work free. This is part of what I have learned in my crash course in public education for kids who don't fit the system.

There are reasons why the existing programs within our district didn't work for Bekah. As the parent of one of these children, you should know—although it won't help—that the existence or lack of the right program does not alter the system's obligation to provide an appropriate education.

What we went through applies to many young people with different profiles. Their pictures usually don't appear in the newspaper under "school stars" or "applause," although they sometimes show up under "obituaries." I hoped it was in my power to catch Bekah before she hit bottom. Many times the outcome could easily have tipped the other way. We worked incredibly hard, both Bekah and I, and we were just lucky enough to pull it off.

Today's legislation not only allows all children to attend school but demands that they do so. The law places obligations on both sides. It's far easier to force parents to comply with attendance statutes than it is to get district-level personnel to admit they've heard of the laws requiring them to provide an "appropriate" education. Even when the parent names the law and cites its provisions and the administrator is responsible for ensuring compliance with that law, compliance may not happen. In case you need to know, the first law you quote is Section 504 of the Rehabilitation Act of 1973 (29 U.S.C., Section 794), enacted twenty years before my daughter needed it. Its implementing regulations are at 30 C.F.R., Part 104.

I had to do a lot of research before I learned to question the administrators' ignorance. I didn't start researching for a while, because I thought the schools and I shared an interest in finding the easiest way to educate my daughter.

Sometimes responsible behavior looks like the worst sort of irresponsibility. When it became obvious that the school was making Bekah certifiably nuts, I spent four years at risk of prosecution and jail because I didn't force her to attend. I contributed to her truancy. A *truant* is a beggar or a vagabond, one who is a miserable wretch.

There were two ways out of my legally vulnerable position. I declined both.

First: I could have signed a paper. I had several opportunities. The paper first appeared at a meeting I requested with district officials just after my daughter stopped attending school. I still thought help might be available from the system that required her attendance. An administrator offered me a packet of materials on home schooling. It included resource lists, a bibliography, and forms, which I was encouraged to sign. The forms would have transferred responsibility for her education to me and absolved the district of any involvement other than annual testing.

As a single parent with a full-time job and no child support, I had no business signing on as a home educator. I needed help. I needed their expertise. I needed an education for my daughter.

Second and later, I could have allowed the district to classify Bekah's "lack of adjustment" as an emotional disability, called ED in the lingo. This category is used for kids who have serious problems, like schizophrenia and autism. It opens the door to services under the more powerful set of federal laws governing special education, the ones everyone still calls P.L. 94-142.

This is shorthand for a series of legal tools including the Education for All Handicapped Children Act of 1975 (the real P.L. 94-142) and its amendments, one of which renamed the law the Individuals with Disabilities Education Act (IDEA) and brought a new number into the literature, if not conversation (P.L. 101-476). Look for it at 20 U.S.C., Sections 1401–1468, with implementing regulations at 34 C.F.R., Parts 300 and 303.

I don't want to know all this. The laws morph constantly, although the baselines—

FAPE and "zero reject"—have been in effect for long enough that ignorance is hard to believe when invoked by guys with advanced degrees in education. (We dealt with few women.)

ED classification would have remained on Bekah's record forever and might have limited her future options. Because Bekah was only emotionally disabled in school, I refused this path as well.

I became civilly disobedient.

My daughter sobs hysterically in the passenger seat of the van, which I've pulled up at the front curb of the elementary school. Her reactions intensify as the situation repeats and she gets older. She clearly believes that entering the school will cause her greater distress than we are both experiencing in the car—which is a lot.

We have an ally inside the elementary school. Bekah trusts the guidance counselor, and most days I can convince her to go into the building as far as this woman's office. Then I breathe deeply, and arrive at work late again. The scene repeats the next day.

In junior high, someone in the attendance office may see us out front and call the psychologist, who covers three schools and 2,500 students. Bekah has no power except resistance. Over time, she also has several therapists. Some test; some talk. All charge. Insurance doesn't pay much.

We find the path of least resistance, although all paths have resistance. At the elementary school, the psychologist runs Bekah through intelligence and achievement tests "as a favor," because of her pattern of screaming on the curb and then making an inconvenient transition through the counselor's office. He is not required to support this child, because her grades are okay. He tells us she's very bright, and suggests "private school, if possible—this system can't meet her needs." We haven't been forced to study the law and don't know about "zero reject." I'm still grateful for his honesty. He was right.

We confer with the teachers, who have no time, no aides, no interest. One says, with Bekah sitting next to her, "Bekah is a social zero," as if she were discussing the weather. Another says, "We don't believe in bored," and suggests it is Bekah's responsibility, at age ten, to design an alternative curriculum if she needs challenging tasks. No, they can't modify the assignments.

Bekah transfers to a newly opened, local, private elementary school for a year and a half. At the time I think this is expensive, but I have no idea how much more expensive the future will be.

Then we're out on the curb again. The private options in our area end at sixth grade.

*   *   *

Bekah's placement in classes at the public junior high seems random. Despite attention from mother, father, and stepmother, within the first two weeks of school she has been bounced between eighth, ninth, and seventh grades. She spends four hours each night on ninth-grade algebra problems. The math teacher can't meet with us for two more weeks.

By then, Bekah refuses to go into the building and the psychologist has run out of patience. I finally reach the principal by phone (although I'm in the school building daily). He refers me back to the counselors. A computer-generated letter arrives saying Bekah has been truant and we are in violation of the law. I write asking that the school apply the hours I'm spending in the counselors' office to her attendance quota. No response.

I have *got* to have more information. I take Bekah to the city an hour away and pay a thousand dollars I don't have for comprehensive psychoeducational testing. I learn later that the district is supposed to provide this. When the district finally did some tests, they located a neurological slowdown in her brain/hand coordination and "gaps" in math and spelling skills. No one seemed to know what to do with the information, or with the reports from Denver that they received a year earlier.

In Denver, three psychologists interpret Bekah's results for me. She's even brighter than we thought. On one test, she successfully answered questions at a level called "adult superior III." The staff explains how the testing indicates Bekah's learning disabilities and strengths. They aren't surprised that she spells badly and can't remember math facts.

"Don't hold her back," they say. "Give her a spellchecker and a calculator and let her go."

We also learn that Bekah's handwriting is four times slower than it should be. Her difficulty with the algebra homework was mechanical.

The private psychologists write up recommendations for Bekah's educational program. Copies are mailed to the school district. They offer to talk with school personnel.

And the director of the testing center says, "Get her out of there. It's killing her."

Bekah runs into her room again. Slams the door again. Sobs again. Lashes out again. I pick up the notes from under the door. I paste each small scrap on a huge mural in my mind. The images rarely connect. At stoplights I lower my head to the steering wheel and cry until the traffic begins to move. Then I pull myself together and go on.

*   *   *

A few images coalesce, and they include a dog. Bekah's father and stepmother suggest that Bekah needs a friend other than the adults who make up her world. They locate an Australian shepherd named Heather who is being retired from a kennel's breeding program.

Bekah works with Heather on obedience training, and they move together through beginning and intermediate levels. They continue with Canine Good Citizen testing and then with qualification for work as a therapy dog. Bekah and Heather earn certificates together.

For both of us, Heather's greatest gift is our laughter. She's dignified and elegant. In obedience she does what she's told, but always as a favor. Bekah has to lie down on the floor at the training facility and wave her arms and legs to get Heather to hurry.

Heather moves us into a different world, one where Jack Russell terriers bound vertically as if on springs and labs lope along looking for balls to retrieve and Danes survey the world from an absurdly high vantage point. We laugh at the puppies, and at the individual genius of each dog. We laugh a lot at the dog classes.

My book and phone bills mount. There isn't much written about these kids. I read about giftedness and about learning disabilities; I try to extrapolate. I labor for deeper understanding of subtest patterns. I try to tell the administrators what my understanding is becoming, ask for their opinions. Apparently, these ideas are new to them.

When most desperate, I'll call anybody, anywhere. I talk to researchers and their assistants. I ask if the district people would consider contacting the people I've found who might be able to help. They write down the names and file them.

A lawyer in Virginia provides information but seems to have burned out on special ed law. I end the phone call near tears, but with citations of cases. I locate the legal papers. I call a lawyer in Utah, who recommends one in Texas. They're all busy or going in another direction, and I can't afford a lawyer anyway.

A meeting is about to start. Sometimes these meetings occur in the elementary school, sometimes at the old high school, sometimes at the new high school, sometimes at district headquarters. If there is a woman present other than me, that fact is memorable. Most often, the other woman is a psychologist whom I pay to act as Bekah's advocate. "Pay" includes two hours of driving time. No advocate in town wants to risk offending the school district.

There's a routine. So-and-so can't be here today; so-and-so (who I've never seen before, never will again) is here instead. Someone important will be absent or an hour late. The meeting will end in an hour. The papers will be filed. Even if I write a report of the meeting and send copies to all persons present, implicated, or absent, little will happen and that little will take months. More testing, maybe. Everyone seems to hope we'll get tired and go away.

The day's errand list says *bread, milk, dog food, finish planning documents for work, get parts to fix toilet, file civil rights complaint.*

Civil rights complaints of this type can only reflect violations that have occurred within the past six months. No lawyer is required. The complaint that I file on Bekah's behalf fills 125 pages.

A nonprofit organization in Denver has published a very helpful *Handbook of Rights to Special Education in Colorado: A Guide for Parents.* They, and the state Department of Education, have urged me to pursue the complaint process. A staff member reads the file, tells me that I've done a wonderful job, that there's a case here, that she'd love to meet Bekah and perhaps some time when we're in Denver we could have lunch, that the organization's funding is limited and their mandate right now is to serve kids who've been actively expelled, so they can't help any further.

The federal Department of Education's Office for Civil Rights has recently changed its tactics and is taking a "more cooperative" approach to working with school districts.

They still have some clout.

The district provides Bekah with a small amount of tutoring and pays for a few college-level courses (also available to regular students). This is enormously helpful. It's still not an education.

I'm writing for Kyle, who attends one class a day. His mother has quit her job to make sure he gets the rest of his education.

My idea of satisfactory bedtime reading does not consist of the volume I'm balancing on my knees. It's over 1¼ inches thick and bound in innocent-looking blue paper. It's titled *Sixteenth Annual Report to Congress on the Implementation of The Individuals with Disabilities Education Act, 1994.* The bigger type on the cover says *To Assure the Free Appropriate Public Education of All Children with Disabilities.* The author is the U. S. Department of Education, required to prepare the report by Section 618(g)(1)(b) of the Individuals with Disabilities Education Act (20 U.S.C. 1401 et seq.).

These code numbers are becoming familiar.

The word *assure* is comforting.

The word *all* sounds like it should include my child.

Turns out there's no comfort, and my child's rights are worth nothing to the public system—like the rights of other children and parents whom I have met in the years since. I recently attended a meeting with about 175 people drawn from this district alone. The buck gets passed, the forms get filled out, the files get fatter. The parents give up. The children . . .

The meeting was in memory of one child. His mother, who never quit but didn't succeed, gave introductory remarks between tears.

Oren committed suicide at thirteen. After his death, his mother helped put together our city's first seminar for parents of children with ADD.

It takes me years of boring reading, of frustrating meetings, before I figure out that we're on our own. By then, Bekah is almost sixteen and we're running out of time.

We go to Denver again and spend another thousand dollars I don't have hiring an educational consultant who works on matching kids to educational environments. We find a private school two thousand miles away that Bekah likes and that likes Bekah. The school is willing to take her even though she's on medications to handle the depression that's a side effect of the school-induced trauma and she's on Ritalin to help her concentrate. I think she lost the ability to concentrate by being bored for too long. That's another story. They offer her a partial scholarship.

On the day when I am to take Bekah to start classes at this school, she falls as we walk toward the rental car and she breaks a front tooth. I hold Bekah's hand through the dental treatment, stay as long as I can, leave her in her dorm room. I have to go. Two staff members offer to look in on her. She spends the next two days in bed under the covers, then slowly emerges to try to cope with this new environment.

At Thanksgiving, friends ask whether Bekah likes school. She says, "No, but it's where I need to be." She's right. She always has been. Only now she has a basis for comparison, and she can speak.

She returns to school after the break.

We both begin to move forward.

My decision to stick up for my daughter came close to destroying my life. However, I found it relatively easy to make that decision, and to continue remaking it daily. I had to at least give the job my best shot. Otherwise, the situation would almost certainly have destroyed both of our lives.

At nearly eighteen, my daughter is an honorable person. Her values inform her behavior. Home for spring break, she rereads Jane Austen and watches French movies while waiting for the financial aid offers that will help determine what happens for her next.

Meanwhile, I take stock of my own life. Most days I am disproportionately tired. I suspect several stress-induced ailments I've recently endured held off until Bekah didn't need me so much. During the year when she left home, I experienced migraines and major surgery, which nudged me further into a general withdrawal from social activities I used to enjoy, like dancing and music and visiting with friends. I no longer have a life partner, and one man I dated—rare people, uncommon events—called my efforts on Bekah's behalf "psychologically twisted." He told me I should have abandoned her.

I have no idea when or how I will get rid of my debts. My house is in a shambles. There are papers everywhere. Nearly fifty three-ring binders, most of them three inches across the spine, are filled with the evidence of our effort to obtain that elusive *free, appropriate public education.*

This is a success story, though, remember? The kid's okay. So am I, I think.

Yet this is not the life I wanted. It's not the life I hoped for. I don't think this is the life I deserve.

The trick is to make the best of it anyway. I'm tired of making the best of things anyway.

Still, if I had it to do again, I'd make the same choices. I wish the paths had been easier and had led, for me, to a different place. I hope I've gained some wisdom and that a few of the things I intended to do with my own life are still attainable.

I ask Bekah, who knows about such things, how long Rip van Winkle spent in his other reality. She says twenty years, during which the entire American Revolution came and went.

Blinking, I turn back toward the light.

THE LONG TREK TO TRUTH

by Beth Crothers

My son, who's not yet eight years old, will enter undergraduate studies in math and physics in the coming year. Less than two years ago, he was in a remedial first-grade math class. Home schooling and an appropriate diagnosis have made the difference for him.

When my son began experiencing trouble in school, I wanted to do whatever possible to help him, but all the so-called "help services" were concerned with was finding an appropriate tag for him. We were told that he had bipolar disorder. He didn't. We were told that he had Asperger syndrome. He didn't. While professionals treated him for disorders that he didn't have, we persisted in trying to find ways to help him feel better.

In the eighteen months since our son received an appropriate diagnosis and began home school, he has really blossomed socially and academically. I am still in shock by how much! The appropriate medication hasn't helped him become any brighter, but it has helped the rest of us realize how bright he is. The changes in Tosh were dramatic from his first day on medication. Imagine having hives in the brain and spending all day every day trying to scratch what you can't reach! The medication is like the calamine lotion, and really does ease the extreme frustration and anxiety of such pain. We have really had to fight the system to get his needs met and all of us carry the scars. For now, though, things are looking better every day.

He has become happier, more confident, and more self-controlled. He really enjoys learning now that it is no longer associated with the teasing, bullying, and boredom that he experienced in school. He has made several really lovely friendships and has quite a busy social calendar. He also is receptive to his own needs and the needs of others, taking time out of his own accord when he feels stress. He has not shown any head-banging or screaming behaviors for many months. It has been a long trek.

Our son was reevaluated using the WISC III while medicated and scored in the 150–155 range, maxing out on most subtests. He recently underwent the Stanford Binet-LM to see how the WISC-III ceilings had affected his test score. He measured 180+ on this test, which we were told means he has at most three out of a million people as intellectual peers. This sobering thought has helped us understand just how isolated he must have felt in school. Tosh's father and I are not in this range, yet we remember the isolation we felt as intellectually able youngsters in a society and school that frowned on any ability outside of the normal academic range, yet nurtured sporting and musical talents to the full.

Many psychologists have wanted to grab whatever label they could stretch to fit our son's behaviors. Very few people were prepared to perceive what was going on within schools as systematic child abuse, or to question the current practices in education and their suitability for profoundly gifted children. Before he was four years old, we had very few problems. He was a happy, bright little boy who had taught himself to read and use various learning tools. Because of his abilities, I had him tested prior to starting preschool. His IQ was measured at 155.

Sometime after his fifth birthday things started to go awry. He was often the object of bullying and teasing, and at one point I had to withdraw him from school for his own safety. The bullying and teasing deeply affected him. He was placed in a remedial math class, had illegible handwriting, and demonstrated no interest or ability to participate in class activities. He was unable to make friends and could not sit still for ten seconds, even to listen to a story or to draw. He was retested and his IQ was measured at 115. His behavior became unpredictable. He would talk to himself for extended periods and was not interested in leaving his fantasy world.

I was never willing to interpret the behaviors that my son displayed after being beaten at school or stressed in other ways as typical behaviors for him. When our son was at home, he sometimes was hyper and unfocused, but rarely encapsulated in his own world or overly depressed or anxious, unless school was in his thoughts.

We kept looking for answers. The behavioral services shrinks from our local department of education were the ones who told me that he had Asperger syndrome, based on lists completed by his teachers, with questions about eye contact and the like. I told the psychologist looking after his case that he hadn't always behaved like this, and that his problems had started as he became the object of severe bullying and teasing. Before then, he was a fairly normal, yet obviously gifted little boy. She did not choose to hear me.

Tosh's diagnosis came into question at an Asperger support group meeting. These great moms saw straight away that my son was not typical of children with this diagnosis. The members of this group had experience with a wide spectrum of autism, and felt that it was unlikely that Tosh had any of the autism spectrum disorders. In the support group, Tosh had no problems at all socializing. The support group understood what the professionals had failed to comprehend.

I kept searching. I went back to the behavioral services people for an assessment by someone new, and also made an appointment to see a really good child psychiatrist with Tosh.

The behavioral services people had us complete surveys, and the new diagnosis became bipolar disorder. Since our son expressed excitement and joy when doing anything related to his interests, they decided he was having abnormal mood swings and suggested medication. The child psychiatrist spent four or five hours with Tosh, and his assessment was completely different. He basically said that our son was eccentric and injured, but apart from that, okay.

I arranged to see a pediatric neurologist at about the same time, because I wanted the bipolar disorder neurologically diagnosed if Tosh was to need medication. The neurological assessment discovered the attention deficit disorder (ADD), instead of bipolar disorder or Asperger syndrome. I was skeptical at first, but I really trusted this doctor. He listened to me! He explained how hormones affect dopamine production. He also said that because so many kids are now labeled ADD or ADHD, professionals often have trouble diagnosing extreme cases. He knew of several misdiagnosed kids. My son suffers from a neurochemical imbalance, and now he takes Ritalin to correct it. His attention deficit disorder could not be treated with behavior management, although an ongoing behavior management program does help him understand the needs of others and the requirements of society.

Our son could have started treatment much earlier if we'd had a diagnosis based on neurological assessment instead of behavioral surveys. The delay in diagnosing and properly medicating Tosh led to real emotional trauma for an extended period, well over two years. Peer pressure, educational environment, and social stigma contributed to his plight. We're still working through the damage. It's a slow process, but at least now there is light at the end of the tunnel.

Not yet eight years old, our son already is studying math and science at high school level and other academic subjects four years ahead of his age peers. I do not want to think what would have happened to him if we had trusted the first misdiagnosis, or even the second. His brilliance could have been destroyed by the wrong treatment, and by diagnosis based on behaviors that resulted from an inappropriate learning environment. Some so-called experts in the field of "psychology of gifted children" also discussed his case with their peers and other parents in the public arena, without our permission. As our pediatrician put it, "These kids are so rare that it is obvious to anyone knowing the child whom the professionals are talking about. It's not like there are half a dozen of them in this city."

I am now a staunch advocate of second opinions served with generous portions of self-gathered source materials. We've found some very disturbing commonalities when dealing with psychological and child health officials, which have led us to question the ethics and motivations of every professional who deals with our son. After all of our struggles with the school and professionals, we've found some success through home school.

Deidre Lovecky says, ". . . It is the exceptionally gifted whose needs are more difficult to meet by virtue of being so few in number and because of the differences of their cognitive skills." Home school not only provides adequate intellectual stimulation, but also allows a child the opportunity of enjoying learning without having to worry about being "outside of the norm" to the nth degree. I educate my child at home solely to preserve my child's mental and emotional health. People who knew him during his period of schooling now comment on how mature, happy, and responsive he has become since he's been at home. We do not "unschool," but we are fairly flexible. When we initially tried unschooling, Tosh would start something, but five minutes into it decide that it was too much effort and give up. Then he would go on to the next thing. We decided to try this home-cooked method of a twenty-minute minimum per subject. Since we've had this system going, he has been known to immerse himself totally for hours on a project. The twenty-minute rule is great for subjects he hates yet has to do daily, such as occupational therapy and handwriting for his poor fine-motor skills. It also helps motivate him to do what he likes to do but hates to prepare, and gives him an honest chance to choose what to invest time in. It's still obvious that he has a hurdle to cross ten to fifteen minutes into any activity, but his self-control does appear to be getting better. He still goes to school for arts, crafts, and drama. He has a tutor, and he goes to the university for physics labs and mentoring once a week. It costs us a small fortune but it has proven to be worth every cent. It's just appalling that the laws for providing adequate education don't cover kids like ours—at least not without a full-time advocate and an on-call legal team. Our long trek to truth brought us back home.

RUNNING START

by Stewart Matthiesen

My high school experience was not particularly pleasant. My school offered little for the "normal" highly capable student and even less for someone with vision problems. Problems stem more from my handwriting than anything else, because I was almost blind as a small child and I couldn't see the letters properly when learning to write. My vision is now mostly correctable. I don't have problems reading or driving (although I barely pass the vision test) as long as I'm wearing my glasses or contacts. Handwriting just isn't a good way to get me to communicate anything I learn. Teachers have trouble reading it, and I have to slow my thinking to be able to write out my thoughts. Sometimes it can be hard to communicate this to teachers—who haven't had any training on working with gifted disabled students—in a small rural high school whose classes already are too large.

After I scored significantly above average on the Scholastic Aptitude Test at age twelve, my parents borrowed money to buy a computer system. They felt that learning to type would help me overcome my handwriting problems. We also connected to the Internet. In 1993 we were one of the early few in our community. It took a while, but now I type almost everything I write, reserving my pen for only short notes or poems.

We knew that high school would be something of an uphill battle. Middle school was hard enough, and we'd been working with teachers and counselors for years. I started out skipping freshman general science and freshman English and moving into biology and English with the sophomores. Biology seemed to work. I was two years younger than all the other students (having skipped the fifth grade as well as individual classes), but my teacher was helpful and the age difference didn't seem to matter much in that class. English was a bit more of a problem. I just didn't feel comfortable in the class. Everyone's knowledge base differed from mine. They built a lot on freshman English and a lot of books I hadn't read yet. We decided that I would "compact" freshman and sophomore English and do them in one year. This plan was more or less forced upon the only freshman English teacher at the school. We had the predictable problems. I didn't want to write papers, and I wasn't interested in the books she wanted me to read. (I read a tremendous amount, just not the books she liked.) I planned to type most of my work on our computer at home, or to tape some of it. I suppose this plan would have worked had my teacher felt the same way, but she disapproved of my wanting to do things differently from the other students.

For me, compacting classes and accelerating were temporary solutions. I was a little happier in biology, and I'm glad I didn't have to go through both those years of English (that one was bad enough), but in the end I really just ended up running out of classes to take. Due to the size of my school, any student on the conventional plan could take almost every class offered before graduating. Since I skipped a few there wasn't a lot for me to do. By my sophomore year, I ended up in the so-called "slacker" classes because they seemed the easiest and most fun, even if I wasn't learning much.

The saving grace of my educational career was a Washington State program called Running Start. Students participating in this program had to pass at a certain level on a standardized test and then they would be allowed to take classes at the community college level for high school credit, with tuition paid by the state. Most students in the program would take a couple of classes at the college level and the rest at their high school. Unfortunately the nearest community college was more than an hour away, and I wasn't up for commuting. I chose to go all the way: I enrolled at the college full time and moved into its small dormitory. I was fifteen.

It was not an easy transition for a fifteen-year-old student to go straight from the tenth grade into a community college whose average age student was thirty-five. I would not recommend it for most students, but I was left with little choice. I could either stay at my high school and let my mind decay in boredom, or jump into college to see if I could hang on and learn something. I wasn't entirely alone, though; I brought along a friend of mine from high school who ended up being my roommate. The college counselors were very helpful, and my parents were also very supportive of me.

I was lucky to spend my first semester at the college in an experimental class called a learning community. I signed up for one fifteen-credit class that ran from 11 AM to 4 PM every day and gave me credit for introductory biology, literature, and composition courses. The professors were present most of the time, and I had the same classmates for all of my classes. This structure gave me time to settle in and concentrate on meeting people for a little while without having to worry about managing separate classes. I got a 4.0 my first quarter at the college, as opposed to my 3.6 high school GPA.

I found my early college experiences much more exciting and interesting than my two years of high school. I could take classes I liked, although I still had requirements to meet, both for my high school diploma, and for the associate of arts honors degree I was trying to earn. To compensate for my handwriting problems, the school allowed me to take my new laptop computer and printer to class for writing assignments. Maybe I looked a little funny to my classmates, but it didn't matter. We had two park rangers, some loggers, and a couple of retired people in class. What was another teenage kid with a laptop computer? The diversity of the community college made it much easier for me to blend in. Most people would have never guessed that I was only fifteen, and I didn't normally volunteer it. There was even an official policy that professors could not ask students if they were in Running Start, just so that we would not be treated differently.

I also developed close relationships with my professors, being invited to their houses for dinner, or chatting in their offices. I even got a job working with my physics professor as an instructor for the hiking class. In college I found a new sense of independence and responsibility, as well as people who could understand me better and be good role models.

As with any sort of grade skipping or acceleration, there were some social difficulties at first. I guess it made it easier that I wasn't all that attached to my high school life. It wasn't that I was unpopular or anything; rather, I just didn't have that many important relationships to release. It did take some time for me to make new friends and find things to do out of class, but the dormitory lent a sense of community to the eighty people living in it. In my second year in the program, my senior year of high school, I really developed my closest friendships, much closer than I had ever had with anyone in high school.

Dealing with my high school was still a battle. When I first started Running Start there was an agreement in place that guaranteed my high school diploma if I should earn an associates degree. Halfway through they revoked this and told me I wasn't going to graduate unless I took some additional classes, ones that would no longer fit with my current planned schedule to earn my degree. With many petitions and meetings with the counselors and the principal we finally reached an agreement which let me earn my degree and my diploma.

In June of 1997, at the age of seventeen, I attended two graduation ceremonies. I graduated high school with a 3.65 GPA, and I graduated from the community college with a 3.73 GPA. I was ready for a four-year college now, and two full years ahead as well. I knew that I'd made the right decision.

STARBURST IN A NIGHT SKY

by Jim Sinclair,
Autism Network International

This chapter began as a response to questions from a parent of a child who was both gifted and autistic. The parent wanted my opinion about a school's offer to advance his son several grades. My replies to his questions formed the foundation of this writing.

Was I aware of my own giftedness? I was aware—to the extent that I was aware of other kids at all—that they couldn't read or do math or remember things as well as I could. But I didn't think of that as anything significant because I wasn't aware that I was expected to be like other kids. It had no social relevance whatsoever, because autism is such an all-pervasive factor in social relationships that unless a person has reached a certain level of social awareness (which for me happened around the age of twenty-seven), intellect is almost irrelevant. It didn't matter whether people were my age or older or younger, at my academic level or not, gifted or average or retarded—I didn't relate to them.

I began relating to a few people at a very minimal level at about twelve to fifteen years of age, at which time I happened to be attending a special school for gifted students. It was my readiness to communicate that prompted the change of schools, not vice versa. I asked my parents not to send me back to the public school for eighth grade, and they enrolled me in the gifted school.

My parents had considered transferring me to the special school several years earlier. I had reacted so badly to skipping a single grade within the same school, and I became so upset at any mention of changing schools, that they left me in the public school. Although this choice meant that I remained for several years in the intellectually under-stimulating environment of a rather poor public school program, I think they made the right decision by not forcing another traumatic change on me until I requested it myself. In terms of special considerations required, autism trumps giftedness: An autistic person, however high- or low-functioning, needs a lot of careful decision making and support around changes and transitions.

One of the things I kept hearing from teachers and administrators at the private school was that gifted children have social difficulties because they don't have friends who can relate to them at their own level. This concept didn't mean anything at all to me at the time (not that

I spent any time dwelling on it; it was just one of many incomprehensible things I heard people say). I didn't realize what it meant until 1989, when I gave a talk to an audience of "average" people and tried to respond to their comments. At some point after graduation from college, I had finally reached the level of social awareness most people are born with: When I saw human beings, I recognized them as things to be communicated with. And I reached this level of awareness while functioning in an academic environment where almost everyone I dealt with was a professor or fellow graduate student who, if not brilliant, was at least very intelligent. That talk was the first time it hit me that most people in the world are not particularly bright. It was quite a shock.

For me, social functioning during childhood was so abnormal that grade placement made little difference. The first time I skipped a grade was a highly negative experience because of the way the transition was handled (in March instead of near the beginning of a year or semester; without asking about my preferences, or even notifying me until after school on Friday that I would be in a new class the following Monday; and with no support—in fact, with active hindering of adjustment—by the new teacher). But when I skipped the last two years of high school, it was at my own request and against the advice of teachers and one parent, who were concerned that I wouldn't have enough opportunities for social development as an early college student. People said I would be socially isolated. I said I was already socially isolated in high school, and bored besides. I'd rather be socially isolated and intellectually stimulated than socially isolated and bored. At the time I still had no conception of being socially nonisolated; that idea wasn't part of my personal reality.

As a prepubescent college student, I was asked by parents of other gifted children whether I thought they should let their children skip grades. I told them to explain the options to the children and let them decide. They asked if skipping would cause social problems. I told them to consider how the child was doing socially in the current grade. If the child was able to make friends easily, he or she would probably continue to make friends in a more advanced grade. If the child didn't have any friends at all, he or she certainly wouldn't be any worse off socially in another grade, would at least be happier with more interesting academic material, and might even get along better with the older kids. But if the child had a hard time making friends and was finally starting to make some in the class he or she was in, then it could be too disruptive to change classes.

Are grade advancement and the provision of "gifted" programs a justification for the school to determine that a child does *not* require special education services for autism? Not unless he learns to apply his academic skills to areas that for most people are nonacademic. My academic skills haven't kept me from being unemployed, homeless, malnourished, intentionally victimized by people who would exploit anyone who was vulnerable, unintentionally victimized by people who didn't recognize that I was vulnerable, and endangered by my own lack of functional living skills. I don't consistently remember to eat, and don't have the organizational skills to shop regularly. I forget to shower or change clothes, sometimes for days at a time. Not only do I have minimal housekeeping skills, but I don't even have enough spatial orientation ability to keep track of where I am and what's happening in my own home. (One time I lost the broom while I was in the process of sweeping the floor.) At this point in my life, the most noticeable effect of my intellectual abilities is that they prevent me from receiving needed assistance from an adult service system that's geared for mental retardation.

With an autistic child there are additional social issues. He's not going to fit in and be "just one of the kids" no matter what grade he's in. He's going to need special help if he's going to be socially integrated in any class. I can't speak from experience about that, because I didn't have that kind of help. Would the school recognize the need for an aide if your child were in a class with older children? Would the older children be more open to accepting him and acting as social tutors and mentors for him? Or would they only resent him? And if they would resent him, would they resent him more or less than the younger kids will? (Gifted kids in regular classes are resented, by other kids and sometimes by teachers as well. It's a fact of life.) Whatever the decision, don't think in terms of a child being "as normal as possible." I think normalcy is neither an achievable goal nor an appropriate one, for either gifted children or autistic ones. A child with autism is not going to have a normal life no matter what you do. The question is, what would allow him to have the most productive and fulfilling life? What skills does he need to develop, and where could he best learn them? What activities does he enjoy, and where would he be happiest? Who are his friends, or does he have any friends, or is having friends even important to him?

Whatever class he's placed in, I think you should provide (*not* force) opportunities for him to meet and socialize with kids of all ages. He might get along best with ten-year-olds now, but if all his friends are that much older than he is, things could get rough when they're all teenagers and he's only ten years old. If he still has some opportunities for contact with other ten-year-olds at that time, he *might* become interested in getting to know some of them. I didn't start learning to appreciate six-year-olds until I was about thirteen, and I started helping out in a lower school classroom as my "community duty" assignment at school. *Then* I discovered that I like working with children and that I'm good at it. I was never good at getting along with children when I was a child myself! Along with little kids whom I could play and be silly with, the people I was most interested in as a teenager were college students I could exchange ideas with. I never have learned to communicate with teenagers; eventually I just got old enough that I was no longer expected to do so.

I'd recommend providing opportunities for any autistic, gifted student to have contact with other autistic children and adults. Through Autism Network International (ANI), an international peer support and advocacy organization run by and for autistic people, an autistic community has formed. Within this community, autistic people can share understanding, support, problem-solving strategies, and the simple enjoyment of being among people like ourselves. Autistic children and their parents can meet autistic adults, and start to get some ideas about what their own lives might be like in the future—things they can look forward to, and supports that they may continue to need. At a very fundamental level, contact with other autistic people has finally allowed me to understand what it means to meet friends who can relate to me at my own level, and what it is to be socially nonisolated. I've found others I can understand, and who can understand me, without the need for the complex monitoring and calculating and translating that are required to communicate with most people. I am able to connect in a shared space where I don't need to stay in intellectual overdrive. Other autistic people often share my social instincts and intuitions. When those instincts and intuitions actually work, our communication is like a starburst in a night sky.

The benefits of this kind of community are not limited to autistic people who are considered high-functioning. All autistic people, by definition, have some significant areas of being "low-functioning," or else they would not met the criteria for a diagnosis of autism. And I believe that all autistic people, given a proper environment and supports, have some areas in which they can be "high-functioning." I know people who are considerably lower functioning than I am in the areas typically measured by IQ tests and school grades, but are much higher functioning than I am in practical areas like daily living skills.

In my years of coordinating ANI, I have had many opportunities to see and be part of "first contact" experiences when a new member comes to a gathering to meet other autistic people for the first time. Occasionally during the early years, when I knew that a highly gifted autistic newcomer was going to come to a gathering where there also would be much more obviously impaired people, I wondered how the newcomer would respond to seeing such "low-functioning" people as peers. I found that there was no need to worry. There are certain autistic commonalities that we can see and relate to, whether autistic people can talk or not; whether they can read or not; whether they are toilet-trained or not. Just as a gifted person may value the company of other gifted people—whether disabled or not—in order to connect on a level of "giftedness," an autistic person may also need contact with other autistic people—whether gifted or not—in order to connect with others who share the world of autism. If you look for it, that starburst shines through the thickest clouds.

A gifted child with autism is going to need help with exactly the same things any other autistic child needs help with. He may be able to be helped with some things by turning them into cognitive tasks, but his cognitive abilities aren't going to make him any more able to cope with the world without special preparation. Don't let the school use his intelligence as an excuse to deny him one bit of the preparation he's going to need for nonacademic real life.

IF GIFTED = ASYNCHRONOUS DEVELOPMENT, THEN GIFTED/SPECIAL NEEDS = ASYNCHRONY[2]

by Lee Singer

Martha Morelock and the Columbus Group have suggested that "asynchronous development" is the defining characteristic of gifted children. Most of the literature on gifted children describes children whose asynchrony is mainly in the differences between their intellectual (mental) ages versus their chronological or emotional ages. I do not want to minimize the problems of meeting the needs of children who have mental ages more than 50 percent higher than their chronological ages. As Linda Kreger Silverman so aptly describes it, ". . . gifted children develop in an uneven manner, . . . they are more complex and intense than their agemates, . . . they feel out-of-sync with age peers and 'age appropriate curriculum,' . . . the internal and external discrepancies increase with IQ, and . . . these differences make them extremely vulnerable."[1]

Gifted/special-needs children develop in an even more extremely uneven manner. They are more complex and intense than their gifted agemates, and no single grade-level curriculum will meet their needs. These discrepancies are even greater than those of other gifted kids, making them even more vulnerable. In addition to having asynchrony between their intellectual and physical development, they have extreme asynchrony between intellectual development and the ability to express or use that intellect.

So what does it mean to be gifted/special needs? If gifted = asynchronous development, then gifted/special needs = asynchrony[2].

For my son, who is gifted and mildly dyslexic, it means being bored to tears in math and science classes because they are too easy, while struggling to read grade-level books. It means not being able to read books that discuss science and other topics at his level of understanding. It means finding the reading of class books challenging, but the classroom discussions excruciatingly boring.

For my son, who is gifted and has dysgraphia (extreme difficulties with writing), being gifted/special needs means having his hands get cramped and tired after only one page of writing. It means being unable to write and think at the same time, so that his written work doesn't

---

[1] Asynchrony, by Linda Kreger Silverman, Ph.D.

come anywhere near reflecting the depth of his thoughts. It means he is thinking about math concepts that his teachers don't understand, but having trouble writing them down.

For my son, who is gifted and has ADHD, being gifted/special needs means getting assignments wrong because he missed some of the instructions and therefore did the wrong thing correctly. It means getting in trouble for not paying attention because he is incapable of focusing on multistep oral instructions, but seems too smart to not understand what he is supposed to do. It means getting in trouble for losing control at the end of the day, when he is tired and his medication has worn off because "you're too smart to forget the rules."

For my son, being gifted is not enough to compensate for the combined effects of the dyslexia and the ADHD-caused auditory processing problems, which make it nearly impossible to learn a foreign language. My son is a visual-spatial learner but the dyslexia makes it hard to associate written and spoken words in a foreign language. The inability to attend to auditory stimuli consistently makes it almost impossible to associate the sounds of a foreign language with their meaning. So, being "many times gifted" means feeling hopeless and stupid in language class.

For me, having a child who is "many times gifted" means trying to find a school that can accommodate a highly gifted child with special needs, while living in a state where "gifted" is a dirty word. It means finding that private schools are not equipped to provide the special services for my son's learning disabilities, while the local public schools have no gifted programs. It means trying to convince schools that my child needs special education services even though he is working at grade level, because that is still far below his intellectual capacity. It means having a child who is simultaneously under- and over-challenged, who spends each day alternating between extreme frustration and extreme boredom, who is miserably unhappy at school and begs for home schooling. It means tears and battles over homework at the end of a long day, when the ADHD medications have worn off.

What does my son need? He needs support and accommodations for both his special needs and his giftedness. If I could design the perfect program for him, it would include occupational therapy for his physical problems with writing, allowing him to dictate all his work until he is physically ready to keyboard, and one-on-one instruction in writing until he is no longer convinced that he "can't write." It would include subject acceleration in math and science, so that he could be learning the subjects he most loves at his own level. It would include finding a math mentor who can explore advanced mathematics with him. It would include short school days and a light homework load, so that he has time outside of school to decompress and think and explore and just be a child. Most important, it would include teachers who understand that a child can both be highly gifted and have learning challenges and that inconsistent work is a sign of ADHD rather than of "not trying," who support him where he is weak while helping him soar where he is strong, and who appreciate his sparkle, creativity, and humor.

Having said all this, I am the one who is "many times gifted," because I have a beautiful, sensitive child whose gifts lead him to see the world in creative, unexpected ways, and whose intelligence and learning disabilities help make him a sensitive and loving child who brings me great joy and

LIVING WITH CONTRADICTIONS

by Michael V. Rios

I never use the term "gifted" anymore.

I have long felt that the use of the term has caused many of the problems we experience when trying to get resources we need for our children from various institutions, or to have a sympathetic conversation with other parents. Instead I describe my profoundly gifted son as having "ADS—asynchronous development syndrome" (usually preceded by "severe"). I find people then ask about it, and I start by explaining his least developed areas (such as handwriting, compositional ability, or organizational skills), some of which may be below his chronological grade level. I mention how he has long ago mastered the rest of the material in the grade that his weak areas would normally place him, leaving him with endless hours in class without a single new piece of information. He cannot be in any one grade without complex accommodations. I then talk about the social disadvantages and difficulties, that the kids he can play sports with are never the kids he can do homework with or play strategy games with, so it limits and fragments his interpersonal experiences.

The vast majority of the time, this has had the desired effect. As soon as I use the word "syndrome," people put on a sympathetic mind-set. As I describe the situation, the difficulties become quite clear before the extent of the giftedness is shown. I find many people, with whom the subject happened to come up at one time or another, regularly initiating conversations about him, asking me about how he is doing, with genuinely heartfelt concern.

I was forcibly confronted with these issues when my son was nine years old. We knew virtually nothing about giftedness at the time, nor had any clue about the extent of his abilities. His attitude and general personality had deteriorated over time, to the point that he had gone into a civil-disobedience mode with the school. He would walk into the classroom, but would refuse to participate in any way, even to the point of sitting on top of a desk, facing away from the teacher, and reading—and heaven help the teacher who tried to interfere! His behavior in or out of school was sullen, hostile, angry, at times even violent; he now succinctly describes his condition at the time as "insane."

We had tried dozens of different approaches without success, and finally took him for psychological testing. When we had him tested, he maxed the IQ test he was given, and his academic knowledge and ability ranged from two years behind grade level in writing to that of a college senior in science—a discrepancy of 4.5 standard deviations!

That discrepancy (which is the definition of asynchrony) is precisely what defines an identifiable learning disability (LD) for federally mandated services. Many parents have unnecessarily avoided this route, perhaps out of fear of stigma or of loss of control of the process. The guidelines for learning disabilities require accommodations in all areas that will help the child have a successful school experience, not just in the identified area of weakness; by having him identified as LD, we have been able to get the accommodations that we needed. We cited a Connecticut study that showed that learning disabilities in gifted kids improve the most by ignoring them, which gave us almost complete flexibility in his individualized educational plan (IEP). And the IEP cannot be legally put into place without the signatures of the parents, so the ultimate control remained in our hands.

When I have suggested this approach, some parents have had a hard time identifying in their own children the disabilities that virtually all these children have. The issue, though, is not about how talented our kids are, but the difficulties they face daily from their asynchrony: the child who can discern music far better than her fingers can play, or visualize better than she can draw.

Asynchrony emphasizes the real issue, and usually the greater the giftedness, the greater the asynchrony. We have kids who may need calculus before they're completely dry at night. We have kids who may have the professional skills of an adult, but the emotional maturity of an eight-year-old. We have kids who can produce and direct an award-winning video, but cannot write four sentences describing it. We have kids who can handle college-level science courses but don't have the organizational ability to get their lab reports from their backpacks into the teacher's hands.

Perhaps one of the most extreme asynchronous areas for many exceptionally gifted children is organizational ability. Too often, the child is considered lazy, unmotivated, oppositional, or worse, when the truth is that the child is incapable of maintaining organization. Organization requires certain types of neural development, just as walking and writing does; no amount of training or motivation will help until those developments occur. For many asynchronous children, without accommodations, this disability can cripple their attempts to function in an accelerated learning environment. And the effect of having a neurological deficiency treated as a moral or personal failing can have a devastating effect on a child.

If our kids were uniformly advanced, they would have far fewer problems; it is precisely the asynchrony that creates the special needs. Often, when an accommodation is needed for a gifted child, the issue is raised that other children should receive the same "benefit." This perception can result in gifted classes being watered down to accommodate nongifted children, or in the resource being taken away entirely. But kids who aren't asynchronous don't need accommodations to do well in a regular classroom.

Our "insane" nine-year-old is now a popular twelve-year-old, with a variety of accommodations and supports that allow him to have a patchwork of courses that reflect his varied abilities. He can handle advanced calculus, does well on tests, but can't get the homework done consistently. The teacher has accommodated this, with the IEP to back him up, and our son is able to stay challenged but not overwhelmed.

As parents, we're not asking for special privileges for our kids; we are asking for what they need to function in an appropriate environment. Without that, there is a loss of interest in school, depression, and even suicide. The emphasis on asynchrony as a syndrome, even a pathology, can help others realize that we are only concerned parents helping our children cope with their greatest challenges. Other parents can then see that we face the same issues that they do; and rather than being elitist, we are asking only that the schools and society make a place for *all* children, ours included.

PAIN, WASTE, AND THE HOPE FOR A BETTER FUTURE: "INVISIBLE DISABILITIES" IN THE EDUCATIONAL SYSTEM

by Margi Nowak

A few years ago, when my then preteen son and I went to Olympia to learn how to advocate for people with disabilities at one of the Advocacy Day Wednesdays held during the legislative session, I met a woman whose attempt to triumph over inexpressible pain stunned me to the point of mute but profound admiration. She was one of the "lunchtime mentors" to those of us who had come for the day to introduce ourselves individually to our state representatives, and she was also the mother of a son who had died of Niemann-Pick Type C—a hideously relentless neurological disease that inexorably kills male children who begin developing normally and then slowly lose all functions, inevitably deteriorating and dying before their teen years are over. This woman knew a kind of parental pain that the rest of us hope never to experience, let alone understand—a pain which might be seen as being at the extreme end of a continuum embracing all manner of disabilities ranging from those that guarantee acute physical suffering and premature death, to those which are virtually invisible. Deeply grateful for my experiential ignorance of the former kind of disability affecting a child of mine, I am, however, very familiar with the latter kind of pain: being the mother of a child whose disability is hidden rather than obvious. In extended family gatherings, in the classroom, in informal groups among age-peers, and in society in general, such children may at first glance appear to be "just like everyone else," for they use no wheelchairs, have no feeding tubes, and show no physical signs of pathology. But make no mistake about it: invisible neurological disabilities—particularly those which give rise to behavior patterns that differ from the expected norm in ways that bring forth negative judgments about child and parents alike—can indeed cause tremendous emotional pain for such children and their parents too. As a member of an international online community focusing on one such disability, I have four years' experience reading the stories shared on a private listserv by hundreds of other parents as well as adults who themselves have the same neurological condition. I have also participated actively in a Washington State support group for people affected by another neurological condition, and I regularly read an online support newsgroup related to this disability too. In addition, I am also a cultural anthropologist and an educator who has created a course on disability at my university.

My observations concerning the situation of children with invisible disabilities within the educational system are thus filtered through several different but complementary lenses: emotionally involved parent, theoretically informed researcher, pragmatically interested professor. No matter which way I look at the situation, however, my conclusion is the same: for such students and their families, the educational system is the site of far too much needless pain even as it wastes far too much human potential. At the root of this unnecessary suffering and waste, I believe, is not simply the bureaucracy, with all its entrenched, inflexible, and even Dilbert-like propensity to make positive and creative systemic (as opposed to incidental) change well-nigh impossible when proposed by relatively powerless people from the bottom of the system. In addition to this structural tendency for systems—however terrible they might be for some individuals—to stay basically the same as a whole, I believe there is also a corresponding ideological reason for this state of affairs. At issue here is the underlying question of expertise. The determination of what is true or acceptable or best in a particular social (or educational) system is typically made, in the end, by those with the power to make the determination stick. In the words of a phrase suggested by Michel Foucault, these "regimes of truth" thus operate in an inherently circular manner, with the "legitimate knowledge" of the gatekeepers and decision makers depending for its legitimacy on the assent of those whose "legitimate" expertise has put them into positions of power in the first place. How does this translate into the real lives of students with invisible disabilities? Typically, it involves what their parents see as an almost unwinnable (even if not formally declared) battle between two competing camps of "experts": the bureaucratically and hierarchically organized school system, fighting to break even if not win a numbers game against the scarce resources and limitations of budget, space, personnel, technology, training, and even taxpayers' good or ill will toward public education, versus the comparatively tiny, desperately pieced together, much less "legitimate" circle of people who, for reasons of love, commitment, and sometimes money (for those families who can afford it), act as advocates for such a student.

The very first campaign of such a battle—getting the child officially recognized as having a disability requiring special accommodations—can confront the parents with an even more painful shock than the one they had to face when they initially recognized and acknowledged that indeed their child was "not normal." In the vast majority of cases, students with hidden disabilities are not labeled as such in their infancy. Rather, parents have to absorb, little by little, the painful fact that their child is undeniably different from other children in the family, neighborhood, day-care center, play group, or preschool—and that this difference is causing their child to be left out, humiliated, taken advantage of, and above all, negatively judged by children and adults alike. As difficult as it might be for parents to accept this reality and then try to move on and help their child navigate through life, if the disability in question happens to be one not well known by the general medical and educational community, the parents then have to face the second painful shock: doctors and educators typically do not appreciate being told by "mere parents" that their label for their child's difference (e.g., behavior problem, or attentional difficulties) is wrong or incomplete, and that something else is going on with this particular child. In fact, getting the proper label can occupy years of the child's early educational career. To illustrate with one particular disability, Asperger syndrome (a variant of high-functioning autism) is a neurobiological condition marked by, among other characteristics, serious social skill deficiencies, especially with age-peers. It is often accompanied by moderate to severe executive dysfunction—that is, the individual can have enormous (and in some cases irremediable) difficulties planning, initiating, organizing, prioritizing, and completing required tasks.

At the same time, however, many children with AS are highly verbal, especially with adults, and another characteristic of the disorder—fascination with, and astonishing expertise concerning, a special area of interest (e.g., dinosaurs, sports statistics, trains, sharks, carnivorous plants)—makes them seem, in their early educational years at any rate, like "little professors," hardly needing remedial academic attention. And so, the stage is set: the parents, hearing the child come home from school day after day with tales of woe, especially from the nightmare periods of the school day for such a child—recess and lunch—see their child as having enormous needs for help and special consideration, while the teachers and other school personnel, seeing the same child reading considerably above grade level, often determine that the real problem here is an overprotective mother who refuses to allow her child to face the consequences of his inappropriate and blameworthy behavior. In the meantime, the child, who, because of his "weirdness" in his peers' eyes, will inevitably have attracted the attention of predatory types of students, will find himself set up again and again as prey. This is the child who is the perfect "victim" for setups. His neurological wiring is very likely to make him hypersensitive to stimuli involving sounds and touch as well as to obsessive-compulsive mental looping over perceived injustices. A soft, insistently repeated noise, inaudible to the teacher but calculated to "unnerve the nerd"; a tiny, personally meaningful object such as a special pencil, taken and "only borrowed" from such a student; a quick poke here, a "misplaced" lunch there—and the "weird kid" can be counted upon to explode in what to the predators is a highly entertaining display of socially inappropriate, clumsily expressed rage.

Eventually, after such a student accumulates sufficient battle scars from such episodes and attracts sufficient negative attention from teachers for not turning in work, his parents' first campaign in their battle to secure some sort of accommodations for their child will be over: He will very likely become a focus of concern. The official, bureaucratically bestowed label he will probably receive at first is not likely to result in a placement or system of accommodations that special education or 504 law so ideally seems to promise. Instead, such a student will typically be squeezed into whatever existing places and services his school already provides for "kids with problems," and he is all too likely to be labeled as qualifying for these services on the basis of having some "other health impairment" such as severe behavior disorder (SBD), oppositional defiant disorder (ODD), or attention deficit disorder (ADD).

Such a label, typically involving at least partial-day placement in a learning resource room (LRC) will then, because of limitations of space and personnel, typically put the student in what one researcher of Asperger syndrome has called the worst possible environment for this type of child. What this individual so desperately needs is constant, supportive, guided exposure to the very best peer-age role models in the school building, and what he often gets instead is a segregated experience with special-needs students whose different issues and problems make them the very last people on the planet likely to tolerate, much less nurture, the "Forrest Gumps" of the world.

If this all-too-typical train of events is not already depressing enough, it is, in addition, highly likely that at least some of the students with hidden disabilities such as Asperger syndrome may also be gifted (even though their work output may still be "substandard" according to "normal" criteria such as grade averages). Here a sad and sorry waste compounds the personal tragedy of "wrong placement": neither the student nor society in general is ever likely to benefit from what could be exceptional intellectual or artistic abilities. Instead, in these sorts of cases such talents will appear merely as quirky flashes of odd genius, garnering for their holder none of the specialized and sustained guidance needed for these gifts to develop to their full potential. All too often, school systems justify their refusal to let such students gain entry to special programs for the gifted and talented by citing the "normal" requirements, forgetting or ignoring the fact that for these students, life is never going to be normal. Furthermore, what the gatekeepers often confuse in such situations is the difference between exceptional abilities and the "normal" display of these qualifications. Some disabilities, particularly those that involve executive dysfunction, mean that for the person's entire lifetime, his or her ability to meet certain standards of achievement is always going to be compromised. How sad for the school system to use one or several of the symptoms of an invisible disability—which is emotionally painful enough as it is—as justification for exclusion from what could otherwise, if done right, be a genuine avenue for success. Even without the issue of giftedness complicating the situation of students with hidden disabilities, the problem of securing the proper fit between student and program typically involves endless and exhausting negotiations between home and school. While perceptive and caring individual teachers may, here and there throughout a particular student's career, make a tremendous difference in one or another classes such a student may take, the educational system as a whole is woefully unable to maximize the potential of all the square pegs who just cannot be made to fit into round holes. Privately, among themselves, many parents of children with such disabilities have often had furtive thoughts of wishing for a temporary switch: "Just for a few days, let them see my child in the body of a Stephen Hawking. Perhaps then maybe they'll notice that not all brain impairment equals intellectual impairment, and also, perhaps—God forbid—if my child looked so disabled, perhaps then we could finally stop fighting to get appropriate services."

As more than one such parent has further observed, the prevailing wisdom among the battle-weary is that the decision makers in the educational system all too often wait for the child to fail (or the parents to threaten to take legal action) before finally deciding to allocate funds and resources to provide more appropriate accommodations. And, in line with the observation that educational bureaucracies operate as "regimes of truth" (with the legitimacy of the gatekeepers' power determined by the very same criteria of expertise that determine who gets to wield that power), the school system also controls the definition of what it means to "fail." A student whose disability severely impacts his ability to hand in homework "normally," but who is bright enough to pass standardized exit tests, will probably manage to squeak by and pass most of his required courses. That student's parents, who fear, with every fiber of their being, that their child's eventual high school diploma will guarantee him virtually no viable future after they are dead, may plead and plead that the "failure" is taking place right now, but since their expertise as parents is structurally positioned at the bottom of the chain of decision makers, their concerns and ideas have no effect on comprehensive, long-range policy decisions. Instead, such parents are "cooled out" by district-level administrators who listen but who are "tone-deaf" to hear, and worn down by the sheer number of steps required to secure the genuinely appropriate, system-wide (rather than haphazard and piecemeal) set of accommodations that would make all the difference for their child.

This is not what the law either intends or even permits. Section 504 as well as special education laws provide ample legal grounds for the creation of truly individualized educational programs for students with disabilities, but if the disability in question happens to be one that is not familiar to school staff and administrators, and/or if the parents request accommodations that have never been heard of let alone tried before, the chances are almost certain that the only accommodations the child in question will have received by the time he or she exits the supposedly "free, appropriate public education" system will have been a patchwork of cobbled-together partial adjustments that have had to be hammered out anew every September, with each new year's slate of teachers taking at least three months to even begin the realize the extent of the disability's impact on educational performance. When the vast majority of these teachers are indeed caring, capable educators, who often would help provide more appropriate accommodations—if they had proper support from higher up the chain of command—the waste of potential here is even more tragic. A sadly perfect illustration of this tragedy (insightful planning, worthy intentions, and hard work never finding their mark) is the contrast between the wonderfully well-done individualized education plan and 504-related material posted on the OSPI website—in particular, the 67-page online brochure entitled "Ladders to Success: A Student's Guide to School After High School" (http://inform.ospi.wednet.edu/sped/transition/ladders.pdf)—and the shocking lack of mention if not awareness on the part of high school educational and administrative staff that this document (and more important, the impulse behind it) even exists. Transition services for special-needs high school students may be promised by law and described in hope-affirming words in official documents, but in the trenches no one seems to know much about this phrase, let alone how to implement it appropriately, when the student in question is not "seriously" or "obviously" disabled. Perhaps some gatekeepers to these kinds of services believe that preparing "these kinds" of special-needs students for a college and post-college career is an exercise in delusional thinking, but personal biographical stories shared in online support groups by bright, articulate adult survivors who have precisely these kinds of disabilities (invisible conditions that resulted in their being judged incompetent and lazy themselves throughout their early school years) reveal the possibility of far more hopeful post-high school outcomes.

What would it take for these hopeful outcomes to become more of a reality? How could the pain and waste that is currently so operative in the lives of students with little known, invisible disabilities be ameliorated?

Three related suggestions come immediately to mind:

All teachers and administrators (rather than only special education experts) need more adequate training for dealing with the special needs of students with disabilities who are increasingly populating regular education classes. Clearly it is not possible for all teachers to be instructed in advance concerning all possible disabilities, but there needs to be a system-wide network of support for school personnel, beginning with an efficient, administratively sanctioned delivery system of information, custom-tailored to address the particular strengths and weaknesses of each individual student identified as having special needs. Many parents try mightily to educate their child's teachers by filling their school mailboxes with relevant information gleaned from excellent, up-to-date Internet Web sites devoted to the disability in question, but with no legitimization given to this material from the top of the bureaucracy, overworked teachers are likely to merely file these pages away for future reference. Another key role for this administratively sanctioned information delivery system could also be that of working to close the knowledge gaps that exist between those (typically, parents and advocates) who know what education law intends and promises, and those (typically, school personnel) who may actually be less knowledgeable in this respect, but who still control access to services.

Distinct from the special education department in each school, and integrated within the entire complex of school programs, facilities, buildings, and personnel, there should be a permanent, daily, clearly recognized person, place, and position (perhaps filled by social workers) to serve as an immediately available resource for students whose special needs are likely to involve them in social misunderstandings and conflicts with others in the school. Such a person would be trained to serve as the student's advocate vis-à-vis teachers and students who do not understand the effect of the student's disability, and the room itself would serve as a safe haven for, among other things, the student's self-initiated removal from potentially explosive situations. Dividing up such services ("If you're in a crisis situation on a Tuesday morning, go to the guidance counselor; if she's busy, wait for the assistant principal or make an appointment to see the school psychologist next week") engenders a feeling of wandering hopelessness for the student, which can quickly cancel out any previously made gains in self-reliance and trust in others. Legitimate recognition should be given to the hard-won expertise of parents regarding the complexities of their special-needs child. Of course professionally trained teachers and administrators have vastly more collective and pedagogical experience with thousands of students "who are not like this one," but the parents of a special-needs child have infinitely more experiential wisdom about what is likely to work or cause more problems with precisely this one. While special education law is very clear about the crucial importance of incorporating parental input into such students' educational plans, the social and political realities of the status contests and insecurities displayed at parent-teacher meetings greatly compromise the good intent of the law. What is important to recognize in the end, however, is that whether the parent is a suit-clad professional or a single mother who comes trembling to school meetings wearing sweat pants and an attitude, she, more than anyone else in that meeting room, is most likely to be locked on to the most important target of all underlying her child's education: providing the best possible answer to the question "What will happen to him when I'm no longer here?"

All other educational goals and objectives pale in comparison to the need to address and continually keep in mind this absolutely fundamental priority. For parents of children with disabilities, it is this question more than any other which motivates them to keep persisting, through all the inevitable as well as sadly unnecessary pain and waste of potential, to fight for a better future.

ONE LAST WORD

by Ameli Cyr

There's something I want you to know.
You can't help us that much.
The only thing you can do is,
don't yell or push.
It just won't work.
You've got to be gentle with us,
and gentle with animals,
particularly the ones who are becoming extinct
in certain places.
We're just
like them—
we're rare
but precious.
There are twice-exceptional students,
and there are talented students.
I think I'm both.
Some of us are like that.
If we're one, we're the other.
You can help us.
Be gentle with us.
That's all I want to say.
Gotta go.

TEACHING STRATEGIES: LEARNING AND LEADERSHIP

Individualization may be the only lifeline that some twice-exceptional children have in a school environment. Research has shown that a child in crisis needs one good, kind adult in order to have a handle on the positive aspects of life. If family life becomes chaotic, children and teens often turn to a teacher. I used to think that all of the teachers should accommodate the special needs of my children. After all, Section 504 law demands it. The Individuals with Disabilities Act demands it. Yet, how is a teacher with twenty-five or more students in a classroom supposed to provide learning opportunities for every one of those intellectually diverse students? In the upper grades, when a teacher sees those students for less than an hour before getting a whole new group, what is she or he supposed to do? Standards-based teaching has become popular, as teachers strive to ensure that their students meet a certain level of competence. This philosophy is anathema for twice-exceptional students. I think it's time for a revolution in education and teaching strategies, a revolution that celebrates the individual rather than the mass approach. Teaching to the middle means that somebody loses learning time. Standards-based education means that teachers feel compelled to teach standards instead of teaching children. These teachers and parents explore some answers.

PARADOXES:
A PARENT/TEACHER PERSPECTIVE

by Amy Bailey

One of the great paradoxes of giftedness is that it can be coupled with disabilities. When I first began teaching over twenty years ago, the profile for a gifted child was clear cut and simple: gifted children were good at everything. The truth is that most gifted children have a far more uneven development. In fact, over the years, I have come to believe that the children with the most phenomenal gifts often have severe deficits and that they compensate for these deficits in novel and unexpected ways.

As the parent of a twice-exceptional child and a teacher of the gifted, I have spent many hours in both personal and professional reflection of the paradox of these children. I have come to one conclusion: We must address the learning difficulties of gifted children by promoting their strengths instead of dwelling on their weaknesses. This is true for all children, but with gifted children it is vital to offer the experiences and intellectual stimulation that will lead them to offset their weaknesses in their own unique ways.

Chances are you are searching for answers on how to meet the needs of a child who seems to defy the standard expectations. Although my comments are addressed to parents, they also apply to the many concerned teachers looking for ways to help these special children reach their full potential. The answers center on three basic areas of concern: placement, balancing a curriculum that is challenging yet not overpowering, and finding appropriate extracurricular activities.

Finding the right placement: Where does my child fit in?

Many twice-exceptional children miss out on participation in special programs for the gifted. Sometimes their deficits mask their gifts and they are not identified. Sometimes they are seen as lazy or uncooperative because their abilities shine through, and teachers assume they just aren't applying themselves. Often parents fear that the work will be too demanding and that the child will suffer a sense of failure, and so they opt for a less challenging course of study. On the other hand, many twice-exceptional children hide their weaknesses so well that they miss out on important opportunities to learn strategies to help them overcome their disabilities—lessons that will make not only school easier, but which may give them lifelong benefits. They spend extra hours struggling to complete what their peers do in minutes, convinced that they just need to work harder, when in fact, they really need to learn to work smarter.

Most twice-exceptional children can reap important benefits from a gifted curriculum, but it is important to create an individual education plan (IEP) that addresses gifts as well as identifies problems. Your child may need assistance from an LD resource teacher who should be an integral part of the teaching team, and modifications may have to be made to accommodate the child's particular learning style.

What if the school says my child doesn't score high enough on the standardized test to be admitted to the gifted program?

Programs for giftedness may follow guidelines from the state, school district, or even the individual school. There are no standardized federal guidelines, so it is difficult to generalize about programs. If your child has a documented disability and is qualified to receive special services under IDEA, use the clause that says such students must be placed in the least restrictive environment. This clause usually means that a child should be mainstreamed, whenever possible, in a regular-education class. In the case of a twice-exceptional student, it also means that the child should be placed in a gifted program when it is clear that the child would benefit from an academically challenging placement.

Often standardized IQ or academic achievement test scores determine placement, but these tests are not always valid for children with learning disabilities. For example, a child with a language disability would be at a disadvantage if given an IQ test that relied heavily on verbal skills. It would be much more appropriate to use a test like the Test of Nonverbal Intelligence (TONI). Many school districts also use a multifaceted portfolio. Consider gathering your child's outstanding work and presenting it as proof of abilities. Don't limit the portfolio to written work or even schoolwork. For example, your child may have created a complex science experiment at home just for the fun of it. Take photos of the completed work, or videotape your child explaining the project and the steps taken to complete it. You might include letters from adults in a position to comment on your child's gifts, such as a scout leader or athletic coaches, or camp counselors at summer enrichment programs. Familiarize yourself with the characteristics of gifted children so that you can identify those behaviors and point them out to the educators who will be making the placement decision about your child. Collecting this type of information will help you provide the placement committee with a more accurate picture of your child's special gifts.

How is a gifted curriculum different from a regular curriculum?

The curriculum for a gifted student has been modified in one or more ways. These modifications include enrichment, which is common in, although not limited to, elementary schools. Enrichment means that in addition to the material in the regular curriculum, children are exposed to more advanced ideas or given extra opportunities to explore a subject in depth. It is the regular curriculum with a bit more added on. In a pull-out program, a special teacher takes all of the children from a grade or school and pulls them out of regular class for enrichment. Another modification might be curriculum compacting, in which the class moves much faster than in the regular curriculum. A gifted class of fifth graders might complete regular fifth-grade math and begin working on sixth-grade concepts, thus compacting an extra half year of work into a single year. Skipping a grade is also a form of curriculum compacting. It is important for you to understand which type of modifications are already in place and use that information to make decisions about further modifications for your child.

What are the advantages of placement in the gifted program?

For the majority of twice-exceptional children, placement with gifted peers can have long-term benefits. Foremost is the chance to enhance self-esteem. Students have an opportunity to have true intellectual peers. These peers not only validate the child's own sense of self-worth, but also give a sense of social connection and a sense of social responsibility. When the child has a chance to explore stimulating new ideas with gifted peers, learning becomes exciting rather than routine. I have found in my work at the high school level that gifted students tolerate differences much more than typical teenagers do. Since these students value intellectual abilities, they will respect the gifts of their twice-exceptional peers and view their difficulties with understanding.

Now that my child is in a gifted program, how do I make sure he or she is not overwhelmed?

For true inclusion, the regular classroom teacher, the gifted teacher (if the program is a pull-out enrichment program) and the learning disabilities resource teacher must work together as a team. Make sure that your child's IEP stipulates that the LD resource teacher give input. This stipulation can be handled in a number of ways. The child may see the resource teacher at regular intervals to work on areas of concern, or the resource teacher may actually come into the class to observe and assist, or meet with the classroom teacher to discuss modifications. The LD teacher is an expert at working with children with learning disabilities, and must be involved. Don't be afraid to ask the LD resource teacher if he or she feels that the regular teacher is following the suggestions made, and likewise, be sure to ask the regular teacher if the LD resource teacher works actively on the teaching team.

How do I know if all members of the IEP team are working together?

You might ask for a regular progress report that tells what each member of the team is doing as well as the progress your child is making. Such reports encourage everyone to work together and give you important information about your child. You might consider designing the form yourself so that you can specify the types of information you would find most helpful. Make it a simple form, perhaps even a checklist with space to write in subjects covered or modifications made. Good forms actually evolve as the year progresses and you tailor them to the needs of the teacher, the parent, and the child. Listen to your child. Does he feel overwhelmed? Is she spending hours on homework every night? If so, take this as a red flag to investigate the problem and get the teaching team to brainstorm possible solutions. Do not automatically assume that the program is not right because it is too demanding. Think outside the box and ask "How can my child demonstrate his or her abilities in spite of the learning disability?" Older children should be allowed to give their own input as well. I find they come up with much more creative alternatives than I do.

My child needs extra time to complete assignments, and this modification is a part of the IEP. Won't it be impossible to keep up in a class that utilizes curriculum compacting?

Curriculum compacting is possible because gifted children do not need as much practice to absorb concepts as their less gifted peers do. It doesn't mean that they do twice as much work, but rather that they can learn twice as fast. Teachers of the gifted understand the concept that less is more, so they can understand that a child might not need to complete volumes of work to show mastery. This in itself can be a boon to children overwhelmed by what amounts to, at least for them, mindless busy work in the regular classroom. For example, an ADHD child might have trouble focusing on twenty-five math problems, especially when the concept has already been mastered, but might be asked to complete the five most difficult. In a compacted curriculum, this type of modification would already be in place. If your child needs extra time, the IEP can include that need.

In what ways can the gifted curriculum be modified to meet the needs of a twice-exceptional child?

I advise parents and teachers to become familiar with the characteristics of their child's learning disability. The first step in meeting needs is to understand what those needs are. From there, be creative. I try to approach modifications with a clear idea of the concept I am teaching. How can a student demonstrate mastery of the *concept?* This doesn't mean my standards are lower, just that my means of assessment are different.

Common accommodations allow students to use technology to compensate. Dyslexic students often use books on tape, and students with written language expression can create audio- or videotapes to show mastery. Is this "cheating"? Do these students get out of doing work? No. They must be held to high standards for their alternate demonstrations of mastery. I seldom have been disappointed by these alternate assessments. Many times, this type of modification actually helps a student make the connections needed to overcome the disability.

Let me give you a specific example: W was a student in my tenth-grade academically gifted English class. He was very verbal, contributed great ideas to class discussions, and did very well on tests of reading comprehension. When it came time to write essays, his written work in no way reflected the depth of his understanding. I learned from his parents that in the fourth grade he had been tested privately and it was determined he had a disability in written language expression. Nothing was done since he was so gifted; he had no serious problem until he reached the more demanding English courses in high school.

How could W compensate for his disability and still master advanced expository writing? I analyzed his work and realized that his biggest problem was organization. He found it literally impossible to create an outline for a composition. The assignment was to take two poems and a short story and write a paper that discussed some common thread that ran through all three works. I realized he was highly visual and delighted in drafting and mechanical drawing, so I asked, "If these three works of literature were three pieces of a machine, could you draw a schematic in which you show the points at which they make contact and how those points function together?" I certainly could not have made such a drawing, but W smiled and said, "Sure." He began sketching and we labeled the parts of his "machine" to correspond to the works of literature and the common thread in each. The next day he had complex drawings with several views, which he had to explain to me, but it was clear he had the concept. Now I had a concrete way to help him make the connection between the picture in his mind and the more conventional written outline form.

For several months W "drew" outlines and we worked together to get his ideas in written rather than visual form, but little by little, he made the transition and his writing improved greatly. We were willing to think outside the box. Focus on the gifts and allow them to compensate for the disability. You might not be able to tear down a mountain, but it is possible to build a road that goes around. W did.

Other than placement in a gifted program, is there anything I can do to ensure that my twice-exceptional child finds school challenging, rewarding, and fun?

Try to remember that there is more to education that just academics. We sometime feel twice-exceptional children "waste" too much time pursuing eclectic interests rather than putting that effort into schoolwork. A few years back I had a conference with a parent who felt her twice-exceptional son spent too much time on art projects and that they interfered with his work in English. She confirmed that he had expressed an interest in a career in commercial art. I went on to explain that I used art concepts to help him relate to English. For example, his understanding of drawing in perspective helped to clarify the literary concept of point of view. Sometimes early interests turn into rewarding careers, and we need to take the time to let children find out what they are good at, and give them the freedom to pursue what they love.

Can some of my child's interests be bad?

Yes, there can be problems. If you find your teen only wants to spend hours engrossed in interactive role-playing games with peers you find questionable at best, don't ignore this and assume that he is simply pursuing what he loves. There are important considerations, especially for teens. If you find the child's interest is self-destructive, shuts him off from family and former friends, or has gotten him in trouble with authorities at school or in the community, intervene. But I believe that certain steps can be taken to keep this type of self-destructive interest from taking over. Steps could include paying careful attention to how and when the child focuses attention, and providing opportunities for healthy outlets, such as sports or productive group activities.

What can I do to head off these kinds of problems?

One of the best ways to discourage your child from the wrong activities is to involve him or her from an early age with constructive ones. Let your child try a variety of things and when something clicks, encourage it.

What types of activities are best?

At the top of my list is Odyssey of the Mind, a creative problem-solving competition. I have had great success with OM teams with members who were twice-exceptional. Because teams are made up of seven members working together, the child learns teamwork, and since a team needs members with a wide variety of gifts, there is usually a niche for almost every child. Music and band are also great activities. Again, students learn to work together and share the common interest in music. For athletic students, sports offer the same recognition. Drama, debate, art, dance, mock trial, and other activities are great as well. Also consider special summer camps. I have seen many twice-exceptional children gain self-confidence and leadership skills from participation in a Junior ROTC program or the study of martial arts. As your child approaches teen years, consider seeking out a mentor. For example, if your child has a strong interest in architecture, see if a local architect will be willing to consider an internship. Many professionals are delighted to find young people interested in their own fields. Many schools offer internships and apprenticeships, and programs like DECA can also help your child seek out mentors for future careers.

No hard and fast rules exist, but if we trust these children, value their strengths and support them as they deal with their weaknesses, they have a chance to reach their full potential and will grow up to do wonderful, amazing things.

SPECIAL ED OR GIFTED? IT MAY BE HARD TO TELL

by Susan Winebrenner

In spite of all the time and energy educators spend trying to match the right special-needs label to the right child, a child who is "twice-exceptional" will probably be identified only for her "disability" and rarely for her strengths. Two of the many children I have taught over the years exemplify the complexity of identification and strategy implementation for twice-exceptional students. Readers of these case studies could consider how these students might be served within the existing system.

In fourth grade, Elias's deficits are apparent. His writing is illegible, he still hasn't mastered his number facts, and his skills in math and language arts leave much to be desired. His articulation problems make him sound like a much younger child. But Elias is a maven when it comes to maps, U.S. geography, and national parks and monuments. When his family takes a trip, Eli plans it. He can recite and describe the daily itinerary from every one of those trips for the past four years. He kinesthetically understands all the basic map terms and simply lights up when talking about his favorite national parks and monuments.

The class is about to begin a unit on map terms and skills and Eli reminds me that he already knows "that stuff." I tell him, and the entire class, that the end of the unit test is available for anyone who believes they can demonstrate mastery before the unit is taught. Eli easily scores in the A range on the test, and is therefore excused from having to do the work that is planned for those who still need to learn the essential information about maps and geography.

Now I experience a dilemma. How should he spend his social studies time during the next few weeks? Shall I allow him to work on an extension activity, or would it be better if I used that time to have him work on those areas in which he is so woefully inadequate? The deciding question is this: Is Eli truly exceptional in his ability in this particular content? Clearly, he is. Therefore, is Eli as eligible for differentiation in this area as someone who is "gifted across the board"? Clearly, he is. So I follow the same guidelines with Eli I would use with any other student eligible for differentiation. From a menu of extension activities I have prepared during my planning for this unit, Eli chose a task that matched his learning style strengths: kinesthetic and visual. He will create an imaginary country, using instant papier-mâché. On the model, he will locate examples of at least ten terms and concepts the class will be learning. He will be expected to follow certain working conditions in order to be eligible to continue working on his project day by day. He will keep a daily record of his project on a log I have provided.

Four weeks later, as the map unit ends, Eli presents his project to a spellbound class. Naturally, other students think it would be a fine idea to create a country too. So for the next three days, they work in small groups to do the job, and during that time Eli serves as the "create-a-country consultant."

That experience had profound, long-lasting effects on Eli and his classmates. Even during times when his deficits were visible, everyone could remember how Eli was able to demonstrate dramatic strength and talent in his area of expertise, and students could learn how to better appreciate the strengths and weaknesses in every person, including themselves. Eli is clearly a child who is twice-exceptional. Significant learning disabilities plague his academic progress in almost all of his schoolwork. Yet, he has equally significant strengths in one or two areas that should allow him to be eligible for the differentiation that is the educational right of any gifted student, since those opportunities will lead him to reach his learning potential. High success in this project could lead to better success in those areas that give Elias trouble. Emphasizing his strengths will give him more chance to access those strengths in all areas of learning.

Donna, on the other hand, began with a different set of needs. Donna had striking features, and she was loudly aggressive, under incredible stress from a home environment that provided more ups and downs than a roller coaster ride. She was in a small elementary school where a close-knit group of caring teachers provided stability, support, and dependable routines through all of Donna's elementary years.

Donna participated competently in the gifted program at her school, in a resource room program for gifted students that met one day each week. Although she often got into altercations on the playground, she usually responded positively to the staff's efforts to keep her on a steady course and got through most school days without serious temper flare-ups or physical outbursts. On bad days, she would spend some time in the "responsibility training room," where she learned more appropriate ways of interacting with her peers and teachers.

In junior high school, things were different. There was a no-nonsense discipline code, which was strictly enforced. More often than not, Donna was in the school office, sitting through yet another forced exit from her classroom for not following the rules. The most absurd outcome of this discipline plan was that Donna had accrued so many strikes by the middle of March, the only thing that was left for her to lose was her eligibility to attend the end-of-the-year school picnic on May 27! Needless to say, Donna did not qualify for any of the accelerated sections that were available in that school in reading or math. One frustrated teacher even commented, "Donna doesn't deserve to be gifted!" She probably meant that, in her opinion, Donna's behavior contraindicated her placement in any gifted education program, which some of the teachers believed should be reserved for kids whose exemplary classroom behavior entitled them to such "special services."

I absolutely believe this teacher was sincere in her convictions, and did not understand the reality that kids who have exceptional abilities are entitled to appropriate educational services. Very often, in regular classrooms, gifted students must first demonstrate neat, legible, and accurate productivity on the grade-level work before they are entitled to progress to enrichment or extension activities. This is ironic, because gifted kids need something different from the regular curriculum so they can experience the promises made by lofty school missions statements, not simply because they are gifted.

Children with learning disabilities, behavior disorders, or other types of school problems who are also gifted in one or more areas must be allowed to be gifted in their areas of strength while they receive assistance in their areas of need. The discrepancy between their superior abilities and their dramatic weaknesses results in feelings of inadequacy, frustration, and hopelessness. Many are at high risk of becoming school dropouts. It is simply not effective or fair to bring sanctions against any child which prevent them from experiencing differentiation whenever necessary.

In many parent-teacher conferences regarding twice-exceptional children, parents often express confusion about the child's inability to concentrate at school. Mom or Dad will describe how Jonathan can stay on-task for lengthy periods when he is working on a project or subject that absorbs his interest. Everyone wonders, "How can the same brain be ADHD and not ADHD at different times?" Parents offer the hopeful suggestion that perhaps Jonathan is not really ADHD. Closer to reality might be the fact that if the teacher can find ways to allow Jonathan, and others like him, to learn the required standards through a topic of consuming interest, the student might exhibit fewer ADHD behaviors at school.

When teachers understand and use the processes of compacting and differentiation, these fears can be put to rest. Compacting, a term created by Dr. Joseph Renzulli and Dr. Sally Reis, is the process of allowing highly capable students to demonstrate their previous mastery of some of the required curriculum. Compacting also occurs when students are allowed to demonstrate that they need less time than their age-mates to learn new material. When the evidence of the need for compacting is present, differentiation steps in. This means that students who demonstrate that the regular curriculum or pacing is not providing the appropriate challenge for them, different topics or activities should become available. As a matter of fact, this reasoning should be all that parents need to use to convince educators that differentiation is appropriate. We ask for it, not because a student is gifted by whatever definition, but because that student is as far removed from the age-appropriate learner as is a student whose ability is two standard deviations below average.

For all students in a class to accept the presence of differentiation opportunities regarding curriculum, teachers need to help all students understand and appreciate individual differences. We spend lots of school time teaching kids to be tolerant of cultural and ethnic diversity. Appreciating the reality of diversity in learning ability is a natural extension of that concept.

When asked to differentiate the curriculum for a twice-exceptional child, the teacher may express concern about the reaction from other students if she allows this modification for Jonathan. She may expect that other students will ask something like, "How come Jonathan gets to do something different? Why can't we do the topic we want, too?" I firmly believe that differentiation opportunities should be offered to any student who can benefit from them. For example, a student such as Elias (described previously), who can demonstrate mastery level on upcoming curriculum before it is taught, should have the opportunity to demonstrate that mastery in a way that is learning-style compatible and experience the differentiation opportunities. By learning-style compatible, I mean that if they have difficulties in writing, they should be able to dictate the evidence of mastery into a tape recorder, or type it out on a computer. In the words of Dr. Kenneth Dunn, "If they're not learning the way we teach them, let's teach them the way they learn!"

Happily, solutions for these dilemmas are surfacing. Within the gifted education community, the issue of appropriate interventions for students who are "twice-exceptional" is a hot topic. Groups are forming in several states to aid educators and parents in dealing with this special challenge. A network supporting this movement can be accessed using information from the Resources Section at the end of this chapter.

Some classroom practices are appropriate for these students whose giftedness is often obfuscated by their glaring learning weaknesses. Several chapters in this book contain information about useful strategies. There is an abundance of written resources to help frustrated youngsters, their parents, and teachers understand this dilemma of being twice-exceptional. Several publishing houses provide catalogs listing more material than most persons have time to peruse. Sometimes, family counseling with a therapist who understands the dynamics created by the presence of gifted children, with or without disabilities, can facilitate the use of techniques that help the family understand and accept realities and choose responses to family situations that facilitate harmony.

The following are considerations that may allow twice-exceptional students to become more productive and comfortable at school.

1. Teachers and parents should create a learning atmosphere in which individual differences are valued, where kids can really learn from their mistakes, and where positive growth is noticed.

2. Students should be taught in their learning-style strengths before remediation is practiced. There should also be regular opportunities for students to express what they are learning in nontraditional ways. These include: drawings, making tape recordings of what they have learned, using visual organizers, using computer-assisted learning programs, spell-check and grammar-check programs, and using video and other visual formats for teaching.

3. In testing situations, teachers should allow students to work where they can apply compensation strategies such as: working without a time limit, reading the test items aloud or having someone else read them, or listening to soothing music as they work. If teachers really want to test what these kids know, the students should be allowed to finish the incomplete items at another time and record them informally for home-school use only. Naturally, this data would not be sent to the standardized testing agencies.

4. Teachers should teach students to set short-term realistic goals and to take credit for partial amounts of work. Setting a goal for each instructional period regarding the amount of work the student predicts she can complete by the end of the period can help turn hopelessness into productivity.

5. Teachers can find the areas of learning in which students have a passionate interest, even if it is outside the parameters of the regular curriculum, and find ways to allow the kids to work on those topics now and then

6. Teachers must avoid entreating these kids to try harder. When the message that the senses are perceiving gets mixed-up on its way to the brain, it's more helpful for someone to demonstrate how a task should be attempted than it is to talk about effort. Teachers need to remember that the demonstration should include several concrete examples of how the task might be attacked.

There are many students in all classrooms whose giftedness is masked by a learning disability or challenge. They have noticeably uneven abilities from subject to subject, and may experience great frustration in some types of schoolwork. It is very important to be able to notice and attend to their giftedness while simultaneously helping them learn compensation strategies for their weaknesses. It's a daunting task, but one we can accomplish by using the resources contained in this book.

RESOURCES:

For more information about the twice-exceptional network, contact Daphne Bowers in Cherry Creek, CO at (303) 486-4230. Several books also may be helpful:

Baum, S., S. Owen, and J. Dixon. 1991. *To Be Gifted and Learning Disabled.* Mansfield Center, Conn: Creative Learning Press.

Bireley, Marlene. 1993. *Crossover Children: A Sourcebook for Helping the Learning Disabled/Gifted Child.* Greyden Press.

Dixon, John. 1983. *The Spatial Child.* Springfield, Ill.: Charles C. Thomas.

Dunn, Rita, and Kenneth Dunn. 1987. *Teaching Students Through Their Individual Learning Styles.* New York: Prentice Hall.

Freed, Jeffrey. 1997. *Right-Brained Children in a Left-Brained World.* New York: Simon and Schuster.

Lee, Christopher, and Rosemary Jackson. 1992. *Faking It: A Look into the Mind of a Creative Learner.* Portsmouth, N.H.: Heinemann.

Lyman, Donald. 1986. *Making the Words Stand Still.* Boston: Houghton Mifflin.

Vail, P. 1987. *Smart Kids with School Problems.* New York: Penguin Books.

CATALOGS FOR FURTHER MATERIALS

Free Spirit Publishing, Minneapolis, MN, 1-800-735-7323.

How Difficult Can This Be? Video demonstrates actual conditions experienced by persons with learning disabilities. PBS video. 1-800-344-3337.

The ADD Warehouse, Plantation, FL, 1-800-233-9273.

GIFTED/SPECIAL NEEDS, THE INTERNET, AND ME

by Meredith G. Warshaw

Knowing how to parent a gifted child can be an extremely difficult experience. The same is true of parenting a special-needs child. When you have a gifted/special-needs child, the confusion and frustration can be truly overwhelming. Finding information, resources, and emotional support are critical in direct proportion to the difficulty of finding them!

In recent years, the Internet has turned the world into a global village. For many of us with gifted/special-needs kids, this global village has been a lifeline. There are several reasons that the Internet can provide us with help that is not available in "real life":

1. **Numbers:** In any given school system, there may be very few kids who are gifted/special needs. Professionals there seldom, if ever, will have encountered a child like ours. If a group comprises just 0.1 percent of the population, however, there will be 200,000 members of that group in a country of 200,000,000 people.

2. **Expanded knowledge base:** Not much research exists on the needs of gifted/special-needs kids. For some special needs, there is not much research in general, whether for gifted or nongifted kids. By having contact with people in many different settings, and with many different areas of expertise, we expand the likelihood of finding someone who knows the research. Plus, Internet databases help us find resources that may not be available in our local libraries.

3. **Anonymity:** Parents may not want to discuss their children's "twice specialness" with people they know in real life. The Internet provides a place where we can discuss our children's special needs without worrying about how people will react to our child, or where we can complain about school problems with less worry that our child will experience a backlash from upset school faculty and officials.

These properties have helped many of us get needed help and support via the Internet for the challenges of parenting and educating our gifted/special-needs children. I will provide information on how to find these resources (with the caveat that information on specific resources may become outdated very quickly).

Information

The Internet provides access to two important types of information: (1) "Factual" information—articles, bibliographies, lists of resources, etc., and (2) "Personal" information—discussion with other parents who have BTDT ("Been there, done that") and can share their experiences of what has worked for them, what hasn't worked, and what has failed miserably. As one parent wrote, "I could use an instruction manual on this kid. But he didn't come with one. So I'm spending an awful lot of time trying to build my own instruction manual for this amazing kid."

For factual information, there are several Web sites that are particularly good starting points:

1. ERIC (Educational Resources Information Center) at http://ericfac. piccard.csc.com/ is a wonderful resource for research (both personal and professional) on education topics. For research purposes, the Search ERIC Database (http://ericir.syr.edu/Eric/) and AskERIC (http:// ericir.syr.edu/Qa/userform.html) are both invaluable.

    In addition, the ERIC Clearinghouse on Disabilities and Gifted Education (http://www.cec.sped.org/ericec.htm) is hosted by the Council for Exceptional Children (http://www.cec.sped.org/home.htm). Through this clearinghouse, it is possible to get ERIC digests, fact sheets, and minibibs (http://www.cec.sped.org/ericec/digests.htm). ERIC digests are short reports (1,500 to 2,000 words) that provide a basic overview, plus pertinent references, on topics of interest to the broad educational community. ERIC digests are in the public domain and may be freely duplicated, but please acknowledge your source. Minibibliographies (or "minibibs") contain annotated readings on a particular topic. In some cases, the "Readings" may be combined with "Resources" on a specific topic.

    ERIC lists gifted education mailing lists at http://www.cec.sped.org/ ericec/gifted.htm and learning disabilities/special education mailing lists at http://www.cec.sped.org/ericec/ld-sped.htm. ERIC also has links to Internet resources for gifted education at http://www.cec.sped.org/ faq/gt-urls.htm.

2. Hoagies' Gifted Education Page (http://www.ocsc.com/hoagies/gift.htm) is by far the best starting point for any search of Internet resources on giftedness. Topics include: Articles & Research (including ADHD as well as Gifted), Books, Education Programs, Summer / Saturday, Education Tools, Internet Investigations, Journals & Magazines, Kids and

Teens Stuff, On-Line Support, Organizations & Conferences, Parent to Parent, and A Lighter Note.

3. LD Online (http://www.ldonline.org/) is a great starting point for Internet resources on learning disabilities/special needs. It includes sections on the ABCs of LDs, Internet resources, and more in-depth information.

4. The Mining Company has some comprehensive sites for special needs. Their ADHD site at http://add.miningco.com even has a section on gifted/ADHD. There is also a site for parenting special-needs children at http://specialchildren.miningco.com/, and a site for parents of children in grades K-6 at http://childparenting.miningco.com/ that includes links for both gifted and special needs.

5. Britesparks (http://britesparks.com/) is a new site from Australia that is also an excellent resource. In particular, it has a very comprehensive section on special needs (http://britesparks.com/currents/index.htm) including a great collection of essays on GT/special needs kids.

Support

In many ways, the most important thing I've gotten from the Internet has been the emotional support of other parents in the same boat. It is a relief to have a place where I can discuss the problems of having a child thinking many years above grade level without it sounding like I'm bragging! It is also a relief to have a place where I can discuss the problems of dealing with a child who has attention deficit hyperactivity disorder, without worrying that people will think I'm a terrible mother who just can't control her son! To quote another parent:

> Besides knowledge, the most important result of the Internet is learning that other parents go through the same parenting-a-gifted-child-with-LD joys and frustrations that I do. I now have GT/LD "cyber friends" . . . other parents with children who share similar traits to mine. Across the cyber-highway we bounce ideas and share frustrations. Most important: we have keen empathy for each other's tough times. We know. We have been in similar circumstances. I find this tremendously comforting. It is nice to not have to hack this journey alone.

GTWorld (http://www.gtworld.org) is a group of mailing lists related to giftedness. The list GT-Special is specifically for families with gifted/special-needs kids. My friend Janis Ossman and I started it because we weren't getting what we needed from either the gifted kids' lists or the special needs lists. We needed a place where we could discuss our gifted kids'

ADHD and other problems without constantly being questioned about whether ADHD was real, berated for using medications (or for *not* using meds), or having to justify and explain the behavior problems we deal with every day. On the other hand, we needed a place where we could discuss our special-needs kids' giftedness and the problems it presents without seeming like we were bragging to parents who were trying to get their kids to read and write at grade level. GT-Special is a safe place where we can discuss our twice-special children, and the problems we face in helping them (and others) understand and deal with their differences, while also encouraging them to develop and enjoy their exceptional intellectual abilities.

GT-Special provides both support and information. It is a safe place (with very strict rules to protect people's privacy and emotional safety) to ask for help and information. Equally important, it is a haven filled with other people who have BTDT—people who empathize with our struggles and exhaustion (and those of our children), exult with us when we have successes dealing with the schools or our children make breakthroughs, provide shoulders to cry on, humor to help us carry on, and understanding of the joy we get along with the frustration from our truly twice-special kids.

One Story

I'd like to end with one parent's story. When I began to write this article, I asked parents on GT-Special if there was anything they wanted me to include. One mother wrote to me:

> The Internet has been a lifeline for our family. We live in a town of 300 people. Our school district has one elementary and one high school, one class/grade. They had no idea why we were asking such strange questions and making such unusual requests. They thought our sons were quite typical and couldn't understand why we said they were so unhappy with school. By fifth grade our son was so unhappy he asked to drop out. The emotional pain was so intense I was afraid I'd lose him. The only useful piece of advice I received from the school system was from the school superintendent, who said, "With a kid like this, you need to connect to the Internet NOW." I did. I found others with the same kind of kids. Through the Internet we found out about Dr. Linda Kreger Silverman and traveled to Denver to have the kids tested at the Gifted Development Center. Both kids were highly gifted and twice-exceptional. The oldest is likely profoundly gifted; at ten he had reading comprehension at the college senior level and a vo-

cabulary of someone age thirty. They helped us through radical acceleration and dealing with areas of ADD and LD. I don't know what would have happened to our family without the connections the Internet has provided. I shudder to even think about it. I had consulted educators, child development specialists, occupational therapists, physical therapists, and psychologists. None of them knew anything about highly gifted children. The Internet was a lifeline for us. We will always be grateful for that simple advice to connect.

Many of us have similar stories. Whether our children are moderately or profoundly gifted, whether they have ADHD, Asperger syndrome, dyslexia, or depression, whether we live in big cities or small towns, we all need the information and support that we can find through this truly World Wide Web. In addition to the information and support I have gotten through the Internet, I have made close friends from all over the world—and they are friends who can truly understand and help. I am profoundly grateful for all the resources the Internet has provided to my child and me.

CONSTRUCTIVE INSTRUCTION:
ACCEPTING AND ADAPTING TO STUDENTS' LEARNING STYLES

by Marea Nemeth-Taylor

Children who are gifted as well as learning disabled do exist! The label is not an oxymoron. We comprehend the fact that someone may be gifted in sports but have difficulties with schoolwork, or the converse, where someone is gifted academically but has "two left feet and is all thumbs." It is more difficult, however, to comprehend that someone is gifted and disabled in the same area. Some children are gifted verbally but have enormous difficulty putting their ideas down on paper.

Assessment of children who are gifted in some areas of intellectual ability and have other learning differences usually occurs through an intelligence test such as the WISC-III. The overall IQ, however, is only an average of all the subtest scores. The GLD (gifted learning disabled) child generally has statistically significant variations between these subtest scores. Hence, providing only an average IQ score is misleading. An average score ameliorates the differences between the extremes, and thus does not reflect the true ability or disability the child experiences. Imagine standing with one foot in a bucket of ice and the other foot in the fire so that on average you are comfortable. The IQ averaging of subtests would be comparable.

If a child's disability affects understanding of language, as with a receptive language disability, then the child may be penalized during the assessment situation. The child's disability will hinder how well he or she understands the instructions given with regard to each subtest. Similarly, if a child has an expressive language disability, that is, difficulty in saying what they know, the child will be penalized on the subtest where the child is asked to express the answer verbally. The IQ scores thus gained will not reflect the true ability of the child.

The true ability of the child also will be misrepresented if the child processes information slowly, is reflective, or is a perfectionist who must have everything right before proceeding to the next item. For these children the timed subtests, the majority of the performance sub-tests of the WISC III, will not reflect their true ability. The timed subtests have a hidden additional factor in heavily weighted bonus scores for those children who perform these subtests faster than the norm.

Each child must be allowed to be an individual and to express his or her unique learning style. In my private practice, I have had a student who would sit quietly, absorbing new information. When she was asked to apply that knowledge, she would spin on a swivel chair while she thought about the answer. This child, who detested oral reading, would read aloud if she were allowed to spin on the chair. The spinning helped her read. Another child would jump out of the chair like a jack-in-the-box whenever he solved a mathematical problem. On days when everything went well, he was hardly ever in the chair. A teacher, especially in a one-to-one situation, must accept physical movement as a valid learning style and not automatically label "excess" movement as attention deficit disorder or attention deficit hyperactivity disorder. In the kinesthetic approach to learning, the child needs to be physically involved in order to learn successfully.

As an educational pathologist, I present information to the children at levels commensurate with their abilities or strengths, and expect them to perform the tasks commensurate with their disabilities. For example, a child who has a spelling disability would be presented with spelling rules or word attack knowledge at the appropriate high ability level, regardless of age, but would be expected to apply this knowledge at a level that takes disability into account. If the child has concomitant handwriting difficulties, I either write the word as the child orally spells it, or we use a movable alphabet.

I have found through years of experience that most GLD children who have difficulty with reading and/or spelling have trouble with decoding and encoding language. Encoding is educational jargon for spelling, to put sounds into code. Decoding is educational jargon for reading, to make sounds out of the code. These skills need to be taught explicitly, so that the child can add them to their existing tool belt of skills. Many of these children have developed strategies that work for them, and they get into difficulties when their strategies no longer work. They often cannot develop new, effective strategies on their own.

When I teach reading and spelling, I ensure that my students all have phonemic awareness. They become aware of the sounds within words. I use a top-down approach to teach the concepts. The student needs to understand that sentences are made up of words and that these words can be distinguished as discrete units, and then syllables are identified and stated. At the next level, the onset and rhyme within words is identified and stated, and sounds (not spelling) within words are identified and stated. Once these skills have been established, I then work directly on spelling rules and sound groups. These sound groups are identified and then written. I use a systematic phonics program with added branches and loops wherever the student needs them.

A similar approach works for a child who has written expression difficulties. The different methodologies available to commence writing are presented and discussed at the ability level of the child. We then either work together using a method or the child expresses their ideas verbally while I act as a scribe. A tape recorder can be used instead of a scribe, and those with access to a computer can use a dictation program. Using a dictation program can present problems, however, in that there are many new skills for the child to learn. Even though a dictation program obviates the necessity of writing, the planning steps still need to be followed so that the overall objective is not lost. Through the use of a computer, the drafting and redrafting stages often present less of a problem because cutting and pasting on a computer are far easier and much faster than rewriting.

I teach mathematics through the use of a hands-on approach with lots of things to manipulate. If the child does not understand the task at an abstract level with symbols and mathematical terminology, then we move to the concrete level that uses objects and everyday words. A solid grounding in numeration is established before I teach any other concept. If the child is interested in algebra, for example, but has not mastered the basics, then algebra is used to teach the skills the child has not mastered. Again, the concepts are presented at the ability level of the child even though the actual arithmetic used is at the level just below which the child experiences difficulty. This way, the child maintains interest and achieves success with the tasks.

Using a metacognitive approach to teach any skills to GLD children works well. Metacognition in this context involves teaching children how to identify their own thinking styles and how to communicate about how they think. With this type of approach, when the child is made aware of his or her own thinking, the child can identify what works. For example, the visual spatial learner may think in pictures, and can use that knowledge to create mental pictures of how to solve a specific problem. I then ensure that the child transfers this awareness of thinking to the new skills being taught. The child needs encouragement to transfer this awareness across tasks as well. I achieve this by asking constantly how the child knows that the answer is correct, what method was used to arrive at the answer, and whether an alternate method could have produced the same answer. Transference within a content area occurs as a child learns to use a syllabic approach to spelling words; I suggest that the child looks at the spelling words for that week and breaks them up into syllables in order to learn how to spell the words. To facilitate transference between content areas, I encourage the child to approach an apparently large task in a similar manner; i.e., to break the large task into smaller sections just as the large word was broken into syllables.

My methods are not fixed, because each child is an individual and unique in his or her own right. I adapt my methods to meet the needs of the child rather than expecting the child to conform to fixed methods. Every program I use is modified to meet the needs of the child at that time with that content. Some of my students spin on their chairs while they work, and others are like jack-in-the-boxes. If children appear to need physical movement in order to concentrate, they can move. Other children ask all kinds of questions, which I answer even when the purpose may be one of distraction. I find children attempt to distract me when the work appears to them to be unpleasant, impossible, or boring. I explain to the child that this work was prepared especially for him or her, so even though it looks unpleasant, impossible, or boring at first, I know that the child is capable of doing the activity. I am there to ensure that each child succeeds.

A SECOND LOOK AT ATTENTION DEFICIT DISORDER

by Jeffrey Freed and Laurie Parsons

It's the catchall term of the decade: attention deficit disorder, or ADD. It seems that most of us either are parenting or have some connection with a child who's been diagnosed with ADD. Some experts say that five to ten percent of the juvenile population "suffers" from ADD: Children are lining up in schools for their daily doses of Ritalin, which some critics assert is passed out like candy. Why is this happening? What is this mysterious condition? And is it necessarily "bad"?

ADD is described in current literature as a neurological syndrome that has three major components: impulsivity, distractibility, and hyperactivity. At one time, ADD was referred to as "minimal brain dysfunction." Typically when we hear of ADD, it's in the context of a youngster who has failed or fallen short of expectation in some manner. He may be struggling in school, sassing his parents, or getting in a fistfight with another student on the playground. The term itself certainly carries with it a negative connotation. The words "deficit" and "disorder" are not going to do much to build the esteem of a child who's already having difficulties.

The child with ADD typically has two speeds: full tilt and collapse. He has a consistently short attention span, which means he fails to hold a thought or stay on a task for more than a few minutes. He doesn't have a "brake" in his brain that tells him to look before he leaps. His lightning-fast mind flashes from one random thought to another. He may be physically and socially clumsy. He may be organizationally challenged. These traits are all the negatives of a child with ADD, flaws we hear about all too often. Sadly, for many children, labels such as "disordered," "disabled," or "defiant" become a self-fulfilling prophecy.

Indulge me as I offer a new perspective on children with ADD, one that comes from more than twelve years of working one-to-one with many of these fascinating young people. While they certainly face many challenges, they have a surprising number of strengths. I have delighted in uncovering the many gifts these children possess and demonstrating them for the world to see. In a way I feel that I'm getting even with all the teachers who failed to understand me. I struggled in school and have been diagnosed with ADD.

I've found that children with ADD share a strikingly common attribute: They have a visual, right-brained learning style. The right side of the brain is the hemisphere that's linked to spatial and artistic ability, emotions, and holistic thought. Right-brained children are intensely creative, can do difficult math problems in their heads, and are excellent speed-readers. They have a powerful visual memory, easily retrieving information stored on their mental blackboards. They are more likely to be gifted than others are. Many of them are born perfectionists and are extremely competitive. They are super-intuitive and can read you like a book. They are good at building things, think in three dimensions, and notice patterns and connections.

Right-brained, ADD children are hypersensitive in almost every sense of the word. They likely have acute hearing, "eagle eyes" that can pick up on the most minute detail, a keen sense of smell, and tactile defensiveness. Their emotions are close to the surface. If they can survive traditional education, they may emerge as great leaders and thinkers. Albert Einstein, Thomas Alva Edison, William Butler Yeats, George S. Patton, and others were identified early as having learning disabilities, but they succeeded in life despite the constraints of the schoolhouse.

Children like this tend to do poorly in school for a couple of reasons: first, because their antennae are always up, they are easily distracted by external stimuli; second, educators tend to be left-brained, detail-oriented auditory processors who view visual learners as "flawed." What many of these children need isn't a prescription for a pill, but a prescription for a different teaching method.

My teaching techniques have evolved over the years, and I have to confess that the foundation of the work that I do is fairly simple: I take traditional teaching methods that don't work with these kids and reverse them. For example, if a student struggles with phonics and "sounding out" spelling words, it doesn't make sense to hammer away at an area of weakness. Instead, I attack spelling by using an area of strength: the student's sharp visual memory. I've had excellent success teaching many right-brained students to spell, not through drill and repetition, but by holding up colored letters on a white piece of paper and asking them to remember words by the way they look. Phonics can then be used as a finishing tool. Many of my students who couldn't spell anything longer than a five-letter word can now routinely spell words such as *existentialism, antidisestablishmentarianism,* and *parapseudomicrobrain-scanology*—both forward and backward.

Math can be taught in a similar fashion. Because many students with ADD have difficulty with fine-motor skills, they may struggle with doing math using pencil and paper. Children are amazed at what they can do when I take away pencil and paper and ask them to do mental math, completing a series of computations in their heads. The right-brained child can develop his ability to visualize and hold numbers to solve challenging problems without having to labor through a series of painful written steps. I've worked with several of these students who are practically human calculators!

How many times do we tell children with reading difficulties to slow down? Again, my method reverses the traditional manner of teaching reading. I've found that right-brained children can attain better comprehension through speed-reading passages several times. The first time they scan the material to get the big picture; then in subsequent readings they can fill in the details.

In short, I teach children with ADD *a different way to learn.* If I can harness the visual memory, I can instruct them to use their mental blackboards to place spelling lists, times tables, math formulas, maps, and periodic tables. The right-brained child can retrieve the images from his mind as easily as the left-brained child looks up the answer in a book.

My teaching methods also utilize a great deal of psychology. I've found that if you believe in the abilities of children with ADD, they'll go to the moon for you. These children need to have a parent or mentor who recognizes their abilities and believes in them. Because they're so intuitive, they know if you think they're failures, and they'll live up to that expectation. My methods also use humor as well as challenges. Children with ADD love jokes and puns. As perfectionistic and goal-oriented as they are, these youngsters will focus better when tackling a more difficult problem. When doing mundane work, their minds may wander and they make careless mistakes.

It's clear that by dwelling on their flaws, our education system is failing many right-brained children with ADD. Rather than working with strengths that are intrinsic to the brain's right hemisphere and looking for innovative methods to produce results, we use a "one size fits all" approach that attempts to remediate weaknesses. Ronald D. Davis and Eldon Braun write in *The Gift of Dyslexia* that, "The problem (ADD) has been around ever since teachers have attempted to teach students subjects that didn't interest them. In most cases, it should be described not as a learning disability, but as a teaching ability." Rote learning, drill, and repetition are ineffective in inspiring these bright children who need to get the big picture to learn effectively. Trapped in the auditory classroom, their divergent minds wander easily, particularly if the material is dry and there are many diversions.

Thomas G. West writes, in his pioneering book *In the Mind's Eye,* of the double bind of having a strong right brain: "an imagination that is so powerful and so rich that it can produce the most original and profound conceptions . . . but which may be so enticing (especially in youth) that it is extremely difficult for the affected person to focus on an assigned task or on tumbling symbols on a lifeless page."

This collision of left-brained teachers and right-brained children will only intensify as we enter the new millennium. We know that because of the malleability of the human brain and its continuing development through infancy, childhood, and adolescence, early childhood experiences actually alter the structure of the brain. Pathways that are reinforced thrive, while those that are not used atrophy and die. As our children are exposed to television, computers, video games, and other outside stimulation, I believe it's making them more visual and right-brained than they were genetically programmed to be. If you want the short course on why children think differently, spend a few minutes watching *Sesame Street* or MTV. See how you respond to the dizzyingly rapid-fire images and visual chaos. Imagine what's happening to the brains of our children, who may spend more time watching television than in the classroom.

I believe that earlier identification and greater understanding of the right-brained child with ADD will result in less ostracism and shaming. We must respect the differences in these children, and see them in a more positive light. Thomas Armstrong, in *The Myth of the ADD Child,* prefers to think of the "hyperactive" child as "energetic," the "impulsive" child as "spontaneous," and the "irritable" child as "sensitive." The "daydreamer" who studies cloud patterns from the window of his classroom may go on to become one of the great thinkers of the next century, helping us to solve problems in fresh and creative ways.

THE OUTSTANDING, BUT OUT-OF-SYNC, STUDENT

by Carol Stock Kranowitz

Liz, a sophomore, is the brightest student in her high school. With an ear for languages and a head for history, she aces her AP courses. She's Debate Club president and Student Government secretary.

"Liz the Wiz" should have a sky-high sense of self-worth, but she's miserable. "Liz the Mis" would be a more accurate nickname, she thinks. Her unhappiness stems from being doubly different: incredibly clever, and incredibly klutzy. She is acutely aware that intelligence can't help her body to function smoothly. She knocks into people, bumps against furniture, trips on air. She avoids sports because she is too clumsy, too cautious, and always the last to be picked, anyway.

What interests Liz is not athletics, but dramatics. She's a good memorizer and loves literature. Gathering her courage, she decides to try out for the lead in the upcoming production of *Hedda Gabler.* At the audition, she stands awkwardly, feet planted to the boards, shoulders hunched, and elbows fixed to her sides. She begins to read the lines—and speaks with convincing passion.

The drama teacher is surprised and impressed. This ungainly girl can act! She wants to see more and asks Liz to demonstrate how the distraught Hedda might whirl and crumple, after receiving terrible news.

Liz freezes. She can't do that—she'll lose her balance! How will she get down? How will she get up? Why didn't she foresee that a tryout would include movement as well as speech? She has ruined her chances! She bursts into tears and stumbles out. Oh, why can't she just be normal?

Joe, seventeen, has learning problems. He spends his school day with an army of special educators, troops of other struggling students with whom he has little in common, and a laptop. His laptop is his survival kit and best friend, and he couldn't function without it. It allows him to take notes, find addresses, keep his calendar and schedule straight, and, best of all, draw dynamic, sensuous, vigorous figures that look three-dimensional.

Joe's major difficulty is an auditory-language processing deficit. Because decoding the words he hears and reads is very challenging, he does poorly in all subjects except geometry and art. As he misses the subtleties of spoken language, doesn't get jokes, and misinterprets social cues, his interactions with others are unsatisfactory.

In addition, he always seems to be on the warpath. The message his perpetual scowl sends is, "Don't touch me!" If someone jostles him, he becomes angry and aggressive. Regarded as a problem student, he is "noncompliant," "hostile," "inflexible," "inattentive," and "self-absorbed."

When the last bell rings, Joe lopes home and works out on his backyard trampoline for thirty minutes. Jumping and jolting improve his spirits and clear away the mental cobwebs. Then he heads for his workbench and begins his real work.

This youth, who can neither write a sentence nor comprehend algebra nor tolerate the touch of another person, is a sculptor of exquisite talent. His medium is clay and he is most content when he is up to his elbows in it. His subject is the human form—and he has the rare gift of infusing his figures with life and spirit. Sculpting comes by gestalt.

He dreams of going to art school where his talents will be recognized. But he figures that with his luck, he'll end up as a bum, or a day laborer, or some other kind of social outcast.

Difficult? Inflexible? Fussy, picky, touchy? Clumsy, impetuous, distractible? Insecure? Hard to reach or teach? Yet very, very bright? Do you know these students?

Many teenagers who are twice-exceptional may have sensory integration (SI) dysfunction. This subtle problem is an obstacle that hinders an adolescent's ability to learn, play, relate easily to others, and function smoothly in everyday life. In addition, it is an obstacle for the teen's family, teachers, and classmates.

Why do uniquely gifted students often seem to have SI dysfunction? We don't have the answers now, but someday we may. Sensory integration is diagnosed and treated with delicacy, and the disproportionate numbers of gifted students who have this dysfunction will benefit from further research and study.

Conversely, why do students with SI dysfunction often seem to have rare gifts? One reason may be that their deficit in making sense of certain sensations forces them to develop other skills. Just as the blind person often develops precise hearing, the girl who fears movement can develop a beautiful speaking voice, and the boy who responds atypically to touch sensations can turn his visual-spatial and tactile skills into works of art. Before reading about SI dysfunction, it is important to understand what sensory integration is, and why we need that integration.

Sensory Integration: A Necessity of Life and Learning

Sensory integration is the neurological process of organizing sensations for our use in everyday life. Normally, our central nervous system:

- efficiently receives sensory messages from our bodies and surroundings;
- interprets and integrates these messages; and
- organizes them for purposeful responses.

For instance, we take in a teacher's instructions, understand what we need to do, and do it. Or we get unexpectedly bumped off center, interpret this loss of equilibrium as nonthreatening, and regain our sense of balance. Life's little demands do not dismay us; we can adjust.

This three-part sequence is a sensorimotor experience. "Sensory" refers to sensations that the brain takes in and integrates; "motor" refers to the movements (or spoken words or emotional expressions) that our bodies produce in response. Some essential sensorimotor skills are:

- responding appropriately to light, unexpected touch, such as when an insect alights on our leg;
- discriminating what we touch or what touches us;
- moving smoothly through space, i.e., across the classroom, around obstacles, or down the street;
- balancing;
- changing and holding our body position in resistance to gravity;
- forming a mental plan of how to act and then doing it; and
- using both sides of the body together in a cooperative manner.

All our actions—conscious or unconscious—are sensorimotor. To perform any action, to express any thought, to reach any goal, we must integrate millions of bits of information through all our senses.

While seeing and hearing are our most obvious, familiar senses, we have other, "hidden," senses that are even more fundamental. These include:

1) The **tactile** sense, which provides information, primarily through our skin, about the texture, shape, and size of objects in the environment. It also helps us distinguish between threatening and nonthreatening touch sensations.

2) The **vestibular** sense, which provides information through the inner ear about gravity and movement, and about our head and body position in relation to the surface of the earth.

3) The **proprioceptive** sense, which provides information through our joints, muscles, and ligaments about the position of our body parts and what they are doing.

These three basic sensory systems start developing in utero, are functioning at birth, and continue to develop throughout our lives. When they function well, then self-control, motor skills, and higher-level functions such as visual perception, auditory perception, and academic skills can develop according to Mother Nature's plan.

When these sensory systems work inefficiently, however, a person may show unusual responses to touching and being touched, to moving and being moved. He often has problems with attention, learning, and behavior. He may have great difficulty functioning in daily life— not because he *won't* do what is expected, but because he *can't*.

A person with SI dysfunction may have a sensory regulation problem and/or a sensory processing problem, described below.

Two Types of Sensory Integration Dysfunction

Sensory regulation—A sensory regulation problem is the over- or underreaction to sensations. A person's central nervous system misgauges the significance of ordinary sensations. As a result, a person has difficulty regulating, or modulating, reactions to sensations. Atypical reactions may occur with *frequency* (several times a day), *intensity,* and *duration* (lasting for an unusually long time).

Hypersensitivity is overresponsiveness to sensory messages. Seeking self-protection from ordinary stimulation, the student has *sensory defensiveness.* When a person can tolerate only the least intense sensations, he avoids experiences that others enjoy or ignore. For instance, Liz is uncomfortable with the vestibular sensation of falling, and Joe cannot bear the tactile sensation of being brushed against in the hallway. They cannot make adaptive responses to ordinary situations, and so their modus operandi is fight, fright, or flight.

Hyposensitivity is underresponsiveness to sensory messages. Ordinary sensory stimulation is insufficient. The hyposensitive person needs frequent, intense, vigorous sensory experiences to get into gear. Joe, who has hyposensitivity to some sensations and hypersensitivity to others, finds that jumping on the trampoline gets him organized and in sync.

Everybody, from time to time, is out of sync and has trouble regulating sensations. Fatigue, hunger, extreme weather conditions, lack of exercise, mental stress, or emotional ups and downs can cause anyone to over- or underreact to sensory stimuli.

Most people can recover fairly easily. To calm down, maybe they take a bath, sip a cup of tea, or listen to Mozart. To become awake and alert, perhaps they take a shower, crunch on a granola bar, or jog around the block. They instinctively know how to get a balanced *sensory diet,* which is comprised of daily, multisensory experiences that one normally seeks to satisfy one's sensory appetite.

However, twice-exceptional students, with their unique nervous systems, may have trouble keeping—or regaining—their equilibrium. They may have trouble automatically balancing their sensory diets, as well.

Sensory processing—A sensory processing problem is the misinterpretation of sensory information coming from a person's body and from the environment. The person's central nervous system is inefficient at analyzing, organizing, and synthesizing—i.e., integrating—sensory messages in order to use them for meaningful responses. The person may have little self-awareness or comprehension of what is happening in the world around him.

Liz's poor processing of vestibular sensations, for instance, affects her muscle tone, body expression, and motor planning. Inefficient motor planning, in turn, affects her ability to visualize the motor requirements of unfamiliar tasks. Joe's difficulty in interpreting many kinds of sensory cues affects his sense of belonging.

In short, a student with regulatory and/or processing problems may have trouble learning new skills, taking calculated risks, exploring the environment, developing and maintaining friendships, and performing ordinary tasks. Life seems uncertain and unpredictable; life is hard.

Common Symptoms

SI problems are not always easy to recognize. People with these difficulties often behave in ways that suggest other diagnoses (subjects of other books and chapters). These include attention deficit disorder, learning disabilities, allergies, nutritional or vitamin deficiencies, and vision dysfunction.

So how can we tell the difference?

SI dysfunction is a strong possibility when a person exhibits unusual responses to touching and being touched, and to moving and being moved.

It is important to understand that one of the hallmarks of SI dysfunction is inconsistency. For instance, a student may overreact when another person accidentally grazes her foot under a table, but underreact to the pain of a broken collarbone. The student may be uncomfortable moving through open space, but have no aversion to being touched. Also, he may be out of sync on Monday, but in sync on Tuesday!

Dysfunction looks different in every person. Some people will exhibit many of the following characteristics; others will exhibit few. Many of the symptoms have some similarities, in that people with SI tend to have trouble regulating and organizing the stimulus that comes to them through their senses. With these caveats in mind, take a look at some of the common symptoms.

The Tactile Sense

The student with the *sensory regulation problem of hypersensitivity* to touch sensations may:

- Have *tactile defensiveness* (oversensitivity to unexpected, light touch), rubbing off kisses or casual touches.
- Exhibit a "fight, fright, or flight" response when standing in line or in a crowd, pushing others away or striking out to avoid closeness.
- Dislike messy activities (cooking, painting, and using chalk or tape).
- Be bothered by certain clothing fabrics and styles, and be particularly sensitive to sock seams, shoes, and tags in shirt collars.
- Dislike having skin exposed, always wearing long sleeves and pants, even in summer; or, dislike having skin covered, wearing as little as possible, even in winter.
- Become anxious or aggressive on windy, "hair-raising" days.
- Be a picky eater, avoiding certain foods (rice, chunky peanut butter, lumpy mashed potatoes, lettuce) because of texture, or preferring food to be the same temperature, either hot or cold.
- Dislike swimming, bathing, brushing teeth, or having hair cut.
- Have difficulty initiating or processing interactions in peer relationships.

The student with the *sensory regulation problem of hyposensitivity* to touch sensations may:

- Touch people and objects constantly.
- Not realize he has dropped something.
- Seem unaware of touch unless it is very intense, showing little reaction to pain from bruises or cuts, and getting hurt without realizing it.

- Have poor body awareness, requiring firm pressure to know where one's body was touched.
- Be insensitive to room temperature.
- Be a messy eater and be unaware of messiness on his face, especially around his mouth and nose.
- Chew on inedible objects (fingernails, hair, pencils, shirt cuffs).
- Physically hurt other people or pets, seemingly without remorse, but actually not comprehending the pain that others feel.
- Have poor peer relationships, inappropriately "invading others' space."

When *processing* touch sensations is the problem, the student may:
- Seem out of touch with his hands, as if they are unfamiliar appendages.
- Have trouble holding and using tools (pencils, scissors, forks).
- Without the aid of visual cues:
  - Be unable to identify what body parts have been touched.
  - Be clumsy performing tasks such as zipping, buttoning, unbuttoning, tying shoes, and adjusting clothes.
  - Be unable to identify familiar objects solely through touch, e.g., when reaching for objects in a pocket, box, or desk.
- Avoid initiating tactile experiences, such as picking up objects that are attractive to others.
- Have trouble perceiving the physical properties (texture, shape, size, density) of objects.
- Prefer standing to sitting, to ensure visual control of his surroundings.
- Squirm or sit on edge of chair.

The Vestibular Sense

The student with the *sensory regulation problem of hypersensitivity* to sensations of gravity and movement may:
- Be intolerant to movement, and therefore avoid it.
- Overreact, negatively and emotionally, to ordinary movement sensations, possibly misinterpreting them as life-endangering.
- Dislike physical activities such as running, biking, sledding, or dancing.

- Be cautious, slow-moving, and sedentary, hesitating to take risks.
- Not like the head to be inverted, as when being shampooed over the sink.
- Be very tense and rigid to avoid changes in head position.
- Be uncomfortable on stairs, clinging to walls or banisters.
- Experience motion sickness when riding in a car, boat, train, airplane, escalator or elevator.
- Appear to be willful, manipulative, uncooperative, or a sissy.
- Demand continual physical support from a trusted peer or adult.
- Have the additional problem of *gravitational insecurity,* which is a high degree of fear disproportionate to the movement she is experiencing. Usually, the stimulus is passive movement against gravity, such as riding in an elevator. This great fear of falling is experienced as primal terror.

The student with the *sensory regulation problem of hyposensitivity* to sensations of gravity and movement may:
- Crave intense, fast, and spinning movement (using a rocking chair, turning in a swivel chair, jumping on a trampoline, riding on roller coasters, careening around corners)—and not get dizzy.
- Be a thrill seeker and daredevil.
- Need to move constantly (rocking, swaying, spinning, jiggling, shaking her hands or head, fidgeting) in order to function. The student may have trouble sitting still or staying in a seat.
- Enjoy being upside down, such as hanging over the side of the bed.
- Have poor balance, falling easily and often.
- Bump into objects and furniture, apparently on purpose.

When *processing* sensations of gravity and movement is the problem, the student may:
- Easily lose her balance when climbing stairs, riding a bicycle, stretching on tiptoes, jumping, standing on one foot, standing on both feet when eyes are closed . . . or swooning like Hedda Gabler.
- Move in an uncoordinated, awkward way.
- Be fidgety.
- Have low muscle tone, and seem to be "loose and floppy."

- Tire easily during physical activities.
- Have poor posture and difficulty remaining upright when seated.
- Be confused about whether she or something else (a train, a tennis ball, or another person) is moving.
- Have problems with directionality, often moving in the wrong direction.

The Proprioceptive Sense

When *regulating and/or processing* sensations of body position, the student may:
- Have problems with touch and/or with gravity and movement, as well.
- Have a poor sense of body awareness.
- Be stiff, uncoordinated, and clumsy, falling and tripping frequently.
- Lean, bump, or crash against objects and people, and invade others' body space.
- Have difficulty carrying out unfamiliar and complex motions, such as putting on ice skates for the first time.
- Be unable to do ordinary, familiar things without looking, such as getting dressed.
- Manipulate hair clips, lamp switches, pencils, and classroom tools so hard that they break.
- Have difficulty ascending and descending stairs.
- Slap feet when walking, sit on his feet, stretch his limbs, poke his cheeks, pull on his fingers, and crack his knuckles (for additional sensory feedback).
- Pull and twist his clothing, such as stretching his T-shirt over his knees or chewing sleeves or collars.

Additional Symptoms

SI dysfunction also hinders the smooth development of skills that everyone needs to perform successfully, in and out of school. A fine line exists between a young person with a few of these symptoms, and a young person with many of the symptoms or some in extremis. Careful observation over time can aid in distinguishing between SI and the natural developmental stages of youth and adolescence. Difficulty in one of the areas discussed below suggests that SI dysfunction may be the underlying cause, particularly if several simultaneous symptoms are in evidence.

Fine-motor skills involve the precise use of small muscles. The student may lack effective *hand coordination,* necessary to manipulate pencils, rulers, and other classroom tools. He may have inefficient *eye-motor (oculomotor) skills,* necessary to focus on other people or objects, keep both eyes fixed on one target, watch his own hands perform a complicated task such as writing, and follow along a line of print as he reads. He may have poor *oral-motor control,* necessary to coordinate the tongue, lips, and muscles of the mouth for fluid speech and accurate articulation.

Muscle tone is the degree of tension normally present when our muscles are in a resting state. Regular exercisers typically have firm tone; "couch potatoes" have *low tone.* The student with low tone, like Liz, can compensate for a "loose and floppy" body by holding herself stiffly and rigidly, but at a great cost of energy. She may tire easily and have difficulty maintaining an upright posture, sitting and standing without slouching, and keeping a firm grip on a pencil.

Visual perception, the ability to understand what the eyes see, is a complex skill that is learned over time, after many sensorimotor experiences. The student may have inaccurate *visual spatial perception,* necessary for interpreting the position and orientation of letters and numbers in order to read and write, and for knowing where he is in space, how to move around an obstacle, and how to visualize abstract concepts. He may lack good *visual figure-ground perception,* needed to distinguish the foreground from the background of objects and symbols in order to pick out pictures, words, or figures on a printed page, and to look up at the chalkboard and down at his book without losing his place.

Often, students with SI dysfunction process visual information inadequately. Some of them rely on rudimentary senses of touch and movement to get information about their body and the world around them. Others may depend highly on visual input, although it is inefficient, because other senses may be even less efficient. Like Joe, they may also rely on their computers to organize and make concrete the abstract symbols of language. They may think and read aloud to mediate their vision, and their modus operandi is frequently *high verbal, low performance.*

Bilateral coordination is the ability to use both sides of the body as a team. The student may have difficulty alternating feet to climb stairs or ride a bike, stabilizing a paper with one hand while writing with the other, or catching a basketball with both hands.

Motor planning is the ability to conceive of, organize, sequence, and carry out a complex sequence of unfamiliar movements. Threading a belt through the loops of new trousers, completing a lab assignment, mastering a locker combination, and following a drama teacher's instructions to swoon are tasks that require effective motor planning. Many students with SI dysfunction know what they are expected to do or want to do, but they cannot plan how to carry out the action.

Associated Problems

A twice-exceptional student may have other problems that are not necessarily caused by sensory integration dysfunction, but that are frequently exacerbated by it. Students may be picky eaters and have problems with digestion and elimination. They may have sleep irregularities. In addition, dysfunction may affect their auditory-language processing and emotional security.

Auditory-language processing is the ability to listen and communicate verbally. A student like Joe may have difficulty attending to what others say, appropriately answering comments or questions, phrasing or rephrasing thoughts so that others can understand, reading, and writing. Social interactions with peers and adults may be hard.

Emotional security is the sense that one is cherished, that others are trustworthy, and that one has the skills to function effectively in everyday life. Students like our Joe and Liz, however, may have a tentative hold on their sense of self-worth and belonging. If uncertain about his or her abilities, then even the best-loved student in the world may feel unloved and unlovable.

Helping Twice-Exceptional Students

What can parents, teachers, coaches, grandparents, and other caring adults do to help twice-exceptional students? Here are some ideas:

Observe the student's choices of self-therapy. This self-therapy may be fidgeting with paper clips and locks of hair (for tactile organization), chewing cuffs and collars (for oral-motor stimulation and organization of the entire central nervous system), turning in circles or getting into upside-down positions (for vestibular input), or cracking knuckles and filling pockets with rocks (for proprioceptive feedback). Perhaps the behavior begins when the student is anxious, hungry, bored, or restricted in movement. Look for patterns, which will help you determine appropriate strategies.

Don't take self-therapy away. Instead, foster it! Offer frequent resistive activities (using a punching bag, lifting weights, raking, shoveling); deep-touch pressure to the student's muscles and joints (massages, bear hugs); and other safe, appropriate activities that provide the sensorimotor experiences he craves. Does he gnaw on pencils? Give him a pretzel or a wad of chewing gum. Does he rock in his chair? Keep a small trampoline nearby for frequent movement breaks. Does he bump and crash into objects and people? Give him hard-work activities, such as carrying boxes of books and moving furniture, for sensory input.

Guide the student into a regular physical activity. Athletic prowess is less important than daily movement. Sports such as track, gymnastics, and swimming are excellent choices for individuals who probably won't ever be MVP of the football team. Being active is essential for the mind, body, and spirit. Being active keeps people healthy. Being active can suppress hypersensitivities and satisfy hyposensitivities. Furthermore, having some athletic skill can be a key to ensure a student's sense of belonging and acceptance by his peers.

Consider occupational therapy, or another form of professional treatment. Some people with SI dysfunction instinctively know how to satisfy their need for stimulation. Others, however, do not know how to get the sensory diet their nervous system needs. Support such as occupational therapy, which addresses an individual's sensory needs, can do wonders to help these students flourish.

Help the student break tasks into small, manageable parts. She probably has great difficulty getting organized to produce her masterpiece, term paper, or science project. Why? Because the essential sensorimotor skills of bilateral coordination, fine-motor dexterity, motor planning, visual perception, etc., may be lagging far behind. Problems with motor planning, organization, and visualization can interfere with kicking a soccer ball, becoming a good problem solver, driving, making change, or planning ahead to ask someone to the prom. With help, many highly-motivated teenagers can learn to accomplish these goals.

Pay attention to feelings. Understand that sensory integration dysfunction evokes profound emotions—especially when the dysfunction has been overlooked for years. Why shouldn't a person be angry if he puts enormous effort into completing assignments, but is told that he "isn't working hard enough"? Why shouldn't a person be withdrawn and depressed, when she hears, "Someone with an IQ of 160 ought to be able to hit a tennis ball! You could do it if you tried."

Sensory defensiveness can cause school phobias and anxieties. When a student somaticizes, i.e., comes up with symptoms of illness such as a stomachache prior to entering the noisy and visually confusing cafeteria, chances are that the stomach really aches.

Don't try to jolly a person out of "irrational fears" or "unreasonable anger." The emotions may seem unjustified to you, but they are legitimate to the person who does not feel in control of his body or his environment. Give the student what psychologist Carl Rogers calls "unconditional, positive regard."

Acknowledge unusual talents. A person like Joe with language problems may be unable to grasp Shakespeare but be a genius at interpreting maps. A person with severe tactile defensiveness, who shuns physical contact, may become a professor who shines from behind a desk. A person with poor motor coordination may mature into an extraordinary poet, photographer, or composer. If possible, encourage your student to "follow his bliss," the counsel of mythologist Joseph Campbell. *At every opportunity, let students like Joe and Liz know how much you appreciate their unique contributions of creativity, sensitivity, and very existence!*

BRIDGING THE PERSPECTIVES

by Daphne Pereles Bowers

Despite my extensive teaching experience with twice-exceptional students, the most rewarding educational encounter I have had with these amazing children is watching my own children as a parent. I believe they have taught me more than I could ever have gained in any class or by teaching any number of these students. The reason I have learned so much from them is that as a parent you are privileged enough to see the whole child. You watch them develop and grow into these incredibly divergent, creative thinkers. You also witness the growing frustration with a school environment that increasingly becomes more difficult for them. You watch while that incredible creativity slowly becomes stifled as they try their hardest to get their thoughts on paper, to finish lengthy assignments, and to be successful. Little by little the successes become fewer until you begin to see them giving up. As they release their dreams and ambitions, they begin to falter academically. The emotional concerns increase and the school focuses heavily on these.

I believe my experience as a professional and as a parent of these unique children provide me with two interesting perspectives. Respect for the various perspectives of these kids forms a crucial first step in beginning to address their vast and varied needs. It also provides an opportunity to consider programming options through collaboration when a self-contained option is not available.

The term "twice exceptional" brings with it many questions that vary depending on your perspective. As a classroom teacher, you may tend to think, "Oh no, another label. What will be required of me now? How many of these kids could there really be anyway?" As a special education teacher, you may ask, "What strategies can I use to help remediate the problem? Why doesn't this child seem to fit into my existing special education classes?" As a gifted and talented teacher, you wonder, "Why can't this child show what he can do in the classroom? Why, if he is so bright, is he failing? Why can't he keep up with his gifted peers in my classes?" As a parent, you think, "Could that be my child? Why doesn't he just learn and do his schoolwork like everyone else? I know he is bright, so why is it difficult for him to get his work done? Is there a real reason for his behavior?"

Trying to understand what it means to be bright and to have learning difficulties at the same time is challenging regardless of your role. Developing the concept of what it means to have some sort of processing deficit or attentional concern impeding potential is a crucial step. A learning disability by definition is a discrepancy between actual cognitive ability and academic achievement. This discrepancy can be an indication of some sort of a processing deficit (i.e., visual sequencing, auditory short-term memory, etc.) that is called a learning disability.

Appropriate placement remains crucial. Many students referred for special education services are of average intelligence and demonstrate well below average achievement within the regular classroom setting. It makes sense to most classroom teachers making the referral that these students need help to be brought up to grade level. It does not make a lot of sense to refer a child who may be functioning, for the most part, on grade level. While these bright children may very well be functioning on grade level, the frustration and emotional stress they are experiencing are just as significant, if not more so, than their cognitively average peers with similar disabilities. Twice-exceptional children tend to be highly sensitive and emotionally fragile. Again, depending on your perspective, you may be aware of the impact underachievement is having on these students or it may be hidden. If you are the parent of one of these children, you know how emotionally painful it is for your child because s/he will usually feel safe enough to pour those feelings out at home.

Learning disabilities may look like lazy behaviors to the untrained, unknowledgeable observer. As we learn more about these intriguing children, we find that there are many common characteristics among them. What we call these characteristics can vary depending on the perspective. What may look like attention deficit to one person may look like gifted over-excitabilities to another. The characteristics are very similar: moving around while completing work, impulsively calling out and answering questions out of turn, drifting off into creative thought, and losing focus on the task at hand. What may look like lack of effort or laziness to one may look like a processing deficit or a learning disability to another. Again, the characteristics are similar: inconsistent completion of assignments, erratic work effort, or poor organizational skills.

Whatever they are called, many of the characteristics of these children interfere with their ability to be successful in a school setting for many reasons. Oftentimes only the gift is spotted and unrealistic expectations are set for the student with no understanding of the existing deficit. In other cases, the deficit is obvious and becomes the focus of academic programming with little thought to the gifts or passions. Other times, probably more times than we are aware of, these students are not found because they have learned to compensate well enough to get by, yet not enough to achieve their true potential. Their disability is masking the gift and their gift is masking the disability. Perspective again plays an important part.

As we begin to understand that the various perspectives on these children play a crucial role in gaining a greater understanding of the whole child, we realize the necessity of these views to facilitate appropriate programming options within a learning environment. Educators are allowed to see a small part of the whole child. What we see is what s/he chooses to share with us. In some cases, it is extremely limited, especially if the child is not particularly verbal. There should be an understanding that the parents bring valuable information about their children for us to use as teachers. Parents see the child at home growing up whereas educators see the child who sits at a desk at school. As parents, we do not know what our children choose to share of themselves in that environment. There should be an understanding that the teacher's perspective of our child is also valuable and reflective of what s/he may look like in a school setting. Without that mutual understanding, it is difficult to address the varied needs of twice-exceptional children.

In addition to the perspectives of the classroom teacher and the parent, the perspective of the child himself is imperative. Often programming may be done for a student without his/her input. The child often holds the key to what may spark his interest and make him willing to take on the learning challenges he may face. The special education process seldom integrates interests into its programming. The focus is usually identifying what is wrong and how it can be "fixed." The gifted and talented identification, if in place, oftentimes focuses on academic abilities, and twice-exceptional students typically do not fit into the rigorous production-focused classes. Some exploration may be necessary to help the child get a better understanding of what types of activities engage his mind, but the time is well spent. No one knows better than the child does himself what makes him more receptive to learning.

Bringing together the various views of the twice-exceptional child is an important step in recognizing his/her full potential and to build a program that will encourage growth and foster success. This collaborative approach is something that can be done in any school building. Accumulating existing data, allowing participants to think of their concept of the child's strengths, interests, and challenges, and setting up a meeting to include all of the people working with the student are all steps in this process. The most valuable part is building a team approach to supporting a child with diverse needs and interests. This approach provides built-in support for all of the teachers working with this child. These children are not easy to teach or to parent, and the more support for all involved will provide the twice-exceptional child with a more cohesive educational experience. This collaboration is an ongoing process and should be continued throughout the twice-exceptional child's school career. Through a collaborative approach that emphasizes sharing their diverse perspectives, teachers and parents can invigorate the love of learning inherent in twice-exceptional students.

IS THERE A PLACE IN COLLEGE
FOR THE STUDENT WITH LEARNING DISABILITIES?

by Barbara Priddy Guyer

In 1981 I tested a young man who had been asked to leave a university four times because of academic problems. His grade point average was one of the lowest I have ever seen—1.86. When I talked with him, I was convinced that he was unusually intelligent. His use of vocabulary was excellent, and his math skills were appropriate for his educational background. Since he was a finance major, one would hope that he had outstanding math ability. He had a very alert, inquisitive expression in his eyes, but best of all, his smile was infectious. When Bob smiled, it was difficult not to smile back at him. It was almost impossible to stay angry with him for any period of time.

One of the reasons that I was interested in testing Bob was that he impressed me as being a person who should be an honor student. The fact that he was anything but that made the mystery of why he was an academic failure one that needed to be solved. The results of his evaluation revealed that his IQ was in the borderline genius range, but his reading comprehension skills were at the ninth-grade level. His attention span was very short, and he was easily distracted by almost anything. These frequent failures in college had bruised his self-esteem. This was compounded by the fact that most of the other members of his family had graduated from college and were otherwise successful. His family's success raised his level of anxiety about college.

When I spoke with my husband that night, I told him how touched I had been by Bob's sad story of academic failure. "What we need at Marshall University is a support program that will make it possible for students who have learning disabilities to attend college," I exclaimed to my husband.

His response was, "Why don't you begin a program yourself?"

I felt that it would be too expensive, and my husband suggested that I write a grant for start-up money. When my grant proposal was approved and funded, we began a program entitled Higher Education for Learning Problems (H.E.L.P.) in the fall of 1981 with three undergraduate students (Bob was one of the three) and two graduate assistants. I received one-half release time to work on establishing H.E.L.P. Today we have approximately 200 undergraduate students with nearly 50 employees. Thirty of these employees are graduate assistants who work twenty hours per week tutoring, receive a stipend, and have their tuition costs waived. We have six full-time employees and fourteen part-time employees. The latter are teachers from the community who work in H.E.L.P. after school. Some of the teachers are learning disability specialists who work with H.E.L.P. students in the areas of reading, spelling, and written language. They try to help the students learn to write and read more effectively. Professors sometimes respond when they are asked to provide accommodations in testing, "I can provide a time extension on this test as you request, but what is this student going to do when he has to go out in the 'real world'?" When I can tell the professor that the student is working diligently to improve his reading and written language skills, the professor becomes visibly relieved and much more cooperative. Professors do not want to graduate students from their departments who are not capable of functioning as skilled professional people who are a credit to their university.

We often encounter students at the college level who cannot read because of learning disabilities not addressed at the elementary, middle, and high school levels. We have taught many college students to read through the H.E.L.P. program. Although it is sad indeed that intelligent students with learning disabilities arrive at college unable to read, it is gratifying to know that they have not given up and are still willing to try. Unfortunately, school systems in this country often discontinue teaching reading after the elementary school years. Instead, students are taught "bypass skills," which means that they are given oral tests, assisted in writing reports, etc. Some educators feel that if one hasn't learned to read by the early teen years, that it is pointless to continue this instruction. Perhaps one of the reasons that our students make such good progress in reading and spelling is that the college students are old enough and mature enough to understand the necessity of being literate. This was probably not so with many elementary age students with learning disabilities. I have attempted to teach a significant number of younger students to read, and they (usually boys) have often failed to cooperate. Instead, they have exhibited an air of, "Just try to teach me something. Go ahead—I dare you!"

H.E.L.P. provides qualified students with LD or attention deficit hyperactivity disorder (ADHD) the rights they are guaranteed under Section 504 of the Rehabilitation Act. These are students with average to superior intelligence who can successfully attend college with appropriate assistance and with sufficient dedication and hard work.

During the last eighteen years the following services have been provided through H.E.L.P. to more than 1,200 graduate and undergraduate students and more than 400 medical students and physicians from 45 different medical schools. (Medical H.E.L.P. is a support program for medical students and physicians with learning disabilities who are having difficulty passing tests and board examinations.) The services available through H.E.L.P. include:

- Assessment to determine the presence of LD and/or ADHD
- Tutoring in course work, note taking, study skills, organization, and memory improvement
- Remediation in reading, spelling, and written language skills by learning disabilities specialists
- Liaison between professors, H.E.L.P., and students
- Arrangement of accommodations in testing
- Counseling for problems of self-esteem and severe test anxiety

All tutoring is one-to-one and is done in a small, quiet room where distractions are at a minimum. Each tutor works with H.E.L.P. students only in areas where the tutor has had training. All tutors are taught how to teach material in a different manner from the way it was taught in the classroom. A multisensory approach to teaching is strongly encouraged. Tutors are also taught how to work with students in improving their note-taking skills, test-taking strategies, etc. Tutors are taught the warning signs of depression, alcohol or drug abuse, etc., as well as what they should do when they are suspicious of a problem in this area.

The Advantages of Having a Learning Disability

There are many problems associated with having LD, but we are discovering that there are also many advantages. For example, hyperactive children can become adults with endless amounts of energy that can be channeled wisely with guidance. Many of the most creative people have had LD, and this creativity can lead to personalized and original modes of self-expression. People with LD often have extremely well-honed spatial orientation and coordination, too. Some of our greatest athletes have learning disabilities, coupled with outstanding ability to coordinate their physical actions and to orient themselves spatially with incisive acumen. Many people with LD also have a unique understanding of the needs and problems of others, an attunement to the needs of other people, and a high level of empathy. They often have superior math ability, or exceptional verbal ability that may help to compensate for the deficits in written language.

Modifications Made for LD Students

When appropriate, and when recommended by a qualified professional person, the following accommodations may be made for LD students:

- Time extensions allowed on tests
- Oral testing provided
- Foreign language may be substituted with approved courses such as Spanish culture, classics, and religion courses. Substitution must be approved by Modern Languages Department
- Isolation from class allowed during testing and other in-class written work to avoid distractions
- Tape-recording of lectures permitted

Modifications Not Made for LD Students

Although many modifications are made for LD students, some changes are not allowed.

- LD students must attend class with other students. Additional help is provided *outside* the classroom
- Every student must successfully complete a transitional class in math or English if ACT or SAT scores are low in those areas
- LD students must know the material in each class on an acceptable level, although they may express that knowledge differently
- Mathematics is usually not substituted because it is believed to be an integral part of the curriculum

Typical Problems of LD College Students in the Classroom

- Problems with reading, writing, spelling, and math may make academic success more difficult than it is for other students
- Short attention span may make it difficult to concentrate and listen to a professor's lecture

- Hyperactivity/restlessness may make it difficult to sit reasonably still in class
- Organization deficits may cause the student to waste time, etc.
- Expressive language is poor, making it difficult for the student to excel in class discussions so that the professor may learn that the student knows the material
- Social perception problems may create problems in interacting with peers and professors
- Inadequate self-esteem may cause the student to be the class clown, or even withdraw from school
- Discrepancy between ability and achievement causes frustration for the student
- Difficulty with time and space may cause the student to be late for class
- Memory deficits may cause the student to have significant problems in learning material for tests
- Text anxiety may make taking a test an extremely unpleasant experience for the student
- Because of anxiety, skills may deteriorate in class, especially when taking a test or making an oral report, resulting in low or failing grades

How to Have a Learning Disability and Succeed in College

When a college student has a learning disability, it is very important to do everything possible to ensure academic success. Some of the things that H.E.L.P. students have learned significantly improve one's chances of succeeding are:

Study Habits

- Find a quiet place to study
- Exercise, get enough sleep, eat well, and take sufficient breaks while studying
- Plan two hours of study time for each hour of class (not usually in unbroken two-hour blocks)
- Schedule study hours at the *same time each day*
- Study no more than one hour before taking a break. Plan in advance the length of the break. Time study and break sessions
- Schedule study periods before and after classes whenever possible

- Work on most difficult classes when you are the most alert
- Use a multisensory approach: read aloud; write dates, names, etc., on desk top with index finger while saying aloud
- Reward yourself for using study time effectively
- Allow time for fun

Scheduling

- Put all assignment due dates on large desk calendar (can't lose it!)
- Post your schedule on dorm wall to remind you when you are to be in class, be tutored, etc.
- Carry a reduced course load until you know that you can successfully enroll in more classes. Don't set yourself up for failure by registering for eighteen credits your first semester.
- Make out a weekly schedule showing due dates and study times. Post on dorm wall
- Color-code schedule: blue for classes; red for tutoring; green for study; and yellow for fun time

Studying for Exams

- Find out what will be covered on each exam from professor—not another student
- Attend classes faithfully, especially before a test
- Set up temporary, more intense study schedule to prepare for a big test
- Catch up on missing assignments, blank spaces in notes; read over old tests to see why you made errors
- Make up study aids to review (main idea lists, definition lists, time lines, or flash cards)
- Reread and memorize highlighted material in text and notes
- Read aloud and visualize what you read
- Read recently covered material because it may be on the test
- Participate in a study group. The discussion may help you to pick out important material you have failed to emphasize
- Take a trial test. Predict what will be on exam

- Get a good night's sleep the night before exam
- Stay away from anxious students who may upset you before the exam
- Relax and arrive early for the test

Reading Textbooks

- First, read the introduction, table of contents, and look at pictures and charts to familiarize yourself with overall purpose of book
- Learn to read selectively. (Those who do not read well need to learn *what* to read.)
- Read the main headings in a chapter first and then highlight them
- Next read supporting information. Highlight in a different color. Highlight as little as you can. A phrase may be enough
- Read the summary and questions at the end of chapter so you'll know what author thinks is important
- If you have a problem with reading or tire easily when reading, order Textbooks on Tape from Recordings for the Blind and Dyslexic, Princeton, NJ
- You may benefit from using a computerized reader such as the Arkenstone Reader, WYNN Program

Writing a Paper

- Always begin with a structured outline such as is found in Project Read from the Bloomington, MN, public schools
- List the main ideas first. This will help you to see overall picture. Then add supporting ideas
- Read directions from the professor for the style you are to use in writing the paper
- On your weekly schedule, plan specific times for library research. Ask tutor to help you learn to gather information for paper
- Use index cards. Write author, title, etc., at top. Paraphrase material on card
- Using an outline, write the paper. Write one or more paragraphs for each main idea, depending on desired length and topic of paper
- Proofread paper. Arrange for someone else to proofread your paper as well
- Begin working when assignment is made. Do not put off until last few days!

Problems may manifest themselves in the classroom in a variety of ways. These students may read slowly, and comprehension deficits may require rereading material several times. Their written language may be poorly organized with deficits in grammar and syntax. Spelling may be creative but unacceptable, with frequent reversals, transpositions, omissions, and insertions. Handwriting may be difficult to read, and students often exhibit distractibility and short attention span. Due to these difficulties and other factors, students' knowledge may be far greater than test scores indicate.

Summer Program

H.E.L.P. has a required summer program for all incoming students. Each summer around the middle of June there is a 4½-week program, which is held each weekday from 12:30–4:30 p.m. There are no more than five students per class with a learning disabilities specialist as teacher, as well as a graduate assistant. The group addresses improving basic skills in spelling, reading, reading comprehension, written language, math, skills, and self esteem. Every effort is made to utilize all of the student's senses in learning.

Summer H.E.L.P. students also enroll in one university class in the morning. During the afternoon they work through this class to teach note-taking skills, study skills, and test-taking strategies. Summer H.E.L.P. is required for new H.E.L.P. students, as it seems to improve the success rate of students when they return to campus to begin their fall classes. Most incoming students complain bitterly about being required to attend the summer program, but when the session ends, they agree that it was a worthwhile experience. The students usually say that they are glad that attendance was required in the summer program because they wouldn't have participated in it otherwise.

Conclusion

The students in the H.E.L.P. program are a very special group of people. They are usually willing to work much harder and longer than the other students on campus are, once they have realized the benefits of the summer program and other H.E.L.P. supports. The good work ethic that they develop while in college makes them excellent employees following graduation. Students who have never had to study to make good grades often reveal their lazy behavior and poor work ethic after they become employed. This type of problem rarely happens with a

H.E.L.P. graduate. Our students have gone on to be quite successful. Some of them today are working as executive officers in national companies, lawyers, business owners, and physicians in every aspect of medicine. These students have found that having a learning disability has many advantages and that LD has not kept them from reaching their goals.

Bob, the young man for whom I originally began the H.E.L.P. program, completed the requirements for a degree in finance. His grades slowly improved as he learned to comprehend what he read more accurately. His improved study and test-taking skills made it possible to make better grades on examinations. Bob's skills improved so much that he made the dean's list his last semester in college. Today, fifteen years after graduation, Bob is leading "the good life." He is happily married, the father of three children, and the vice president of operations for a national company. He is very actively involved in improving the quality of life in his community. It is certainly doubtful if Bob could ever have realized his dreams if he had not participated in an in-depth support program such as H.E.L.P. Bob is one of many LD students who required academic support if graduation were to be possible. We must continue to create new support programs and to improve existing ones so that capable young people who have learning disabilities may thrive. Staff members who supply academic support services need to be aware of the special factors that influence twice-exceptional students, and how to work with these students in order to enhance their strengths and help them overcome organizational deficits. Counselors may be the ones to whom students and teachers turn when academic difficulties arise in the classroom, and teachers might notice trouble before anyone else does. Instead of blaming the student, or labeling the student in a negative way, it is essential that they know to consider appropriate interventions for twice-exceptionality when a bright student seems to have learning problems.

TEACHING THE TWICE-EXCEPTIONAL CHILD:
AN EDUCATOR'S PERSONAL JOURNEY

by L. Dennis Higgins and M. Elizabeth Nielsen

A Personal Encounter

I knew that my daughter was twice-exceptional from the first day she spent in preschool. Something was uniquely different about her. Her kindergarten teacher confirmed the concept, which was validated by every subsequent teacher. At a young age, she displayed use of high-level verbal vocabulary, unique creativity, intelligence, and high levels of problem-solving ability. She also demonstrated a low tolerance for frustration, poor organizational skills, highly anxious behaviors, and fierce independence. She seemed very protective of her abilities.

I was a trained educator of gifted children when she started her school career. In short, I knew bright children. After many conferences with her teachers, verification came that she truly was unlike the other children (gifted or nongifted) in her classes. She danced to her own drummer. She followed her own rules (unless the rules set by teachers passed her own). She did not, would not, disclose what her requirements were for successful participation in class activities. She truly was a mysterious entity in the classroom, a conundrum. And frankly, it concerned me.

Over the years, the educators in her life responded to her needs in unique, creative, and ultimately successful ways. She was served in general education, gifted education, and finally in twice-exceptional programs. Now as a young adult, she struggles still with her dual exceptionalities. She is enrolled at the university level in another state away from her parents. She carries her challenges with her. In ways I never expected, her life experiences set my own educational destiny.

In 1988, the Jacob Javits Educational Act served as a national catalyst for researching and serving special populations of gifted children. The act provided federal grants to institutions that might best be in a position to conduct research. The University of New Mexico was awarded one of these grants. This grant, a collaborative project between the University of New Mexico and the Albuquerque Public School District, became known as the Twice Exceptional Child Project. The goal of the grant was to identify and to serve a population of twice-exceptional learners (Nielsen, 1989).

When I became coordinator for this Twice Exceptional Child Project, I knew that the experience could provide answers to the questions parents and educators of twice-exceptional children had been asking for years. I hoped my own questions about my youngest daughter would also be answered. I reluctantly left a ten-year team-teaching position, teaching first-order gifted children with my teammate and friend, Sandy Lethem. I soon found just how this choice would change my life.

For the next six years as coordinator of the Twice-Exceptional Child Project, I learned much about the twice-exceptional population, published information about them, and made countless presentations in their behalf. After helping to identify, place, and serve more than 250 gifted children with disabilities, I decided to return to the classroom setting. I left my position with the Twice-Exceptional Child Project to try my hand at teaching a population of twice-exceptional learners within the Albuquerque Public School District (Higgins, 1998).

The first few months within this classroom setting forced me to change what I thought were appropriate methods for teaching this population. I did not, however, change my philosophy about these students. Philosophically, I believe this population is epistemologically grounded in its nature and tied to its abilities and disabilities in inexplicable but fundamental ways. These children are who they say they are and we as educators can't change that fact.

Characteristics of the Twice Exceptional and the Relationship to Educational Needs

Research indicates that twice-exceptional students are highly intelligent, have diverse interests, are creative in task performance, and possess critical thinking skills (Waldron, 1991). However, twice-exceptional students also demonstrate an uneven pattern of behavior with manifestations taking the form of aggression, withdrawal, frustration, and/or lack of impulse control (Van Tassel-Baska, 1991). These students may attend to irrelevant stimuli in the classroom. They demonstrate short- and long-term memory problems. They require the general education teacher to make intense modifications in their instruction. Whitemore and Maker (1985) indicate that these children may have low impulse control and may be aggressive and disruptive in class. In turn, this creates a true dilemma. How does a classroom teacher provide appropriate programming for these children while at the same time help them overcome their frustrations and successfully complete classroom activities?

An extensive amount of research concerning this population has been generated over the past years (Baum, 1988; Betts and Neihart, 1988; Fox, 1984; Higgins, 1995; Nielsen, Higgins, and Hammond, 1993; Nielsen, Higgins, Hammond, and Williams, 1993; Nielsen and Mortoff-Albert, 1989; Schiff, Kaufman, and Kaufman, 1981; Whitemore and Maker, 1985; and, Wilkinson, 1998). The research forms a basis for and demonstrates that the needs of the twice-exceptional student must be addressed in ways that are not typical and certainly not traditional. Research provides a basis for honest decision making about how best to serve the population of twice-exceptional learners.

No universally accepted model for a twice-exceptional program exists. To date, the approach has been pragmatic at best. As Waldron (1991) indicates, "students who are both gifted and learning disabled need to allow their own unique learning differences form the basis for successful enrichment and remediation" (p. 40). Hence, it seems appropriate to provide special classes for these unique learners (Higgins, 1998; Nielsen, 1989). The following components recommended by the authors are essential for the basic operation of a twice-exceptional program. These components are grounded in both personal experience and years of classroom teaching with these unique learners. Orchestration of these components may occur in an infinite amount of ways. Use of the Autonomous Learner Model (Betts, 1985; see Appendix B) for the gifted is highly recommended, and the scope and sequence of content must be carefully considered, designed, and delivered.

Components for Teaching the Twice-Exceptional Child

Several essential components combine to create a comprehensive program for twice-exceptional learners. Although the overall approach is provided by the Autonomous Learner Model (Betts, 1985), the components are derived from the research in the field and the experiences I have found successful during three years as a classroom teacher. Some of these components are grounded in readings, personal beliefs, and my work with Sandy Lethem. Most of the components are confirmed by the responses of the twice-exceptional children in my classroom. The driving forces behind programming for these students must include futures studies, thematic instruction, movement activities and instruction, simulations, social and emotional well-being, technology, the design of teaching space, and specific educational plans.

Developing a Future Positive Perspective

Future studies focuses on the student's predicted and planned future. It involves the individual in local, national, and global contexts. Futures studies helps the student develop the skills and attitudes needed in the near, far, and distant future. It encourages children to become proactive rather than reactive to the future and helps them understand that they do have a certain amount of control in the future. The studies consider what the future may bring in the larger political, philosophical, and environmental sense. Thus, by envisioning and creating the future, the student may more closely define the future and his or her own place within it.

Twice-exceptional children dream of the future in positive but perhaps impractical ways. Incorporating futures studies to develop a future-positive perspective builds the skills of the future, incorporates real data and real problems for students to discuss, and sends the message that the individual does have a certain amount of control over the future based upon their actions. Futures studies, an extremely abstract metadiscipline, are an important aspect of programming for this very special population.

Twice-exceptional learners tend to have strong positive views of their personal futures concerning their education and possible career, but lack understanding of how to attain the desired goals. Dewey (1916) believed that encouraging individuals to take charge of life, without also supplying the means to help them do so, created a valueless future. Based upon his philosophy alone, it would be difficult to justify not including futures studies with these children.

In two recent studies of twice-exceptional students (Higgins, 1995; Wilkinson, 1998), virtually 100 percent of the students stated their intent to finish high school. Most of these students fully intended to complete their education with advanced degrees. Finally, 70 percent and 62.5 percent of these students aspired to having managerial or scientific careers as adults.

Educators of twice-exceptional children hold the responsibility of teaching these students specific methods for achieving their goals, so that these students will be encouraged to fulfill their dreams. Suggested avenues for helping these learners to view and understand their personal future include providing a course in futures studies, involving students in the Future Me Program (Higgins, 1999) and/or placing students in a mentorship/internship program. Students should be encouraged to study the future through seminar topics, service learning activities, or any one of the vast amount of materials available through commercially appropriate vendors.

Themes and Subthemes

Most twice-exceptional learners require the "big picture" in order to understand curricular expectations. In response to this characteristic, curriculum that is abstractly theme-based as well as concretely content-based is an absolute necessity. Theme-based teaching tends to focus on the whole student. This instruction, which must address the cognitive, affective, and psychomotor domains, is useful for focusing and refocusing students who need help with their organizational skills (Lewis, 1993). This work encourages the preorganizational skills that have proven to be important for these students. This population responds to both an overarching conceptual theme as well as to concretely based subthemes. Although the overarching theme must remain constant through the school year, the related subthemes must change from grading period to grading period. Discussions and activities concerning these themes should ultimately culminate in valid generalizations.

Three-Year Cycle

Based upon the model set forth by the Albuquerque Public School District for twice-exceptional learners, teachers of twice-exceptional children must be prepared to teach these children in the classroom for a two- to three-year time period. As a result, the curriculum must reflect at least a three-year cycle. A thematic structure, related to the curricular philosophy designed by researchers at the University of Kansas, offers this overarching conceptual backdrop. Based on this model, a three-year curricular cycle for students is relatively easy to plan. The design encourages educators to provide major themes and minor subthemes for each year of the three-year cycle. In this way, no child will repeat any content area, enriched or otherwise.

Children brainstormed a list of concepts. This list was developed in relationship to the theme "Delicacy" and its corresponding subthemes, *wind, sand, stars,* and *waves.* Students in the class brainstormed content areas they might like to study in relation to these subthemes.

Hands-On, Interdisciplinary Assignments

Since many twice-exceptional students have great difficulty with paper-pencil tasks, hands-on assignments become an appropriate response to this situation. The use of manipulatives that test and strengthen the student's fine and gross motor skills and yet provide a content base is essential. Although these assignments must be tied directly to the conceptual themes that are part of the curriculum, they also must be tied to the core curriculum. Since twice-exceptional learners are also classified as gifted learners, an interdisciplinary approach seems to be most appropriate.

For example, the theme "Delicacy" may be studied in an interdisciplinary way. A lesson designed to enrich a mathematics concept in multiplication also would ask that students use the vocabulary from a social studies perspective. This combination requires the incorporation of many aspects of instruction. A teacher might combine the idea of bead making as a "delicate" craft. This instruction must include the cultural aspects of the uses and importance of beads across culture and history. The mathematical concepts of classification, attribute listing, and nonlinear ordering might be incorporated into the lessons.

First, the teacher asks the class to examine beads from a variety of perspectives (craft, culture, historical importance, material, shape). The teacher then introduces a problem. In this case, the problem is the "unorganized bead maker" who consistently mixes up the beads that are created. Students solve the problem by finding a way for the bead maker to organize the creations in a bead cabinet of their design. The culminating product of this interdisciplinary math lesson would be to create the design of a cabinet that the bead maker would use to display these very delicate beads (Dubois, 1977). In a typical assignment, students are introduced to bead making from an historical and perhaps cultural perspective, and then help the bead maker to construct cabinets for easy storage and retrieval of the beads. This classification process has its roots in multiplication principles. For example, if the beads are made with bone, wood, and ceramic (materials) and were either oval or square (shape), students must decide how many cubicles the bead maker would need to incorporate in a display cabinet in order to keep all of the beads organized (a 3x2 categorical display). Students design this cabinet and represent the design using construction paper. Students are then asked to share their specific creations, many of which are unique within the class and are one-of-a-kind creations. Suppose the bead maker decides to add blue, red, and green (color) to the inventory. How many cubicles would the bead maker need now (a 3x2x3 categorical display)? How might the display cabinet change?

Movement Activities and Instruction

Movement studies can include adventure trips that involve extensive movement on the part of the individual students, involving the student as a whole, kinesthetically connected learner. In some instances, movement itself can be the source of knowledge, through dance or action. In other circumstances, movement across time and space becomes primary.

Wilderness Trips

The twice-exceptional program supports wilderness activities, including an overnight camping experience. This experiential component addresses many of the goals of the program and ties directly to Dimension Three of the Autonomous Learner Model—adventure trips.

As is true in many states, New Mexico is rich in potential for wilderness trips for twice-exceptional children. One such trip, experienced by the class of 1998–99, included a three-day/two-night camping trip to an ancient Anasazi Indian archeological site known as Chaco Canyon. The canyon is located in the western part of New Mexico, 250 miles west of Albuquerque. Students were responsible for planning the agenda of the trip (although actual lesson plans for the trip were not part of student responsibility), the sleeping arrangements, the daily menus, and the grocery list. For this trip, each student was assigned a pueblo in which to become an expert (Chaco Canyon is an historical site that boasts eight major pueblo ruins within an eight-mile range). Each student would become the tour guide for individual pueblos, and was assigned a scientific role to perform at each pueblo. For example, the tour guide at Pueblo Bonito was also the botanist for the canyon. After the tour of the pueblo was finished, the scientific portion of the visit began. In this manner, the botanist would report on all of the plant life in each pueblo but also would be the expert on the assigned pueblo (Lethem & Higgins, 1988).

Frequent Changes in Activities

This population often exhibits difficulty in sustaining attention for an extended period of time. Frequent changes in daily activities in order to ensure motivation are often required. These changes must also include opportunities for student selection. The teacher must ensure that the overarching theme and related subthemes are continually addressed through the use of advanced organizers. In this way, the student's cognitive structure is strengthened and the teacher is able to organize and convey large amounts of information (Joyce, Weil, and Showers, 1992).

A weekly schedule that reflects such changes can meet the demands of this component. Thursday is the beginning of the workweek and Wednesday is the end of the workweek. Work assigned on Thursday is due the following Wednesday. All direct teaching, spelling tests, and language arts assignments occur in the middle of the week, on Wednesday.

Structured time for outside activities such as jumping rope, walking, hanging by the arms on the jungle gym, throwing and hitting balls, and any positive activity that allows students to keep moving help twice-exceptional students of all ages. These activities must occur throughout the day to break up long periods of academic work.

Some of these students might have sensory integration difficulties. Providing a "fidget bag" for the student's use throughout the day is highly recommended. The fidget bag contains small tactile items that serve as calming devices. The basic rules for using the items contained within this bag might include:

1.   The item chosen may not get in the way of instruction.
2.   Fidgets may be used only during certain hours of the day.
3.   The fidget chosen must be the result of a singular random pick.
4.   The item chosen must satisfy the need for the manipulative.
5.   If the item gets in the way of learning, it is put away.

Fine-Motor Control Practice

Some twice-exceptional children may have great difficulty with the writing process. They also often exhibit difficulty with cutting and pasting, and with general use of the small manipulative items (crayons, paper clips, rulers, protractors, etc.) found on the typical student desk. Practice with fine-motor control in the form of illustrating, painting, and calligraphy often helps with these skills.

Small Group Settings

Since the needs of this population are diverse, intense, and extreme, these students require an educational setting that is conducive to 1:1 teaching and interaction. The Albuquerque Public Schools has created classroom settings that restrict the number of students to an absolute capacity of eight students. The twice-exceptional population operates within this definition. Without this type of intervention, needs are extremely difficult to meet. A full-time assistant often helps in the classroom.

Educational Strategies

These students thrive on the traditional strategies used in gifted education (i.e.:, interpretation of data; inquiry; metaphorical thinking; creative problem solving; application of generalizations). However, traditional data input must be modified for these students. Twice-exceptional students are not likely to receive the data from reading alone; they need alternative ways for data input. These students have the same level of conceptual ability, the same vast amount of knowledge, and the same curiosity as the "traditional" gifted child. Once the data has been acquired (tested through Bloom's Taxonomy), twice-exceptional students are able to perform to the level of gifted students. The remedial needs of this special population cannot be ignored and must not go unaddressed in the classroom. A 60/40 blend works well. At times, a 60 percent gifted education and 40 percent special education should be delivered. Other times, the inverse would be true. No schedule can be set for this pattern of instruction; it depends on the specific class of students. This pattern will ensure that essential remediation does not monopolize the student's time to the exclusion of enrichment.

Social and Emotional Development

Although not all twice-exceptional students have identical profiles, many of the characteristics include, at a minimum, the following social and emotional characteristics: low academic self-concept; high levels of frustration; unrealistic self-expectations concerning achievement; hyperactivity; and low self-esteem but positive self-image (Nielsen, 1989; Sowa, McIntire, May, and Bland, 1994; and, Wilkinson, 1998). These students often feel unique. As one twice-exceptional student explained, "I had to leave my old school because I know too much and I know too little. I want to be a regular kid. I want to shrink my memory." The following practices have proven successful with diverse learners.

Address Social-Emotional Issues

This population is particularly emotionally fragile. Emotional needs tend to take time from the actual teaching of content and requires 1:1 attention from the teacher in the program. Unless these emotional issues are addressed, the absolute cognitive level of the student cannot and will not be reached at its potential level (Betts, 1985). Although many teachers and administrators will say that this is not the job of the teacher, for this population it must be a number one focus.

School Counseling

Directly connected to the social-emotional issues, whole group counseling on a weekly basis helps establish the social-emotional climate and the group dynamics of the class. These students often have deep insights, and can help each other as well as themselves. In a discourse on communication, one student said, "Language can be very violent. We commit toward ourselves through self-talk, by stopping ourselves from learning and growing, by not allowing ourselves to make mistakes." The counselor involved should be one who cares about the high-ability, low-functioning individual and is aware of the characteristics as well as the low vulnerability of this population. Typical activities must include role playing, values clarification, autonomy, and self-discovery activities. It is reasonable to think that this type of counseling, coupled with social and emotional awareness, will plausibly refocus the twice-exceptional student's desire to become goal oriented and redirect him to a more desirable internal locus of control.

Student Awareness of Abilities and Disabilities

Twice-exceptional students often become aware of the difference between what they can intellectualize and what they can produce as compared to other children with the same intellectual potential. This awareness can be a source of frustration and a cause of anxiety and so must be addressed with counseling and directed attention. Under Individual Development, Dimension Two of the Autonomous Learner Model (Betts, 1985), students have the opportunity to explore this in a structured environment with a teacher/facilitator who is knowledgeable and concerned about the information discovered. This teacher/facilitator should be willing and able to help these students come to terms with who they are.

Technology

Historically, traditional school has not worked for many twice-exceptional students. Desks arranged in linear rows, a daily schedule that splices the day, and obtaining information largely from books has proven to be unsuccessful. Instead, an environment needs to take advantage of current and available technology.

Because of their disabilities, twice-exceptional students tend to rely on a variety of technologies in order to successfully approach and complete schoolwork/assignments. These technologies include computers, spellcheckers, authoring systems, multimedia encyclopedias, synthesizers, books on tape, tape recorders, presentation packages, grammar checks, and language master machines. Emerging new technologies are essential components to twice-exceptional programming.

CD-ROM Technology

Although not unique, the use of the CD-ROM has proven to develop student independence and success. Students are able to gather a tremendous amount of information using this technology and are able to replay various sections of a lesson to hear what they missed, gain new understanding of a complex subject, or review material before a test.

CD-ROM materials offered by commercially oriented vendors such as Tom Snyder Productions (1999) and Sunburst (1999) provide a tremendous avenue of success for the twice-exceptional learner. Opportunities to do problem-based learning, critical thinking, and even basic skill development exist within these well-developed products. For example, in the Voyages of the Mimi 1 & 2 (Sunburst, 1999), students are able to use portions of the CD-ROM for video editing purposes, in effect creating their own version of a whaling adventure or of an archeological dig. Using the Decisions, Decisions series or Great Ocean or Solar System Rescue (Tom Snyder Productions, 1999), students understand more about oceanography, astronomy, colonization, or immigration through simulation packages. Both companies, and many others not listed, have a fine array of materials that offer the unique modifications that are just right for the twice-exceptional learner.

Design of Teaching Space

Low/Soft Lighting

Learning style personalities of the twice-exceptional benefit from differentiated lighting different from what is typically found in the classroom setting. Natural lighting and lighting from floor and table lamps provide a calm, harsh-free setting in which these students must work. Specialized wall and track lighting systems might also be utilized. This specialized lighting creates a soft, warm atmosphere and encourages the twice-exceptional learner to become more relaxed and more willing to participate in all activities, thus becoming more productive. Ultraviolet lighting, unique modular configurations, fiber-optic plumes and sound/light walls can benefit these students.

Nontraditional School Furniture

The learning environment is extremely important for this special population of gifted learners. If possible, the physical environment should be divided into separate rooms with distinctive features for each room. One "room" in the classroom, labeled the "hard area," might be filled with traditional student desks and large tables used for work surfaces. Another area, labeled the "soft area," might be filled with low tables, sofas, overstuffed chairs, special lighting, and large pillows.

Twice-exceptional children often prefer working on the floor with soft pillows, using a clipboard as a desk or working as a group around low tables no more than three feet in height. Overstuffed chairs and sofas also facilitate the learning process. An array of plant and small animal life strategically placed throughout the classroom can affect learning in a positive way. Although each student has a traditional desk in a specified area of this unique classroom environment, students are free to work anywhere in the classroom they wish. Direct teaching is facilitated at the traditional desk location and desks are positioned in a horseshoe configuration, but assignments are usually completed in other locations. These students demonstrate a need for both the soft, comfortable asymmetrical furniture and furniture arrangements in which to sit and do their work and the traditional school furniture to store school supplies and to participate in direct academic instruction, so administrative support is essential. An outdoor learning area so students may work outside in an environment would incorporate low water plants, a garden, and shade.

Music as a Background

Twice-exceptional students use quiet study time or "downtime" well if they have soft, wordless music as a permeating background throughout the day. A musical background creates a unique, "filled" environment. They also work well if they have control over that music. Free selection of music is recommended and appropriate. In addition, these students benefit from tonal sounds that register in the very low frequencies.

Quadraphonic sound can fill the classroom. Music with lower frequencies and unique studio mixing is being produced to see what effects this will have on the student population. This music could act as a "white noise" backdrop for the classroom setting to create a calming environment that stimulates the learning process.

Nontraditional Methods and Materials

Twice-exceptional students reject traditional materials just as they resist traditional teaching methods. A hands-on, experiential approach to learning is preferential to traditional textbook learning. These students prefer activities conducted outside of the classroom setting that emphasize group problem solving. Certainly, wilderness activities serve this purpose. Activities might include any of the low ropes or high ropes courses, experiential group problem solving using metaphorical analyses of their experiences, twenty to thirty minute jaunts to locations around the school, or conducting "Here, Hear, and Now" observations. The "Here, Hear, and Now" observations are activities that provide a nonthreatening experience that strengthen auditory observational and recording skills. Students find a location somewhere on school property and sit (the Here), listen intently to any sounds that occur (the Hear), and record that information on special paper that is separated in thirty-second intervals so as to record "sound bites" (the Now). By separating the students by distance, they essentially create a "sound map" of the school for a 15-minute interval. Students are always amazed at how much life there is on school property.

Since students enjoy and benefit from hands-on construction activities, the classroom is stocked with 1½-inch PVC pipe with a variety of related fittings (these inexpensive pipe and fittings are available at any hardware store). Students are allowed to work on the playground, putting together unique complex structures (none may be taller than six feet) and solving problems from a variety of teacher-made task cards that parallel math, science, and language arts activities. After activities are complete and evaluated, the structures are disassembled and materials put away.

Finally, at the end of each day, all students perform their daily restoration assignments. By "restoring the environment" on a daily basis, the room is put away for the day and readied for the next day. These assignments range from vacuuming the carpets to feeding and watering the animals to watering the many plants in the room.

The Individualized Educational Plan (IEP)

New Mexico is unique in that gifted children are contained under the umbrella of special education. Thus, each child in the program must have an individualized education plan (IEP). It is beyond the scope and intent of this chapter to discuss the legal issues of the IEP. An important aspect for programming rests on the IEP's goals and objectives. The type of individual consideration for these students is intensified by the unique, excessive need for individual help and unique programming. This consideration must play a strong role in the programming for and instruction of these children.

An actual IEP must include several parts, starting with the present levels of performance (PLP) and ending with an evaluation component. Since this program has been designed to address the whole child (not just the academic side of the child), this information is gathered from a variety of sources. These sources include formal testing, interviews, writing samples, anecdotal records about kinesthetic levels, and any information that might be gleaned concerning social or emotional status. Goals and objectives match the needs of the students.

Lethem and Higgins (1988) have created goals and objectives for all dimensions of the Autonomous Learner Model. This document of goals and objectives can serve as a foundational, working document, to build the actual goals and objectives for children within the program. A team of individuals including teachers, parents, diagnosticians, and even the student creates the actual and final goals and objectives. No IEP ends up exactly the same as any other.

Essential Classroom Activities

The following classroom activities have been designed considering the characteristics of the twice-exceptional learner. All activities have been classroom tested and are consistent features within my classroom designed for these students. Modifications are recommended to fit specific locations.

Seminar

Based on their unique characteristics, twice-exceptional children must have opportunities to successfully express their ideas and their interests with a group of children who share similar characteristics and interests. The seminar is designed to allow students to pursue "passion areas" and "related passion areas," as appropriate. The seminar process also encourages library and Internet searches thus reinforcing research skills, provides opportunities for home discussions, allows for formal discussions in the classroom using a variety of strategies such as Interpretation of Data, requires the gathering of topical readings, encourages much discussion and interaction with peers, and has a strong evaluation component. As the students become more confident, they are encouraged to facilitate the discussion of the assigned topic. This includes encouragement of the less verbal, ensuring that no one student dominates the floor and brings the discussion to a close.

Obviously, the amount of written work in preparation for the seminar must be minimal. Although these students have the global and conceptual thoughts of the typical gifted student, they do not have the ability to generate the equivalent amount of written documentation. In order to modify this requirement, "seminar prep" times must be incorporated into the weekly schedule. During these times, the teacher of the twice-exceptional student must provide simple readings, CD-ROM opportunities, and videotape introductions to the topic. Lectures that minimize the writing process must also be included. Finally, students must be given the time to prepare for the seminar. A bulletin board, divided into quadrants, lists the topics at least one month in advance and must be a central part of the classroom. This bulletin board is in a constant state of change, taking a completed seminar topic down, rotating the existing topics from quadrant to quadrant, and placing new topics up as space permits.

Seminar topics are always asked as an open-ended question. Since there is no one right answer to the question, an exploration of alternative points of view is encouraged.

Future Classics Presentations

Twice-exceptional learners often tend to be poor to average readers, although some of them read voraciously and well. Like other learners, they need to share information about books they have read. The Future Classics Presentation replaces the traditional book report (Lethem and Higgins, 1988), yet allows the student to respond to what was learned about the book, to share personal feelings about the book, and provide any recommendations concerning the book. This component of the program encourages communication skills, provides a variety/choice of hands-on projects, reinforces the skill of summarization of literature, provides a "safe" audience for sharing information and projects, encourages access to quality literature, and allows for a student evaluation and/or recommendation of the book to other readers. The sharing of information is accomplished through a variety of recommended hands-on projects that students must complete on a monthly basis.

Two-Minute Presentation

Twice-exceptional students traditionally have a great deal of difficulty finding and using factual information. Their disabilities, including poorly developed reading skills and poor organizational skills, often prevent them from successfully completing this task. A method designed to help students develop these skills is the weekly two-minute/one-minute presentation. This component introduces students (even low readers) to the concept of informational summaries, reinforces communication skills, teaches organizational skills, builds self-confidence, provides opportunity for public speaking, utilizes synthesis skills, and allows students to practice extemporaneous speaking.

The two-minute/one-minute presentation requires the student to read a one-page informational card (from a variety of topics), study the card for two minutes, and then provide a one-minute presentation summarizing the facts found on the card. The card (usually a Time-Life fact card) contains charts, pictures, large print, and graphs the student uses to glean the information quickly and easily. It also helps the student with extemporaneous speaking. After the one-minute presentation, the student must then answer questions about the card from other students.

Folderwork/Holistic Assignments

One difficulty for twice-exceptional students is the fragmentation of the school day. By either switching from classroom to classroom or routinely dividing the day into subject or content areas (i.e., math then reading then spelling then social studies, etc.), the student often has difficulty organizing both the physical and the emotional parts of the day. Instead, twice-exceptional students must have an integrated, interdisciplinary curriculum. Still, these students need a flexible but fixed schedule. This is the purpose of the folderwork assignment.

Folderwork or holistic assignments provide students with schoolwork in content areas, address themes and subthemes, provide opportunities to make personal choices in their work throughout the day and evening, and encourage autonomy. As one student noted, "Being autonomous doesn't come from this classroom, it comes from within, it is who you are."

Although folderwork assignments are individualized, they do allow for some repetition from student to student, making the folderwork more manageable for the teacher. Often, the folderwork contains information about upcoming assignments, words of encouragement to the student, miscellaneous information concerning an historical event or astronomical feature that might occur during the week, or even a small message to parents. Folderwork assignments are assignments for the week, assigned on Thursday and due on the following Wednesday. This is not to imply that a teacher does not become involved with the organization or with motivation to get all assignments complete. In fact, the folderwork assignment is designed with individualization in mind. The daily/weekly schedule is organized so the teacher can work with individual students on all assignments.

Theme Books

Every Monday morning, the week begins with a quality literature book connected to the theme and subtheme. I call this the "weekly theme book feast." Theme books are a gentle, peaceful way to begin the week. Among the positive aspects, theme books encourage the examination of quality, succinct writing, build a strong relationship and foundation to the curriculum, create an awareness of quality illustrations, encourage a "love" for reading, and provide a unique opportunity for discussions about a variety of topics.

Art Activities

Art activities have both a therapeutic and calming effect with the twice-exceptional learner. Art activities that require large sweeping effects with the hands and arms help develop fine and gross motor coordination. Art activities must reinforce any therapeutic avenues that are pursued. Art activity often helps these students through a difficult but immediate emotional crisis based on an event that might have occurred during the course of the day. Of course, art activities are tied to the working themes.

Conclusion

Self-contained programs for twice-exceptional students are unlike self-contained remedial programs or self-contained gifted programs. The self-contained twice-exceptional program truly is its own element. The intensity of the population is labor intensive and physically exhausting. These students have self-determination skills that take tolls on classroom teachers. This magnifies when these children are grouped together, as they should be, for a majority of the day. A nondogmatic educational assistant skilled in working with delicate emotional issues is best.

Education for twice-exceptional learners is an exercise based on and driven by the needs and nature of the population. Twice-exceptional children are unique in the world of exceptional children, fitting neither under the rubrics of a gifted population nor that of a learning disabled population. Teachers must make appropriate provisions and modifications—addressing emotional, social, and cognitive areas—in response to the characteristics of these children. These students thrive on opportunities for self-exploration in a structured but safe manner. Teachers must help students come to know and understand their strengths and weaknesses and help these students come to terms with those conditions.

Twice-exceptional children can and must develop strategies to help them cope with or overcome their difficulties and challenges. A variety of opportunities is required during their educational day, including hands-on problem-solving activities, academic instruction in a traditional sense, remediation, opportunities for creativity, activities that help develop a positive future image, discussions with other learners concerning passion areas, and open opportunities to safely discuss their emotions with other learners or a facilitator. Most important, these students need to spend a significant portion of their day with other twice-exceptional learners. These students must have the opportunity to be who they are in a comfortable, accepting, and safe environment.

REFERENCES

Baum, S. 1988. An enrichment model for gifted learning disabled students. *Gifted Child Quarterly* 32: 226–230.

Betts, G. T. 1985. *The Autonomous Learner Model for the Gifted and Talented.* Greeley, Colo.: ALPS Publishing.

Betts, G. T., and M. Neihart. 1988. Profiles of the gifted and talented. *Gifted Child Quarterly* 32(2): 248–253.

Dewey, J. 1916. *Democracy and Education,* New York: Macmillan.

Dubois, D. W. 1977. *Mathematical Models for Teachers.* Unpublished manuscript. University of New Mexico.

Fox, L. H. 1984. The learning-disabled gifted child. *Learning Disabilities* 3(10): 117–128.

Higgins, L. D. 1999. In press. *Future Me Program: A Futures Simulator.* Greeley, Colo.: ALPS Publishing.

———. 1998. A profile of a twice-exceptional program: A personal journey. *Highly Gifted Children* (12)2: 18–27.

———. 1995. *Educating the first generation of the technology age: An examination of attitudes toward technology among twice-exceptional learners.* Unpublished doctoral dissertation. Greely, Colo.: University of Northern Colorado.

Joyce B., M. Weil, and B. Showers. 1992. *Models of Teaching.* Boston: Allyn and Bacon.

Lethem, S. L., and L. D. Higgins. 1988. Unpublished manuscript. *Program Guide for a First-Order Gifted Self-Contained Classroom.* Zuni Magnet School. Albuquerque Public Schools, Albuquerque, New Mexico.

Lewis, M. E. B. 1993. *Thematic Methods and Strategies in Learning Disabilities.* San Diego, Calif.: Singular Publishing Group.

Nielsen, M. E. 1989. *The twice-exceptional child project: Identifying and serving gifted/handicapped learners.* Application: Javits Gifted & Talented Students, SAI# R206-A-90151-90/92.

Nielsen, M. E., L. D. Higgins, and A. E. Hammond. 1993. Twice-exceptional child project: Identifying and serving gifted/handicapped learners. In C. M. Callahan, C. A. Tomilinson, P. M. Pizzat (eds.), *Contexts for Promise: Noteworthy Practices in the Identification of Gifted Students.* Storrs, Conn.: National Research on the Gifted and Talented.

Nielsen, M. E., L. D. Higgins, A. E. Hammond, and R. A. Williams. 1993. Gifted children with disabilities: Albuquerque's twice-exceptional child project serves "nontraditional" students. *Gifted Child Today* 16(5): 9–12.

Nielsen, M. E., and S. Mortoff-Albert. 1989. The effects of special education service on the self-concept and school attitude of learning disabled/gifted students. *Roeper Review* 12(1): 29–36.

Schiff, M., A. S. Kaufman, and N. L. Kaufman. 1981. Scatter analysis of WISC-R profiles for learning disabled children with superior intelligence. *Journal of Learning Disabilities.* 400–404.

Sowa, C. J., J. McIntire, K. M. May, and L. Bland. 1994. Social and emotional adjustment themes across gifted children. *Roeper Review* 17, 95–98.

Sunburst. 1999. Educational Catalog Pleasantville, N.Y.

Tom Snyder Productions. 1999. Spring/Summer Catalog. Watertown, Mass.

Van Tassel-Baska, J. 1991. Serving the disabled gifted through educational collaboration. *Journal for the Education of the Gifted* 14 (3): 246–262.

———. 1994. *Comprehensive Curriculum for Gifted Learners.* Boston: Allyn and Bacon.

Waldron, K. A. 1991. Teaching techniques for the learning disabled/gifted student. *Learning Disabilities Research & Practice* (6) 40–43.

Whaley, C. E., and H. F. Whaley. 1986. *Future Images: Futures Studies for Grades 4–12*. New York: Trillium Press.

Whitemore, J. A., and C. J. Maker. 1985. *Intellectual Giftedness in Disabled Persons*. Rockville, Md: Aspen.

Wilkinson, S. C. 1998. Unpublished doctoral dissertation. *Influences on the academic performance of twice-exceptional high school students* An exploratory study of risk, resilience, and achievement*. Albuquerque: University of New Mexico.

ON HIGH POTENTIAL AND ANTISOCIAL BEHAVIOR

by Ken Seeley

As I was preparing this chapter, a terrible tragedy descended on my community. On April 20, 1999, two teens entered Columbine High School, killed a teacher and twelve of their class-mates, and wounded twenty others before taking their own lives. These students were of high ability, good achievement, and from upper-middle-class homes. As I write, many of the details are still unfolding. All of us become victims of this tragedy. As educators, parents, human services providers, we ask how it could have happened. Capable, achieving students from good homes are not supposed to commit such crimes. The horrific and tragic event at Columbine became the catalyst for this chapter, and I hope can serve all of us who must heal and learn.

My definition of "at risk" is the greater likelihood of failing to achieve at least a basic quality of life relative to physical and psychological safety, education, health, or economic self-sufficiency. Quality of life is an illusive concept and may ultimately be one's own perception. When applied to giftedness, "at-risk" is a difficult concept. If one has the potential to achieve at a high level but never finishes high school but otherwise has a satisfactory quality of life, is that so bad? We advocates could see the great intellectual loss to self and society. Others would argue that happiness should be the barometer. As educators of young people we must have zero tolerance for loss of potential. Isn't developing potential really what good education is?

Giftedness and Delinquent Behavior

The prevailing views of the connection between giftedness and delinquency are para-doxical. One explanation, the "risk" theory, states that talented youth are more vulnerable to unfavorable environmental influences due to their heightened sensibilities and greater percep-tual ability. Giftedness itself can make a child feel different from peers and less likely to fit in to groups. This vulnerability might lead a youth to join fringe groups of other social outcasts who are being adversely affected by problems at home or at school.

The other competing perspective is that talent is a protection against delinquent behav-ior. High levels of intellectual ability with greater insight into their own behaviors allow tal-ented youth to see the long-term consequences of criminal activity. As a result gifted youth are better able to understand and cope with negative influences.

Overall, the research on the family experiences of gifted and average delinquents tends to support the protection perspective. Talented youth who become delinquent often have experienced particularly unstable homes with family separation and conflict. At the same time, our research from Arapaho County gifted delinquents found no predictive factors about giftedness and unstable homes. Gifted delinquents were as likely as not to come from good homes as unstable homes.

The interaction of talent and delinquent behavior is affected strongly by environmental factors, age, and gender. A deep hostility and alienation drove the two boys who murdered their classmates at Columbine High School. They were social outcasts at their school, the targets of bullying from other students, and loners in their neighborhoods. They had a preoccupation of studying war and violence in great depth. They set up a Web page for their own little clique. We begin to see some of the characteristics of the disaffected gifted child in reflecting upon their traits. Ultimately, psychological profiles will emerge and we will know more. If these youth were gifted, we need to analyze what, if any, influence their high ability could have played in this terrible incident.

Some evidence suggests that specific factors within giftedness can influence either the risk of delinquency or protection from delinquency. High verbal ability would add to a youth's skills to adapt to the environment in more socially acceptable ways, a protection against negative influences. This cluster of verbal abilities is referred to as "crystallized" intelligence, on which there is extensive professional literature. Teachers reward this type of intelligence because it conforms to school learning requirements of taking in information and giving it back on tests and projects. Crystallized abilities are more helpful to gifted youth in social adaptation, enabling them to verbally analyze and explain the complexities of human behavior.

Another cluster of abilities is characterized as "fluid" intelligence. This intelligence is a more spatial or figural understanding of the world with a quick perceptiveness often lacking verbal labels. Some evidence, although dated, indicates that gifted delinquent youth possess very high levels of fluid ability and low levels of crystallized ability. All of us have both clusters of abilities, but it seems when they are out of balance toward the fluid type, there is a greater vulnerability to negative influences. Students high in fluid but low in crystallized ability are not often recognized as good learners in schools. They understand information more conceptually and spatially rather than in step-by-step analysis using verbal explanations. They often can answer a teacher's questions correctly, but be unable to explain how they got the answer. These learners usually are not rewarded in classes and may be accused of cheating because they lack the "rule-oriented" requirements of schooling.

In summary, fluid abilities tend to be intellectual capacity that is independent of experience. This fluidity involves the ability to solve creative problems and process novel material. Crystallized abilities are basically learned knowledge involving information retrieval. Assessment of delinquent youth has found these to be out of balance among gifted delinquents. Common terms for fluid ability might be "innate or instinctive ability" or "street smarts." Since this ability is not encouraged in school, students who use high fluid ability to solve problems may not experience high achievement usually associated with giftedness. The thinking style of these youth is characterized by a quick perceptiveness. Many experienced educators can see these abilities as "raw" intelligence and describe the gaps between verbal performance and ability on report cards with the famous "capable of doing much better" rating, as if these youth are intentionally holding back their true talents.

These observations are a very scant beginning of a theory about the development of delinquency in gifted youths. Below is an outline to help identify factors that protect youths or increase their vulnerability to delinquency.

TYPE OF TALENT

Fluid Ability: figural creative, performance IQ, spatial ability
Crystallized Ability: verbal creative, verbal IQ, grade point average

Family Environment
Stable
Unstable
Disintegrated

School Environment
Achievement
Peer support
Extracurricular
Hostility toward school or from school
A caring adult at school

The interaction of these factors in the lives of gifted youth will determine how protected from or vulnerable to delinquency they are. It is important to take an asset-based approach and try to build the protective factors through interventions at home, at school, and in the community.

Using Assets to Build Resilience in At-Risk Gifted Youth

Assuming that we actively look for at-risk gifted youth in our identification strategies, we need to develop individual plans that incorporate the youth's total environment. These youth are more difficult to identify because they are typically underachievers and may have high levels of fluid ability. On standardized achievement tests and classroom verbal tasks they might appear average. Special identification procedures are needed to find their assets. Procedures might include interviews, product reviews, nonverbal intelligence testing, peer nominations, and interest surveys.

At-risk gifted youth and their families need to understand that they have talents and learning styles that may differ from the high achievers. These students often hear that they are not working up to potential. We should not focus on deficits, but build on strengths. If a youth has a strong interest and ability in science, but is mediocre in all other areas, their individual learning plan should develop other areas from the base in science. They could study biographies of scientists who struggled in school, and be allowed to do advanced science. Most important, the student and family should design the bridge from her or his interest to the academic requirements at school.

The family and home must be integral to an individual learning plan for an at-risk gifted youth. This may involve home visits or special outreach to parents to recruit them as allies and participants. If for whatever reason the parents are not responsive, the school must work with some responsible family or community member, perhaps identified by the student, to participate in the learning plan. This may be a grandparent, other relative, or a pastor. The home–school connection is absolutely essential if we are to see any progress.

Underachievement typically breeds low motivation. It is the reverse side of "nothing succeeds like success." Educators observe a low achieving, poorly motivated student who seems to have potential. It is too easy to label the student "lazy" and let ourselves off the hook for any responsibility to build success with different approaches. Motivation is a state of mind that varies with the student's interests. It is not static and pervasive. The challenge is to form a compact with the youth to achieve in areas of their interests, and to also complete work that they might find unpleasant or difficult. Life is full of things that we are not motivated to do. Completing unpleasant work in order to get on to more interesting things is an important lesson to teach and learn.

Overcoming difficult environmental factors for at-risk gifted youth is perhaps the greatest challenge for educators. We cannot cure poverty or racism, but we can help youths to recognize their talents and use them to build resilience to negative environments. First and foremost, the student must have at least one caring adult at school in a sustaining relationship. All children and youths need to count in someone else's life outside their family. What better place than school to find that relationship? If they do not get that opportunity at school, they may find it in gangs or delinquency. Social connections through youth groups, clubs, scouts, churches, or other community resources build resilience. Developing these social skills helps build an interest in academics through positive peer interaction.

Afterword

Feelings of alienation and isolation are common among at-risk gifted students. A sense of "community" at school helps overcome the inevitable hostility that results from being an outcast. Opportunities to recognize and use their talents is a wonderful way to reach at-risk gifted students. Their desire to find a caring environment at school is tied to their need to be caring and giving about something important. School-sponsored service learning opportunities are a great way to involve these students who might not choose sports or pep club as a way of feeling connected to a community.

We will never know if any of these alternatives might have prevented the tragedy at Columbine High School. The two student murderers had many characteristics of at-risk gifted youth. The school's ability to recognize the problems of these two boys and to connect them to a positive community may have helped. We must keep developing alternatives for the hard-to-reach students and not let them or ourselves off the hook on the way to finding a positive future.

TECHNOLOGY: TRANSFORMING THE CLASSROOM FOR GIFTED STUDENTS WITH DISABILITIES

by Sandra Berger

Research has discovered that students learn best when they can connect new ideas to what they already know and have experienced; they are actively engaged in applying and testing their knowledge using real-world problems; they can organize their work around clear, high goals with lots of practice in reaching them; and they can use their own interests and strengths as springboards for learning (Resnick, 1987).

Mason, a high school junior, is both gifted and learning disabled. He uses a computer to bypass his illegible handwriting and illustrate his papers. For a science fair project, he used a digital computer camera and a series of still clips to make a motion-picture explanation of his experiment. "It visually shows what is happening and how I got my data much better than any picture could," Mason said. "If a picture can tell a thousand words, a movie can probably tell a million." Tommy, age seven, had a passion for and understood much about space and aviation, but he was unable to read at a first-grade level despite special services and much effort on his mother's part. Using text-to-speech software, he was able to circumvent his limitations. A considerable auditory memory allowed him to understand basic principles of physics and construct the mini-gliders that he was so interested in. Bob, age eleven, is dyslexic, and has difficulty decoding words and deciphering instructions. A software instructional program for computer keyboarding, designed to allow students with disabilities to acquire keyboarding skills through a visually-cued, split screen, alphabetical approach, solved the problem. Barbara, who is visually impaired, talks about her experience in a "special" class for children with disabilities (Cline and Schwartz, 1999). Because teachers were focused on helping children with far more serious disabilities, Barbara complained that she was not learning anything and was transferred to a regular classroom. She received no additional assistance until eighth grade. Barbara was able to use her considerable intelligence to figure out ways to see the blackboard, textbooks, and her own written work. In ninth grade she was at last given an optical device and magnifiers. Teachers were amazed to learn of Barbara's impairment. With the use of sophisticated optical equipment, Barbara graduated cum laude and earned a doctorate from an Ivy League university. She teaches at a major university, and contributes to her field. Barbara's story is more about persistence than technology, but without the technology, she might not have reached a challenging and fulfilling level of education.

Mason, Tommy, Bob, Barbara, and hundreds of others represent examples of how assistive technology and human resilience can alter the future for learners who are gifted and have disabilities. Imagine the frustration of a gifted student who delights in generating complex problem-solving ideas at an unbelievably fast rate, but cannot express those thoughts verbally or in writing. One of the ways to assist these students is through assistive and adaptive technology. Assistive technology (AT) is any item, piece of equipment, or system that helps people bypass, work around, or compensate for learning difficulties (Raskind, 1996). AT devices may be high technology, which usually incorporates a computer chip, or low technology, a device that one might buy at a hardware store or make on a home workbench. Examples of high-tech devices might be optical character recognition (OCR) calculators, word processors with spelling and grammar checking, word prediction, voice recognition, speech synthesizers, augmentative communication devices, alternative keyboards, or instructional software (Behrmann, 1994). Low-tech devices include note-taking cassette recorders, pencil grips, NCR paper/copy machine, simple switches, head pointers, picture boards, audiotaped instructions, or workbooks. Assistive technology devices include hardware (the actual equipment) and software (the programs that run on computers).

Assistive technologies are changing the world for Mason and others, much like fax machines changed the way we conduct business. Computers, new software, CD-ROMs, scanners, speech synthesizers, highlighters, speech-to-text printouts, and other equipment can enhance an individual's ability to communicate, work at a level of challenge, and have a fulfilling life. For example, in some school districts, the extension of infused adaptive technology (text-to-speech synthesizers, special keyboards, speech-to-text, etc.) enables students with cerebral palsy or muscular dystrophy to succeed in college preparatory tracks and in skill classes such as computer-assisted design (CAD) (The Smithsonian Institution Innovation Network, 1995). Students create sophisticated CD-ROMs, videotapes, and other types of multimedia presentations. Depending on the specific disability, a variety of high level and low level technologies can allow students to bypass their limitations. Graphic organizers; electronic mnemonic (memory enhancing) techniques; multimedia presentations; or the "integrative strategy" instruction model (Ellis, 1993) can all help "level the playing field" for these students (Howard, 1994). In fact, some researchers believe that dyslexia can be seen as an advantage in this computer-driven information age (West, 1997). Dyslexic people find it difficult to understand letters, numbers, symbols, and written words. They are visual, multidimensional thinkers, often intuitive and highly creative, and may excel at hands-on learning (Davis and Braun, 1997). Their strengths are ideally suited to graphics-based Web pages.

Identification and assessment of giftedness in students with disabilities

Gifted students with learning disabilities typically fall into one of three subgroups: (1) students recognized as gifted whose disabilities have not been noticed; (2) students recognized as having disabilities but not identified as gifted; and (3) students in the regular education classroom who are gifted, have disabilities, and, because their giftedness and disabilities mask one another, are not recognized as either gifted or disabled (Baum, 1990). The first and third groups may achieve at what seems like a normal or average rate until school becomes more rigorous and they start falling behind peers. At that point their academic difficulties may be much more obvious. If they can't keep up with work or maintain quality, frustration and self-criticism become part of their daily grind until someone intervenes. In some cases, their level of underachievement invites testing for a learning disability. However, if a learning disability has been diagnosed, that does not guarantee intervention because the discrepancy between achievement and ability, as measured by standardized tests, might be so narrow that the student would not qualify for special education services (Brody and Mills, 1997).

What does technology have to do with recognizing giftedness? The most important thing to remember about the population is that they are both gifted *and* have limitations that interfere with expressing giftedness. One role of technology is to enable students to circumvent their limitations successfully so that giftedness can be expressed. For example, if a dysgraphic student is given a word processor, the quality of handwriting becomes less of an issue. The use of text-to-speech software can promote learning for students with nonverbal learning disabilities who cannot read, have a good auditory memory, and have the ability to manipulate abstract concepts and talk about their ideas.

Despite the use of technology to enable students, giftedness may still be extremely difficult to recognize. Students who have cerebral palsy and other orthopedic or communication disabilities are likely to have limited life experiences, which artificially lowers their test scores (Beckley, 1998). The same is true of gifted students with sensory impairments, either vision or hearing. Vision impairments can limit a person's ability to generate visual images, which may be manifested as developmental delay in young students. Some with severe hearing or visual impairments are not recognized as gifted until college, simply because no one knows how to recognize their intellectual capabilities (Cline and Schwartz, 1999). The irony is that when students successfully mask a disability, standard testing accommodations might not be offered simply because no one suspects that the student might be gifted.

Speech or hearing therapists and other special education teachers may be the first to recognize giftedness because they assist many students with similar disabilities and can see the differences among those students. Students who are gifted often use their problem-solving prowess in some resourceful ways. Using extraordinary visual observation, young gifted hearing-impaired students have been known to teach themselves to lip-read. Limited vision can be augmented by a host of low-tech and high-tech devices; Braille can be transformed to print for the teacher. When provided with appropriate accommodations, gifted disabled students learn quickly—at a much faster pace than other students with identical disabilities—and often display a highly sophisticated sense of humor or other traits that are typically associated with giftedness. Gifted students with physical and sensory disabilities need environments that stimulate performance if they are to use their strengths to fulfill their potential. There are many different types and levels of interventions; there is no best solution for meeting the educational needs of gifted students with disabilities. People who assist these students must be creative in their search for solutions. They must work with two types of educators—gifted educators and special educators—finding an optimal match for each student's strengths and limitations. The goal is to provide students with the means of using their intellectual capabilities and to be alert to the possibility that a student who is gifted and disabled may demonstrate advanced intellectual capability in some unusual ways (Willard-Holt, in press; Willard-Holt, 1994).

How can technology assist gifted students with disabilities?

Adaptive technology can aid many students in communicating and learning. Adaptations can range from increasing the print size on a monitor to providing sophisticated electronic input devices. All of these devices can "level the playing field." Research studies indicate that gifted elementary students with learning disabilities have a powerful fear of failure resulting from high expectations and low achievement (Vespi and Yewchuk, 1991). The children believe in themselves, but do not see themselves as academic achievers. The type of intervention that is needed focuses on the students' strengths but schools tend to focus directly on correcting disabilities at the expense of recognizing strengths (Howard, 1994). When educators focus on developing and nurturing students' strengths while providing them with challenging learning experiences, increased self-esteem and a belief in self-efficacy are the results. Computers in particular help students compensate for limitations, are nonjudgmental, provide instant feedback, and make learning fun. Students who use desktop publishing can now develop real products for real audiences. They can use two of their greatest strengths, abstract reasoning and problem solving, without expending their energy to compensate for weaknesses.

The use of assistive technology also facilitates learning by making learning interactive instead of passive, and by providing students with a sense of responsibility and independence. They can begin to feel responsible for themselves, and less dependent on others. A federally funded project on technology, literacy, and disabilities surveyed teachers on their use of technology (The Council for Exceptional Children, 1999). Teachers found that the effects of technology were positive catalysts for student success for the following reasons (The Council for Exceptional Children, 1999):

1. Increases access to information. Students have access to information that otherwise would have been difficult to retrieve. In one sense, technology "gets rid of" the student's limitations so that the student can focus time and energy on creating or producing. Learning is enhanced.

2. Reinforces information with drill and practice. Although drill and practice should not be used with most gifted students, those with disabilities benefit because they get one-on-one assistance and immediate nonjudgmental feedback from a computer that is eminently patient. A computer is an ideal tutor, willing to repeat again and again without stating the often heard "You are so smart. Why can't you remember this one little thing?" Since gifted students are highly sensitive and vulnerable, practicing with a patient, noncritical computer can be a pleasant experience compared to other learning methods (Bennett, 1999).

3. Provides motivation and changes everyone's expectations of a child's ability and potential. Gifted students with disabilities can become very discouraged and self-critical. Some "feel" smart, and don't understand why certain tasks are so difficult. Experiencing success can provide freedom and an incentive to go on. They become active, focused learners, in charge of learning and creating. Their expectations of themselves and the expectations of others provide positive reinforcement, an "I can do it" attitude.

4. Makes learning more interesting and reduces frustration. Using technology can be a more interesting way to learn, although some students become distracted by the process and have to be reminded that technology is a tool, a means to an end, not an end in itself. Learning becomes fun, leading to more learning because of the technology. Some students tend to stay on task longer because they are no longer exhausting their energy by compensating in time-consuming ways. The intellectual excitement that all gifted students crave becomes part of

the learning process. Technology broadens the available options for the creation and presentation of student products. For example, a keyboard allows an individual with dysgraphia (the inability to write properly) to present readable information and to rewrite by cutting and pasting. Rewriting is far less arduous. Students who have difficulty with oral expression can use adaptive communication devices such as text-to-speech software. Assistive technology helps the students work around problems by focusing on their strengths rather than their limitations.

5. Offers independence. Computer technology allows the most orthopedically disabled students additional control over their lives. One gifted student with cerebral palsy uses a head switch to look through a CD-ROM encyclopedia. When fine motor control is a problem, adaptations can augment a standard keyboard. Instead of having to dictate their work to an assistant, students can use speech recognition software.

6. Allows students to work more rapidly and produce a finished or more finished product. Gifted students with disabilities never have enough time. Since technology makes certain tasks easier, a student might finish earlier and take time for in-depth learning. Enrichment becomes possible, and learning is fun.

Technology also offers gifted disabled students who are homebound or home schooled a number of options that previously did not exist. The use and sophistication of the Internet have exploded during the past few years, creating a great many distance-learning opportunities. For example, the regional talent search programs—Institute for the Academic Advancement of Youth (IAAY) at Johns Hopkins University in Baltimore, MD; the Duke University Talent Identification Program in Durham, NC; the Rocky Mountain Talent Search at the University of Denver, Colorado; and the Center for Talent Development (CTD) at Northwestern University in Evanston IL—provide distance-learning experiences during the summer as well as during the regular school semester. Other university-based gifted programs offer a variety of virtual options that might be the ideal program for gifted students with disabilities who need or want additional stimulation. The added advantage is that students tend to maintain the relationships after the program experience ends. Appendix A includes contact information for university-based programs that offer a variety of services. Most programs require SAT scores for eligibility. Students who need testing accommodations should make arrangements at the beginning of the school year. Contact information for talent search programs is available at http://ericec.org/fact/gt-asso.htm.

Technology and computers empower students to do more and be more, and to set and achieve goals in ways that did not exist a few decades ago. Technology is bursting into the classroom at every level, as a tool for teachers to develop, monitor, and provide instructions, and for students to access and engage in learning. *Assistive Technology for Children with Learning Difficulties,* a publication of the Parents Educational Resource Center (Raskind, 1996), lists eighteen different technologies categorized by (1) written language, (2) reading, (3) listening, (4) organization/memory, and (5) mathematics. Virtual schools are springing up everywhere. Not all of these schools are accredited, so consumers must take care to ask good questions and request documentation for any claims made by such schools.

The Internet and World Wide Web

In less than ten years, the Internet has developed from a communication system intended for use by the military and universities to a highly sophisticated graphics-based hyperlinked multimedia technology used by millions of "ordinary" people. The Internet has grown faster and changed teaching and learning more rapidly than almost any other tool this century. The current administration has put its weight behind Internet connections for every U.S. school and library. Funding in the form of discounts (called the E-rate) on all commercially available telecommunications services, Internet access, and internal connections is available from the U.S. Department of Education to schools and libraries that qualify (Fulton, 1999). (Information on the E-rate is available at http://www.slcfund.org.) The Assistive Technology Act of 1998, P.L. 105-394 (Tech Act), was designed to enhance the availability and quality of assistive technology devices and services to all individuals and their families throughout the United States. Regional Technology Education Consortia (http://rtec.org) provide technical assistance to school personnel. When parents or teachers do not know the type of assistive technology that will help a student, the Internet offers several federally-funded Web sites where sophisticated databases can match disabilities and software with a simple keystroke. For example, Abledata (http://www.abledata.com) provides a searchable database with access to hundreds of technologies. An online list of databases developed by Jim Lubin, a quadriplegic who works eight to ten hours a day at his computer, is also available on the World Wide Web—http://www.eskimo.com/~jlubin/disabled.html.

Gifted Disabled Students and the Web

Many gifted students with disabilities encounter isolation and loneliness. They have a difficult time finding others like themselves. The Web offers many well-established organizations that sponsor "key pals" and other ways for students to communicate with one another about weather conditions and other geographic differences. Students who are working on a unit like the one described above might communicate with children in Great Britain to discuss castles—what happened to them, how they are used now, and so forth. The Web has removed barriers to international communication and collaboration.

Hyperlinked pages are the essence of the Web. The links designate a computer that could be anywhere in the world. One of the advantages of using Web sites as resources is their thematic structure. A Web page may represent a small part of a Web site, which is a collection of pages that pertain to a similar topic or unifying theme.

Imagine for a moment that you are designing a unit on the Middle Ages for a wide range of abilities. You are looking for resources that might be incorporated in several different ways, and you find a Web site that looks promising. The first page describes the Middle Ages by providing a broad overview. There's a highlighted reference to castles. Clicking with your mouse on the word "castles" leads to a graphic illustration and description of castles during the Middle Ages. In that description, there's a reference to knights and knighthood. Clicking on it leads to a graphic illustration of a knight wearing a suit of armor with another illustration on how to make a helmet from cardboard. The knight's family tree is explained in another link. At this point you know that some of your students can learn basic skills by using their own family tree. Some of your students will want to look at armor and different types of heraldry. The students who can conceptualize abstractly can develop a multimedia presentation on the day in the life of a knight, using material from the Web site as well as classroom resources. The unit could easily incorporate all of the academic subjects—math, social studies, language arts, science, and even art and music.

Technology can address the needs of students who have a wide range of abilities and skills, including gifted students with disabilities who prefer complexity and are capable of mastering complex ideas but who are limited by a disability. Hyperlinks on the Web enable students to satisfy their thirst for knowledge and delve into a subject to learn everything possible. They get immediate feedback from the computer, which satisfies their impatience and instant need to know. Many, perhaps more than half of these students, are visual spatial learners, and will learn more from the graphics interface than they would from a teacher lecture or from a book. Gifted students, with or without disabilities, focus intensely when learning about topics of interest. This can be frustrating for a teacher who has to cover a certain portion of the curriculum, and equally frustrating for the parent who would like the entire family to eat a meal together. Because technology is close at hand—in the classroom, in the public library, or in the home—students have much greater control, which may result in greater independence and responsibility.

Teachers and the WWW

Using the World Wide Web can expand the educational options for teachers as well as students. Teachers who are working with a wide range of abilities and disabilities often need a wide range of curriculum-enhancing resources. Several Web sites focus on providing teachers with time-saving suggestions and activities to involve one's students on the Web, while demonstrating how to integrate technology so that it becomes a useful tool. The Teaching with the Internet Web site (http://www.enmu.edu/~kinleye/teach/Inetch.html) charts a variety of effective teaching strategies and delivery systems that are appropriate for students with disabilities (e.g., cooperative learning, note taking, group discussion) and links you to Web sites that support these systems. The ERIC Clearinghouse on Information and Technology has launched GEMS, a huge lesson plan database, which will eventually link directly into other sites that provide lesson plans. Additional sites are listed in the appendix to this book (see Appendix A). In the not too distant future, accessing the World Wide Web is likely to occur as part of the daily classroom routine. The ability to acquire and use Web-based information to bring meaningful learning experiences to the classroom will be part of every teacher's repertoire.

If you are designing thematic units and looking for subject-oriented content, it's best to use one of the big libraries like Berkeley, listed in Appendix A. There are sites that provide a hotlist of sites grouped thematically, like The Well-Connected Educator. Time barriers cease to exist. Virtual museums abound on the Internet, and many of the world's finest museums offer a virtual tour of artwork. By providing a wealth of resources, the WWW has solved many of the problems teachers encounter when teaching gifted students. The references at the end of this chapter include major Web sites in the academic subject areas, and Web sites of special interest to parents, children, and teachers.

Accessibility Issues

Accessibility for people who have limited vision or are blind is a critical element of designing and choosing Web sites. If you want to see if a Web site you have designed is accessible, *"Bobby"* is the most advanced tool available to the public. *Bobby* is a Web-based public service offered by the Center for Applied Special Technology (CAST) that analyzes Web pages for their accessibility to people with disabilities as well as their compatibility with various browsers. The analysis of accessibility is based on the working draft of the W3C's WAI Page Author guidelines with the Page Authoring Working Group's latest revisions. All pages on your

Web site must meet these requirements to display the *Bobby* Approved icon. *Bobby* was created at CAST. Founded in 1984, CAST is a not-for-profit organization whose mission is to expand opportunities for people with disabilities through innovative uses of computer technology. *Bobby*'s URL is http://www.cast.org/bobby/.

Finding Your Way

In an information-driven society and economy, information about information reigns supreme. Information retrieval is an essential skill in this age of gigabytes and millions of computer servers. There were approximately five million Web sites in January 1998. With so many resources available, how can a teacher use the WWW efficiently to assist gifted students with disabilities? Internet search skills may be as important as knowing how to use a dictionary. Exploring the Web without a guide can easily turn into a daylong process with nothing to show for the time spent. Therefore, one of the first things to learn is how to use search engines, indexes and directories, and electronic libraries, and to try to get accustomed to some of the language used in this new culture. Once teachers master these skills, they can teach the students. Many gifted students with disabilities have the ability to conceptualize at advanced levels, and they enjoy problem-finding and problem-solving activities. Learning and teaching Web search skills are consistent with the students' intellectual capabilities. So although this chapter is about using technology to transform the classroom for gifted students with disabilities, we'll take a short side trip for a brief explanation of search engines, directories, and libraries.

The difference between search engines and directories is that search engines, such as Infoseek, Excite, and Altavista, are based on computer programs that index all or most of the servers on the Web. Search engines are searchable by keyword and may allow for advanced (Boolean) searching using the Boolean operators, AND, OR, and NOT. Directories are collections of resources that are created by a human being rather than by a computer program. They may be general or subject specific, and may include a keyword search to their site only. Yahoo is an example of a directory. To use Yahoo, one chooses from a menu the category that seems most promising, then views either a more specialized submenu or a list of sites that Yahoo technicians thought belonged in that section. In sum, use a search engine when you have a focused topic and want to combine terms. Use a directory when you are new to the Net or not quite certain what you are searching for. Students should be taught to use directories, and several are designed for that purpose, like http://www.rcls.org/ksearch.htm.

A third type of searching resource, online libraries, are directories of directories or online databases and files. Usually, library collections are carefully chosen and evaluated by librarians who are concerned about the validity and quality of resources. The Librarians Index to the Internet (http://sunsite.berkeley.edu/InternetIndex/) is one example. Some of them, such as the Brittanica and the Argus Clearinghouse listed in Appendix A, rank sites by criteria you can find on their Web sites.

A fourth means of searching is called meta-searching because it searches the search engines and reports back on the Web sites that match the user's criteria.

Evaluating Web Sites

If the Internet is to be an effective tool for learning, students must learn how to search efficiently and think critically about evaluating the quality of the information they find. The appendix includes Web sites that teach the skills of analysis, synthesis, and evaluation. The following are six basic questions that can be used as starting points:

Authority—Who's in charge? edu? org? com?

Design/Style—Organization

Navigation—How easy it is to move around?

Content—Accurate, up-to-date, without bias?

Performance—Download quickly?

Curriculum Connections—Does the content support and enrich the curriculum? Interactive? Useful?

Filtering Software

We all know of places where we would not want our youngsters to go because they're not safe. The Internet is no exception. Parents and teachers who are concerned about their children's safety will find filtering software on the Web that can be downloaded and used without incurring a fee. By logging onto NetParents (www.netparents.org), adults can find out which Internet Software Providers offer filtering software for free or at low cost, and get tips on child safety on the information superhighway. The American Library Association launched an effort called The Librarian's Guide to Cyberspace for Parents and Kids that will help parents find positive sites for their children.

Nobody knows what sort of technological advances the future will bring. We do know that for the first time in history, gifted students with disabilities have an opportunity to work at their level of challenge. If we deny the technological advances on behalf of our students, we will deny a future for people like Stephen Hawking, the famous physicist who communicates with a computer-driven voice output device. Who knows what we will lose as a society? Appropriate technology for high-ability learners with disabilities is not really a choice. It is a necessity, for it offers these students the opportunity to pursue their interests independently, to live with the possible instead of the impossible, and to enjoy the pleasure of lifelong learning and contributing to a field of endeavor. As Yogi Berra once said, "The future isn't what it used to be."

How can parents and teachers select the appropriate software for gifted students with disabilities?

The *Parents Educational Resource Center* recommends the following steps:

- Determine a child's specific difficulty.
- Identify the child's strengths.
- Include the child in the selection process.
- Narrow down the types of technology that might be helpful, based on the child's strengths and weaknesses. Aim for as close a match as possible.
- Examine the specific settings where the technology will be used.
- Think about portability when selecting assistive technology.
- Select technologies that work together.
- Choose technologies that the child can easily learn to operate.
- Select products that offer technical support.
- Research the reliability of the product.
- Consider your personal technical support network.
- Consider the cost of the technology when compared to others that accomplish similar objectives and goals.

REFERENCES

Baum, S. 1990. *Gifted But Learning Disabled: A Puzzling Paradox.* ERIC EC Digest #E479.

Behrmann, M. M. 1994. Assistive Technology for Students with Mild Disabilities. ERIC Digest #529. http://ericec.org/digests/e529.htm.

Bennett, F. 1999. *Computers as Tutors: Solving the Crisis in Education.* ISBN 0-9669583-6-5. http://www.cris.com/~Faben1/.

Beckley, D. Spring 1998. *Gifted and Learning Disabled: Twice Exceptional Students.* Storrs, Conn.: National Research Center on Gifted and Talented.

Berger, S. 1996. *College Planning for Gifted Students,* 2nd edition. Reston, Va.: The Council for Exceptional Children.

Brody, L. E., and C. J. Mills. 1997. Gifted children with learning disabilities: A review of the issues. *Journal of Learning Disabilities* 30, 282–297.

Cline, S., and D. Schwartz. 1999. *Diverse Populations of Gifted Children. Meeting Their Needs in the Regular Classroom and Beyond.* Upper Saddle River, N.J.: Merrill.

The Council for Exceptional Children. 1999. *CEC Today* 5(5), December/January.

Davis, R. D., with E. M. Braun (contributor). 1997. *The Gift of Dyslexia: Why Some of the Smartest People Can't Read and How They Can Learn.* Perigee Books.

Educational Testing Service. 1998. *Computers and Classrooms: The Status of Technology in U.S. Schools.* http://198.138.177.34/research/pic/cc-sum.html.

Educational Testing Service. 1998. *Does it compute? The relationship between educational technology and student achievement.* http://www.ets.org/research/pic/dic/techtoc.html.

Education Week. 1998. *Technology Counts '98: Putting School Technology to the Test.* http://www.edweek.org/sreports/tc98.

Ellis, E. S. June-July 1993. Integrative strategy instruction: A potential model for teaching content area subjects to adolescents with learning disabilities. *Journal of Learning Disabilities* 26(6): 358–383, 398.

Fulton, David. 1999. *E-Rate: A Resource Guide for Educators.* ERIC Digest ED420307. Syracuse, NY: ERIC Clearinghouse on Information and Technology. http://www.ed.gov/databases/ERIC_Digests/ed420307.html.

Howard, Judith B. 1994. Addressing needs through strengths: Five instructional practices for use with gifted/learning disabled students. *Journal of Secondary Gifted Education* 5(3): 23–34.

National Center for Education Statistics. February 1999. Issue Brief. *Internet Access in Public Schools and Classrooms: 1994–98.* http://nces.ed.gov/pubs99/1999017.html.

President's Committee of Advisors on Science and Technology, Panel on Educational Technology. 1997. *Report to the President on the Use of Technology to Strengthen K–12 Education in the United States.* http://www.whitehouse.gov/WH/EOP/OSTP/NSTC/PCAST/k-12ed.html.

Quality Education Data (QED), a Scholastic Company, 1700 Lincoln St., Suite 3600, Denver, CO 80203. 800-525-5811; Fax: 303-860-0238; http://www.qeddata.com/.

Raskind, Marshall. 1996. *Assistive Technology for Children with Learning Difficulties.* Pasadena, Calif.: Frostig Center. Available from the Parents' Educational Resource Center, 1660 South Amphlett Blvd., Suite 200, San Mateo, CA 94402.

Resnick, L. B. 1987. *Education and Learning to Think.* Washington, D.C.: National Academy Press.

Southwest Educational Development Laboratory. 1998. *The Research Exchange* 3(3): 1–3. National Center for the Dissemination of Disability Research. http://www.ncddr.org/researchexchange.

The Smithsonian Institution Innovation Network. 1995. *Kern High School District & Project 2000—Technology as a Catalyst for Change.* http://innovate.si.edu/smith/1995/longsum/ea13.htm.

Tomlinson, C. A. 1995. *How to Differentiate Instruction in Mixed-Ability Classrooms.* Alexandria, Va.: Association for Supervision and Curriculum Development.

Vespi, L., and C. Yewchuk. 1991. A phenomenological study of the social/emotional characteristics of gifted learning disabled children. *Journal for the Education of the Gifted* 16, 55–72.

West, Thomas G. 1997. *In the Mind's Eye: Visual Thinkers, Gifted People with Dyslexia and Other Learning Difficulties, Computer Images and the Ironies of Creativity.* Updated edition. Available from: Prometheus Books, 59 John Glenn Drive, Amherst, NY 14228-2197; World Wide Web: http://www.prometheusbooks.com

Willard-Holt, Colleen. In press. ERIC digest. Reston, Va.: The ERIC Clearinghouse on Disabilities and Gifted Education. (*Note:* An ERIC number will be assigned and available by the time this book goes to press.)

Willard-Holt, Colleen. 1994. *Recognizing Talent: Cross-Case Study of Two High Potential Students with Cerebral Palsy.* Storrs: National Research Center on the Gifted and Talented, University of Connecticut.

The World-Wide Web Virtual Library: Evaluation of information sources URL: http:/www.vuw.ac.nz/~agsmith/evaln/evaln.ht)

RESEARCH AND THEORY: DISCOVERING POSSIBILITIES

When a school failed to identify and serve our children, we found solace among researchers and theorists who understood the nature of our children's challenges. We read books, articles, essays—anything that would help us cope with the work and create beauty and order in our lives. We started going to conferences, hoping against hope that somebody somewhere would have some kind of answers. Research provided the link between what we knew to be true in our own family constellation, and the possibility of answers to our myriad questions.

Sometimes the research readings were complex, and our family found that we had to learn a whole new jargon about what was happening for our own children. We searched the Internet, magazines, research journals, libraries, and bookstores for the latest research on our children's needs. Every book recommended became another book read, until our eyes grew red and weary. Where were the answers? What was happening? How could we help? Finding an answer, finding research that supported our family's existence, became a kind of treasure hunt. The researchers in this book are among the finest treasures of our trek.

THE TWO-EDGED SWORD OF COMPENSATION:
HOW THE GIFTED COPE WITH LEARNING DISABILITIES

by Linda Kreger Silverman
Gifted Development Center

Highly-gifted individuals appear to have significant discrepancies between their strengths and their weaknesses. This is one of the attributes of asynchrony that marks the development of the gifted throughout the life span. Asynchrony comprises several interrelated components: advanced cognitive abilities, heightened intensity and complexity, uneven development, unusual awareness, feeling out of sync with societal norms, and vulnerability. Uneven development is a universal manifestation of giftedness (Silverman, 1995). All gifted children develop at a faster rate mentally than they do physically. *Mental age* denotes the rate of cognitive development, while *chronological age* is more correlated with physical development. The intelligence quotient (IQ) originated as the ratio between mental age and chronological age. Therefore, the higher the IQ, the more asynchronous the child or adult.

Asynchrony is magnified when high levels of intelligence are combined with disabilities. However, Maddi Wallach (1995) suggested that asynchronous development in childhood causes "arrival at adulthood with extraordinary abilities and unusual deficits" (p. 36). If all highly-gifted individuals have "extraordinary abilities and unusual deficits," how does one differentiate between those with disabilities and the rest of the highly-gifted population? This is not a simple question.

What Is Compensation?

Recognition of learning disabilities among the highly gifted is made extremely difficult by virtue of their ability to compensate. Compensation is the mind's ability to solve a problem in another way than is typical. The highly gifted excel at problem solving. The more abstract reasoning capability one has, the more one can use reasoning in place of modality strength to solve problems. Let me give you an example. A highly-gifted child turned his mother's face toward him when she spoke and intently studied her face. In school, he sat in the front row and watched his teacher just as intently. He was in second grade before it was discovered that he had a 98 percent hearing loss (C. J. Maker, personal communication, July 8, 1998).

Compensation enables one part of the brain to take over a function when there is injury to another part of the brain. Both sensory equipment and the processing of sensory information can be more acute in the remaining senses when one or more of the senses are impaired. The most dramatic example is Helen Keller—blind, deaf, mute—whose sense of smell (as well as taste and touch) was so finally tuned that she could detect a storm hours before there was any visible sign.

> I notice first a throb of expectancy, a slight quiver, a concentration in my nostrils. As the storm draws near my nostrils dilate, the better to receive the flood of earth odors which seem to multiply and extend, until I feel the splash of rain against my cheek. As the tempest departs, receding farther and farther, the odors fade, become fainter and fainter, and die away beyond the bar of space (as quoted in Ackerman, 1990, p. 44).

Compensation is, indeed, one of the miracles of the mind.

But compensation is a two-edged sword. While it helps an individual to adapt, it also acts to prevent accurate diagnosis and recognition of disabilities by oneself and others. Many forms of compensation are unconscious. A child whose eyes do not team properly may see doors an inch to the right of where they really are. After bumping into several walls or doors, the mind automatically adjusts the child's perception one inch to the left to enhance the survival of the organism. Instead of allowing the recognition of the problem, so that it can be remediated through exercises or lenses, the mind adjusts the perception—at least in some situations. This process occurs with all of the senses.

Some forms of compensation are conscious. Special educators attempt to teach children to compensate for weaknesses by consciously developing their strengths. And many determined individuals teach themselves to compensate for injuries or disabilities through years of practice and exercise. One gifted woman I know with cerebral palsy had to teach herself to walk three times. Even if the process of learning how to compensate is a conscious effort, the compensation itself eventually becomes automatic or unconscious, and the individual comes to rely on that capacity to compensate in order to function in the world.

The problem is that while modality strengths can be counted on consistently, compensation tends to be unstable. Under a variety of conditions, the mind stops compensating adequately. Fatigue, illness, and stress all have an impact on compensation mechanisms. When I am tired, my eyes cross. A person who has taught herself a set of organizational routines to help her deal with being organizationally impaired may not be able to rely on those strategies if she suffers a loss of a loved one.

Compensation requires extra physical, emotional, and cognitive energy. When the body is fatigued, when it does not receive proper nutrition, when illness occurs, there is often insufficient physical energy to compensate. Likewise, when a person is emotionally wounded, there is less emotional energy. After exerting a tremendous amount of mental energy concentrating all day when concentration is difficult, an individual may feel "brain-fried"—unable to take in any more cognitive information. At all these times, disabilities may be more evident or appear more severe. Sometimes a person can have a surplus of cognitive energy, but not have enough physical energy to do anything but watch TV. One cannot borrow from one energy source to replenish another. All three sources of energy must be present for functioning to be optimal.

Age is another variable that affects compensation. A highly-gifted child may be sort of spacey in elementary school and still maintain a B+ average. However, by junior high school, when hormones kick in, and the work becomes more difficult, the student's grade point average may drop to C. The compensation strategies that the mind developed for coping in the first twelve years of life may not work as well during the preteen years. Compensation can also be situation-specific. It works in some situations and not in others. New strategies may need to be consciously developed when the automatic mechanisms no longer do the job.

Unfortunately, since compensation occurs at an unconscious level, individuals are rarely appreciative of their own heroic achievements. Instead, they berate themselves for their weaknesses or inconsistency of performance. They *expect* the compensatory mechanisms to work all the time, and they blame themselves if they don't. This undermining of self-esteem is often the by-product of the lack of understanding they received as children from the significant adults in their lives. I recently worked with a highly-gifted teen who is dyslexic. Her well-meaning teacher set standards for her based on what she demonstrated she could do on one occasion. The teacher assumed that if she failed to live up to her previous performance, she must not be trying hard enough. So she was penalized for succeeding once when she was unable to repeat the performance.

Rose, my friend with cerebral palsy, provides another poignant example. Her high intelligence has enabled her to compensate well enough to pursue graduate studies in mathematics and live independently. However, there have been many ups and downs along the way, with accompanying self-deprecation during the down times. Last week, Rose visited a center for the disabled and came to the realization that she had been denying the impact of the cerebral palsy on her life, diminishing its importance since she could "pass as normal." She also realized that in doing so she failed to give herself credit for what she had accomplished in coping with her disability. Rose had difficulty accepting herself as gifted, since she was unable to do so many things. When she finally understood how giftedness and disability interact, she was able to describe herself in her journal as gifted for the first time in her life, without putting gifted in quotation marks.

The Importance of Early Detection

It is essential to the well-being of the individual to have disabilities diagnosed as early as possible. Early diagnosis enables early intervention. Early intervention is particularly important in the case of motor delays, since the optimal time period for their correction is under the age of eight. Too many educators and pediatricians adopt a "wait and see" attitude, advising that children often "outgrow" these fine motor or gross motor problems. The window of opportunity for remediation of sensory-motor dysfunctions may be over before everyone takes the problem seriously. In my practice, I have found a startling number of highly-gifted children with sensory-motor delays. Many were the product of very long labor, emergency C-sections, a cord wrapped around part of the body, or the necessitation of oxygen at birth. A neuropsychiatrist in Denver hypothesized that in some of these cases perhaps one part of the brain is hyperoxygenated while another part has oxygen deprivation. A pediatric occupational therapist should be contacted to evaluate any signs of clumsiness, switching hands when engaging in activities, or difficulties with writing or drawing. Also, when highly-gifted children hate puzzles, that is another red flag. Although some children may exhibit these traits without having a disability, early diagnosis will enable early treatment for those children with those needs.

We have also found that chronic otitis media—more than nine ear infections in the first three years—can result in auditory processing impairment with concomitant problems in attention, listening skills, spelling, rote memorization, and handwriting. In highly-gifted children, otitis media is often difficult to detect, since the number one sign is irritability. Many highly-gifted children are just naturally irritable—with or without an ear infection! Frequent well-baby checkups are advised. Better yet, a young mother of a gifted child should have an otoscope and instruction on how to check her baby's ears daily. By the age of seven, children who have had chronic otitis media should receive a full audiological examination, including a central auditory processing battery.

Children who begin reading at two, three, four, or five years old may be bringing naturally farsighted eyes into near-point focus, leading to slight muscular imbalances. Don't hide the books and the cereal boxes. A behavioral optometrist who specializes in vision training can retrain the eyes within six months. Some highly-gifted children have tracking problems (they lose their place when they are reading) or near-far/far-near focusing problem (they find it difficult to copy for the board). Some have poor binocular fusion, depth perception, visual discrimination, visual-motor coordination, or visual perception. High verbal IQ combined with performance IQ that is fifteen or twenty points lower should signal the need for an optometric evaluation. Regular eye exams can detect these difficulties. If vision training is recommended, the exercises should be practiced for fifteen minutes a day, every day, with at least one parent, for about six months. These exercises work for adults as well as children, and should be considered in the event of closed head injuries.

In assessing highly-gifted children, whether intellectually or in terms of modality strengths (vision, audition, kinesthetic abilities), it is vital for the examiner to compare the child's strengths to his or her weaknesses, rather than to the norm for average children. Highly-gifted children often have strengths at the top of the test and weaknesses within the average range. The uninformed interpreter will not realize that those average scores are being inflated (compensated) by high intelligence and actually represent disabilities. On a Wechsler scale, for example, a discrepancy of nine points is significant (Kaufman, 1994)—even if the high score is 19 (the ceiling of the test) and the low score is 10 (exactly average). From a normative viewpoint, the scores are averaged and the child is seen as having moderate abilities with some unusual strengths. Instead, the strengths should be seen as the approximate level of the child's actual abilities, and the low scores should be interpreted as significant weaknesses, possibly improvable through therapeutic intervention.

Perils for the Highly Gifted

I know a half dozen highly-gifted women who have sustained closed head injuries or other cognitive impairments—from car accidents, falls, and Lyme's disease. All of them had cognitive assessments ordered by their insurance companies. None received insurance compensation. Why? Because their high intelligence enabled them to score within at least the average range on these assessments, especially when their strengths and weaknesses were averaged. Their previous accomplishments and expected levels of continued achievement were dismissed as "overachievement"! In the majority of cases, there were no IQ scores available prior to the insult to the nervous system, which could have served as a basis for proving to the insurance company that losses had occurred. Even in cases in which that documentation has been available, psychologists have ignored the significant losses, attributing them to "depression," etc. A person is considered "normal" (unimpaired) if he or she scores anywhere within the normal range on assessments. This normative basis of evaluation, which is prevalent in psychology, discriminates against the highly gifted. I wish this discrimination could be challenged legally.

The good news is that the mind's power to compensate really comes to the forefront when there is cognitive injury. It may take several years of exercises and practice, and some processes will never be as rapid as they once were, but in many cases it is possible to regain most of one's functioning abilities in time. Since the process is lengthy, it may be terribly discouraging, but retraining and practice eventually pay off. When brilliant violinist Nadia Solerno Sonenberg accidentally cut off one of her fingers, she was able to reteach herself to play the violin with four fingers, and eventually achieved the same level of expertise that she demonstrated before the accident. Mobilization of the will is the key to compensation.

Conclusion

It is difficult to determine whether a highly-gifted person has disabilities or just the natural asynchrony that accompanies that degree of difference from the norm. When the weaknesses pose a problem for the self or for others, it is wise to seek professional diagnosis. To be highly gifted is to be idiosyncratic. There are no two highly-gifted people who are alike. In fact, highly-gifted people differ from each other to a greater extent than other groups. Self-acceptance may be hard won, especially accepting one's weaknesses. But it is important to raise the question, "To what extent could I be more effective (or fulfill my potential) if my weaknesses were ameliorated?" Detection and amelioration of disabilities can dramatically affect the quality of one's life. They enable the appreciation of one's self and the development of conscious strategies of compensation. They shift attitudes toward oneself during periods when compensation is faulty. Highly-gifted people with disabilities are heroic. They are to be admired when their compensation attempts work and supported when the mechanisms are inconsistent. Only then will they develop the confidence to fulfill their own unique purpose in the world.

REFERENCES

Ackerman, D. 1994. *A Natural History of the Senses.* New York: Vintage Books.

Kaufman, A. S. 1994. *Intelligent Testing with the WISC-III.* New York: John Wiley.

Silverman, L. K. 1995. The universal experience of being out-of-sync. In L. K. Silverman (ed.), *Advanced Development: A Collection of Works on Giftedness in Adults.* Denver: Institute for the Study of Advanced Development.

Wallach, M. 1995. The courage to network. In L. K. Silverman (ed.), *Advanced Development: A Collection of Works on Giftedness in Adults.* Denver: Institute for the Study of Advanced Development.

VISUAL PROCESSING DEFICITS IN THE GIFTED

by Rebecca E. Hutchins

Visual processing deficits often go unidentified in gifted children. I am a behavioral or developmental optometrist and I am frequently asked to evaluate gifted children whose parents have been told by their eye care practitioners that the child has "perfect 20/20 vision," yet other professionals are recommending further visual testing. How can this occur?

As we know, a gifted individual is frequently a good reader and learner, excels at problem solving, and often has learned to compensate for any areas of weakness. Whereas in another school-aged child learning and reading problems are usually the flags that force evaluation for vision deficits, these flags often are not present in the gifted population. In this population, the most common referral criterion is a discrepancy between verbal and performance scores on the WISC-III. The child has knowledge, but lacks the visual processing, auditory, or sensory integration skills to perform at the same high level on tests which include a performance criteria.

A child or adult may have perfectly adequate hearing, be able to hear all frequencies in the normal range, yet does not respond appropriately when asked to perform with oral directions. Does this individual have a hearing problem? No. An auditory processing deficit? Yes. There is a major distinction and it is similar in the visual arena. Many individuals are screened or examined in complete, "thorough" visual evaluations and yet are told that they have no problems, "perfect vision." They may have 20/20 acuity or clarity of sight, no problems with crossed eyes, good eye health, but other aspects of the visual system were not explored. In my experience, all eye care professionals do an adequate job of examining for the presence of disease, an obvious eye turn, and the refractive status (that is, whether the person is obviously near- or farsighted).

I explain this phenomena with a computer metaphor. A computer includes hardware (the machinery) and software (the programs). A deficit in either one will cause problems. It is always important first to make sure that the hardware is working. Sometimes the problem is as simple as the fact that the computer is not plugged in. If this is true, it doesn't matter what software we try to use, nothing will run. A regular visual evaluation will examine the hardware of the visual system. What is missing is an examination of the software. That's where the developmental or behavioral optometry specialty comes in. Let's quickly enumerate the visual skills that need to be evaluated to check out visual processing. To make this easier to remember, I'll use the mnemonic of the five Fs.

The first skill is tracking, which also can be called FOLLOWING. Tracking is a common area of deficit in the gifted children who have been referred to my practice. Megan was brought to me when she was six years old. She read for me during the exam, and I was sure that her parent's report that she was reading at a fourth-grade level was accurate. However, when I evaluated her tracking, it appeared two to three years *below* what I expect in a six-year-old. She moved her head initially instead of just her eyes. When I touched the top of her head to remind her to keep it still, her eye movements were jerky in the horizontal and vertical areas. When I went into rotation, she totally lost her ability to look at the target. On questioning, I discovered that she had begun reading to herself after memorizing books read to her at about age four. In my experience, the visual system is not yet ready to perform smooth tracking at this age, and many of the early readers I see exhibit poor tracking, yet report they are good readers. How can this be? Data has shown that a child might read only 6 percent of the words and comprehend text up to the fifth-grade level to compensate. You can imagine how the reading takes off when the tracking problem is treated. This is most prevalent, as in the case of Megan, in children who began to read at age five or younger. My theory is that the ocular motor system is not yet developed enough to perform smooth tracking, and once s/he can read, never has a need to change the following mechanism unless it is isolated and identified.

The next skill is aim, or the second F, FIXATION. Eyes may have a tendency to over- or under-aim when they look at an object. This problem will make the person think that the object is a bit closer or farther away than it actually is. If this tendency is present at near, and the person aims beyond the object, it is called a convergence insufficiency, a jargon term but important for insurance companies. If the eyes aim closer, it is a convergence excess. What these terms mean in real life is that the child must work hard to get the eyes to see the object without seeing two, or, alternatively, must ignore one eye—both of which consume energy. Jonathan was an exceptionally bright fifth grader. He scored at the ceiling on most of the intelligence subtests, yet had a score in the second percentile in coding. When his fixation was evaluated, he exhibited an obvious convergence insufficiency, or a tendency for the eyes to under-aim when looking close up, as in reading and writing. It is easy to see why he would have trouble looking back and forth and copying symbols if his eyes aren't aiming together to begin with, and then are asked over and over again to re-aim back and forth along the page.

The third F stands for FUSION, or the ability to take information from each eye and fuse them together into one single image. When fusion is present, the child will easily appreciate depth and can excel at fine motor tasks. A deficit in fusion can be caused by problems in either FIXATION or FOCUS or a combination of the two. Hetty had gotten good grades before she moved to this area. Right after she entered school, she was put into special education for reading. The parents noted that she had undergone surgery for a crossed right eye at age two, but had been checked since then, and except for needing to wear glasses in the classroom, had no visual deficits. Binocular testing showed good gross depth perception, but lack of fine stereopsis. Testing in a telebinocular or stereoscope, as is used at the driver's license bureau, determined that although she could use both eyes together, she usually only used her right eye and ignored or "suppressed" the left one. She would lose fusion easily and frequently and this, coupled with her deficit in the area of following, definitely explained her reading problems.

Another skill important in schoolwork is the fourth F, or FOCUS. If the focus system is inefficient, the child will see blurry whenever looking, for instance, from distance to near. Rose enjoyed and excelled in most areas of her schoolwork, but hated to copy off the board. She frequently forgot her homework assignments, as she did not copy them down each day. Visual evaluation identified the problem: she had trouble changing focus. When she looked up at the board and then back at her desk, she'd have to wait to focus in and see clearly there, only to look back at the board again and refocus. Some children can change focus for a while, but then tire as they lack the stamina to change focus to copy a long passage off the board, or perhaps they may be able to do fine in the morning, but not by the end of the school day.

The fifth or final F in this sequence was just alluded to: FLEXIBILITY. Aim and focus must be accurate *and* flexible for an efficient visual system. We want single, clear, comfortable binocular vision at all times. This requires cooperation of eye movement, eye aim, eye focus, and all the visual software needed to run these systems. Rose obviously has a problem with flexibility.

Even if we have adequate basic skills, we may still find deficits in the perceptual skills such as form discrimination, visual spatial system, visual motor integration, visual memory, and finally, visualization. In fact, when basic skills are inadequate, I expect that perceptual skills will not be up to par, as they are built on the base of the child's visual space world.

A binocular vision evaluation with a developmental or behavioral optometrist can identify areas of visual processing deficits. They may be treated with lenses, rarely prisms, and usually, vision therapy. Vision therapy is a medical treatment plan that incorporates office and home activities designed, over time, to teach the child to organize his visual software to perform all five Fs comfortably and efficiently. Once the basic skills are present, we frequently go on to work on perceptual abilities, which contrary to popular belief, can be affected by training.

CREATIVITY AND ADD:
A BRILLIANT AND FLEXIBLE MIND

by Thom Hartmann

People with ADD are the descendants of Hunters! . . . They'd have to be constantly scanning their environment, looking for food and for threats to them; that's distractibility. They'd have to make instant decisions and act on them without a second's thought . . . which is impulsivity. And they'd have to love the high-stimulation and risk-filled environment of the hunting field. . . . ADD! It's only a flaw if you're in a society of Farmers!

Many teachers, psychiatrists, psychologists, and others who work with ADD children and adults have observed a correlation between creativity and ADD. Experts define the following personality characteristics as most necessary for creativity:

• **The willingness to engage in risk taking.** Daring to step out into unknown territory is almost by definition a creative effort. Picasso, Dali, Warhol, Salinger, Hemingway, and Poe all struck out in profoundly new and original directions—and were first criticized for their efforts. It's a risk to be original, to try something new. Yet risk taking is essential to the creative process, and is one of the classic characteristics of the Hunter.

• **Intrinsic motivation.** Creative people, while often not motivated by extrinsic factors such as a teacher's expectations or a job's demands, usually have powerful intrinsic motivation. When they're "on a job" that's important to them personally, they're tenacious and unyielding. Parents of ADD children often report the apparent incongruity between their ADD child's apparent inability to stick to his homework for more than fifteen minutes, and his ability to easily spend two hours practicing his guitar, absorbed in a novel, or rebuilding his motorcycle.

• **Independent belief in one's own goals.** Creative people, often in the face of derision and obstacles (look at Sartre or Picasso, both ridiculed for their early ideas), believe in their own ideas and abilities. When allowed to pursue those things which they find interesting (their intrinsic motivations), they can be tenacious for years at a time, often producing brilliant work.

• **Tolerance for ambiguity.** While Farmers generally prefer things to be ordered and structured, and think in a linear, step-by-step fashion, creative Hunters often have a high tolerance for ambiguity. Because their attention wanders easily, they can often see a situation from several directions, noticing facets or solutions that may not have been obvious to "normal" people. Einstein, who flunked out of school because "his attention wandered off," often pointed out that the theory of relativity didn't come to him as the result of tedious mathematical equations. Rather, the theory was a flash of insight that struck when he was considering the apparently ambiguous nature of the various natural forces. He pointed out that, "The whole of science is nothing more than a refinement of everyday thinking" (*Physics and Reality,* 1936). Similarly, Carl Jung, when talking about the ability of creative people to let their minds wander among seemingly ambiguous paths, said, "Without this playing with fantasy, no creative work has ever yet come to birth. The debt we owe to the play of imagination is incalculable" (*Psychological Types,* 1923).

• **Willingness to overcome obstacles.** Creative people are often described as those who "when given a lemon, make lemonade." Thousands of businesses and inventions originated with this ability of creative people, often after dozens of different tries. There's an old model of "horizontal" and "vertical" problem solving: When a person who's a vertical problem solver comes to a door that's stuck or locked, he will push harder and harder, banging on it, knocking on it, and, ultimately, kicking it in. Conversely, a horizontal problem solver would look for other ways to enter the house, trying windows or other doors. While this is a simplistic view of different problem-solving methods, it does demonstrate the difference between "linear" and "random" ways of viewing the world. Creative individuals more often tend to fall into the latter category. They're usually the ones who devise new ways to do old tasks or to overcome old problems.

• **Insight skills.** Creative people can make links between seemingly unrelated events in the past, to develop new solutions for current problems. This apparently relates to the ability to think in more random, rather than linear, ways—one of the cardinal characteristics of the typical ADD thought processes.

• **The ability to redefine a problem.** Rather than thinking of a problem in the same fashion, creative people often reframe it entirely. This enables them to find within the problem itself the seeds of a solution. Often, they discover that what was viewed as a problem in the past is, in fact, a solution to something else altogether. (The notion of viewing ADD as a Hunter trait might be considered an example of this "reframing" process.)

Nurturing Creativity

When you look through this list of creative characteristics, it reads almost like a recompilation of the American Psychological Association's assessment criteria for diagnosing

ADHD. And, reviewing the biographies of some of history's most creative individuals, we discover that they have much in common with ADD Hunters, and, in fact, were most likely people who were "afflicted" with ADD.

A creative Hunter adult describes the experience this way: "The Hunter trait of a constantly shifting point of view is a fabulous asset here. It's what lets you see unexpected things where others see only the obvious. It's like looking for one elusive piece of a jigsaw puzzle, picking something up, and discovering you don't have what you sought but you found something even better instead—it fits somewhere unexpected."

Unfortunately, the risk taking so necessary to creativity is often pummeled out of our children in school. Robert J. Sternberg, the author of numerous books and articles on the creative process, points out that risk taking is often discouraged, or even punished, in a school situation.

Sternberg suggests that our schools, which are largely staffed by earnest non-risk takers and Farmers, are sometimes unintentionally organized in such a fashion as to discourage both creative people and the learning of creative skills. Similarly, many jobs demand that people not innovate. There are risks in coming up with something new that may not work, so risk taking is generally frowned upon in corporate America. These anticreative models are also, probably not by coincidence, anti-ADD/anti-Hunter models.

An educational model that's more experience based will better preserve and nurture the creativity of the Hunter personality. This is not to suggest that the basics of education can or should be ignored; instead, we should consider establishing public-school classrooms and systems that encourage activities to bring out the creativity that's wired into the brains of so many Hunter children.

In the workplace, Hunters may want to consider career or position changes into areas where creativity is encouraged rather than punished. In my years as an entrepreneur in the advertising and marketing industry, I've noticed a very high percentage of Hunters who are drawn to that business.

Hewlett Packard was famous in the 1960s for its workplace model that encouraged engineers to pursue areas of independent research, following their own intrinsic motivations. In *In Search of Excellence*, Tom Peters points out that Hewlett Packard had a policy of "open lab stock," actually encouraging engineers to take things home for their own personal use and experimentation. Two of their engineers, Steve Jobs and Steven Wozniak, came up with an idea for a computer that Hewlett Packard rejected, a computer that Jobs and Wozniak then built in their garage: it was the first Apple computer. Bell Labs, too, has historically offered their engineers a similar wide latitude in pursuing creative impulses. The transistor, the integrated circuit, and superconductivity are the result, revolutionizing our world.

Hunters frequently find the abilities that come with ADD too valuable to sacrifice with medication that modifies the disabilities. Many writers, artists, and public speakers with ADD report that, while their lives become more organized and their workdays easier when taking the drugs, their creativity seems to dry up. One novelist told me that he uses Ritalin when doing the tedious work of proofreading, but drinks coffee instead when he's writing: "Coffee lends itself to flights of fancy; it seems to make me even more ADD, which allows my wandering mind to explore new ideas, to free-associate. Ritalin brings me to a single point of concentration, which is useless when I'm trying to find that random spark of inspiration about how my character is going to extricate himself from a snake pit in India, or escape a horde of Mongols."

A professional speaker told me, "I made the mistake once of taking Ritalin before giving a three-hour speech to a group of about 100 editors in Washington, D.C. Normally when speaking, I'm thinking ahead about what I'm going to say next, formulating concepts into pictures in my mind, dropping in examples before I say them, and continually scanning the audience for cues that my words are either boring or exciting them. But with the Ritalin in my bloodstream, I found myself having to refer back to my notes for that speech—something I haven't done in years. It was a painful and embarrassing experience, and convinced me that Hunters make great public speakers, whereas Farmers, while probably well-organized in their material and presentations, are often boring to an audience because they're not continually scanning their environment."

A writer in the *New York Times Magazine,* describing his diagnosis at age thirty of ADD and subsequent successes with Ritalin, also commented on how much he enjoyed those days when he didn't take his medication. He found that the Ritalin, while smoothing out his emotional swings, stabilizing his time-sense, and giving him the ability to concentrate on his work, also took away a bit of his spontaneity, humor, and sense of the absurd, which he enjoyed. Reflecting on the dozens of successful public speakers, actors, magicians, other performers, and writers I've worked with and known over the years, I'd guess that many, many of them are ADD adults.

DYSLEXIA AND THE SEEDS OF GENIUS

by Ronald D. Davis and Abigail Marshall

When one thinks of genius, the inventive minds of Einstein, Edison, or Leonardo da Vinci typically come to mind. These individuals are also reported to have experienced early learning problems that are now typically associated with dyslexia. This combination is no coincidence: the same mental thought processes that give rise to genius also are at the root of dyslexia.

Parents of highly-gifted children are often baffled when their youngsters, who show amazing mental prowess in other areas, are unable to learn the times tables or seem clueless when it comes to spelling even the simplest words. The child's giftedness often is overshadowed by their difficulties. A nine-year-old who cannot read is usually not seen as a candidate for accelerated coursework. Rather, the child may instead be labeled as "learning disabled," a term commonly associated with slow learners and, within school settings, usually addressed through placement in remedial classrooms.

The mental process that gives rise to dyslexia is a gift in the truest sense of the word, however—a natural ability, a talent. It is something special that enhances the individual.

Dyslexics don't all develop the same gifts, but they do have certain mental functions in common. Here are two basic abilities all dyslexics share:

1. They think mainly in pictures instead of words.
2. They have vivid imaginations and can experience their own thought processes as reality.

These talents, if not suppressed, invalidated, or destroyed by parents or the educational process, will result in two characteristics: higher than normal intelligence, and extraordinary creative abilities.

Picture Thinking

The primary thought process of the dyslexic is a nonverbal picture-thinking mode. Dr. Linda Kreger Silverman of the Gifted Development Center in Colorado coined the phrase "visual-spatial learner" to describe this thought mode, which her research showed to be characteristic of the most highly-gifted children she tested.

Picture thinking allows the person to think much faster than verbal thought. This can be illustrated by the old adage "A picture is worth a thousand words." A picture thinker could think a single picture of a concept that might require hundreds or thousands of words to describe. Einstein's unified field theory came to him in a daydream in which he traveled beside a beam of light. His vision lasted only seconds, yet spawned scores of textbooks that attempt to explain it. To Einstein, the concept was simple; to the average person, it is nearly incomprehensible.

A picture thinker can manifest a prodigious memory. In the classic work, *The Mind of a Mnemonist*, Russian psychiatrist A. R. Luria chronicled his decades-long study of a young man with an uncanny memory whom he called Sharashevsky. This young man could easily memorize a long series of random letters or numbers, or a passage in a language unfamiliar to him. Moreover, he could recall these memorized sequences flawlessly even after the passage of many years. His secret was simply that he converted every symbol to mental imagery, using his imagined scenes to summon up the details.

Most picture thinkers are not aware of the individual pictures as they occur. The thought process happens too fast, often on a subliminal level. For a child, this rapid shuffling of images can mean almost instantaneously "seeing" the solution to a problem or puzzle, without being able to explain why or what process of reasoning led to the result.

That is, the picture thinker's brain gets the thought, but the person isn't consciously aware of it. This commonly is understood as intuition, because picture thinking is the same as intuitive thinking. The person becomes aware of the product of the thought process as soon as it occurs, but is not aware of the process as it is happening. The person knows the answer without knowing *why* it is the answer.

One reason that picture thinkers have difficulty with developing the skills at the foundation of literacy is that they do not naturally develop an ability to think in linear and sequential fashion. Picture thinking is evolutionary in fashion: that is, new facts and knowledge may augment the picture, but the thinking process is not sequential, and does not naturally follow a series of discrete steps.

Until reaching school age, the picture-thinking child may never encounter the need to think in sequential fashion. To read, write, or spell, one must perceive letters one by one, in a set order; but to the picture thinker, the very notion of understanding ideas through linear analysis of component parts is foreign. To the child who perceives and understands the concept of a dog without a need to separately process the information of teeth, fur, floppy ears, four legs, and a tail, the concept of sequencing the letters "d" and "o" and "g" makes no sense. The steps involved in long division, for the picture thinker, may seem as nonsensical as trying to dissect a dog in order to explain it.

The school setting aggravates this condition, especially when great emphasis is placed on teaching reading through emphasis on sequential, sound-letter correspondence, and math "facts" through rote memorization of sums and timed tests. Unfortunately, in the course of their schooling, students are typically taught to invalidate this process, and instead encouraged to rely on verbal thought.

Schoolteachers typically require their pupils to write out problems and answers, showing an accepted sequence of steps to a solution. A correct answer with an unconventional explanation, or none at all, will be deemed to be wrong. Teachers also expect their students to structure their thought processes around words, insisting that they take written notes of lectures and regiment information into outline form. These processes are unnatural to the picture thinker, who is far more comfortable with mental visualization than with breaking down learning into a series of separate, sequential steps.

Thus, rather than learning to enhance a natural talent, the gifted student often is led to question his own abilities and judgment, and to slow down his mental processes in order to complete the requisite series of steps. This external invalidation not only inhibits the flowering of a natural talent; it also creates reactions of frustration and confusion that give rise to the symptoms commonly described as dyslexia.

Vivid Imaginations and Altered Perceptions

Although we are using the phrase "picture thinker" to characterize the dyslexic learner, the thought process actually involves three-dimensional imagery and utilizes all of the senses as well. It is far more than merely perceiving a series of images; rather, the mind of a dyslexic person creates a virtual reality.

This multidimensional, virtual-reality form of thought also enables the dyslexic to experience thoughts as realities. This ability can lead to extraordinary feats of mental prowess, but it can also cause confusion. The engineer Nikola Tesla complained that in childhood, he suffered from a "peculiar affliction" where imagined images accompanied by strong flashes of light impeded his sight of real objects; spoken words would sometimes evoke such powerful images that he could not distinguish between thought and reality.

As he grew older, Tesla turned his overactive imagination to his advantage. He experimented with mental exercises until, at age seventeen, "I observed to my delight that I could visualize with the greatest facility. I needed no models, drawings, or experiments. I could picture them all as real in my mind." In fact, Tesla not only constructed his inventions in his mind, he also used his brain as a testing laboratory, where he mentally operated his prototypes and observed the effects of modifications and improvements as efficiently and accurately as if his constructions had been real.

Tesla's self-reported "affliction" illustrates how a powerful imagination can lead to confusion and disorientation. The potentially dyslexic child often experiences similar effects. The child's brain no longer sees what the eyes are looking at or hears what the ears are hearing, but perceives internal thoughts as though the sights and sounds were real. This disorientation often leads the person to become engrossed in their own inner world, while others perceive that the child is inattentive or daydreaming. But it can also lead to the distorted perceptions of letters and words that typify dyslexia. For the dyslexic child lives in a three-dimensional world, where objects may commonly be rotated or observed from many perspectives. The child who looks at the letter *d* and simultaneously sees *p* and *q* and *b* is using an innate quality of his visual-spatial prowess, but he is also lost, as no sense can be made of shifting and turning letters.

Just as Tesla learned to use his overwhelming imagination to his advantage, however, the dyslexic child can learn to control the mind's mechanism that causes disorientation. Not only is the dyslexic child able to perceive thought as reality—a true asset—but the child also has the ability to control this ability to alter and create perceptions. This ability to control the disorienting power of the mind is something that must be learned. Once the child becomes adept at recognizing and controlling the states of orientation versus disorientation, the child can perceive consistently, accurately, and reliably. With that ability, the picture-thinking child is able to acquire the skills needed for survival and communication in the world of words.

The Gift of Mastery

The true gift of dyslexia is the gift of mastery.

The gift of mastery develops in many ways and in many areas. What mastery means is that the dyslexic child will be able to become proficient in many skills faster than the average person could comprehend them.

The gift of mastery is an accumulation of various characteristics of the individual's basic abilities, beginning with the characteristic of nonverbal thought. These abilities are enhanced by the qualities of high awareness of the environment, originality, intuition, insight, and intense curiosity—all natural outgrowths of reliance on mental imagery rather than words to form ideas.

If the child is encouraged to invoke and exercise the natural inclination to understand through visualization, and to apply these skills as well to the tasks that typically are resolved through verbal reasoning, the dyslexic child easily and regularly acquires a faster, more thorough understanding at each level. The knowledge acquired by incorporation into a world of creative mental imagery is not a mere recitation of words or language, but a grasping of a perceived reality that becomes an abiding part of the individual's store of knowledge.

With mastery, the dyslexic child does not merely remember an idea or concept; rather, the individual *understands* and *owns* it. What is learned is permanent, and becomes a springboard for new exploration and discoveries. There are no limits. As Albert Einstein said: "Imagination is more important than knowledge. Knowledge is limited. Imagination encircles the world."

ALBERT EINSTEIN'S BRAIN:
ATYPICAL ANATOMY AND IMPLICATIONS
FOR TWICE EXCEPTIONALITY

by Kiesa Kay

Albert Einstein imagined himself flying through space on a light beam, and the mind storm sparked by his flight of fancy became the quantum theory of light. In a single year—1905—he originated this theory—the special theory of relativity—and proof of the atom's existence. He had the ability to think in ways that bent time and space, and an inability to conform happily to a traditional classroom structure. New research into the structure of Einstein's brain reveals neurological anomalies that indicate twice exceptionality. His neurological anomalies may have contributed to his frustration with school, as well as to his brilliance. He so loathed memorization and obedience that he nearly gave up science entirely.

"One had to cram all this stuff into one's mind for the examinations, whether one liked it or not. This coercion had such a deterring effect on me that, after I had passed the final examination, I found the consideration of any scientific problems distasteful to me for an entire year," Einstein asserted (Lewis, #122).

This genius dropped out of school at age fifteen. Einstein's teacher asked him to leave school because he incited the other students to disrespect. Before he became famous for his brilliant theories, he toiled as a patent clerk.

Recent research by Sandra F. Witelson, Debra L. Kigar, and Thomas Harvey has revealed that Einstein's brain differed from the brains of others not only in form, but also in content. The size of Einstein's brain was comparable to the size of the control brains in the study, but the parietal lobes proved to be 15 percent wider than the lobes of others.

"Visualspatial cognition, mathematical thought, and imagery of movement are strongly dependent on this region," wrote Witelson, et al. "Einstein's exceptional intellect in these cognitive domains and his self-described mode of scientific thinking may be related to the atypical anatomy in his inferior parietal lobules. Increased expansion of the inferior parietal region was also noted in other physicists and mathematicians" (Witelson, *The Lancet*).

So the structure of his brain significantly affected his learning style. This advantage was offset by an unusual absence of the parietal operculum, which has been identified as important to acoustic-phonetic processing and other associative functions. Einstein was known not to have started talking until he was three years old, which worried his mother. He would sit at parties saying nothing, thinking to himself.

And what thinking it was! Einstein's brain also had axonal connectivity, an anomaly of the Sylvian fissure, and a larger expanse of a functional cortical network. The parts of his brain that think separately in most people seem to have been working together for him. His intuitive insights may have been facilitated by the interconnections in his brain.

At the same time, classroom learning often bored or annoyed him. Einstein himself perceived the restrictions of education as detrimental to the benefits of thinking alone, and most of his work in mathematics occurred far from anyone's classroom.

"It is in fact nothing short of a miracle that the modern methods of instruction have not yet entirely strangled the holy curiosity of inquiry; for what this delicate little plant needs more than anything, besides stimulation, is freedom. It is a very grave mistake to think that the enjoyment of seeing and searching can be promoted by means of coercion and a sense of duty," he stated (Lewis, #42).

He couldn't learn by rote, and ignored whatever bored him. Einstein flunked the entrance exam at Zurich Polytechnic, unable to handle French, chemistry, or biology. His mathematics and science scores were so high, though, that a professor allowed him to audit classes. Even after acceptance there, professors decried his style, and one called him "a lazy dog" (Brian, p. 18). Once he left traditional school, Einstein took pleasure again in learning, and vowed not to let his education get in the way of his intuitive leaps in physics. The unusual structures in his brain may be analogous to the differences in the brains of other twice-exceptional learners. The constantly expanding study of the science of the mind continues to shed light on how gifted, creative minds work. In combination with intellectual acuity, traits that seem like disabilities in the context of a traditional school environment could be the very traits that allow brilliant persons to achieve insights of universal significance. By learning more about how these deep thinkers think, we will learn not only how to help them, but also how to get out of their way so that they can complete their own, important work in this world and beyond it.

REFERENCES

Witelson, Sandra F., Debra L. Kigar, and Thomas Harvey. The exceptional brain of Albert Einstein. *The Lancet* 353, no. 9170, June 19, 1999. www.thelancet.com/newlancet/reg/issues/vol353no9170/body.history2149.html.

Altman, Lawrence K. So, is this why Einstein was so brilliant? *New York Times,* June 18, 1999. www.nytimes.com.

Brian, Dennis. 1996. *Einstein: A Life.* New York: John Wiley & Sons.

Caplan, D., D. Gow, and N. Makris. Analysis of lesions by MRI in stroke patients with acoustic-phonetic processing deficits. *Neurology.* February 1995. 5(2): 293–298.

Center for the History of Physics. Formative Years I. American Institute of Physics, 1996. www.aip.org./history/einstein/early1.htm.

Einstein, Albert. Why socialism? *Monthly Review,* New York, May 1949. www.geocities.com/Athens/Delphi/4360/whysoci.html.

Einstein's Quotes on Education/School. http://stripe.colorado.edu/~judy/einstein/education.html.

Levenson, Thomas. How Smart Was He? (Really Smart.) *Nova Online.* www.pbs.org/wgbh/nova/einstein/genius/index.html.

Lewis, Morgan. Eclectic Quotes from Albert Einstein. www.geocities.com/Athens/Delphi/4360/q-eins.html

MSNBC News Services. Einstein's Brain was Anatomically Distinct. June 17, 1999. www.msnbc.com/news

ASYNCHRONY AND MENTAL HEALTH SYMPTOMS:
A MODEL FOR UNDERSTANDING THE RELATIONSHIP

by Marlo Payne Rice
The Center for Education Enrichment

Children, regardless of their gifts and deficits, must balance their input of information, the level at which they are able to process that information, and the rate at which they can successfully demonstrate new learning. Furthermore, children's level of sensory integration must be consistent with their cognitive energy to appropriately stimulate their thinking processes. When these things do not balance, asynchrony in learning occurs. Many asynchronous children are labeled with attention deficit hyperactivity disorder (ADHD), anxiety disorder, or have other mental health diagnoses. In my opinion, disparities in learning are often responsible for the difficulties we see in attention and emotional functioning. Although attention disorders and emotional difficulties may exist without incongruities in learning, the high incidence of ADHD or other disorders diagnosed in the highly-gifted population may be caused by the characteristically asynchronous development in their skills.

Sensory integration is the primary building block for all learning. When a child is exposed to new information, a complex series of events must occur for that information to be processed successfully by the central nervous system. Simplified, the sensory system must take in and accurately register input. In the case of gifted children, heightened neurological response may increase the sensory input and provide them with the necessary amount of stimulation required to activate their cognitive energy. This increased sensitivity can result in equilibrium between their advanced cognitive processing abilities and their rate of sensory integration.

However, a child also must filter out nonessential information. As we block out certain input, we are better able to focus our attention on relevant information. When sensory input increases, highly-gifted children may or may not possess the ability to filter as much information as they can take in. This can result in hyperfocusing (blocking out all other input) or inattention (blocking any input).

Additionally, once the information has been successfully filtered, it is processed for transmission to the brain. In the case of academic learning, information most often passes through the eyes, the ears, and the system of touch. Therefore, relative skill deficits in listening, seeing, or kinesthetic processing will interfere with the rate of acquisition of new learning.

This interference, in turn, may lower the level of cognitive energy and decrease cognitive stimulation. The brain then seeks greater input from the sensory system, continues to have difficulty processing the information, and perpetuates the cycle until the entire system becomes overloaded and shuts down through inattention.

Cognitively, a child must not only receive a clear signal, but must accurately process the new information. Poor reception or processing often leads to a misdiagnosis of attention deficit disorder. Children with visual deficits employ visual scanning as a technique to increase input, which may appear to others as hyperactive behavior, while children with auditory deficits may appear inattentive and distracted. It is also important to understand that visual and auditory learning styles may or may not be determined by physiology. For example, auditory sequential learners can have poor hearing, and visual-spatial learners may have poor vision. This will further confuse the diagnostician.

Children must also be able to proficiently demonstrate their learning. Thus, speaking, writing, and building are necessary to complete the learning cycle. When a child is unable to express information, anxiety is often the result. When unattended, anxiety can spiral into depression. Strong motor skills, organizational skills, and the ability to speak and write frequently decrease the anxiety level of the asynchronous child.

Furthermore, the entire learning system cycles through the states of sensory processing, attention, and emotional response, creating even more complexity within the system. A simple model of these relationships is as follows:

An example of how this works is illustrated by "John," a recent client. John was referred for evaluation for reading problems by his private school. He had been diagnosed with ADHD, and his parents reported that the prescribed medication made him irritable and hyperactive. In testing, John demonstrated phenomenal strengths in abstract reasoning for both verbal and perceptual information processing. However, his visual-motor skills were in the low-average range. This was combined with poor auditory sequencing and slow visual processing speed. An interview with the parents revealed that John had always had tactile defensiveness and was clumsy in sports. Based on our test results, we referred him for a vision evaluation by a developmental optometrist, as well as screening by an occupational therapist in the areas of motor processing and sensory integration. John's visual and motor skills were weak when compared to his strengths, while his sensory system was reported to be in a state of overreaction. In John's case, his capacity for sensory input was high, while his filtering mechanisms were average. His inability to filter out sensory information created feelings of anxiety and a constant rigidity in his muscle tone. In order to compensate, John had learned to internalize his feelings and block out all input. The internalization made him appear off-task and visually inattentive. His trial on Ritalin had created increased cognitive energy and had raised his level of sensory input. Without improvement in his filtering mechanisms, this increase overloaded his system, with resulting hyperactive behavior. Several months of vision and occupational therapy helped John with his tactile defensiveness, gross- and fine-motor skills and visual processing speed. Subsequently his attention improved, he was taken off the medication, and a tutor was able to support him in the areas of sequencing and organization. John finally improved his writing and reading skills and, for the first time, reported feeling organized and focused.

Although the model explains the relationships between learning and mental health in a simplistic way, it can help parents and professionals understand the significance of these relationships. One of our primary functions as humans is to learn. When we focus on a mental-health diagnosis, we frequently fail to analyze the dynamic of learning, and may treat the symptoms, not the underlying learning problems. As a society, we often seek the simplest and fastest cure for our children's problems. We eagerly accept a diagnosis and a medication that promises to help. However, highly-gifted children don't fit the normal criteria for diagnoses. I believe that we must first assess and accommodate for asynchronous learning skills before we can successfully diagnose or treat the mental-health issues. Through collaboration of professionals in multiple disciplines, we will better assess and deal with the peaks and valleys of our highly-gifted children. Only then can we be confident that the frequent mental-health diagnoses we place on our asynchronous children are appropriate.

THE SOCIAL BRAIN

by John Ratey

Phineas Gage, a mid-nineteenth-century railroad man, survived an accident in which an iron rod was driven through his skull. Although he survived and returned to work, over time he suffered a complete personality change. From being an even-tempered, hard worker, he became an irresponsible, profane rogue who was often compared to a dumb beast with no social or moral sense.

Using computer technology to reconstruct a three-dimensional image of Gage's brain from photographs to assess probable brain damage, Hanna Damasio and Thomas Grabowski found that the regions most likely to have been affected by the penetration were the ventromedial frontal lobes, known to be crucial to decision making. This area is also the funnel through which emotional information from the limbic system enters the frontal cortex. It is here that we become aware of what we are feeling, gaining the understanding that is crucial to allowing us to feel for ourselves and empathize with others. It seems that Gage's injury ruined his ability to make choices that benefited his social survival because his center for matching emotions with reason was destroyed.

While Hanna Damasio was struggling with whether this conclusion made sense, her husband, Antonio, began to treat a patient named Elliot, a man who had at one time been a capable businessman and a good husband and father. As Antonio Damasio describes in *Descartes' Error*: *Emotion, Reason, and the Human Brain* (New York: Avon Books, 1994), Elliot had developed a meningioma—a noncancerous tumor—in the middle section of his brain, right above the nasal cavities, that compressed both frontal lobes upward from below. During the operation, some surrounding tissue from the ventromedial frontal cortex also had to be removed.

After the operation, Elliot began to recover normal functioning. He moved and spoke as before, but began to make bad personal decisions, both short and long term. He eventually lost his job because he could not manage his time or prioritize his work in any way. He would often get hooked on an insignificant detail, such as obsessing for an entire day about how to sort a stack of documents—by date, size, or name. He still had the same business skills and knowledge, but didn't seem to know when to use them, or to care whether or not he was failing.

When Elliot came to Antonio Damasio for treatment, he seemed unemotional. Lab tests showed that the damage to his brain was greater on the right side. He performed well on measures of intelligence, showing a good grasp of current events, including politics and economics. Damasio tested Elliot's perception, short-term memory, long-term memory, learning, language, and math skills. All were normal. He also did well on the Wisconsin Card Sorting Task, which measures the brain's ability to reason quickly, and on the Minnesota Multiphasic Personality Inventory, which provides a basic view of an individual's personality and general disturbances of personality. Even when he was tested on different aspects of social decision making, Elliot chose many correct options to hypothetical problems, but acknowledged that, based on his recent experiences, he was incapable of making such decisions in real life.

Damasio decided to focus on Elliot's emotions. Elliot didn't seem to show any, recounting even his own sad story in a detached way. Damasio wondered if this deficit could be affecting Elliot's decision-making ability. To test this idea, Damasio showed Elliot disturbing pictures of violent and sexual acts and played him similarly disturbing audio material, while he was hooked up to a machine that measures the skin's electrical conductance. Normal subjects who see and hear this material have very strong reactions, giving meaning to the phrase, "it made my skin crawl." Remarkably, Elliot had no response at all.

Damasio reasoned that, like Phineas Gage, Elliot had no emotional guide to direct his activities, no gut response that he was aware of to tell himself to get on with a task or drop it. He had no emotional compass to guide him. He also could not plan ahead, because he had no sense of what he wanted or of what was important. Damasio reasoned that Elliot's lack of "gut reaction" was due to brain damage, and was causing him to have poor judgment in the social realm. Being reprimanded and then fired from work, being cheated by con men, and associating with prostitutes didn't bother him, so he didn't choose to avoid these situations. Damasio became convinced that Elliot suffered from the same type of brain damage as Phineas.

The cases of Elliot and Phineas Gage indicate that lack of emotion leads to poor reasoning and ultimately to poor social judgment, even when factual intelligence is still intact. In fact, the Damasios have identified twelve other patients with similar prefrontal damage, and all have a comparable lack of emotion and a history of terrible social decision making. Most of us have some trouble knowing what we want, but these people have the problem to a much greater degree. For example, they often fall madly in love and are guided in every way by the other person; for the first time in their lives, life is worth living, and they want only to live for the other person.

The Aimless Men

People who have trouble forming social relationships and are little moved by emotions belong to a wider group I call the aimless men. They have milder cases—shadow syndromes—of what befell Elliot and Phineas Gage. I currently have a small group of patients who have similar brain complications and corresponding stories. Two of them could be called loners. They have a terrible time making decisions or plans because they are never able to determine what they actually want to do. Both are bright on factual matters, yet did poorly in school because they never knew what was important and they did not see why they should try hard to do well. If it came easily to them, so be it; if not, then they did not get upset despite the fact that their parents were very invested in them doing well.

Aimless men are not often addicted to substances; there seems to be no point to it. They sometimes respond to stimulants since they both have flagging attention systems, a result of their wavering interest and low motivation, which kept them searching for the next stimulus. These shadow Elliots cannot make decisions or plan anything for the future, because they have no intensity of feeling one way or the other. At this time, treatment for the Elliots and those with the shadow syndromes are sketchy and in their infancy. Treatment does include education on building social skills, social groups, motor coordination training like tai kwon do and tai chi, and a variety of medicines for panic, depression, and attention. The real treatment is to get the person to focus on their emotions and try to stay with them as long as possible, to get familiar with them and to make emotions their course of study.

A New View

In my years of experience seeing patients of all sorts, I've become fascinated with the role that the physical brain plays in our being social animals. The newest neurological findings even suggest that the brain itself is a social organ; in the womb, neurons in the developing brain become functional only if they connect with other neurons. If they do not connect and begin talking with one another, they die. Now we are finding that even the brain's most primitive regions—the cerebellum and amygdala—are the very ones involved in the brain's social processing. Indeed, the amygdala has neurons within it that only fire in response to other people's reactions. Furthermore, evolution shows that the brain has changed itself to survive, adapt, and improve the success of its host person in a group of people.

Nonetheless, traditional psychologists and neurologists have been slow to acknowledge that social behavior is, at least in part, a brain function, just like memory or language. The more I see the pieces put together, the more I am convinced that there is indeed a social brain. The pieces have long been identified, but science has not thought of them as constituting a holistic function. Neurologists have shown that damage to the cortex can affect one's ability to be empathetic; that problems in the cerebellum are associated with autism and its social ineptness; that deficits in the right hemisphere can make it difficult to understand life's overall picture. Together, these parts and others make up the social brain.

If we can understand how the social brain works, we can begin to find ways to treat people whose behavior crosses the limits tolerated by our social society. More important, we might find a way to give otherwise isolated and anguished people the ability to make friends, get along with coworkers, and form intimate relationships. Even though we typically think of these capacities as emotional, psychological, or moral, the existence of a social brain indicates they are also biological.

All the different parts of the brain that we've discussed are involved when we interact with other people. We need attention, perception, and memory to recognize another person and recall what we know about them and our past dealings with them. We need emotion to interpret the feelings and intentions of others. We need motor skills and language to respond in socially appropriate ways.

One of the most intriguing aspects of the social brain is that lower and higher functions are equally important to successful behavior. Kids brutally chide their clumsy peers, saying "You can't even walk and chew gum at the same time." Well, social relationships require a lot of simultaneous walking and gum chewing—that is, they require us to be able to pay attention to many stimuli and respond with many actions all at the same time. A simple conversation with one other person at the water cooler requires us to be able to maintain the right distance, a neutral posture, appropriate body language, good eye contact, and a proper balance of speaking and listening—all physical, "lower" skills that have nothing to do with intellect. The innocent child who can't walk and chew gum at the same time may indeed have difficulty handling these multiple motor demands, and so be unable to conduct himself well in social situations. I had two patients from a leading engineering school who, independently, reported that they had a terrible time when they first tried to join a pickup baseball game as children. Each one had been uncertain about everything—being in a group, taking turns at bat, hitting and fielding, and even understanding what the point of it all was. They were subsequently ostracized, and felt overwhelmed with the shame. As time went on, each of them tried new games less often.

This kind of early experience, of course, is the beginning of a slide down the slippery slope to social isolation. A child in this frame of mind may soon be mocked by other children, called names, be given grief, and be left behind. Parents and teachers may conclude that the child is alone because somehow he doesn't want to make friends. Nonsense! The unfortunate outcome, however, is that by the time the child becomes an adult, after years of insult and rejection, he may well not want social relationships, because he has been bruised so much by others along the way.

The hope is that research can find ways to improve a faulty social brain. In the last few years therapists working with autistic children have greatly expanded the use of a technique called "motoring through." A daughter grabs her mother's leg, and the mother walks the child through a situation, again and again, until the right physical schemata is imprinted on the neural firing patterns in the child's motor cortex.

Such repeated patterning strengthens neural connections in the brain by recruiting neighboring neurons to help in the task. "Motoring through" excites more pathways, which causes the mental task to be linked to the physical task. That's the great promise of understanding the social brain. If people who can't walk and chew gum at the same time, who are supposedly antisocial, who can't make friends, who can't form close relationships, who can't sustain the intimate bonds involved in being a husband or wife or father or mother, can strengthen the neural connections in the social brain, they can overcome the debilitating problems that don't seem to respond to counseling, drugs . . . or ridicule.

The beauty of training the social brain is that it can be approached from so many different angles and the more that are tried, the stronger the neural connections will become. Individuals with faulty social brains can improve their behavior by seeing something done properly, hearing it, walking through it, and acting it out in various situations. They can deconstruct the process—break it down into small parts—then practice each one and begin to put them back together again. Just as children use different approaches to learn how to add two plus two—counting on their fingers, drawing pictures, moving blocks on a desktop, and walking in pairs from the walls of a classroom into its middle—the more approaches taken to improve social skills the better.

The lesson is that practice can make perfect. Some schools are realizing this, and are beginning to put class time aside, even if it's as little as fifteen minutes a week, to help children learn how to be friends, how to recognize and talk about different feelings, how to handle anger or pain, and how to express what they like and dislike. Teachers act out situations, such as one picking on another in the playground, and ask the children how each part of the episode made them feel and how they the teachers could have acted differently. In another exercise, they ask the children to act out an incident, such as meeting a new child on the bus. By making believe that they are saying hello and trying to become friends, the children are actually practicing the techniques they will use on the real bus later in the day.

Modern society has canonized successful social relationships as the ultimate in psychological adaptation, and much of psychology and psychoanalysis is based on this premise. But there is a definite neurological component to this exalted function, and the possibility of correcting the brain's social neurology has been largely ignored.

A Combination of Different Structures

The social brain is not a single entity found in any one place. Rather, it comprises a combination of different structures and systems working together in harmony. There are critical periods of development for the social brain, too, just as there are for other brain functions.

Regions throughout the brain contribute to its social capabilities, from the "lower" areas in the lower back of the brain to the "higher" areas in the upper front of the brain. Located at the base of the brain is the cerebellum. Taking in visual, auditory, and somatosensory information, the cerebellum provides a coordinating function for body movements and possibly some mental processes, such as cognition and attention. The cerebellum also has connections to many parts of the brain involved in attention, and is intimately involved with the higher functions, setting the timing and rhythm and other aspects of language, memory, and emotion.

The cerebellum has only recently been implicated in the normal functioning of social behavior. Traditionally, this "little brain" was only recognized for its role in motor control and balance. New research has shown that the cerebellum is important as a mediator in cognition. To perceive an object or event, we must pull together the various sensory qualities and any relevant memories or thoughts in a carefully timed way. When we see an object, we determine it to be a "chair" based on its outline, colors, and position. We may also simultaneously associate it with the place that the cat seems to favor for sleeping. The cerebellum assists in delaying or accelerating these associations, and regulates attentional states.

Coordinating associations and attention is essential to entering into a relationship with another human being. Communication, conversation, and graceful social interaction all depend on being able to pay attention to another person, and one's own internal states, and to alternate easily back and forth between them. Stroke victims with cerebellum damage struggle with simple physical maneuvers, like walking up and down stairs, for the rest of their lives. Instead of being able automatically to put their feet down in the right place on the stairs, they have to consciously think about where to put their feet. But like autistic patients, they also find it harder to shift their attention quickly from one thing to another.

When it comes to social competence, this inability to shift attention can have devastating consequences. Social information, the look on a parent's face, her tone of voice, is fleeting; it happens in a moment and is gone. Indeed, the "social klutz" is just that, awkward, uncoordinated, out of step. He lacks social grace. All of it driven by an inability to properly pay attention, share attention, and coordinate the many simultaneously incoming and outgoing signals.

Frontal Lobes

As human beings have the largest and most fully developed frontal lobes of all animals, it is considered "the organ of civilization" or "the seat of abstract intelligence." The frontal lobes are also important to allow us to have insights, one of the primary capabilities that separates us from the apes. Insight is how we know that we are ourselves, and what particular abilities and weaknesses we have. Insight depends on working memory, which allows us to know what we feel and have felt and thought and done, all at once. Keeping all this in mind is also what allows us to rehearse and plan.

Patients with frontal lobe lesions typically lack knowledge about their own deficits. They are not aware of the significant loss of social graces that often accompanies this handicap, and are unaware that they are different from others in this regard. Insight helps us learn the personal responsibility that is essential for social interaction. Insight into ourselves engenders empathy for others, as we imagine what another mind may be thinking about itself and the world around it. Empathy and "sense of other" is fundamental to the humanness that makes civilization work.

Researchers also now maintain that the frontal lobes are responsible for working memory, and not having an operational working memory makes it impossible to have a meaningful conversation. People with ADHD may have a problem with this type of memory, which can result in a forced conversational style that jumps from topic to topic. The other participant in the conversation ends up feeling that she is not being listened to or paid attention to. The frontal lobe is also responsible for the temporal organization of behavior, which allows us to navigate the complex and ever-changing social world around us. Obviously, these types of communication and organization problems will interfere with social relationships.

Intact frontal lobes are also important for learning new behaviors. Patients with frontal lobe damage can use previously learned skills and carry out temporal sequences of behavior, but learning new skills and behaviors is very difficult. The exciting news is that with learning and practice through social skills training, people to whom socializing doesn't come naturally can route neuronal connections around the deficient frontal lobe area and acquire new abilities. For people who have no social skills, acquiring even one helpful script can be an "in" to a bewildering social world. A patient who can present the same cheerful smile and friendly hello for everyone, even though he doesn't have any conversational interest or skill beyond that, at least has a beginning. Other social scripts can follow.

Feelings and the frontal lobes

The ventromedial cortex is part of the system responsible for the emotion that colors our decision-making processes, especially in the personal, social realm. Contrary to the popular notion that decision making requires a "cool head," feelings point us in the right direction and help us make moral, personal, predictive, and planning decisions. Feelings are generated when the brain perceives the varying physiological states of the body. The body as represented in the brain is the basis for what we call "mind." Many decisions don't have a reasoned, rational basis, and even those that do are still largely made by what our gut has learned from experience and how it guides us.

Damage to the ventromedial frontal cortex is what caused the social problems for Phineas Gage and Elliot. Other historical cases also show the link between frontal lobe damage and loss of social skills.

The neurotransmitter serotonin may be implicated in damage to the ventromedial frontal cortex. Serotonin has been shown to inhibit aggression in primates and encourage social behavior. Monkeys with good social behavior have more serotonin receptors in the ventromedial frontal lobe than monkeys with poor social behavior. The production of serotonin is also mediated by social circumstances. Vervet monkeys, who are at the top of their social hierarchy, have been found to have more serotonin in their brains than their rank-and-file counterparts.

Antonio Damasio draws the conclusion from historical, clinical, and animal cases that damage to the ventromedial prefrontal cortex consistently results in deficits in reasoning and feeling abilities, especially in the realm of social relationships. Connecting the decision-making, emotional, and physiological monitoring processes requires comprehensive knowledge of the social system, and strategies for using that knowledge to make decisions. Further, information from different brain areas regarding everything from the social system to emotions needs to be held in "mind" for a certain amount of time in order for decisions to be made, which requires good working memory. All of these ventromedial prefrontal cortex processes are essential to survival.

The Amygdala

As we move from the lower and upper brain into the middle we find the amygdala, a central component of the limbic system—the system of emotion and motivation that enables us to participate in the social world.

The amygdala's influence on the whole brain is very large despite its very small size. It consists of about a dozen different clusters of neurons that have different functions. Each tiny nodule is connected to a broad range of brain regions, and a complex mix of neurotransmitters and hormones act upon it. The amygdala has been found to regulate autonomic, endocrine, somatosensory, and motor functions, as well as reproduction, memory, sleep, and orientation. Thus understanding its influence on emotions, particularly fear and aggression, is important for the social brain.

Among other tasks, the amygdala is the searcher of the ambiguous. If something is different or amiss, the amygdala fires to find out what has happened. It is especially attuned to social ambiguity. It responds quickly to a fearful face—even more quickly than it does to an angry face. A fearful face indicates that there is danger, but not what or where the danger is. An angry face indicates that there is danger coming directly from the person who is angry. Tests at the University of Sheffield in the U.K. show that people who have normal intelligence but amygdala damage have good recognition of basic emotions such as happiness, surprise, fear, sadness, disgust, and anger, and various facial expressions, yet cannot recognize fearful faces. Research on the connections of the amygdala shows that it quickly triggers autonomic and endocrine responses to social stimuli, from sexual advances to group cooperation. The frontal cortex, responsible for the brain's most complex processing, has the heaviest projections to the amygdala, and the two work together as part of the network that is the social brain.

Output from the amygdala has two components. The first feeds back to the sensory cortex and thalamus areas sending messages to it. The second goes to the hypothalamus, which creates the autonomic and endocrine responses. Meanwhile, the central nucleus of the amygdala sends outputs to the brain stem areas that regulate heart rate and breathing. These connections are important to social behavior because they influence the perception of another animal and modulate the body's reaction.

In much more complex but similar ways, the amygdala helps regulate our production and response to higher social stimuli. Its connection to the cingulate cortex, for example, appears to have a role in speech. Connections between the amygdala and hippocampus provide memories of previous social situations. The amygdala, temporal lobes, and posterior medial orbital cortex constitute a connected system that is important for attaching emotional significance to stimuli.

The amygdala and structures around it called the extended amygdala send information to various parts of the temporal cortex to help the neurons there remember to change, regroup, and recalibrate. It sends cholinergic neurons up to the temporal cortex, making those neurons more likely to fire and fire more easily, thus making it easier for them to encode a memory. They also lead into the cholinergic system of the reticular activating system—the arousal center. When this system gets sensory stimulation, the action of the amygdala can throw it into a fever pitch. In some people, the amygdala may be too impulsive for modern-day life. What was adaptive in the evolutionary environment—the "fight" in the fight-or-flight response—may lead to serious illnesses today, which can range from rage disorder and violent behavior to the high blood pressure developed by the classic Wall Street investor who worries intensely and unceasingly about "the market."

A lot of panic, particularly social panic, is driven by the amygdala. This may beset a person who walks into a cocktail party, feels that she doesn't know anyone and is overwhelmed by the lights, smells, and sounds that all eventually converge in the amygdala. The amygdala goes on alert, looking for danger and responds by flashing: "Threat to survival. Stop. Watch out. Be on alert. Keep wary of strangers." If a link to a memory of previous panic is formed, or the threat or discomfort is high enough, the signals turn on the nucleus basilis, which sends acetylcholine to the sensory cortex. The acetylcholine raises the potential to fire away in the sensory cortex, thus making the likelihood of encoding the events and storing memory of it much greater. This distress is fed back to the amygdala and the sensory cortex is activated further. The whole system jazzes up. There is a reverberating circuit effect, a runaway reaction. Fear begets further fear, and soon the woman runs out of the room, sweating and paranoid. This motor activity, then, helps her calm down.

Alternatively, as the woman's anxiety heightens, someone may approach her who has a friendly expression and a quieting tone of voice and give her a reassuring touch on the arm. This raises the woman's serotonin level, which dampens the alarm network, tells the cortex to shut up and the amygdala to reduce its vigilance, for there is no longer a threat.

When we see a fearful face we are instantly thrown into overdrive to search for more information. But this hyperalerting can also take place in nonthreatening circumstances: a man may get a whiff of perfume that reminds him of the sixth-grade teacher he adored, and he is energized and readied for action.

This kind of disconnect can also be seen in the hothead who loses his temper and then quickly says he is sorry when he realizes he has gone too far. Too much of his cortex is hijacked by the amygdala and thus he can't put on the cortical brakes of reason. His emotional system is activated before the facts are really in, and he reacts before the situation is clear.

If the frontal lobe can't intervene fast enough in these kinds of situations, we latch on to our emotional response and shut off any further investigation of possibilities. In this way, emotion affects social cognition; we get swept away by our feelings, which overrule our better judgment. We "go emotional" and become less cognitive, less logical, since the frontal cortex's reasoning and decision-making apparatus is overwhelmed by the emotional response.

Face recognition

The amygdala plays a crucial role in face recognition. Being able to recognize faces is an important part of the human repertoire of social behaviors. For one thing, it is essential for survival, a key to determining whether a friend or a foe is approaching. It is also essential to maintaining social relationships.

Face recognition points to the power of the amygdala and represents a culmination of its various functions. The amygdala's connections to the hippocampus and arousal systems, and its ability to tie together memory and behavioral responses, are what tell us how to respond when we see a particular face. Humans are "hard wired" to perceive and recognize other human faces. It also seems that the brain handles face imagery as special visual information, which it tends to process in the right hemisphere. When we scan a face, we make a lot of eye movements directed toward the eyes and mouth of the other person. Research shows there are more eye scans in the left visual field. This is odd, even unique to faces, because we scan most stimuli in a symmetrical way. Information from the left visual field goes to the right hemisphere, which suggests that the right hemisphere has a mechanism to recognize faces, similar to the left hemisphere's recognition of words. Tests using "chimeric figures"—faces with the left and right halves made from two different people—support this conclusion. Split-brain patients, who don't have any communication between the hemispheres, consistently identify the chimeric people as the one whose half-face is on the left.

A deficit in the ability to recognize faces is called facial agnosia or prosopagnosia, derived from the Greek words for "face" (prosopon) and "not knowing" (agnosia). Prosopagnosia seems to be a result of an impairment in the medial occipitotemporal cortex of the brain, owing to stroke or brain damage. Although bilateral damage usually causes the full-fledged syndrome, damage to the right hemisphere alone is far more debilitating than damage to the left. Prosopagnosiacs can sometimes use cues such as a mustache or birthmark to identify a face, and most can recognize expressions. It's the specific link between the face and its identity that's the problem.

The opposite of the inability to recognize faces is a disorder called Capgras syndrome, also caused by brain damage to the amygdala and other areas in the temporal lobe. In this heartbreaking malady, patients recognize the faces of family and friends, but there is no emotional input connected with the faces. These patients assume that impostors have replaced the members of their family. Although they usually have many other cognitive abilities, they can become delusional and paranoid when they try to explain what happened to their family members. Fuller understanding of the process by which we recognize both the face and identity of the people we know will increase our understanding of the social brain.

Facial expressions constitute one of the primary methods of communicating information in the social realm. As with face recognition, both the production and recognition of facial expressions are hard wired in specific areas of the brain, notably the occipitotemporal lobes and cortex, and the amygdala. And again, the right hemisphere seems to play a more important role; patients with left hemisphere lesions have difficulty recognizing certain expressions, but patients with right hemisphere lesions have an even harder time.

Creating facial expressions is an innate skill. Infants respond to certain stimuli with prewired facial expression. Unlike adults, however, who create fairly specific faces for each emotion, infants will use the same face for many different situations. As the brain stem and cortex develop, muscles and coordination strengthen, and recognition of different emotions improves, a baby's facial responses become more specialized.

Free will and the anterior cingulate cortex

Another region in the center of the brain that is critical to social function is the anterior cingulate cortex. It is part of the limbic system and it has many connections to other brain areas, and plays a role in social behavior, emotion, and motor functions. It also receives more input from the thalamus—the sensory filter—than any other cortical region.

Electrical stimulation of the cingulate cortex can cause changes in the autonomic system, including heart rate and breathing. Involuntary vocalizations, visceral symptoms such as nausea and vomiting, and automatic movements of the hands and mouth can also result. In some people, damage to or loss of this area due to stroke, tumor, or surgery can have no apparent affect on personality or behavior. In others, it decreases social awareness. Disturbances to this area, owing to lesions, epilepsy, chemical imbalance, or surgery can cause mild modifications or major upheavals in social and emotional behavior. They can range from apathy, impulsiveness, disinhibition, aggression, psychosis, sexual deviancy, obsessive-compulsive behavior, and impaired social judgment to the simple desire to change hobbies or reading habits.

The anterior cingulate cortex also seems to be involved in regulating the emotional content of physical pain in three ways: by determining the emotional meaning of the pain; by initiating a motor response to the aversive stimulus; or by learning how to predict and avoid the pain. Some people have found relief from chronic nerve pain through surgical lesion of the cingulate. They report that they still feel pain, but that they do not experience any emotional reaction, such as despair.

The Social Dance

Doing the "social dance"—physically knowing how to behave with other people—is a very important aspect of social skills. For example, as noted earlier, judging where our bodies are in space compared to those of other people so that we stand at the appropriate distance from someone while having a conversation, is a basic social skill that is not easily taught. The right hemisphere, particularly the parietal lobe, is responsible for analyzing external space and the body's position within it. It is also responsible for pulling together a complete perception of the spatial and social components of the world. Studies of lesions in the right hemisphere indicate that it is involved with attention, music, body image, body scheme, face recognition, and the physical act of dressing. The right hemisphere also plays a role in the attentional system, and in feeling and displaying emotion.

Research has shown that adults with right hemisphere lesions respond with indifference to emotionally disturbing events, and similar damage in children is associated with chronic difficulties in social relationships. Often, the nature of the problem is linked to one or more "nonverbal learning disabilities," such as social dyslexia, which causes people to mistakenly interpret or misread others. People with this difficulty can decode and recognize words easily, but have poor comprehension of what they read. It is hard for them to pick up meanings and innuendoes. One patient who told me that she had a good sense of humor began our session by telling me a joke. However, when I referred to a friend she was mad at, and jokingly said, "You might want to beat him about the head and shoulders," she immediately responded by saying that that would be an overreaction.

People with this kind of brain deficit may use words well in conversation and love to talk, yet they do not get along comfortably with others because they cannot pick up on non-verbal cues like body language, facial expressions, or tones of voice. Though they are intelligent, they can seem dense or obtuse owing to the lack of information they cannot extract from the environment around them. In short, people with nonverbal learning disability cannot put things in context or manipulate them well.

Nonverbal learning disorder, which is coming to be called "right hemisphere deficit syndrome" (RHDS), results from impairment to the right hemisphere during early development. Some 50 percent of people with RHDS have prenatal problems or problems at birth. They are often "difficult" babies—sleepy, inactive, disinterested in social interactions, yet at times over-aroused and hypersensitive. In the first six months there are problems with eye contact. At one year problems with "joint attention" become apparent, and they show a lack of understanding of facial expressions. At two years they fail to develop the "theory of mind" as other children develop. When they begin to explore their environment as toddlers, they show one of two patterns: fearlessness or timidity. The fearless toddlers don't seem to have a clear conception of their bodies in space and are thus accident prone. The timid ones prefer to label objects rather than handle them. Both of these traits, we may speculate, are due in part to a deficit in the ability of the right hemisphere to put the child in space and in the proper dimensional context.

Adults with RHDS may show a lack of awareness of other people's interest in conversational topics. They also may have a flat voice, little emotional expression, difficulty reading others' emotional signals, a limited vocabulary of emotion words, and an inappropriate sense of interpersonal space. There also seems to be a genetic predisposition for this disorder; 50 percent of patients have a family history of social problems.

The social skills problems that right hemisphere damage creates are often mistaken for the social problems of other disorders. Many people with nonverbal learning disorder have been diagnosed with ADHD. There is a difference, however, between the impulsive social behavior of ADD and the unaware social behavior of nonverbal learning disorder. Individuals with a right hemisphere deficit may also be misdiagnosed with autism, but they are more likely to have fluent spoken language, and don't exhibit the stereotypical movements that characterize autism.

One patient of mine, JC, is an extremely smart librarian. He could talk, read, and write at an early age. He was a child genius, and yet through his entire life he has had a hard time with meaning. He is interested only in the literal sense of things. I once suggested increasing the dosage of a medication he was taking, and he balked, saying that that was not indicated on the bottle. He stops all conversations short with "I got it" when he understands the literal meaning of what is being said. He wants to communicate only through words; he refuses to make eye contact. He takes no joy in human encounters. Although he is an honor graduate from one of the world's leading universities and has received many academic accolades, he has an impossible time deciding on all sorts of details for himself, and is extraordinarily dependent upon authority figures. He has an underactive right hemisphere and despite his brilliance is unable to relate to others in any intimate way.

Language

One of the right hemisphere's most critical contributions to the social brain is its role in the social aspects of language. Language, consciousness, and social behavior probably evolved concurrently, each driving and causing the other to expand. Social interactions provided the opportunities to learn new behaviors from others, increasing intelligence. Expanded social behavior patterns, in turn, created a more complex environment that had to be navigated. Language developed as one navigational tool for this journey.

Language, especially syntax, is an essential part of human intelligence and social behavior. Syntax gives us part of our ability to plan ahead. Prosody is the tone of voice in which words are spoken—the emotional content of speech—and is also important as it often provides cues as to other people's moods and intentions. It also contributes to our understanding of humor and metaphor, higher forms of social communication.

As noted earlier, although the brain's left hemisphere plays the dominant role in deciphering the content of language, the right hemisphere seems to hold the most influence over the production and comprehension of prosody. Patients with right hemisphere lesions don't understand metaphors; when people in one group were asked to choose a picture that matched the phrase "give someone a hand," they picked a picture of a platter with a hand on it. These same patients also had impairments in regard to understanding humor; when given a choice of endings to fun stories, they often chose bizarre conclusions instead of appropriate punch lines. They tended to laugh more at humor that relies on the totally bizarre and unexpected than on a subtle switch of meaning, which in fact underlies most of what we encounter as humor. They miss nuances and have a hard time understanding metaphors used in conversation; they will think that the metaphor or hyperbole is real and literal, and be surprised by it.

Language and nonverbal learning disorder point to the importance of the right hemisphere in the social brain. Simply understanding the deficits of the right hemisphere can help people who are so impaired find ways to change their social behaviors. One patient of mine who has right hemisphere problems used to get highly insulted at humor in her workplace. She took everything far too literally. Only by realizing that this was happening, and analyzing her past bouts of anger, could she begin to see her way out of getting furious in response.

When it doesn't work: Antisocial personality disorder

Being socially capable depends on smooth coordination among the different brain regions involved in various aspects of social behavior. But when one or more regions fail, handling social situations can become a nightmare. This is what happens to people with antisocial personality disorder (APD), who are branded as simply socially inept but may actually have brains that are structurally different from the norm. Some of the compromised behaviors in APD can be seen in the activities of many of us "normal" people, too.

A person with this disorder may seem to lack a conscience, or moral sense, regarding other people. Those who have milder cases may even be charming and likable, but may use these characteristics to manipulate others. They may also be impulsive, irresponsible, and sometimes violent.

Research has shown that underactive frontal lobes may be at the root of this disorder. Some studies have indicated that antisocial people are also physiologically underaroused; their heart rate, skin conductance, and EEG readings are lower than those of socially normal people. This underarousal could cause such individuals to seek inappropriate stimulation, or make it difficult for them to learn the rudiments of social behavior. They do not have access to normal emotional cues to help regulate their relationships. Further research has shown that many antisocial people may have prefrontal dysfunction, and dysfunction in the corpus callosum or the region in the left hemisphere, responsible for language.

Adriane Raine at the University of Southern California conducted a study of underarousal in 101 fifteen-year-old boys. He tested them with skin conductance, heart rate, and EEG measures and correctly predicted 75 percent of the criminal and noncriminal outcomes when the boys reached age twenty-four. Another study found abnormal EEGs in 50 percent of violent offenders. Raine explained that much of the underarousal was caused by a combination of genetic and environmental factors, including a compromised structure of the frontal lobes, a lack of neurotransmitters or neurons or both in the region, a paucity of connections to the area, and a lack of practice in using the area.

Overly aggressive people fall into the "antisocial" category of misbehavior. Raine used PET imaging to measure glucose metabolism in the prefrontal lobe of forty-one homicide defendants who were pleading not guilty by reason of insanity. The study had a control group of forty-one age- and sex-matched people. Raine found that the killers had a deficit in the frontal cortex and abnormal concentrations of norepinephrine, dopamine, and serotonin in the area, but that the effects of this could not be picked up on typical psychiatric or neurological exams. The preliminary findings provide initial indications of a network of abnormal cortical and subcortical brain processes that may set up a predisposition to violence in such individuals.

Dysfunction of the left hemisphere that results in loss of control over impulses is another possible cause of antisocial behavior. Lesion studies indicate the possibility that violence also can result from damage to the left temporal cortex, amygdala, and hippocampus.

Social success

Clearly, biochemicals in the brain influence the ability to engage in sex, love, bonding, and child rearing—all fundamental social behaviors. Anthropologists have found that romantic love is universal among all cultures, which provides strong evidence that it is biologically based. From an evolutionary perspective, feelings of attraction and love may have evolved as a way for two adults to bond, conceive, and provide the long-term care that a helpless human infant needs. In the ancestral environment, two adult humans were necessary to protect an infant from predators and provide enough food. Today, we know that two adults together provide a better and more stable learning and growing environment for the developing infant brain. Since evolution has found it most fit for humans to be in long-term relationships, the human brain needs and wants to interact with other people. It longs to fall in love and works at maintaining a primary relationship.

The clear influence of the brain over our ability to sustain love relationships is one strong indication of the power the brain has to influence our social being. The capacity to get along with another person requires a strong social brain as much as any intentional or psychological action. Constructive social behavior requires a healthy social brain—an activation of neurons every bit as intricate as the mechanisms controlling language, movement, or emotion.

For as much as individuals must be able to fight or flee, they need sociability. It is necessary for human survival. Children who are not held or given love when young may grow up disturbed, scared, or dangerous. Adults who isolate themselves from the world are more likely to die at comparatively young ages. We have a central dependence on others. We are designed for group living. If we can begin to understand how the brain affects social functioning, we will have even more success as social creatures in the future.

EXTRAORDINARY DEVIATIONS

by Howard Gardner

When one speaks of extraordinariness, there may be a tendency to focus on the high end of the bell-shaped curve: on those individuals and institutions representing the most formidable accomplishments. Our understanding is enhanced, however, when we examine individuals who stand out because of differences or deficiencies. Moreover, as the concept of fruitful asynchrony intimates, the combination of powers and deficits sometimes turns out to be productive.

Dating back to the classical figure of the archer Philoctetus, Western societies have pondered the relation between the wound and the bow. As the price of the gift of creation, it is argued, individuals must suffer from a defect, some kind of initial or acquired wound. Certainly, there is no difficulty in documenting the many artists who have physical defects (the lame Byron, the deaf Beethoven) or psychic trauma (the neglected Brontë sisters, the schizophrenic Robert Schumann). But because many creators lack such obvious defects, and because the possession of such defects does not itself assure extraordinariness, one can at most identify correlations—à la Virginia Woolf—between kinds of wounds and kinds of accomplishment.

Certain wounds recur in the lives of extraordinary individuals. Prominent is the loss, during early childhood, of one or both parents. Writer Jean-Paul Sartre once remarked that the best gift a father could give his son is to die young. Ignoring the hyperbole and the irony, it does seem that the sustaining of an early loss motivates individuals to create a world that is more perfect in their imagination; on more occasions than would have occurred by chance, such invention has culminated in a life of creativity or leadership. Should there be more than one major youthful trauma, the growing individual becomes increasingly at risk. One has the feeling that Virginia Woolf was initially wounded and eventually defeated by an accumulation of traumas. Clearly, certain traumas are sufficiently devastating that an individual's potential for accomplishment is shattered. One thinks in this context of the survivors of the Holocaust or of the Chinese Cultural Revolution, many of whom have been rendered incapable of productive work.

A neurological condition called temporal lobe epilepsy seems associated with creativity of a very different sort. A manifestation of this disorder, which entails seizures in the parts of the brain involved with language and emotion, is a tendency to write a great deal *(hypergraphia)* and to concentrate on religious themes *(hyperreligiosity)*. In most cases of the "temporal lobe epilepsy personality," the individual behaves bizarrely in interpersonal relations; his or her copious writings are suffused with dramatic spiritual themes, of interest chiefly to the individual author and to those who study this syndrome. It has been claimed, however, that occasionally artists afflicted with this syndrome, like Fyodor Dostoyevsky and Vincent van Gogh, reflect its peculiar worldview in their artistic productions. In these instances, vivid forms of perception, secondary to pathology, may help to generate artistic work of unusual power.

When planning their political or religious campaigns or creating works of science or art, extraordinary individuals can focus their attention for many hours at a time, screening out even the most dissonant of stimuli. Such attention is desirable, of course, but it may be akin to autism—a pathological condition in which attention is so focused that the individual is unable ever to engage in normal human intercourse. It is not surprising that the incidence of autism is higher in the families of individuals who perform at a high level in certain academic disciplines, like mathematics, science, and engineering.

Marked focus is often accompanied by notable energy. Many extraordinary individuals stay up for long hours, need little sleep, walk, run, or talk for much longer periods of time than do their peers—in fact, they often cannot function without outlets for the expenditure of their energy. And they often have voracious appetites—for experience, for food, for sex. We may assume that such generous allotments of energy are not simply an acquired capacity, though the potential to channel them toward one's work may be. And, like preternatural focus, they may relate, in ways yet to be discovered, to clinical conditions like hyperactivity or Tourette's syndrome.

Consider, finally, the apparent correlation between certain deficits and certain gifts. The neurologist Norman Geschwind and his close collaborator Albert Galaburda spoke of the "pathology of superiority." Specifically they proposed an intriguing syndrome featuring associations among left-hemisphere pathology in utero, linguistic problems, and a correlative flowering (more technically, hypertrophying) of spatial and artistic capacities. While their explanation of the syndrome remains controversial, Geschwind and Galaburda's general claim is consistent with our notion of fruitful asynchrony: a deficit in one cognitive or affective area may go hand in hand with the capacity to develop other kinds of strengths. Whether it be the loss of a parent, a rare neurological condition, or an unusual deployment of energy and attention, the sting of the wound can be transmuted into the string of the bow. One must *exploit* the asynchronies that have befallen one, link them to a promising issue or domain, reframe frustrations as opportunities, and, above all, persevere.

PATHOLOGIES OF SUPERIORITY

by Ellen Winner

Atypical Brain Organization

Norman Geschwind was a brilliant neurologist who noticed a strange cluster of abilities and disabilities in certain kinds of gifted individuals. Geschwind was intrigued by his observation that individuals with high right-hemisphere abilities (this would include the spatial domains of math, music, and art) tended to be non-right-handed. Geschwind rejected the notion of a dichotomy between right- and left-handers, and argued instead that handedness was a continuum. Non-right-handers are all those who are not strongly right-handed: strong left-handers, weak left-handers, and those who are ambidextrous. Geschwind noted that these individuals also had a higher-than-average frequency of linguistic deficits—dyslexia, stuttering, delayed language acquisition, even autism, which is associated with impaired language. And they had a higher-than-average frequency of immune system disorders such as asthma and allergies. Geschwind noted that these traits sometimes clustered within individuals, or, if not in individuals, in families.

Geschwind referred to these peculiar clusters of gifts and deficits as "pathologies of superiority." With his colleague Albert Galaburda, Geschwind theorized that the association between right-hemisphere (spatial) gifts, left-hemisphere (linguistic) deficits, non-right-handedness, and immune disorders was due to the effect of the hormone testosterone, which altered the organization of the developing fetal brain.

Geschwind and Galaburda noted that elevated testosterone in utero after the twentieth week of gestation inhibits growth in certain posterior areas of the left hemisphere, because the left hemisphere is slower to develop than the right and is thus more vulnerable to insult. When growth in a brain site is inhibited, there is compensatory growth in parallel areas in the other hemisphere, as well as in adjacent areas in the same hemisphere. Thus, a delay in the posterior left hemisphere (relevant for language) could lead to growth in areas nearby (related to calculation ability) and to parallel right-hemisphere areas (related to spatial and musical abilities). This phenomenon should result in gifts in right-hemisphere skills such as art, music, and math, and in calculation ability, as well as in pathologies of language such as dyslexia, delayed speech, and stuttering.

Such compensatory stimulation of the right hemisphere could also lead to an atypical brain organization called "anomalous dominance." Geschwind estimated that about 70 percent of all people have "standard dominance"—a strong left-hemisphere dominance for language and hand (yielding right-handedness), and a strong right-hemisphere dominance for other functions (for example, visual-spatial and musical processing). Anomalous dominance, defined as any pattern deviating from the standard one, is associated with more anatomically and functionally symmetrical brains, with language less lateralized to the left hemisphere, and visual-spatial functions less lateralized to the right side. In addition, about a third of those with anomalous dominance were estimated to be non-right-handed.

In addition, testosterone can interfere with the development of the thymus gland, known to play an important role in the development of the immune system. Hence, Geschwind and Galaburda argued that excess testosterone exposure leads to immune disorders such as allergies, asthma, colitis, and myasthenia gravis.

Excess testosterone exposure may occur for a variety of reasons. Male fetuses are exposed to more testosterone because they are exposed not only to testosterone provided by the mother but also to that which they themselves produce. (Fetuses of either sex with a male twin fetus are exposed to more for the same reason.) Thus, the syndrome should be more frequent in males. The sex difference favoring males in math would be consistent with Geschwind's hypothesis, as would the fact that more males than females are non-right-handed and have learning disorders. Smoking and stress in pregnancy can also increase testosterone. In addition, some fetuses have more sensitive testosterone receptors, perhaps for genetic reasons.

At its extreme, this syndrome sounds like the savant syndrome: excellence in calculation, music, or art, along with impaired linguistic skills. If the theory is correct, individuals gifted in spatial, "right-hemisphere" skills—mathematics, visual arts, and music—should show the following five tendencies, and males should show more of all of these than females:

1. Superior spatial skills (a measure of enhanced right-hemisphere development)
2. Non-right-handedness (a measure of anomalous dominance)
3. Bilateral representation of language (a measure of anomalous dominance)
4. Language-related problems
5. Immune system disorders

Some intriguing evidence, discussed in the following sections, supports each one of these predictions. Many aspects of the theory, though, are heatedly contested, and many of its specific predictions either have been refuted or have not been clearly supported. Yet some general aspects of the theory may well turn out to be correct, and if so will advance our understanding of giftedness and the brain. Brain researchers can no longer ignore associations between the seemingly unrelated phenomena that Geschwind and Galaburda attempted to explain by one unified theory. At the very least, then, the theory will have stimulated us to think about brain organization and giftedness in a new way. And so far, no new theory has been proposed that can explain these associations.

Superior Spatial Skills

We have already seen that people gifted in math, music, and art have superior visual-spatial skills. One study provides more direct evidence of enhanced right-hemisphere development. Academically gifted adolescents were asked to look at pictures of faces, a visual task known to involve the right hemisphere. The mathematically gifted subjects showed enhanced electrical brain activity in their right hemispheres, an indication that their right hemispheres were more activated during this task than were those of a control group. This is just one study, but it is consistent with the prediction that people with right-hemisphere gifts have enhanced right-hemispheric functioning during tasks known to involve the right hemisphere.

Non-Right-Handedness

Individuals gifted in math, art, and music are disproportionately non-right-handed, in comparison to the population at large.

Math

Mathematicians have a tendency to be non-right-handed, as do those who simply rate themselves as having mathematical ability. For instance, researchers in one study found that 20 percent of those who rated themselves as having special ability in math were non-right-handed, in contrast to only 10 percent of those without any self-reported math gift. And among young adolescents who score at the highest levels on either the math or verbal portions of the SAT, or both, the frequency of left-handedness was found to be more than twice that of the general population. Although these youths had family members who were left-handed (showing a genetic influence), the frequency of left-handedness was higher in the gifted youths than in their immediate relatives (consistent with the possibility that intrauterine hormones played a role). Of those who were not left-handed, many were ambidextrous or had relatives who were left-handed.

One might well expect this finding among the mathematically gifted. While doing mathematical computations and reading and writing mathematical signs are activities carried out by the left hemisphere, conceptualizing mathematical relations and concepts is a right-hemisphere ability. But why should verbal ability (a left-hemisphere function) be associated with non-right-handedness? For one thing, verbal ability was assessed by the verbal portion of the SAT, which is more a measure of verbal reasoning than a measure of pure linguistic ability, such as sensitivity to syntax. For another, perhaps the adolescents with high verbal ability also had fairly high mathematical ability. Thus, their increased incidence of non-right-handedness could have been associated with their mathematical giftedness.

Art

Artists show the same disproportionate incidence of non-right-handedness. One survey of art students found 21 percent to be left-handed (in contrast to 7 percent of other students at the same institution), and 48 percent to be non-right-handed (in contrast to 22 percent of other students). In another study, 20 percent of the children identified by their teachers as gifted in art drew with their left hands. A disproportionate number of non-right-handers also go into architecture, and a disproportionate number of male (though not female) non-right-handers go into chess.

Music

Musicians too are disproportionately non-right-handed. For instance, in one study, 11 percent of people who considered themselves musically gifted were non-right-handed, in contrast to 4 percent of those who did not feel they had musical ability. However, the evidence for a relationship between handedness and musical ability is more mixed than it is for art or math.

There is thus a fair amount of evidence for an association between non-right-handedness and giftedness in math, art, and music. However, two qualifications must be made. First, while left-handers turn up in disproportionate numbers in areas requiring right-hemisphere abilities, most people in all fields are of course right-handed. This leads one to wonder whether, among those who go into such "right-hemisphere areas," left-handers are any more gifted than right-handers. The answer is probably no. Non-right-handers in music, art, or math have not been found superior to right-handers in these fields.

The second qualification is related. When we compare non-right-handers and right-handers taken from the normal population, we do not find higher spatial abilities in the former group. Some studies show no difference, some show higher spatial abilities in non-right-handers; some show just the opposite. Such conflicting findings may arise from non-right-handers being a mixed group. Recall that only about a third of non-right-handers actually have anomalous dominance. Of this group, some may have language in both hemispheres, while others may have spatial skills in both hemispheres. To complicate matters, some right-handers from non-right-handed families also have anomalous dominance.

Those with bilateral representation of language may have poor spatial skills, due to spatial abilities being "crowded out" by language skills, and/or have heightened verbal skills, since their language is more widely represented in the brain. These would certainly not be the non-right-handers who go into art or music or math, but they might be those who go into law or other verbal areas. Those with bilateral representation of spatial ability may have poor language skills due to crowding, and perhaps also increased spatial skills, since these are more widely represented in the brain. These could be the non-right-handers who eschew verbal areas and go into the visual arts.

Bilateral Representation of Language

Since non-right-handedness identifies only about a third of those with anomalous dominance, it would be useful to have a more direct measure of dominance. And there is now some evidence that various forms of giftedness are associated with a more bilateral, symmetrical kind of brain organization, with the right hemisphere participating in tasks ordinarily reserved for the left hemisphere.

Processing words is normally a strongly left-hemisphere task. But academically gifted youth have brains less lateralized for language: they use their right hemisphere as much as their left to process words, in contrast to ordinary people who make more use of their left hemisphere in verbal processing. This can be shown by using what is called an interference task. For instance, mathematically gifted and average students were asked to tap a key as quickly as possible while reading a paragraph aloud at the same time. When one is tapping with the right hand, the left hemisphere is in control; when one is tapping with the left hand, the right hemisphere is in control. Reading a paragraph is a verbal task, and if verbal tasks are processed in the left hemisphere, this should interfere with the tapping rate in the right hand. For the average students, the verbal task slowed the tapping rate in the right hand, but not the left, showing that only their left hemisphere was involved in the verbal task. In contrast, for the mathematical subjects, the verbal task slowed down the tapping rate of both hands, showing that both hemispheres were being used to process the paragraph. Thus, mathematical giftedness was shown to be associated with decreased language lateralization.

Language-Related Problems

The hypothesis that left-hemisphere-related disorders are associated with right-hemisphere talents can be tested either by looking for heightened right-hemisphere abilities in learning-disabled children, or by looking for an elevated frequency of learning disorders in children with right-hemisphere talents. Both ways of testing the hypothesis yield a clear and consistent answer: There is indeed a relationship between visual-spatial abilities and language-related learning disorders.

To begin with, children with language-related learning disabilities display high right-hemisphere abilities. Dyslexic children do very well on tests that assess right-hemisphere spatial skills (for example, making patterns, putting together puzzles), but poorly on tests assessing left-hemisphere, sequential skills (for example, remembering a string of numbers). These findings fit with more anecdotal observations of visual-spatial talent in dyslexic individuals. They also fit with the fact that autistic individuals (who have language and communication impairments) have high visual-spatial skills.

The same association shows up when adults or children with visual-spatial talent are examined for verbal problems. Children with mechanical ability who become inventors as adults often do poorly in verbal areas in school but excel in math. Artists (but not musicians) score poorly on verbal fluency. Art students report more reading problems than do other college students and also make more spelling errors, including more of the kind associated with poor reading skills—nonphonetically-based errors that do not preserve letter-sound relationships. Dyslexic children with high spatial abilities may be just a more extreme case of those many children who are much more gifted in math than in verbal areas.

Musical giftedness may also be associated with language-related problems. In one study, 20 percent of musically gifted individuals reported a history of learning disabilities such as dyslexia, delayed speech, stuttering, math difficulties, or hyperactivity. In contrast, only 10 percent of the nonmusically gifted subjects in this study reported any of these disabilities. And those reporting a history of dyslexia were more likely to report music talent than those without a history of reading problems.

Despite the fact that high mathematical ability is sometimes associated with lower verbal ability, mathematically gifted children do not appear to have reading problems. One reason may be that math involves a strong left-hemisphere as well as right-hemisphere component, as mentioned previously.

From an evolutionary perspective, one might wonder why dyslexia has survived. But of course there would have been no survival disadvantage for dyslexia in a preliterate society. We cannot have evolved from phonologically-based written languages, since these were invented far too recently.

The tendency of artists and possibly musicians to have language problems of some sort may shed light on why children gifted in these areas do or do not go on to become artists or musicians. Reading problems may lead these children to avoid fields that require extensive reading. By default, then, they may drift into music or art. Given that modern cultures place a higher value on language than on art or music, it would not be surprising to find individuals who possess verbal as well as visual or musical gifts being drawn to verbal fields rather than to art or music.

Immune System Disorders

High-IQ individuals have a higher than average frequency of immune disorders of childhood onset, as do non-right-handers. About 60 percent of Camilla Benbow's academically gifted adolescents had allergies, a rate over twice that in the population at large. This effect may have been a function of the high mathematical—rather than verbal—ability of these adolescents, as would be predicted by the theory (Benbow, "Physiological correlates of extreme intellectual precocity," *Neuropsychologia* 24, 719–725). In the 1960s, it was noted that high-IQ children attending a school for the gifted run by Teachers College in New York City had more allergies and asthma than normal. However, because there was no biological theory by which to explain this, the high rate of immune problems was attributed to the strains of urban living. There has been far less research investigating a potential link between immune disorders and either artistic or musical giftedness, and so far only a glimmering of evidence that such a link exists.

In Summary

Although the research picture is mixed, and results of studies are inconsistent, the overall findings can still be summarized. Giftedness in abilities subserved by the right hemisphere is associated with enhanced right-hemisphere development. Consequently, individuals with such gifts are likely to have anomalous brain dominance. They are more likely to be non-right-handed, and possibly also to have language bilaterally represented in the brain, than are individuals in the population at large.

Individuals with such brains are likely to have not only gifts but also disorders of two general kinds: first, language-related learning disorders such as dyslexia and, second, at least among the math gifted, immune system disorders of childhood onset such as asthma and allergies. All of these findings are consistent with the Geschwind-Galaburda theory that testosterone inhibits some areas of the brain while simultaneously enhancing others.

The model may well end up modified and even rejected as we learn more about the brain, especially from brain-imaging studies of high-ability people at work. But no future theory will replace the Geschwind-Galaburda theory unless it can either account for the clustering of gifts in math, art, and music with non-right-handedness, immune problems, and language-related learning deficits, or show that these traits do not in fact cluster.

REFERENCES

Colangelo, N., S. Assouline, B. Kerr, R. Huesman, and D. Johnson. 1993. Mechanical inventiveness: A three phase study. In G. R. Bock and K. Ackrill (eds.), *The Origins and Development of High Ability.* New York: Wiley.

Gardner, H. 1975. *The Shattered Mind: The Person After Brain Damage.* New York: Knopf.

Gardner, H. 1983. *Frames of Mind: The Theory of Multiple Intelligences.* New York: Basic-Books.

Geschwind, N. 1984. The biology of cerebral dominance: Implications for cognition. *Cognition* 17, 193–208.

Geschwind, N., and A. M. Galaburda. 1987. *Cerebral Lateralization.* Cambridge, Mass.: MIT Press.

McNamara, P., K. A. Flannery, L. K. Obler, and S. Schachter. 1994. Special talents in Geschwind's and Galaburda's theory of cerebral lateralization: An examination in a female population. *International Journal of Neuroscience* 78, 167–176.

Mebert, C. J., and G. F. Michel. 1980. Handedness in artists. In J. Herron (ed.) *Neuropsychology of Left-Handedness.* New York: Academic Press.

O'Boyle, M. W., and C. P. Benbow. 1990. Enhanced right hemisphere involvement during cognitive processing may relate to intellectual precocity. *Neuropsychologia* 28, 211–216.

Rosenblatt, E., and E. Winner. 1988. Is superior visual memory a component of superior drawing ability? In L. K. Obler and D. Fein (eds.), *The Exceptional Brain: Neuropsychology of Talent and Special Abilities.* New York: Guilford Press.

Winner, E., M. B. Casey, D. Da Silva, and R. Hayes. 1991. Spatial abilities and reading deficits in visual art students. *Empirical Studies of the Arts* 1, 51–63.

Winner E., and M. B. Casey. 1993. Cognitive profiles of artists. In G. Cupchit and J. Laszlo (eds.) *Emerging Visions: Contemporary Approaches to the Aesthetic Process.* New York: Cambridge University Press.

Zatorre, R. J., A. C. Evans, E. Meyer, and A. Gjedde. 1992. Lateralization of phonetic and pitch discrimination in speech processing. *Science* 256, 846–849.

READING AND WRITING PROBLEMS
OF HIGH SCHOOL GIFTED STUDENTS WITH LEARNING DISABILITIES

by Sally M. Reis

Joe is a tall, heavyset, intense-looking young man with dark curly hair, a beard, and glasses. A college junior, who was a physics major when this study was conducted, Joe had many problems in school because of his learning disability. His father is an attorney and his mother, who has a bachelor's degree in English, conducts title searches for a law firm. She stayed home when Joe was in school. Joe has one older brother who is pursuing a doctorate.

Joe never really had to work in school because he learned quickly. His verbal IQ is over 140 and yet his problems in school began at a very early age. In fact, he had so many learning problems in the primary grades that he was placed in a self-contained, special education classroom for students in grades two through six. During his time in this self-contained classroom, Joe was instructed along with students with mental retardation, emotional or behavioral disorders, or who had specific learning disabilities. He became severely depressed. About this time in his education, he recalled: "It was degrading. I was very resentful of it. I don't really remember that part of my life that well. I've blocked it out. I knew I was different than the other kids." Joe was retained in fifth grade while in the self-contained special education class. He described this by saying that he had become a disciplinary problem while he was in the classroom. Joe's memories of the class were very negative: "They used to send us out to recess with the mainstream kids. I remember being sort of alone and being made fun of. They called me retarded."

Joe recalled that school personnel released him from the special education class in sixth grade because they considered him "cured." "I was the first student to be completely mainstreamed out of the program in its history. The principal used to come down and observe me and they would bring visitors from here or there to talk to me."

These experiences were not the only negative ones that occurred in Joe's education. On a questionnaire for our study, when asked if he was ever identified as gifted, Joe wrote: "I was told that I should have been placed in a talented and gifted class in sixth grade. After taking the entrance exam I was told that I only failed by a few points." Although very involved in a university learning disabilities program, Joe was on academic probation due to required liberal arts courses he had to take outside of his major area. At the current time Joe has dropped out of his university program.

This chapter describes a study that investigated factors that enable some high-ability students with learning disabilities, like Joe, who had consistent problems with reading and writing, to succeed for a period of time in an academic setting. Educational research has expanded in recent years with the study of various special populations, and new theories of intelligence (Gardner, 1983; Sternberg, 1981) have revealed that the potential of some students may not be measured accurately by current measurement instruments. High-ability students with learning difficulties have been studied for many years. In 1937, Samuel Orton found wide ranges of intelligence among nonreaders. His extensive work with a specific reading and writing disability known as dyslexia indicated many high-ability students had learning problems. Some of the nonachieving high IQ students in Terman and Oden's (1947) study exhibited feelings of inferiority, an inability to persevere in the accomplishment of goals, and a general lack of self-confidence. According to current theorists and researchers, these characteristics are common among high ability students with learning disabilities (Baum, Owen, and Dixon, 1991; Daniels, 1983; Whitmore and Maker, 1985).

The examination of the lives of highly accomplished individuals who lived in the past is often used as a rationale for various educational interventions or practices. Eminent individuals, in particular, often experienced difficulty with the educational system. Goertzel and Goertzel (1962), in studying the lives of prominent individuals, found that many avoided school, had different learning styles from those used for instruction, and utilized unique compensation styles to overcome learning problems. More recently, West (1991, 1992) discussed the phenomenon of individuals such as Albert Einstein, Michael Faraday, and James Maxwell who exhibited superior talents in visualization, yet who were, by recent standards, also dyslexic.

The specific research concerning high-ability students with learning disabilities began following the passage of PL 94-142, when the expanded emphasis on the education of students with disabilities created an interest in students who were both gifted and demonstrated learning disabilities. Hokanson and Jospe (1976) found that, among all disabilities, the largest populations of high-ability students were identified as having learning disabilities. Project SEARCH (Hokanson and Jospe, 1976) focused on the identification of high cognitive ability in students with disabilities. In this study, Hokanson and Jospe learned that high-ability students with learning disabilities demonstrated creative ability but were considered only for educational services to remediate their disabilities.

Sporadic case studies also have indicated the presence of artistic talent among students with learning disabilities. For example, Vantour (1976) described gifted students with learning disabilities in the classroom and placed the instructional emphasis on students' artistic abilities rather than their scholastic disabilities. Two years after the passage of PL 94-142, Maker (1977) examined the strengths and weaknesses of gifted students with handicapping conditions, and provided initial suggestions for programs and services for those students. A major concern expressed by Maker was the difficulty of identifying this population, specifically the inflexibility of reliance on IQ score cutoffs. The existence of this population was further supported when Educational Resources Information Center (ERIC) listed the heading "gifted handicapped" in their national retrieval system and when The Council for Exceptional Children (CEC) held two major conferences on this special population.

Research on high-ability students with learning disabilities continues to be difficult because of problems in defining each population. The fields of gifted education and education of students with learning disabilities have long been separated by their own definitions for the population to be served, as well as by their separate professional organizations, journals, and recommended educational practices. Practitioners in both fields have indicated that their respective federal definitions are inadequate (Boodoo et al., 1989; 1989; Renzulli, 1978; Taylor, 1989; Vaughn, 1989; Ysseldyke and Algozzine, 1983).

Students who exhibit characteristics of both the gifted and learning disabled populations pose quandaries for educators. The misconceptions, definitions, and expected outcomes for these types of students further complicate the issues facing appropriate programming for this population (Baum et al., 1991; Olenchak, 1995; Whitmore, 1986). Awareness of these students' needs is becoming more common with both the teachers of the gifted and the teachers of students with learning disabilities, yet most school districts have no provision for intervention programs for this group (Boodoo et al., 1989). And, according to statistics gathered in 1991, only 2.2% of all college students entering institutions across the country had learning disabilities (Henderson, 1992).

Study Design

Qualitative case study methodology was used in this study to investigate the subject's perceptions and experiences which are in turn related to the individual's external behavior—in this instance, overcoming the obstacle of the learning disability. Accordingly, the individual's perceptions are of primary importance in a study of this nature. In order to obtain the most accurate image of the subject's experiences and perceptions, open-ended questionnaires and in-depth interviews were used with both participants in this study and their parents. Miles and Huberman (1984) and Yin (1989) have suggested the case study approach as appropriate methodology for in-depth study of a small number of cases in order to make analytical generalizations.

Twelve currently enrolled college or university students or recent graduates who were identified as having a learning disability comprised the sample for this research (see Table 1). These individuals either were identified as having a high IQ or high ability in elementary or secondary school, but were not identified as gifted and included in the district gifted program. Information such as IQ and/or achievement tests, outstanding performance in one or more academic areas, teacher nomination, and product information from an academic portfolio was used to document the label of giftedness.

Data Collection

Researchers used three methods of data collection in this study: records and testing information, written responses to an open ended questionnaire, and in-depth interviews with each subject and with one of their parents. Researchers determined the number of interviews conducted when data saturation was reached. Data saturation occurs when the subject can only provide information which has become redundant and does not offer useful reinforcement of information previously collected (Spradley, 1979). The open-ended questionnaire served as a preliminary source of issues to be investigated further during the interviews as well as an additional source of information.

Prior to the initial interview, each subject received a biographical questionnaire and written information about the study and his or her anticipated role in it. Parents and/or teachers consented to complete brief written summaries of their perceptions of each subject's academic history and the effects of their learning disability and label of giftedness. Each interview session was used to clarify, verify, and expand upon the subject's responses. The researcher tape-recorded and transcribed interviews, adding the field notes and observations at the time of the interviews. Interviews and other data collection procedures followed guidelines suggested by Spradley (1979), Strauss (1987), and Strauss and Corbin (1990).

Table 1
Summary of Self-Report Questionnaire Data

Participant	Strength area	Nature of the LD	Time period when identified LD	Time period when identified gifted
Arthur	Generally a "B" student	Slow processing of information	4th semester of college	No
Colin	Computer, math, science	Spelling, handwriting, poor short-term memory, reading, decoding	7th grade	Yes, 7th grade
Diane	Sports	Dyslexia, language	college	No
Evan	[None reported]	Spelling, abstract math problems	11th grade	No
Forrest	Not great, but does well in many areas	Dyslexia, concentrating	7th grade	No
Fred	Considered bright; astronomy	Math, spelling, social problems	8th grade	No
Jake	Considered self average	Dyslexia, motor skills	6th grade	No
Joe	[None reported]	Verbal and written expression, auditory	3rd grade	Recommended in 6th grade—not identified
Kate	Not really	Language, spelling, reading	2nd grade	No
Mike	[None reported]	Language, spelling	10th grade	No
Martin	Deeper insights to life	Attention deficit disorder, dyslexia	1st grade	No
Peggy	Standardized tests, yet "stupid" on homework	Slow thought processes, spelling, penmanship, reading comprehension	5th grade	No

Data Analysis

Data analysis was conducted using techniques designed by Strauss (1987) and Strauss and Corbin (1990). As suggested by these researchers, data analysis coincided with data collection and affected the collection of additional data. Data analysis techniques included the use of a coding paradigm described by Strauss (1987) and Strauss and Corbin (1990) as well as coding suggested by the same researchers including three levels: open coding, axial coding, and selective coding. This coding paradigm results in the formulation of a core category or categories of results.

Results

The findings in this study revolve around the core categories for both participants and parents. The major core category found for participants was their negative experiences in school, with a particular focus on reading and writing problems. All of the participants recalled negative, even painful, memories of situations that had occurred during their elementary and secondary school years. It is important to note that these negative school experiences occurred within the context of many positive outside-of-school experiences that provided participants of this study with an opportunity to distinguish between positive life experiences and negative school experiences. *All* of the participants in this study had positive out-of-school experiences, which may have enabled them to survive and even constructively adapt their negative school experiences, resulting in positive personal attitudes that may have enabled them to succeed later. Many of these students excelled in athletics or sports; many had hobbies or passionate interests outside of school; many had spatial strengths that were not recognized, rewarded, or nurtured in the schools they attended that emphasized reading, writing, and verbal skills. For many of these students, the discussion of these school memories was troubling and several indicated that they tried never "to think about what happened to them in school." In some cases, they admitted to "blocking out" memories of painful events that they would rather forget, but each was able to "dredge up" these incidents during the course of the interviews. As Joe eloquently summarized:

> I still have a lot of emotion about it. I had a lot of mistreatment. It [this interview] conjures up memories of things that I don't like to meet.

The negative school experiences that these students encountered included: repeated punishment for not completing work on time; retention (repetition) of a grade, which was attributed to the participants' learning disability; placement in a self-contained special education class in which the majority of students were developmentally delayed or had been identified as mentally retarded; and cruel treatment by peers and teachers. In fact, if these and other school experiences were not related over and over by many respondents, one might consider them to be rare, almost accidental happenings. But they were not rare, and indeed, similar experiences were remembered by all of the students in this study, and in almost half the cases painful memories still remain.

Late Identification of a Learning Disability

The majority of the participants were not identified as having a learning disability until middle school or high school, even though most were referred by teachers or parents for testing or various types of assistance because of difficulties encountered in reading or writing in primary or elementary school. Learning problems were evident in these early grades, although most students who were referred were not identified as having a learning disability until later in school.

The late identification was problematic for the participants in this study in many ways. First, although they were not identified until their later years in school, their academic difficulties began much earlier. Accordingly, because they had difficulty reading, writing, spelling, or with handwriting, they were often criticized, punished, or told to work harder. Most of their teachers realized they were bright and many of the participants had superior oral skills that were not matched by their written or reading skills. This resulted in several teachers urging these students to "shape up" and "work harder." Because of this pressure, some learned to work hard. For example, Arthur described himself as a student in this way:

> Diligent, I cared about my grades. I have always been very persistent. I work slow. It's a good thing with me, working slow. Through high school before I knew anything was wrong, I thought I just wasn't working hard enough and I could get the As, if I really just put my time in it.

Unfortunately, others were quite adversely affected by the criticism and the constant urging to work harder. Diane always believed her learning problems were her fault.

> Diane: I never talked about my work to anybody because I knew it was my fault that I couldn't learn. I just had to work harder. Even my father, when he saw my IQ score said, "You need to try harder."

Researcher: You never thought that you had a problem?

Diane: No! It was always me. I didn't get it or I didn't work hard enough or I didn't try hard enough. I still think that sometimes. . . .

Arthur's mother had suspected for years that he had a learning disability, but he was not formally identified until he was a teenager:

> My mother was very disappointed; she also felt guilty. Because I had been evaluated in seventh grade because of my seeming intelligence and problems in school. I scored super high on the cognitive and the logic. My mother had me taken to a psychologist for that and then she met with the people in the school and they said they couldn't put me in the learning disability program because I was too smart. They had nothing for me.

Arthur was denied access to the learning disability program in his school because he was "too smart," and despite frequent referral because of his reading and writing problems by his teachers, he was never identified as having a learning disability by any of the school psychologists who tested him. Similar problems existed for other participants as well. The duality of being talented often allowed the student to do well on the standardized IQ assessments, which often masked the learning disability and produced confusing and intensely difficult times for the persons in this study. Peggy explained:

> The school psychologist said it was obvious that I was not *truly* learning disabled because I tested so well on the standardized achievement tests. He went on to tell me that I had an "anxiety-induced learning problem" and I would grow out of it.

In the assessment process, several students were told that they had scored very high on IQ tests and two were either nominated for a gifted program or actually identified as gifted. That produced interesting reactions. Explained Jake:

> In high school, they said I was really intelligent, but I was like, well, you know it doesn't mean that much if I can't do the work.

Mike had a similar experience:

> Everybody always told my parents I was bright and I was hyperactive. They just thought I was smart and had a discipline problem.

Negative Interaction with Certain Teachers

All of the subjects recalled negative experiences with some of their teachers. All could specifically remember at least one teacher and most could remember more than one teacher who had been a negative influence in their schooling. Some teachers denied students the right to special education services guaranteed to them because of their learning disabilities. Other teachers constantly told the participants of this study that they were lazy and could achieve if they worked harder. Arthur remembered one secondary English teacher:

> Some of my teachers were awful to me. I remember one English teacher. To this day, I hate her. She would just have the idea that if I couldn't do it, if I couldn't get an essay exam done in the time, then I just didn't deserve extra time. . . . That was the hardest English course I'd ever had, you know, because I couldn't do the work in the allotted time. Because of the essays. . . .

The negative experiences with teachers often caused anger and resulted in retrospective insights about what teachers might have done to improve the school experiences of these participants. Diane recalled:

> I remember being so angry at the kids who would get the As and stuff, because I actually knew more than they did, but nobody would let me say anything. If they had given me oral tests, I could tell them anything that they wanted to know about, but they always gave me the written stuff. I would be on question 3 or 4, and the time would be gone, because it took me so long to figure out what the questions were.

Several participants mentioned specific problems with high school English teachers who often gave writing or reading assignments that they could not complete in the allotted time.

Kate:	I've always had Bs and Cs. I had Ds, but not too many. Not a lot. I know in my senior year I got a D. I just had a really hard time with my English teacher in my senior year. I know I got Ds in her class, but not too many.
Researcher:	When you say a hard time, what do you mean by that?
Kate:	She didn't understand learning disabled, and she was a difficult teacher with everyone, it wasn't just me, but with me, she thought I used my learning disabil-

ity as a crutch, and she gave me a very hard time. I tried to get help with her but she wouldn't. She'd make me feel like an idiot. I had a very bad time with her.

Some of the participants in this study simply accepted what happened to them during their school years, but retained an impression or a deep belief that they were not as intelligent as many of their peers because of their learning disability.

Martin: I am not as smart as everybody else. I think that when that came out more is when I went on in school, I was held back in first grade.

Researcher: You stayed back because of the learning disability?

Martin: Yeah.

Researcher: And they told you it was because of the learning disability, or they said that you didn't have the skills to go on?

Martin: No, they told me, because it was the learning disability.

Problems with Peers

Most of the respondents cited incidents of problems with their peers that almost always began in the elementary grades and continued throughout school. Peggy explained that by fourth grade the kids had picked up on the fact that she couldn't do her work:

They made up songs about me. At the end of doing all of the times tables, you had to take a thing called "The Review." It was flash cards, and it mixed up all the different times tables, and you had to do a certain number of them, and pass the review, and there would be a big thing about, "so and so has already gotten to the review and so and so did it today." I never got to the review, and there was this song about that "Peggy will never take the review" made up about halfway through the school year.

Some passively accepted the type of treatment they received from their peers and some fought back. Kate cried when recalling several incidents related to peer pressure.

I remember an instance when I wanted to die. My girlfriend sat next to me in a high school history class. I don't think she even knew what she did. My history teacher was tough on us. He was an older man, always giving these pop quizzes.

He asked me to read out loud, so I had to read. I only read like one paragraph and I stopped, and he picked someone else in class and my girlfriend turned to me and said, "What's wrong with you, you can't even read?" And I thought, "You're my friend. Why did you have to embarrass me like this?" It was so hard.

Tracked Classes and Lack of Effort in School

Ten of the twelve high-ability students in this study had negative opinions about the tracking system formerly used in most of their high schools; in particular, their placement in lower-level reading and math groups in the elementary school and low-track classes in their high schools, despite their high IQ test scores and apparent ability in some areas. In some instances, their placement in low-skills classes resulted in a lack of effort and in negative opinions about themselves. In Mike's words:

> I couldn't do certain things and the teachers were always hounding me and also I kind of got it into my head that I wasn't that smart. Sort of, I don't know, I think I was kept down. Because I think I could have done a lot more, but they would always put me in low groups and things. I was never in the highest reading groups. Because of the high potential of many of the students in the class, being placed in low-skills classes produced considerable anxiety, frustration, and boredom.

Some of the subjects asked their mothers to intercede for them in order to get them placed in more challenging classes. Fred explains his reaction to low-tracked classes:

> No, I wasn't being challenged. I mentioned to my mother that I felt that I could handle more than I was doing. The reading groups that I was in, I felt that they were still too simple, and so she requested that I have testing, and I found out that [reading group] was really way too slow with what I could handle, and so that worked out pretty well after that.

Martin's parents were so frustrated with the school's inability to challenge their son that they found a summer camp with a stimulating and challenging academic program for students with learning disabilities. Martin's frustration about never being able to move to a higher-track class during the regular school year was evident in his comments. His high school used a three-track system in which track one was the highest track and track three was the lowest. Each year

Martin was led to believe that he would be able to move from the lowest track with special services into a higher track in which he was "mainstreamed."

> Martin: I was ready to go out. Ready to . . . when they were telling me you are going to be mainstreamed, total mainstream, I was ready for it. I wanted to go bad.
> Researcher: And so you weren't able?
> Martin: It was a slow process, because they put an expectation in my mind saying that I was ready, and then the next year would come, and I would schedule for classes but it never happened, and I was always in that low-tracked class.

Commenting on these classes, Martin continued:

> I was in English level three, and in English level three they only teach you at a certain pace. They only require so much. They only give you so much of a workload, but in a level-one class, they give you so much more of a workload, and a higher level of understanding required, and since I was always in level three classes, I was never stimulated.

As a junior in high school, Martin was finally able to take an advanced class:

> I think I could have been in a higher level, but because I had [a] learning disability, I was put in these low levels. I wasn't pushed to excel, or do better, or even try to achieve at higher levels. I was never like that until 11th grade. So in 11th grade I was put in English one, the top-level English class, and I passed, and then [in my] senior year I was also in there and I passed, but all the way up through there I was in level three.

Several other participants mentioned that unchallenging classes resulted in a lack of effort. Joe and several of the other participants indicated that they never worked, never did homework, and drew and daydreamed during most of their classes. When any of the subjects in the study were able to move into higher-tracked classes, the students' learning experiences improved. Kate explained about her high school experience:

> I was in the lower classes, I was getting As and Bs, I mean it was just way too easy. I had this teacher for general bio and she said, "I think you could get into biology." So I could still have her. I switched into it. It was difficult, but it was a

challenge for me then. Like I was getting As all the way through. Everyone copied off of me in general classes, but in college biology, it was more of a challenge, which I liked. I struggled to get a B, maybe even B-, but it was *challenging*.

Several of the respondents also commented on their ability to learn how to work in the higher-track classes when they had never had to work before. Martin summarizes most succinctly his disappointment and the feelings described by several other respondents:

It seemed like I never, as I look back, because of my learning disability, I never got opportunities for learning in my high school.

Difficulty in Reading and Writing

In every case in this study, the specific nature of the subjects' learning disability was related in some way to verbal ability, which they perceived to have had a detrimental effect on every aspect of their schooling. All of the subjects mentioned problems with reading and spelling. Diane explained:

I have a problem with lots of reading. That's always gonna be a problem. I don't have trouble reading, I mean I can read through stuff. It's just running through pages. I mean I can read. I can sit there and read two pages or three pages and realize that I had no concept of what I put my eyes over in the last three or four pages so I have to start over. I can do the same pages a long time before I understand what's happening. I can read through math texts, complicated math texts, just as quick as I could read a cheap novel or something. It's just the process of going through the same way to verbal ability.

Every subject in this study mentioned problems with reading, handwriting, and spelling. Mike found that a word processor for writing and books on tape helped him process and generate useful information. Diane identified her own language disability, while Peggy and Jake reported extensive problems with handwriting. Respondents also discussed the problems with reading. Kate explained:

My learning disability is language oriented. I have a hard time spelling. I can't spell. I even have a hard time reading. I have a very hard time sounding out words. Written expressions, I am very bad. I have a very hard time getting my thoughts down to paper. Basically, that's it, but that's very difficult since languages vary. How I compensate, like say with reading is, since I am visual I'd learn the word, and I learn how to say it and I just remember it, but that's it. I think that's how I learned how to read, 'cause I had a very hard time sounding words.

Diane was able to recall the moment in second grade when she realized what reading was and that she couldn't do it. Some of the participants also mentioned their inability to process and apply certain types of information and concepts. Peggy explained:

I feel like my brain shorted out. I would understand the concept and if someone would walk me through the process I could understand every step of the way, and then I would get home, and I would look at it, and I couldn't apply it. It was very frustrating, and it is very frustrating, because I think at that level, especially [when] teachers say, "Do it my way!" And I couldn't, and I would say, "Well, I can't do it her way, so I am not gonna do it at all."

Discussion

It is clear from the data collected in this study that some high-ability students with learning disabilities have negative experiences in school, and that many of these negative experiences revolve around reading, writing, and verbal expression. It is also apparent that some students in this population succeed in an academic setting despite these negative experiences.

The Combination of the Learning Disability and the Students' Giftedness

The participants in this study were able to resolve the conflict between their abilities and their disabilities in one of three ways. First, some participants struggled to gain the compensation strategies needed to directly address their learning disability and become successful in an area that may have initially appeared difficult if not impossible. This enabled their talents to emerge as they used strategies to overcome or at least compensate for their learning disability. Evan, for example, became a political science major despite a learning disability that hindered his skills in writing and reading. Second, a smaller number of participants selected an academic direction in which they had strengths *and* which was not dependent upon the acquisition of compensation strategies or the mastery of an academic discipline that was affected by their specific learning disability. It is clear that this was only possible because these students were in college and could select a major area in which their specific talent could emerge. For example, Peggy's musical talents caused her to pursue a major in voice, thus enabling her to avoid the continued struggle to compensate for her numerous learning difficulties in academic areas. These options are not available to the elementary or secondary student who has limited academic choices in school. Third, the majority of participants in this study combined the two options mentioned above as they attempted to both compensate for their learning disability and also select a major area of concentration in which their specific learning disability did not affect academic performance. Colin pursued a major in electrical/systems engineering thereby enabling him to focus on his strengths. He had to learn compensation strategies in order to be successful but he did not have to use them to the extent he would have had he majored in an area that required him to use reading and writing skills primarily.

Implications

Several implications emerged from this qualitative study of twelve participants with learning disabilities who succeeded in an academic setting. The implications drawn from this study parallel findings by others who have studied this phenomenon (Baum, 1984, 1988; Torrance, 1982, 1992). Some implications of this research, however, have not been noted in other research studies and may signify the need for additional research.

The Need for the Development of Student Talents

Most of the participants in this study had special talents and abilities outside of school that were identified, nurtured, and developed by their parents possibly more than they might have been if school problems did not exist. Because these problems did exist, parents often looked for other areas in which their child could excel and spent considerable resources in helping to develop these talents. It was the development of these talents that often provided the students with the belief that they could excel in an area outside of school if they worked hard at it. Then, many realized that if they could do that well, perhaps they could do better in school if they applied themselves and worked harder. This belief in themselves often caused them to try much harder at their academic studies. Ironically, the hard work was necessary because of their learning disabilities, but it was the acquisition of this work ethic that caused many of these students to persevere and become extremely successful in college. Many other gifted students seldom have to struggle to excel in elementary or secondary school and consequently, never learn to work and may not achieve the same levels of success as some of the participants in this study. This is not to infer that having a learning disability is a positive experience, for as has been stated earlier, several of these students were in need of counseling and had emotional difficulties to overcome. It is, rather, that in response to their learning disability, many of these participants learned the value of hard work and effort that later translated into academic success. And many of them first learned about work and effort through the development of talents not necessarily associated with academic success in school, which were identified and nurtured by their parents.

It is clear that participants in this study would have benefited from the advice and input that could have been provided by a teacher with training and background in gifted education. Offering enrichment programs *based on students' strengths and interests* would have provided the students in this study with a more positive educational experience than the continued emphasis on remedial techniques. Advice related to the need for appropriate challenge for high-potential students may have helped to avoid the placement of these students in classes or tracks that were not matched to their instructional needs.

Programs designed for high-ability students with learning disabilities may help to improve self-concept and self-esteem of students as well as developing the potential talent that each student possesses (Baum, 1988; Olenchak, 1995). Programs for this population of students have been successfully developed using Renzulli's Schoolwide Enrichment Triad Model (Renzulli, 1977; Renzulli and Reis, 1985; Renzulli, 1994) as the basis for focusing on students' strengths and interests.

The modifications listed below may help to address the unique needs of talented students with learning disabilities. Most of these modifications can be made with minimal funds and minimal investments of teacher time.

Table 2
Possible Modifications in Reading and Writing for Talented Students with Learning Disabilities in These Areas

Reading	Writing
Identify talent areas in reading and encourage students in areas.	Change the format of the materials from which the student copies (i.e., larger print).
Use a scanner and available technology to enable computer reading of content	Dictate writing assignments to someone who will type for the student with the learning disability.

Modify the student's reading material (select shorter books for book reports or books with larger print).

Outline reading material for the student.

Tape-record reading material for the student to listen to while reading the printed text (including commercially available books on tape and those which are taped specifically for the student).

Provide assignments a month in advance to enable students to chunk assignments into reasonable assignments for reading.

Have the student paraphrase material orally.

Give the student time to read a selection more than once.

Supplement books with multimedia materials if available. (Have students watch the film *Johnny Tremaine* while they are reading the novel.)

Make a reading window for textbook use. Student moves window down and across page while reading.

Include high-interest selections from magazines and newspapers in students' reading assignments.

Identify a talented peer to whom the student may turn for help.

Assess student's interest in order to identify high-interest reading material.

Avoid reading situations which might make a student uncomfortable (reading aloud in a group, etc.).

Use a frame or window to cover all material except what is to be copied.

Make sure student proofreads his/her work.

State clearly the expectations between a first draft and revisions.

Tape-record writing assignments.

Use current technology to dictate writing into computer.

Encourage students to use peer conferencing with a peer who is sensitive to the problems associated with having learning disabilities when proofreading.

Have student keep a daily journal in which writing and spelling is not corrected.

Learn to use available strategies for spell checking.

Encourage the use of concept mapping.

Encourage students to be self-advocates and to monitor the use of compensation strategies as specified in their special education plan.

The Need for Professional Development

Classroom and content area teachers, counselors, and special education teachers should be provided with opportunities for training about the identification and programming necessary to meet the needs of this population. Effective training could help to alert educators and parents to situations that may indicate a learning disability in a high-ability student. Students with excellent verbal skills who experience problems learning to read, or who seem very bright but who cannot express themselves orally, should be carefully watched. Unfortunately, the wrong types of teacher assistance seem to have been provided. Considerable efforts were made; for example, to remediate the participants of this study on skills that they had not yet mastered *and that they may never master* but which can be replaced by the use of technology, such as word processors. Staff development in how to identify and nurture talents as well as compensation strategies would help to address this concern. Professional development might also help to provide teachers with ideas for enabling this population to work in a style that is more appealing to them while simultaneously using compensation strategies such as:

- using projects;
- oral and untimed tests;
- using peers for help in note taking by allowing a peer's notes to be copied for the student with learning disabilities;
- assigning activities with alternatives to long writing assignments such as short answers and others;
- providing longer time for assignments;
- enabling students to use pictures, illustrations, drawings, and diagrams as part of written products; and
- enabling students to do taped or live oral reports with a brief outline instead of written reports.

Teachers also should learn how to listen to these students for clues as to how to address their needs as gifted students with disabilities. Participants in this study could seldom choose topics to investigate or modes of learning that were uniquely suited to their own styles, preferences, or strengths, and which took into account their learning disabilities. If these types of opportunities could have been provided for students to select areas of strengths or interests, these students may have had vastly different experiences in school.

* * *

Research for this report was supported under the Javits Act Program (Grant No. R206R00001) as administered by the Office of Educational Research and Improvement, U.S. Department of Education. Grantees undertaking such projects are encouraged to express freely their professional judgment. This report, therefore, does not necessarily represent positions or policies of the government, and no official endorsement should be inferred.

REFERENCES

Bandura, A. 1986. *Social Foundations of Thought and Action.* Englewood Cliffs, N.J.: Prentice-Hall.

Baum, S. 1988. An enrichment program for gifted learning disabled students. *Gifted Child Quarterly* 32(1): 226–230.

Baum, S., and S. V. Owen. 1988. High ability/learning disabled students: How are they different? *Gifted Child Quarterly* 32, 321–326.

Baum, S., S. V. Owen, and J. Dixon. 1991. *To be Gifted and Learning Disabled: From Definitions to Practical Intervention Strategies.* Mansfield Center, Conn.: Creative Learning Press.

Boodoo, G. M., C. L. Bradley, R. L. Frontera, J. R. Pitts, and L. P. Wright. 1989. A survey of procedures used for identifying gifted learning disabled children. *Gifted Child Quarterly* 33(3): 110–114.

Daniels, P. R. 1983. *Teaching the Learning-Disabled/Gifted Child.* Rockville, Md.: Aspen.

Davis, G. A., and S. B. Rimm. 1985. *Education of the Gifted and Talented.* Englewood Cliffs, N.J.: Prentice-Hall.

Denckla, M. B. 1989. Executive function, the overlap zone between attention deficit hyperactivity disorder and learning disability. *International Pediatrics* 4(2): 155–160.

Gardner, H. 1983. *Frames of Mind: The Theory of Multiple Intelligences.* New York: Basic Books.

Goertzel, V., and M. G. Goertzel. 1962. *Cradles of Eminence.* Boston: Little Brown.

Guba, E. G. 1978. *Toward a Methodology of Naturalistic Inquiry in Educational Evaluation.* Los Angeles: University of California Press.

Hallahan, D. P., and T. Bryan. 1981. Learning disabilities. In J. M. Kauffman and D. P. Hallahan (eds.), *Handbook of Special Education.* Englewood Cliffs, N.J.: Prentice Hall.

Hammill, D. D. 1990. On defining learning disabilities: An emerging consensus. *Journal of Learning Disabilities* 23(2): 74–84.

Henderson, C. 1992. *College Freshmen with Disabilities: A Statistical Profile.* Washington, D.C.: HEATH Resource Center.

Hokanson, D. T., and M. Jospe. 1976. *The Search for Cognitive Giftedness in Exceptional Children.* New Haven, Conn.: Project SEARCH.

Jick, T. D. 1983. Mixing qualitative and quantitative methods: Triangulation in action. In J. Van Maanen (ed.), *Qualitative Methodology.* Beverly Hills, Calif.: Sage Publications.

Kirk, S. A. 1963. Behavioral diagnosis and remediation of learning disabilities. In *Proceedings of the Annual Conference on Exploration in the Problems of the Perceptually Handicapped Child.* Evanston, Ill.: Fund for Perceptually Handicapped Children.

Maker, C. J. 1977. *Providing programs for the gifted handicapped.* Reston, Va.: The Council for Exceptional Children.

Miles, M. B., and A. M. Huberman. 1984. Drawing valid meaning from qualitative data: Toward a shared craft. *Educational Researcher* 13(5): 20–30.

Minner, S. 1990. Teacher evaluations of case descriptions of LD gifted children. *Gifted Child Quarterly* 34, 37–39.

National Joint Committee on Learning Disabilities. 1988. [Letter to NJCLD member organizations]. Towson, Md.: Author.

Olenchak, F. R. 1995. Effects of enrichment on gifted/learning-disabled students. *Journal for the Education of the Gifted* 18(4): 385–399.

Piers, E. V. 1984. *Piers-Harris Children's Self-Concept Scale: Revised Manual.* Los Angeles: Western Psychological Services.

Prater, G., and S. Minner. 1986. *Identification of atypical gifted children* (technical report, No. 2). Murray, Ky.: Murray State University, Department of Special Education.

Renzulli, J. S. 1977. *The Enrichment Triad Model: A Guide for Developing Defensible Programs for the Gifted and Talented.* Mansfield Center, Conn.: Creative Learning Press.

———. 1978. What makes giftedness? Phi Delta Kappan 60(3): 180–184, 261.

———. 1994. *Schools for Talent Development: A Practical Plan for Total School Improvement.* Mansfield Center, Conn.: Creative Learning Press.

Renzulli, J. S., and S. M. Reis. 1985. *The Schoolwide Enrichment Model: A Comprehensive Plan for Educational Excellence.* Mansfield Center, Conn.: Creative Learning Press.

Spradley, J. P. 1979. *The Ethnographic Interview.* New York: Holt, Rinehart, and Winston.

Sternberg, R. J. 1981. A componential theory of intellectual giftedness. *Gifted Child Quarterly* 25(2): 86–93.

Strauss, A. L. 1987. *Qualitative Analysis for Social Scientists.* New York: Cambridge University Press.

Strauss, A. L., and J. Corbin. 1990. *Basics of Qualitative Research.* Newbury Park, Calif.: Sage Publications.

Strauss, A., and L. Lehtinen. 1947. *Psychopathology of the Brain Injured Child.* New York: Grune & Stratton.

Taylor, H. G. 1989. Learning disabilities. In E. J. Mash and R. Barkley (eds.), *Treatment of Childhood Disorders.* New York: Guilford Press.

Terman, L. M., and M. H. Oden. 1947. *The Gifted Child Grows Up.* Stanford, Calif.: Stanford University Press.

Van Maanen, J. 1983. Reclaiming qualitative research methods for organizational research. In J. Van Maanen (ed.), *Qualitative Methodology.* Beverly Hills, Calif.: Sage Publications.

Vantour, J. A. C. 1976. Discovering and motivating the artistically gifted LD child. *Teaching Exceptional Children* 8(2): 92–96.

Vaughn, S. 1989. Gifted learning disabilities: Is it such a bright idea? *Learning Disabilities Focus* 4(2): 123–126.

West, T. G. 1991. *In the Mind's Eye: Visual Thinkers, Gifted People with Learning Difficulties, Computer Images, and the Ironies of Creativity.* Buffalo, N.Y.: Prometheus Books.

West, T. G. 1992. A future of reversals: Dyslexic talents in a world of computer visualization. *Annals of Dyslexia* 42, 124–139.

Whitmore, J. 1986. Conceptualizing the issue of underserved populations of gifted students. *Journal for the Education of the Gifted* 10(3): 141–153.

Whitmore, J. R., and J. Maker. 1985. *Intellectual Giftedness in Disabled Persons.* Rockville, Md.: Aspen Publications.

Yin, R. K. 1989. *Case Study Research* (2nd ed.). Newbury, Calif.: Sage.

WHEN INDIVIDUALS WITH HIGH IQ EXPERIENCE SENSORY INTEGRATION OR SENSORY SYSTEMS MODULATION PROBLEMS

by Judith Giencke Kimball

Introduction

Much has been written about gifted individuals with exceptional abilities in math or art, but less well-developed abilities in verbal/language areas (Winner, 1998). Educational programs to improve weaker verbal skills have been used with some success. The opposite case, poor perceptual abilities coupled with giftedness in language areas, is not as often noted to be a problem because language skills, particularly early reading and talking, appear to be prized as the hallmarks of giftedness. When children exhibit problems in perceptual abilities, they often do not qualify for special services because their verbal test scores keep them functioning at an academic level that is well above average. These children, however, can demonstrate dysfunctions that can prove to be very frustrating and demoralizing for them. Sensory integration (SI) theory holds possible explanations for these problems, and occupational therapy using SI techniques offers treatment.

Sensory integration problems were first defined by A. Jean Ayers in the '60s (Ayers, 1965, 1966a, 1966b, 1969, 1972a, 1975b, 1976, 1978, 1979, 1985). She determined that some children and adults labeled as learning disabled had difficulty with issues not commonly associated with learning in the cognitive sense. Their problems involved decreased perceptual abilities (both tactile and visual), poor balance, low muscle tone, poor co-contraction, and difficulty accomplishing nonhabitual movement patterns (dyspraxia). She related these issues to inefficient integration of discriminative sensory input from all seven sensory systems (vision, audition, tactile, gustatory, taste, proprioception, and vestibular/balance), but primarily the tactile, vestibular and proprioceptive systems. Her work has been expanded upon and refined by numerous occupational therapy researchers and clinicians (Fisher, Murray, and Bundy, 1991; Cermak, 1985, 1991; Kimball, 1993; Clark, Mailloux, and Parham, 1989).

Ayers also described tactile defensiveness, which she related to modulation problems in the alert/arousal aspects of the tactile system. Her work in this area has been expanded to include the influence on the nervous system of the alert/arousal components of all the sensory systems. Problems in this area are now referred to as sensory defensiveness (Wilbarger and Wilbarger, 1991).

An explanation of sensory integration problems and sensory defensiveness (also referred to as sensory system modulation problems), can contribute to the understanding of the behavioral and motor output problems that individuals experience which can arise due to less than optimal functioning of central nervous system (CNS) processes.

Sensory Defensiveness

Sensory defensiveness (SD) comes from an overarousal of, or modulation problems in, sensory systems processing. The manner in which the sensory systems process input will influence the child's ability to respond adaptively. In normal individuals, moderate arousal results in optimal adaptive responses, while high arousal initiates an autonomic nervous system sympathetic fight, flight, or freeze response. This reaction is the primary *survival* response of the organism. When arousal gets too high, the nervous system responds adaptively to what it views as a serious survival threat. If the threat is dealt with, the arousal dissipates and the nervous system returns to normal. If it is not possible to fight or flee, the arousal does not easily dissipate, causing stress, anxiety, and difficulty in completing other adaptive responses. Individuals with sensory system modulation problems have sensory systems that are "on alert" more often, do not seem to modulate correctly, and have more changeable arousal reaction levels than normal. This results in problems with adaptive responses as their systems lack predictability and stability. The sensory systems do not function independently; therefore arousal in several systems can combine to produce high arousal. If one remembers that what sensory defensiveness evokes is a survival response, then the intensity of the reaction seen in these individuals is more easily understood.

Individuals with sensory defensiveness have trouble in calming themselves down after arousal. Where a normal individual will be able to experience a sensory event that causes arousal, then be able to calm down to a normal level, individuals with sensory defensiveness experience an arousing sensory event and their systems stay aroused. Any new sensory event builds on that high level of arousal. The person may look calm, but really be close to overload. In this case, a small sensory event that normally would not bother anyone may push the person into overload. A negative emotional response or an explosive reaction sometimes called a catastrophic reaction may occur. The "final straw" is usually not a highly arousing or important event as far as intensity, but the timing is the critical element. Psychologists often suggest finding the antecedent event to the negative behavior and eliminating it to keep the behavior from reoccurring. However, this overlooks the fact that it is not the antecedent event which caused the negative behavior. Any small sensory event could have triggered it due to the fact that the nervous system was in a state close to overarousal.

Optimum responses come with optimum arousal and that lower or higher arousal produces less than optimal adaptive responses. When arousal goes above moderate, disorganization occurs. The normal nervous system understands this disorganization and does something to try to decrease it. If stress-related inputs are not decreased and arousal keeps rising, the person can move into anxiety and negative emotional responses. Some of these emotional responses can be viewed as maladaptive behaviors and persons are often referred to mental-health professionals who deal with the behavior, not the underlying CNS causes. People with normal nervous systems respond to this anxiety as transitory and move back to organization without too much difficulty. The person with sensory defensiveness issues is less able to inhibit these high-arousal states or to move back to normal easily, thus triggering fight or flight responses in situations where they are not viewed as warranted by most people. The responses look out of proportion to the situation to an observer. The person with SD responds as if his body is interpreting the input as a full-fledged alert: "Stay alive, you are being threatened with deadly danger."

Another difference seen in individuals with sensory defensiveness is that the range of optimum performance is smaller than normal. This difference means that the person may go from overarousal to apparent underarousal more quickly than normal and not spend much time in the normal range.

It is also important to note that not all persons who appear underaroused actually are. Some may actually be in a state where the CNS responds to its comprised ability to deal with sensory overload by shutting off further input. These individuals are actually overaroused and adding additional input that they cannot escape from or ignore can put their nervous systems at risk for physiological "shutdown" which can lead to severe respiratory and cardiac irregularities. These severe reactions are rare, but have been documented (Kimball, 1976, 1977, 1988, 1991). Sensory defensiveness is classified as mild, moderate, or severe. According to Wilbarger and Wilbarger (1991, p. 3), elaborated here:

1.   Mild sensory defensiveness: "While appearing quite 'normal,' children with mild defensiveness might be described as 'picky,' 'oversensitive,' 'slightly overactive,' resistive to change,' or slightly 'controlling.' They can act mildly irritated by some sensations, but not by others. They

may be picky about clothes or food. While these children can achieve at age level in school or have good social relations, they may have to use enormous control and effort to succeed in these areas. When they can no longer maintain the level of effort required to do so, they may 'fall apart' emotionally under apparently little or no stress."

2. "Moderate sensory defensiveness is one that affects two or more aspects of a child's life. At this level children often have difficulty with social relations whether being overly aggressive or isolating themselves from peers. Many self-care skills are disrupted such as dressing, bathing, and eating. They have difficulty with attention and behavior in school. Exploration and play may be limited due to fearfulness of new situations and resistance to change."

3. Severe sensory defensiveness: "Disrupts every aspect of a child's life. These children usually have other diagnostic labels for various areas of dysfunction (i.e., severe developmental delay, autism, autistic-like behavior, or emotionally disturbed). Strong avoidance of some kind of sensation or the reverse, intense sensory seeking, are common. Sensory defensiveness may block development and/or interfere with treatment of these children. Treating sensory defensiveness first reduces sensory problems and increases the effectiveness of other forms of intervention."

Treatment of sensory defensiveness takes three avenues:

a) The first is awareness of the problem. If a child's parents, teachers, and other professionals are aware of the problem, they will be more likely to respond in a positive way. Behaviors are related to arousal level. Most children who are sensory defensive have had their behaviors interpreted as being other than what they are, negative reactions to sensation. They have had to train their parents and others to organize their environment for as much sensory safety as possible. These behaviors do not make much sense if viewed individually, but seen together form the patterns of SD.

b) The second is sensory diet. Sensory diet is a concept based on the idea that each individual requires a certain amount of activity and sensation to be the most alert, adaptive, and skillful. Certain types of activities seem to be helpful for individuals with sensory defensiveness and each seems to reduce the defensiveness for a certain period of time. Vestibular activities, particularly rhythmic ones, can provide modulation for up to six hours in the nervous system. Heavy joint and muscle work can provide up to four hours, and deep touch pressure on the skin can provide up to two hours. By careful planning, one can use sensory input to help the child feel safe and organized throughout the day. Specific time-oriented activity routines can be added to the child's day. For instance, jumping on the mini-trampoline or participating in play leisure activities that meet sensory needs can be utilized and changes in routine or in the environment can be instituted. Being aware of the sensory qualities of daily activities is an important first step in organizing a sensory defensive child's sensory diet to provide safety to the nervous system and to begin to make changes in the response patterns. Increasing the intensity, frequency, and/or direction of modulating activities is the goal. Activities which modulate include those that provide deep touch pressure, heavy joint and muscle work, and rhythmic movement.

c)   The third aspect of treatment is a professionally guided program which uses firm brushing with a specific type of nonscratching brush followed by proprioception to each joint. This program utilizes spatial and temporal summation to affect as many modulating receptors as possible. Specific directions for the program are given by the therapist. The key points are 1) that only the special nonscratching brush may be used; 2) the face, stomach, and chest are never to be brushed; 3) the mouth must be done separately because it is innervated separately by cranial nerves. (Finger pressure to the roof of the mouth is used.) Changes in the child's behavior or his responsiveness to this deep touch pressure/proprioception need to be reported to the therapist. *This program needs to be monitored by a therapist specially trained in its use.*

Sensory defensiveness is a separate issue from other sensory integration issues and needs to be treated first to allow the nervous system to respond to other treatment. Sensory defensiveness and sensory integration problems resulting from discrimination-processing deficits (perceptual-motor, vestibular, praxis) are not always seen together. An individual may have one problem, but not the other.

Sensory Integration

Sensory integration (SI) problems are based on processing difficulties in the discriminative aspects of the specific sensory system including the following:

The vestibular system provides us with basic balance and reflexes, lets us know if we are moving or the environment is moving, stabilizes the visual field, and with the proprioceptive systems provides us with background muscle tone and the ability to co-contract (contract antagonistic muscles at the same time to stabilize a body part for function). Low muscle tone and poor co-contraction can be misinterpreted as poor muscle strength because the ability to sustain a motor activity may be decreased. Ability to hold a position in full extension or flexion is normal, but midrange stability is compromised. Vestibular system responses contribute to motor planning (praxis), which will be discussed subsequently.

Proprioception is the sense of position in space and monitoring of tension found in all of our joints, muscles, ligaments, and tendons. It is the sense used when we touch our nose with our finger with our eyes closed. Proprioception is a "hidden sense" in that we cannot see the receptors, but it is an extremely valuable sense that is a major contributor to therapy for sensory integrative deficits as well as sensory defensiveness.

Tactile discrimination lets us know where our body begins and the environment ends, determines the qualities of the touch/pressure input we are receiving, and mediates touch perception in our hands and mouth. The discriminative portions of these three sensory systems in particular influence the development of praxis.

Praxis (motor planning) is the ability to organize the body to accomplish nonhabitual motor skills. Motor planning goes beyond motor coordination to include a type of organizational motor intelligence. Feedback and input from the discriminative portions of the vestibular, proprioceptive, and tactile systems provide information applied to functional activity. Besides the coordination component, praxis forms the basis for the understanding and carrying out of stopping, starting, and sequencing of activities, and organizational abilities. Praxis is the ability of the brain to conceive, organize, and carry out an unfamiliar sequence of movement. This is not based on practice, but is related to building motor sequences and motor repertoire. Praxis is not dependent on effort; trying harder will not improve things. It is based on automatic reflexes and movement patterns in the vestibular system and the proprioception system, as well as the discrimination of tactile input. Praxis results from all systems working together to accomplish an adaptive response. Difficulty with motor planning, called dyspraxia, is partially due to the motor system's not being automatic. The reflexes of the automatic base in balance, equilibrium, and proprioception are not adequately supporting the higher-level motor functioning and sequencing.

One example of how the system normally works is the motor-planning sequence of learning to drive a car. Cognitively planning the physical action needs to occur first. After the physical actions have been planned and practiced several times, they become internalized and increasingly automatic, and then may be transferred to new situations that are similar (i.e., a different car). Children who have motor-planning problems have difficulty in all three areas. They initially have trouble directing their bodies to do efficient nonhabitual movements in order to develop motor plans due to deficient reflexive automatic base (less muscle tone, poor concentration, poor balance, less proprioceptive feedback). Since they have only partial movement patterns in place, they do not internalize them well. When they try to retrieve the patterns for use in situations that are similar, they are not able to abstract the common elements to allow them to only learn the new part of the sequence. They must relearn much of the sequence each time they try it. This makes movement and learning very inefficient. Persons with this problem can accomplish the activity but with less quality and may appear clumsy.

Attention span may also be affected and fine-motor activities may also be involved. While the child may be able to print his/her name if that is the only activity required, when he/she is asked to use printing to express ideas, the ideas may take over and the motor skill of printing may suffer. The concentration and the motor coordination to do both is just not available at the same time.

An additional problem arises in that the feedback the child gets from his/her own body is not always consistent. Some days will be better than others depending on the input that the sensory systems have incurred that day. Never being able to trust his/her own body makes it difficult to know how to respond in any motor situation and makes motor learning much slower. As motor learning is the beginning of the development of the learning of sequences, the child has a great deal of difficulty accomplishing multiple-part sequences. This becomes problematic in school, as most academics are built on sequences as well as starting and stopping, another problem in dyspraxia.

Praxis is diagnosed by an occupational therapist using several standardized tests: The Sensory Integration and Praxis Tests (a two-hour computer scored, in-depth assessment, Ayers, 1989), Imitation of Postures and Motor Accuracy (from The Southern California Sensory Integration Tests, Ayers, 1980) and by nonstandardized clinical observations of hopping, jumping, skipping, jumping jacks, observations of movement, and functional activities (Ayers, 1971).

How SI and DS Affect Students with High I.Q.

Persons with SI problems and high IQs usually have a profile of high verbal abilities and lower performance abilities. Performance IQ abilities include perceptual motor and sequencing. Persons with this profile can usually benefit from SI occupational therapy (OT) treatment to remedy perceptual and motor problems and improve academics (Ayers, 1976, 1978). Persons with the opposite profile—high performance and lower verbal abilities—are usually not good candidates for occupational therapy to help improve academic scores, but are often helped with language based special education remediation techniques. The exception to this rule is the issue of sensory defensiveness, which can be present in both groups and can be successfully treated by OTs.

Praxis Issues

The perceptual motor problems seen with low performance I.Q.s are often associated with praxis problems and are based on vestibular, proprioception, and tactile discrimination inefficiencies but not sensory defensiveness. In gifted individuals, praxis problems can be particularly frustrating. The praxis issue of difficulty with starting, stopping, sequencing, and organization are specifically problematic. It is very difficult to have a body which does not move as fast as your mind. And these individuals are painfully aware that they cannot ever move as well as their peers. They are able to use their intelligence to cognitively figure out how to do movement sequences, but the *quality* of the movements is not the same as their peers as they do not have the same level of autonomic support from the low brain areas that provide the vestibular, proprioceptive, and tactile discrimination necessary for normal praxis.

Additionally, using cognitive processes to direct movement is less efficient, and therefore takes more time. It may take only seconds more, but this time adds up to moving slightly slower than normal and appearing less able in movement or a bit clumsy. This is particularly frustrating for persons with high intelligence—they can see how the action should be done and can even accomplish it with extra work, but the results are not up to normal levels qualitatively and are not competitive with peers. The deficiencies in starting, stopping, and sequencing that come with dyspraxia leave them less able to organize their lives efficiently. Losing homework lists, forgetting books, not being able to organize school projects, and not liking to change classes become issues. Carrying all your possessions in a heavy backpack is a compensatory strategy as well as self-treatment. Having everything with you means not having to organize, and carrying the heavy backpack means the joints and muscles have to work harder which increases low muscle tone and co-contraction.

Perceptual disabilities are often seen in the individual with praxis problems. They result in difficulties knowing where the body or objects are in space and how things relate to each other spatially.

Dyspraxia and its underlying issues can be observed in behaviors starting in infancy. Sucking is the first complex motor skill a child must master to stay alive (after breathing, of course). The first motor sequence is to breathe, suck, and swallow. Difficulty may be seen in this sequence or in the child's ability to master the suck. Developmental milestones (sitting, crawling, and walking) emerge at appropriate ages, but quality of movement is decreased. The baby's muscles may appear "floppier" or "looser" than other baby's. Strength may appear low in some situations but not in others. If these are analyzed one sees that the "weakness" is less than optimal co-contraction in midrange activity and the "strength" is seen when the limb is in full extension or full flexion where only one set of muscles is in primary use. As the baby gets older, other problems emerge. Parents may see more tripping or falling with no apparent obstacles, and difficulty with both the fine motor coordination and the perceptual abilities needed to put puzzles together. Sequencing difficulties are first noticed as an inability to follow Mom's verbal directions around daily skills or safety issues. A direction like "go get a block and put it in the box" may result in a child's putting something else in the box because only part of the sequence was processed.

Articulation problems may become apparent. Articulation is a motor skill requiring much praxis. It is also influenced by muscle tone in the face, mouth, and neck. If the chin is positioned slightly forward due to low muscle tone, articulation becomes more difficult (as does swallowing which could result in drooling). Low tone in the face contributes not only to sucking and articulation difficulties, but to limitations in the quality of facial expression. Much information about feelings and needs is conveyed through facial expression. If a child does not show a range of expressions, parents may not pick up on the child's needs.

Preschool offers additional challenges for the child with dyspraxia. Climbing playground equipment, riding a tricycle (and later a bicycle), and understanding the sequence and rhythm of the day become issues. Changing schedules and therefore the sequence of the day can be upsetting to the child who has a tenuous grasps on sequences, and transitions can be a nightmare. Normally children can understand that when a sequence is interrupted the interruption is a temporary change or an insertion into, or a substitution for, part of the regular routine. The child with dyspraxia only knows that the routine is gone. He cannot access the sequence in the middle and go on, but often must start over from the beginning (which is not usually possible). The child will need time to finish the sequence he was involved in, which is not always clear or convenient for the parents. For example, the child is putting together a wooden train track when the parent arrives late at day care. The father says "Nice job, let's go, we're late" and the child becomes inconsolable. Dad has no idea what happened and the teacher says she has noticed problems with transitions. The child has worked to sequence the track blocks and saw the next piece of the sequence as the payoff that he has been working for—driving the train around the track—or if he is less able to sequence, he just knows he is not finished. Rather than expecting him to leave the train midsequence, Dad might get down on the floor and help complete the sequence. Despite the father's aid, the child may not want to pick up his creation. Transitions need to be viewed in the context of the child's sequencing abilities. (Later we will discuss the "feeling safe" issues in transitions and sequences when we discuss sensory defensiveness.)

School provides many challenges for the child with dyspraxia's view of the world. Poor fine-motor abilities can mean difficulty with cutting, drawing, coloring, printing, and later, cursive writing. Perceptual problems make learning letters, numbers, shapes, and reading difficult. Sequencing becomes more demanding with reading, math, and following directions. Praxis issues become more apparent in gym class and recess.

When children experience SI problems and they are not identified as such, these are interpreted as psychological or learning problems. For example, a child who has trouble cutting out the paper rooster might accidentally cut off its head or legs. Rather than face the humiliation of failure, he might cut more pieces off or rip up the rest of the rooster saying, "There, I killed it." This might earn him a label of aggressive tendencies. Another misunderstanding observed in children with dyspraxia is blaming the environment. They do not understand that they cannot accomplish things, so the failure to cut out the rooster successfully may be blamed on "dumb scissors" or "wrong color paper" or "not enough time" (if the teacher interrupts his labored sequence due to time restrictions). "Aggressive tendencies" can also be a label assigned to the child with poor balance and muscle tone who trips into other kids, or the child who realizes that heavy joint and muscle work can make him feel better and who goes around crashing into other kids or walls, desks, etc. This crashing increases muscle tone, cocontraction, and proprioceptive feedback leading to an increase in praxis, for at least a short time.

"Noncompliant" is another label placed on children with dyspraxia. When the child knows he cannot do the activity to the level of the class, it may appear easier to refuse to try the activity than to be subject to humiliation in front of peers. Refusal at least gets you attention, even if it is negative, for strength at something.

A "dawdling" label might get attached because organizing the body takes longer. And "fidgety" describes the child whose muscle tone, co-contraction, and vestibular issues make it difficult to "just sit" on the floor or in a chair during story time. The usual behavior seen is wiggling, lying back, lying on the stomach, not keeping knees bent while sitting on the floor, or falling out of the chair.

Decreased abilities in sports can lead to decreased self-esteem and difficulty making friends. Boys, especially, bond through sports and many a child with dyspraxia has found himself shut out socially. Gym class and recess can become terrible experiences and the child may become very adept at finding excuses to avoid them, including "getting into trouble" to cause the teacher to revoke the privilege or claiming illness. It should be noted that the motor experience would be very beneficial for the child if there were not such a high social price to pay for trying to participate.

Since the early grades put a high premium on skills with a perceptual motor base, giftedness may not be recognized easily in children with dyspraxia. Their handwriting may be too poor to read and their coordination or opportunity for keyboarding not yet developed. And they hate worksheets! Early reading is appreciated, but the child cannot produce enough written work to confirm that he integrates what he reads.

These children often find solace in fantasy. Video games can become their passion. They do not have to move their bodies to play and the fine-motor skills needed come with constant practice, which is encouraged by the motivation inherent in the game. The video game becomes a source of power and strength that is not available to the child physically or socially. They may revert to game fantasy when not actually playing, seeing the characters as friends with power who are in their control. The line between fantasy and reality may be tenuous, and the fantasy world may become a place to act out the hurt and inadequacy these children feel. As the child gets older, he usually has found ways to successfully avoid having to engage in motor skills, and becomes a "nerd." Also of note here is that children with low muscle tone may look "fatter" than other children and their avoidance of motor skills often leaves them physically inactive and less fit, which can exacerbate a weight problem. This can in turn lead to even less activity and more ostracism by peers.

So dyspraxia is more than a movement disorder; it affects all areas of the child's life. If symptoms of SI dysfunction are not diagnosed, many other inappropriate labels may be given to the child. If dyspraxia is diagnosed, the good news is that it can be treated at any age, even adulthood, by an occupational therapist. Participation in individual sports where the person competes against himself is also helpful. Swimming, karate, running, skiing, wrestling, dance, gymnastics—and even football for the heavy crashing—are examples of helpful activities. Basketball is a very poor choice as are soccer and baseball.

Sensory Defensiveness Issues

Sensory defensiveness results in a different array of problems for the individual. These problems are *totally unrelated to IQ*. No pattern has been delineated. SD appears across all levels of intelligence and presents the same way at all levels. Symptoms are dependent on severity, but some children have the adaptive ability to develop insight into the condition and develop compensatory strategies.

Treatment for SD includes a professional guided deep touch pressure/proprioception program and a sensory diet, and that sensory diet includes accessing modulating input such as deep touch pressure, heavy joint and muscle work, and rhythmic movement (balance/vestibular). Things that produce a condition of "neutral warmth" are also modulating. I like to define neutral warmth as that perfect temperature your bed gets to just before your alarm clock goes off in the morning. It is the light touch which most people find pleasant that negatively affects the individual with SD.

Sensory defensiveness, like dyspraxia, can be seen early. Many mothers, including myself, say that the baby was different even before birth. (My SD child was highly active in the womb and I felt her movement earlier than the other two.)

Babies with SD often have sleeping problems and do not seem able to calm themselves. They are often labeled "colicky." If they are gravitationally insecure (GI), diaper changing can be a problem as movement toward the back, as in placing the child on the changing table or in the crib, can trigger the GI. (Hugging the baby close to your body and moving with him—maintaining pressure as you lie him down—can help.) Some babies with GI cannot tolerate cribs because of the height and are much calmer sleeping on a mattress on the floor. One pediatrician, after reading my OT report on his patient, stated that he had felt a "qualitative difference" in some babies when he placed them on their backs for an exam, but did not understand it until he learned about gravitational insecurity. Babies with SD also may not like to be held and cuddled or might tolerate Mom and Dad but no one else. They may "arch away" when held and be unable to make or maintain eye contact (gaze aversion).

The clothing issues of individuals with SD first become apparent in infancy, and may continue throughout life, especially without treatment. Only a few examples of clothing issues will be given here. Children and adults with SD may be more comfortable in natural fibers (synthetic ones tend to break and "pick" at the skin). They may only tolerate clothes which have been washed many times, and may not tolerate tags in necks of shirts. They dislike anything tight or itchy around the head, face, chest, or stomach, the areas of the body which are the most sensitive to touch. It is very helpful and probably indicative of the increased stress, and therefore increased CNS arousal in our lives, that fashions are becoming more comfortable. For young people, tight jeans are out and in are overalls with waist buttons open, sweat- and windpants and big baggy pants falling off the hips (Janco's). Socks may be worn inside out to eliminate the poking of the seam. Soft fleeces and baggy T-shirts fill out the outfits. However, even with these changes, children with SD may be considered "losers" for wearing the same clothes every day (the only ones that feel totally comfortable), and mothers search for clothes that their children will wear because "they feel right" (a clue: secondhand shops are a good source for acceptable clothes and also eliminates the "new clothes smell" that can bother people with SD). As the children get older, they are labeled "individualistic" or "funky" for their styles, which can be positive with at least some peers.

Other issues around clothing may involve wanting to wear a jacket indoors, not because of being cold, but because the jacket provides neutral warmth and prevents light touch from reaching the skin. Baseball caps worn indoors are a similar sensory issue, but also a social one that has prompted school principals to make "no hat" rules. Heavy backpacks can provide joint and muscle work which will make the child with SD feel more modulated, but again, some schools have banned backpacks. Backpacks have gotten heavier as more and more physical activity is eliminated from children's days. Our bodies are made to do heavy work to relieve stress, so as we adults make the mistake of decreasing opportunities for heavy work, children provide their own.

Food may also be an issue, as the child with SD often limits food choice due to a dislike of the different textures. This oral defensiveness can be severe enough to compromise nutrition. Foods may be used as sensory diet. Qualities of foods which provide modulation include crunchy, resistive, sharp, sour, chewy, salty, and spicy.

Another issue in SD is the compulsivity that develops as a person attempts to keep his nervous system "safe" from overarousal. If the underlying level of arousal is kept near the normal range, the environmental surprises which overarouse individuals with SD will not push them over the edge. One way to keep that level down is to keep as many pieces as possible of one's life routine. Some persons with SD become compulsive in an attempt to feel safe. Quite early they train their parents not to change routines and not rearrange the furniture or move objects in their bedrooms. This can extend to "freaking out" if anyone touches their "stuff" in school, and becoming upset if the normal school schedule is changed even for a special event which they desire to attend. Birthday parties can be upsetting because a balloon might pop at any moment, and the "Happy Birthday" song is loud.

In the school situation, open classroom arrangements meant for exploratory learning can be very upsetting places for the child with SD. Hiding under desks or in corners is not unusual behavior if one is in danger. The problem is, no one else senses danger except the child with SD. Even lining up to move around the school can be perceived as dangerous because the child will be poked and bumped by other children. The only safe place to be is last in line, the place usually reserved for the child being punished.

Children with SD can be labeled as "noncompliant" for not wanting to engage in school activities that they perceive as dangerous, but we, from our own personal frame of reference of normalcy, see as fun. Things like finger painting, pasting, eating in the cafeteria, or even flushing the very loud school toilets can be difficult. Fidgeting or engaging in a repetitive movement like drumming pencils or silverware are common. "Inattentive" or "attention deficit" are also labels applied to persons with SD. SD should certainly be investigated as a contributing factor before the diagnosis of attention deficit is made.

Social issues arise with SD. Persons with SD may want to sit in booths or against the walls in restaurants or cafeterias, or might not want to go to the mall, all actions viewed as "weird" by peers.

Understanding social cues can be a problem. Social distance, teasing, horsing around, and feeling comfortable with social touch are misunderstood issues. In adolescents and adulthood, intimate touching can be perceived as dangerous (remember that much intimate touch is light touch, which can evoke a SD reponse), and the opportunity to discuss what feels safe does not present itself. Society is not yet recognizing SD as a significant issue and we are not good at talking about intimacy and good touch with each other. One adult with SD commented that she always had to have a heavy backrub before she could tolerate being intimate.

Other children often pick up on the vulnerability of the child with SD. Siblings without SD figure out that light touch can really irritate their brother or sister and that most parents will not understand that the light touch can be hurtful. When the child with SD defends himself by striking out, the sibling who touched lightly is not likely to be punished because our frame of reference tells us that light touch is pleasant. The child with SD is punished for striking out when he was only protecting himself. And his nervous system likes the heavy touch. Hitting and crashing his body into things modulates the "itchiness" of the light touch. So he cannot figure out what is happening, as he is often told that he could not be perceiving what indeed he is. He cannot trust his body to protect himself and he cannot trust people to understand and validate what his body feels. This is the perfect setup for emotional and behavioral problems and anger at siblings. One highly successful Ph.D. has never forgiven his sister for holding him down and tickling him as a child. He considered ticking to be torture, as do most persons with SD.

Anxiety attacks also should be investigated to rule out a basis in SD. A gifted college student started having anxiety attacks in the college cafeteria. They completely stopped in one day by paying attention to sensory diet issues. She resumed taking aerobic classes, sat with her back to the wall, ate more resistive foods, avoided very crowded times in the cafeteria, and if she felt any anxiety begin, she engaged in nonobtrusive heavy work like chair pushups, or pushing the heels of her hands together.

Persons with SD can also be sensory seekers, using the qualities of fast movement, heavy joint and muscle work, and heavy touch pressure to modulate their own nervous systems by providing a sensory diet. A high-level executive I know who has been diagnosed as SD spends most of his nonwork time engaged in sports. He skis hard on difficult bumpy trails every weekend all winter, wind surfs all summer, runs or bicycles long distances daily in between, and vacations by skiing, wind surfing, or helping on a relative's farm. His sensory diet must be intense, frequent, and long to modulate his SD, but he feels knowing about SD and how to use sensory diet has kept him from a mental-health diagnosis and has allowed him to succeed at his high-stress career.

If your child is a sensory seeker, the trick is to provide enough intensity safely, within the child's coordination abilities and judgment. There are as many examples of sensory defensive behavior as there are persons with SD. It is not the specific symptoms, but the influence they exert on the person's life that is important. Sensory diet ideas are also as varied; we have only described a few here. If you are SD or your child is SD, consulting with an occupational therapist will help you develop a treatment plan to fit your issues and your lifestyle.

Summary

Awareness of the issues in sensory defensiveness and sensory integration will increase understanding of the reasons people react the way they do. Gifted children experience enough difference; they do not need to have SD or SI issues misunderstood. Occupational therapy treatment can improve SD and SI problems, and make life much easier for these children and their families. Besides the motor and sensory issues, the increased self-esteem that accompanies treatment will help the gifted person realize his/her potential.

REFERENCES

Ayres, A. J. 1965. Patterns of perceptual-motor dysfunction in children: a factor analytic study. *Perceptual and Motor Skills* 20, 335–368.

———. 1966a. Interrelations among perceptual-motor abilities in a group of normal children. *American Journal of Occupational Therapy* 20, 288–292.

————. 1966b. Interrelations among perceptual-motor functions in children. *American Journal of Occupational Therapy* 20, 68–71.

————. 1969. Deficits in sensory integration in educationally handicapped children. *Journal of Learning Disabilities* 2, 160–168.

————. 1971. *Sensory Motor History.* Torrance, Calif.: Ayres Clinic.

————. 1972a. *Sensory Integration and Learning Disorders.* Los Angeles: Western Psychological Services.

————. 1972b. *Southern California Sensory Integration Tests Manual.* Los Angeles: Western Psychological Services.

————. 1972c. Improving academic scores through sensory integration. *Journal of Learning Disabilities* 5, 338–343.

————. 1972d. Types of sensory integrative dysfunction among disabled learners. *American Journal of Occupational Therapy* 26, 13–18.

————. 1975a. *Southern California Postrotary Nystagmus Test Manual.* Los Angeles: Western Psychological Services.

————. 1975b. Sensorimotor foundations of academic ability. In W. M. Cruickshand and D. P. Hallahan (eds.), *Perceptual and Learning Disabilities in Children,* vol. 2. Syracuse, N.Y.: Syracuse University Press.

Cermak, S.A. 1985. Developmental dyspraxia. In E. A. Roy (ed.), *Neuropsychological Studies of Apraxia and Related Disorders.* New York: North-Hollard.

————. 1991. Somotodyspraxia. In A. G. Fisher, E. A. Murray, and A. C. Burdy (eds.), *Sensory Integration Theory and Practice.* Philadelphia: F. A. Davis.

Clark, F. A., Z. Mailloux, and D. Parham. 1989. Sensory integration and children with learning disabilities. In P. N. Pratt and A. S. Allen (eds.), *Occupational Therapy for Children* (2nd ed.). St. Louis: C. V. Mosby.

Fisher, A. G. and W. Dunn. 1983. Tactile defensiveness: Historical perspectives, new research: A theory grows. *Sensory Integration Special Interest Section Newsletter* 6(2): 1–2.

Fisher, A. G., E. A. Murray, and A. C. Bundy. 1991. *Sensory Integration Theory and Practice.* Philadelphia: F. A. Davis.

Kimball, J. G. 1976. Vestibular stimulation and seizure activity. *Center for the Study of Sensory Integration Dysfunction Newsletter* (now Sensory Integration International), July, Torrance, CA.

————. 1977. Case history follow-up report. *Center for the Study of Sensory Integrative Dysfunction Newsletter* (now Sensory Integrative International), Torrance, CA.

————. 1986 Prediction of methylphenidate (ritalin) responsiveness through sensory integrative testing. *American Journal of Occupational Therapy* 40, 241–248.

————. (1988). Hypothesis for production of stimulant drug effectiveness utilizing sensory integrative diagnostic methods. *Journal of the American Osteopathic Association* 88, 757–762.

————. 1991. *Personal Care Records,* Scarborough, ME.

Wilbarger, P., and J. Wilbarger. 1991. *Sensory Defensiveness in Children 2–12.* Santa Barbara, Calif.: Avanti Education Programs.

Winner, E. 1998. Uncommon talents: Gifted children, prodigies and savants, *Scientific American* 9(4): 32–37.

ADMINISTRATIVE OPTIONS: WORKING TOGETHER

Boarding schools, private schools, home school, public education, charter schools: surely, somewhere there's a place for brilliant children who don't think between the lines. The strong academic curriculum of the boarding-school environment appealed to our family, but it comes at a price more emotional than financial. Boarding schools separate children from their parents at crucial developmental times. For some families, this separation may enhance their time together. I found that I wanted to live with my children, to experience their first dates, to have time to sit leisurely together reading. In many boarding schools, overworked teachers live with the teens they teach. Louis Crosier suggested in *Casualties of Privilege* that the house parents in boarding schools should consider that job to be their primary responsibility, and that exhausted, overworked teachers should not receive a free room in a dorm as part of their package. Teaching is a full-time job in itself, and most teenagers need some supervision. Once my research began, I was stunned by the amount of drug use, sexual activity, and physical violence that occurred in some boarding schools. Gifted children with special needs can become moving targets in that kind of environment, with no parents there to offer nurturing or emotional sustenance. Nonetheless, some students have found great happiness and success in the boarding-school environment, and have used the excellent academics there as a springboard to later adult achievement. Private, independent schools sometimes have smaller class sizes and innovative solutions.

Public schools suffer from overcrowding and all the minus signs that extend from the potent blend of too many children and not enough money, plus a need to adjust to legislative changes. The public schools must answer to the laws that govern them and the governmental bodies that control their funding. My children come from a long line of advocates for public schools; their father's Uncle Frank was known as the "Father of the Yellow School Bus" for his work in public education in rural areas. We want to believe in the attainability of a free, appropriate public education for everyone. At the same time, our children need smaller class sizes than most public schools can offer. Public schools also often opt for heterogeneous intellectual groupings, and teach to the middle, at the expense of educational growth for gifted students. Home school offers the greatest opportunity for individualization, but requires a strong time commitment from parents. These school representatives share their ideas of how to fix what's broken, and how to build on the strengths of existing systems and structures that work.

HELPING THE TWICE EXCEPTIONAL:
GIFTED TEENS WITH LEARNING DIFFERENCES

by Diane B. Cooper
Saint Edward's School
Vero Beach, Florida

Being a teenager is a daunting task under the best of circumstances. Being a teenager who is intellectually gifted increases the pressure on the emerging adult. However, being a teenager who is intellectually superior but who is also subjected to the challenges presented by a learning disability of some sort certainly places that student at risk for academic failure, emotional difficulties, and social problems. As the person who meets these adolescents on a daily basis, classroom teachers need to be aware that some children can have two apparently contradictory sets of learning needs: they are academically gifted and learning disabled at the same time. Inevitably, this double label brings a double disadvantage—a learning disability, which may mask their giftedness, or their giftedness, which may mask a learning disability. Thus some of these "twice-exceptional" students may be misjudged as just "average," and thus miss out on the special educational services necessary for them to realize their intellectual potential and bring them the intellectual and emotional satisfaction they deserve.

Since, in reality, classroom teachers interact with both identified and unidentified academically talented students, they need to learn how to spot gifted behavior despite the interference of a learning disability and need to understand what strategies to use, once that identification has been made. Unfortunately, though, deficiencies in the academically talented student with learning disabilities are more apparent in the classroom than are the abilities. Thus, while teachers need to focus on strengthening the area of weakness, they also need to allow special talents to bloom. To help a student become successful in school, the teacher needs to search for strengths as well as to pinpoint weaknesses. For example, Josh, an eighth grader with severe dyslexia, seemed headed for social ostracism and unmitigated unhappiness until the journalism teacher noticed his interest in and talent for photography. She began to give him photo assignments for the yearbook and for the various school publicity needs. He still experiences challenge from his learning disability, but he has a tremendous talent for photography and is receiving widespread praise and recognition for his skill. That emotional boost is helping him keep going in the classroom where life remains difficult, but where he is finding success because he feels good about himself. Teenagers, particularly, need to be approached from many angles in order to develop confidence and pride in their work.

Classroom teachers, especially at the secondary level, frequently make the understandable mistake of confusing an LD/gifted child with an underachiever, because the characteristics are almost identical. For example, gifted kids may be restless and physically active when the tasks they are asked to perform do not capture their interest. Their intensity often leads them into confrontations with authority because they need to be given a good reason to conform. Also, their apparent daydreaming may actually be independent contemplation of complex and creative scenarios. Often, they may even present totally different personas in different situations. They may be socially inept with classmates, yet totally charming with adults, or vice versa. They may be restless and antsy in the classroom, yet sit for hours at a computer. They may be sarcastic and sullen at school, yet compassionate and loving at home.

If a student who exhibits these kinds of behavior is professionally identified as having LD, ADD, or ADHD, the resultant danger is that his or her giftedness may go unnoticed and unattended, because the deficit label will tend to overshadow the giftedness. However, the gifted behavior still will be observable, for example, when a student takes a simple learning task and makes it more complex.

Generally speaking, most gifted students are not learning disabled. Gifted students who *do* have LD can be identified by:

- Extremely uneven academic skills which cause the student to appear unmotivated;
- Noticeable discrepancies between the scores on verbal and nonverbal sections of ability tests;
- Auditory and/or visual processing problems which cause responses, work, and thought processes to appear slow, evidenced by difficulty explaining or expressing ideas and feelings, while often talking around the subject;
- Problems with motor skills, demonstrated by clumsiness, poor handwriting, and difficulty completing paper/pencil tasks;
- Problems with both long- and short-term memory tasks;
- Weak organizational and study skills, resulting in messy and disorganized work;
- Avoidance of many school tasks, causing incomplete homework assignments;
- Issues in self-esteem as shown by anger, put-downs, crying, disruptive behaviors, and apathy;
- Extreme frustration with and dislike of school.

If a student seems particularly frustrated with, challenged by, or uninterested in an intellectually appropriate task, or if you observe unusual discrepancies among specific functions, such as reading and speaking or writing and speaking, you should consider a referral for investigation of learning disabilities according to your school policies.

There is much a middle or high school classroom teacher can do to help a gifted teen who has learning disabilities. First and most important, teach the child and not the ability or the disability. Most gifted children crave the recognition of an adult mentor and flourish when someone takes an interest in them as human beings as well as students. Second, find out what the student knows already and give full credit for that knowledge. Third, find out what he or she is passionately interested in outside of school and allow the student to work on related projects in school. For example, if you are an English teacher and you have a student who is obsessed with marine biology, have her read *Moby Dick* while others in the class are reading *Billy Budd.* Then ask her to share information about whales, their habitat and behaviors, and provide an evaluation of the accuracy of the descriptions of the whale and of the hunter in the novel. Fourth, allow the student to express what he knows in ways compatible with his learning style. If handwriting is a problem, allow use of the computer. If visual presentations are his strength, be sure to provide opportunities to debate.

Strategies for Teaching the Gifted/LD Adolescent

To teach students successfully who are both gifted and learning disabled, the teacher can employ specific techniques which feed into the student's basic learning preferences, with an emphasis on strength rather than weakness. These techniques which follow are valuable for almost all students who struggle academically, regardless of their particular gifts or disabilities.

Give choices

The most powerful motivator for gifted students in any classroom is to consistently have meaningful choices. The easiest choices relate to what students will learn, how they will learn, and how they will express what they learned. For example, if you are studying the Tudor years in English history, you may say, "You can learn about the economic, the social, or the religious issues of the day and how they affected the succession to the throne." Then you might say, "You can either use the Internet, reference books, or videos to gather your information." Then you might say, "You can write a report, prepare a PowerPoint presentation, or make a comic strip which demonstrates what you have learned." The product can be as simple or as sophisticated as is appropriate for the subject and the maturity of the learners. When gifted/LD students can produce something other than a written report, they will often work at surprisingly high levels of cognition.

Make connections to real life

When gifted/LD students are given exciting and relevant material to learn, most of their reluctance and resistance to learning disappears. Their natural intellectual curiosity supersedes their learning hurdles and they involve themselves with the material. All students, but particularly gifted students, get more enjoyment from work that they perceive as relevant, with an emphasis on interpretive thinking and problem solving. Projects can range from a local issue such as traffic or pollution to global concerns such as the ozone layer or overpopulation. One such student, Tom, a junior in high school, compiled a strategy for solving a problem the town was having with traffic flow. He presented his analysis to the town council via slides as the culmination of his project. His ideas were well received, and the council implemented some of them.

Group work also is often effective because it allows the gifted/LD student to contribute his or her superior cognitive skills to the project, while someone who is more skilled at writing or reading can complete that part of the task.

Develop goal-setting skills

Probably one of the most important differences between successful adults and unsuccessful adults is the ability to define and set realistic goals. Students who are unsuccessful either don't set goals, or they set such lofty goals that they are doomed to fail. It is extremely important to teach gifted/LD students that success is not measured by grades or by GPA. Success, instead, hinges on setting and reaching goals. When a student masters that skill, success follows naturally.

One effective way to teach goal setting in a classroom is to break the class period down into segments. Ask the student to predict how much of whatever task you are assigning to the rest of the class they can complete in ten minutes. For example, you have asked the class to learn twenty vocabulary words, giving them practice exercises to complete during the class period and for homework. Ask the student to write down how many words he thinks he can do in that segment. He may say three, so he writes 3/20. At the end of the ten minutes, check with him. If he has, in fact, completed three of the twenty, ask, "What was your goal? Did you accomplish your goal? Who was responsible for completing your goal? How does it feel to complete your goal?" Then let him set another goal for the next segment.

If he did not complete his goal, ask, "What was the goal? Did you accomplish your goal? What plan can you make for the next task to keep the same problem from happening again?" Keep a record of the predictions or goals and the outcomes. Review the record on a weekly basis with the student and seek areas for praise and areas for improvement. For example, one student had terrible difficulty keeping up with his homework assignments. The goal we set was to write down the assignment each day. Once he achieved that goal, the next goal was to put each homework assignment in the designated folder as soon as it was completed. He accomplished that goal with only minor setbacks. Once we both felt that the two behaviors were now habits, then we went on to set the next goal of organizing the backpack each evening according to the schedule for the following day and leaving it beside the back door. This way he would set out for school in the morning already organized, knowing he had his homework and knowing where it was. These simple goals reduced everyone's stress, and his grades rose, hand-in-hand with his sense of accomplishment.

Have your student work on only one area or subject at a time until progress is evident and the student is finding satisfaction from meeting goals regularly. If you add too many subjects too fast, the student may develop a fear of success, thinking: Adults always expect too much of me if I am successful, so I won't do much and they won't expect much.

At the secondary level, undoing habits of negative self-talk and performance take time and require patience on everyone's part. Some of these habits have been part of the student's attitude and manner for years and will be difficult to remedy. Keep practicing positive self-talk, focusing the locus of control for success on the student, rather than on external influences.

Overcome learned helplessness

Successful learners see a relationship between having exerted sufficient effort and success and insufficient effort and the resultant failure. Students who exhibit learned helplessness create a self-protecting set of reasons for whatever happens, all of which gives control to an external force. "I failed that test because the teacher didn't explain it well." Often, even when the student is successful, he attributes his success to "the teacher helped me with it." It is important to teach teenagers to evaluate each success and each failure by training them in positive "self-talk." Write out, rehearse, and use statements such as "I did well on that test because I studied hard and used good study strategies." "I did poorly on that project because the strategies I used didn't work, so I will use a different plan the next time." Then help them outline exactly what it is *THEY* did that was successful or unsuccessful and set goals for the future work. Particularly with teenagers, accepting responsibility for failure does not come easily. With Anna, who was notorious for making excuses, I wrote out the above statements and had her copy them on a notecard that she kept taped to her notebook. Each time she met success or failure, I had her read the appropriate response to me. Within a short time, she was verbalizing her analysis without prompting and was much less likely to blame or praise someone else's efforts for her results.

Design project-based learning

Project-based learning has the potential to "turn on" turned-off students. The same objectives or outcomes can be taught via projects as can be accomplished by traditional teacher-centered classrooms. While some teachers worry that LD students need more controlled learning, not less, in fact, gifted/LD students exhibit the best control when they are allowed to immerse themselves in what they are learning. When they can become cognitively engaged, many behavior problems decrease or disappear. The key to project-based learning is to give the gifted/LD student a planner, which forces him to outline the project and give a step-by-step procedure, including the topic, the subtopics, the sources of information to be researched, and a explanation of the final product. If the teacher does this organizational work carefully, the gifted/LD student will most likely be highly successful in completing the project and will experience a strong sense of accomplishment.

The teacher in these cases must help the student locate and collect sources of information about the topic, provide a place in the classroom for the student to store the information collected, teach the student to look through one source at a time, and record important facts, phrases, and sentences on paper or notecards. Then the teacher should help the student prepare a timeline for completion of the project. To plan the timeline, many gifted/LD students benefit from moving backward from the due date, planning each step from last to first.

Finally, the teacher should help students select a method of presenting whatever it is they have learned. Whenever possible, avoid assigning written reports to students with language disabilities. Instead allow the student to use slides, transparencies, PowerPoint, or other visual presentations. If it must be a written project, encourage the student to do the work on the computer for ease in transcription and editing. Once the work begins, the student should give an oral progress report every day or so to ensure continued meeting of goals. Finally, set a time limit for the presentations, because gifted students who are enthralled by their topic may go on forever if permitted. If the student feels cheated by the time limit, suggest a private meeting time with you to share what other information he or she may have gained.

Allow group responses

When a teacher asks a question and gets a response from a student, all you really know is whether that student knows the answer. By using a variety of group responses, the teacher connects more students to the learning and can also better evaluate the success of the lesson.

There are many familiar ways to do this, ranging from hand signals to colored cards to individual chalkboards. Other less well-known options include "Turn and Tell" and "Fluency Partners." Both techniques are especially effective with secondary students and adult learners.

With "Turn & Tell," students are paired up with someone sitting in close proximity. The teacher, wishing to reinforce a concept or to check understanding, instructs the students to turn to their partner and, taking turns, tell one, two, three, etc., concepts or ideas or facts, that they have learned in the class so far. Usually allowing only two or three minutes provides a sense of urgency and invites more rapid involvement. The teacher uses a signal for returning the students' attention to the teacher to continue the instruction.

With "Fluency Partners," students, using the same partner as in "T&T," are asked to tell their partner in thirty seconds or one minute or whatever time is appropriate, everything he or she heard discussed that day in class. Once the first student's time is up, the other partner begins, and must tell what he or she learned and without repeating anything the first partner said. This activity sharpens listening skills, and reinforces learning through both auditory and verbal practice.

Once students become comfortable with these techniques, they will be able to move quickly into and out of the activity. During the exchanges, the teacher should walk around, listening for misinformation or lack of understanding that she can then address with the whole group.

Use technology

The effective use of technology in the classroom narrows the gap between potential and performance, especially for gifted students with learning challenges. Research shows that student enthusiasm and motivation to learn increases dramatically when technology is used effectively. Students need to learn how to use technology in the same way they learn everything else, through direct teaching that includes practice in thinking out loud. It is important to provide coaching so the gifted/LD student does not become as frustrated with technology as he has with other more traditional types of learning methods. Such tools as word processors, calculators, small electronic organizers, cassette players, CD-ROMs, laser videodiscs, and the Internet are all real-world assists to the learning process and open untold opportunities for gifted students. Christine, who suffered from severe dysgraphia, yet who had marvelous, creative ideas, found her freedom from written failure by using her computer, with the essential spell-check function. Her grades improved tremendously once she began taking tests, doing homework, and taking notes on the computer. She became willing to expand on her ideas, to edit and proofread, and to share her written work with others. Simply by using a machine, she was able to unlock her talents for poetry and short stories.

Miscellaneous Strategies to Enhance Learning

Teaching mapping

A map is a visual organizer which allows students to visualize and order information which may be inaccessible to them strictly through the written word. Mapping is a learning tool which may take the form of graphic organizers, mind maps, flowcharts, timelines, diagrams, cartoons, pictures, Venn diagrams, webs, or any format that helps the student to create a mental picture of the relationships among pieces of information. There are many sources available to stimulate mapping and it is a powerful study tool for gifted/ LD students. Teaching gifted/LD students to use such visual clues can make a tremendous difference in their success.

Teach Chunking

This technique simply reduces the pressure on short-term memory. Students arrange the material to be memorized into small groups and learn the material in that small group. For example, vocabulary words can be broken into subsets with the student learning only three out of fifteen each night. Those three are repeated until the student has mastered them. The next night, three more are mastered.

Create routines and promote the use of a checklist

When it comes to daily routines, make your classroom as predictable and consistent as possible. Begin with a one- or two-item sequence of steps, and then expand it slowly. So, to the gifted/LD student, instead of saying "Close your book, open your notebook, get out your pen, and answer the first five questions on page 100," the teacher would say, "Close your book and open your notebook." Pause. "Take out your pen." Pause. "Answer questions 1 to 5 in your notebook." Eventually, once that sequence becomes routine, the teacher can lengthen the number of directions given to the student.

Another method that reinforces predictability is preparation of a checklist with the student, which the student keeps at his desk. The checklist sequences the steps in the normal routines followed during the day. The teacher keys the student about three minutes before the end of the activity to start working through the checklist. For example, for a routine at the end of class, the checklist may say: (1) Write your name on your paper. (2) Put your homework in the blue folder. (3) Copy today's homework from the board into your assignment notebook. (4) Close your book and notebook and put them in your bag.

Then, when the rest of the class has automatically completed the transition to the next activity, the gifted/LD student will also have completed the transition by working through the checklist. This method also works well in doing homework, placing homework in folders, in gathering books to go home at the end of the day, and in all other routine areas of school life. It is a lifesaver for the student who struggles with organization and greatly reduces stress for everyone. The student should help create the checklists being used and should have time to practice using them, initially with the teacher's or parent's help.

In Summary

Since the learning difficulties of teenaged gifted/LD students are often a combination of boredom and frustration, a lethal condition for learning, middle and high school teachers need to provide alternate learning experiences, instead of relying solely on the work assigned to the midrange student. When these strategies are put into practice, behavior problems and underachievement will greatly diminish.

Teachers need to be aware that, while it may be human nature to expect less of children with disabilities of any kind, such a response severely limits those children from reaching their optimum learning potential. Teachers must take care not to reduce a child to a physical or learning disability condition or to isolate the child in some way solely because of the disability. Neither giftedness nor physical difficulties nor learning disabilities define the child's totality or dictate a child's character, needs, and interests.

Gifted students, particularly, need sufficient intellectual stimulation in order to reach their potential and to make the contributions to society that they are capable of making. If the presence of a learning challenge inhibits the intellectual productivity, the caring and informed teacher can make an enormous difference in the life of a young adult by providing avenues for success.

All professionals who interact with adolescents should remember that the developmental tasks of adolescence are no less challenging for gifted students than for children of normal capabilities. For the student with the double label of gifted/LD, the developmental tasks are often much more challenging. It is evident, therefore, that, in spite of all that is unknown about gifted/LD teens and their educational needs, it remains necessary to examine and to evaluate the programs set before them. Importantly, one teacher *can* make the difference between the smiling image of a student having a satisfying and successful high school career or the sad picture of a person diminished emotionally, with an exceptional intellect unfulfilled.

DUAL EXCEPTIONALITIES IN THE INDEPENDENT SCHOOL

by Tristram Dodge Wood
The Peddie School,
Hightstown, New Jersey

To say that independent schools are relatively new to the field of special education, specifically to working with students who have dual exceptionalities, would be to ignore many of the most successful and most challenging students to have walked our halls. Perhaps they were called "odd," "eccentric," "rambunctious," "hyperactive," or "lazy and unmotivated," but students have been showing us the signs of the gifted/learning disabled since we have had open doors and charged tuition. The question that should be asked, though, is are we serving them, or are we continuing to ignore a population that helps fill our classrooms but usually alternates between driving us to fits of frustration and demonstrating to us the kind of true genius that makes us beam with awe?

I have worked in independent secondary schools for fifteen years, and each year a handful of students have sat in front of me and presented the challenge of students with dual exceptionalities. My first four years were spent working at a school specifically for students who are bright but have dyslexia; since then I have worked at two "traditional" independent schools in New England, and my office and classroom are consistently populated with these challenging and exciting students. These students or ones like them must have been sitting in our classrooms since the beginning of formal education. If these students—the ones who will sit in the back of the classroom and seem to be totally engrossed in their notebook art until you call on them and they can recite, verbatim, your question, the correct answer, and how it relates to an obscure reference that was not offered nor requested, or who can sit and look directly at you while you ask them to do the simplest of tasks and then do something totally different—if they have always been in our classrooms, are we helping them become better students? Are we helping them become better advocates for themselves, better managers of time, better self-editing writers, and better analytical readers, or are we continuing to ignore them because clearly they are "bright" and can understand enough to pass through to the next grade, section, or class?

In my experience working with students who have these exceptionalities, I have found several factors that effect their overall success in school. The first factor is diagnosis or identification. Too often, I have students coming in to my office who have been honor roll students at their previous schools, yet they demonstrate clear signs of having a learning disability. Too often these students slip through the cracks in our system because they are smart, talented, verbally agile, charismatic, or just too quiet to draw our attention to their difficulties. I have found that students who are identified early, through sensitive and astute parents or talented teachers, have the greatest chance for success. They are given the opportunity to develop the strategies they need to survive. They get the kind of support both from schools and families that is needed for them to realize their potential. When we fail to notice and identify students with dual exceptionalities, we often handcuff them in a routine of difficulty and frustration.

Even if students with giftedness and learning disabilities are not identified early, they are not necessarily destined for failure. On the contrary, many students with unidentified learning disabilities develop on their own the compensation strategies that help them overcome their areas of weakness. For some this means avoiding the more difficult math or English classes. For others it means using memorization as a foundation for learning. The variations are endless, but often, due to their cognitive abilities, these young men and women are able to fool us by compensating. These are the students whom we hardly ever hear about. They slide through our educational system, getting high-honors grades in some classes and getting barely passing grades in others. They gravitate toward certain areas of expertise, like computers, the sciences, or poetry. Some even move into technical areas like mechanics, drafting, or art. Regardless of their weaknesses, they get by with some camouflage and some creative course selections. But for our purposes, there are still far too many kids who slip through the cracks. They get to the secondary-school level with unidentified or undetected gaps in their learning abilities.

I worked with a student (I'll call him Abe) who came to our school as a junior from a local public high school. Abe had always received good grades, but he struggled with the amount of reading and writing in our curriculum. After a term of struggling and failing, we agreed that there may be something going on in his learning profile, and an educational evaluation might give us a better idea of his strengths and weaknesses, and why our curriculum was beating him up. When his results came back, they showed that Abe had dyslexia and an overall IQ in the 130s. Several teachers had used the term "limited" when referring to this young man, and yet nothing was further from the truth. Perhaps his difficulty was masked by his previous schools' curriculum, and Peddie's work load of reading and writing exposed something that had always been there, just not on the surface.

The second factor in determining overall success for students with dual exceptionalities is guidance. In my experience, there have been numerous students with dual exceptionalities who have not been diagnosed until they hit the rigors of a more demanding curriculum. Even so, these young men and women were able to develop the strategies they needed to survive and learn, in many cases to the point where to develop further compensation strategies would have been undermining what they had already developed. I find that what gets them to this point is guidance. Usually, a teacher, coach, or parent has taken them under their wing and helped them find ways around their difficulties. These students often get evaluated and identified because of this guidance.

Once we had the results on Abe, we had a clearer idea of how to help him and what he was capable of achieving with accommodations in the classroom and in his study regiment. For Abe, the use of a laptop computer for writing assignments and extra time on tests were provided. At the same time, after a term of feeling inadequate—possibly longer since most students with dual exceptionalities know acutely what their limitations are—Abe was finally able to know that he was smart. Unfortunately, the information and accommodations came so late that to apply to college without further improving upon his weaknesses was considered ill advised. He decided to do a postgraduate year at another independent school with a specialized program for students with learning disabilities and is now a freshman at a selective private college in the Northeast.

A third factor in the success of gifted/LD students is how comfortable they are with their diagnosis. I have worked with students on both ends of the spectrum. Some show the visible sigh of relief that suggests they finally have an answer to why they have always struggled with reading but were able to do calculus in the ninth grade. At the other end are those students who are so entrenched in our paradigms that they cannot break free of the notion that it is impossible to be smart and learning disabled at the same time. They deny this possibility, pretending that nothing has changed, and continue on. Usually, though, they come back after reflecting, sometimes over the course of a year or more, and are open to trying different techniques to help them be more successful. Usually, they return because they can no longer handle the level of work with their preexisting compensation strategies. This is the biggest group of students I work with. They know they are smart but are not comfortable with their differences. I spend a lot of time working with them so that they see that "intelligence" is not a static measure.

I had another student, Beth, who came to our school with no learning evaluation but with all of the signs of an auditory processing problem. After a year of working with her on study skills and time management, I realized that there was more going on than just poor study skills. After having her tested, my suspicions were confirmed by a diagnosis of ADD, combined with an auditory processing disorder related to a previously unknown hearing loss. She ignored the difficulty for a while, but finally came back to my office when her studies started to suffer.

Students with learning disabilities are usually sorely lacking in basic study skills and time management. These students are frequently so used to their own system that when they come to a problem that they are not prepared to handle, they have considerable difficulty. This is particularly true in independent schools, where increased reading and writing loads often cause students initial difficulty. If the student with dual exceptionalities has a gap in his or her skills, the chasm becomes apparent quickly.

The conflict that students have between skill development and intellectual challenge raises an opinion that I have about dual exceptionalities. Again, my experience suggests that to go back and do remedial work with a student who is gifted and has learning disabilities is almost impossible. I say this not because I think remedial work wouldn't help, which in most cases I think it would, but that to be so bright and to have to work at such a simple level is too difficult for most students. For us to force students to relearn remedial strategies is like trying to make a professional baseball player hit with a t-ball stand. Yet, if we can find a way to provide remediation to students in such a way that they are not either insulted or bored with the level at which they must work, we can give them some of the tools they need to find more success.

One way to do this is to have students work in their area of weakness, stressing the remedial while simultaneously having them translate it to higher levels. For example, we can accomplish this balance of remedial and high-level work by having a student read a challenging book aloud. While reading a sentence or two, the student should stop to isolate the difficult phonology, but also be asked questions involving higher-level thinking and deeper levels of literary meaning, such as why a character makes a certain decision, or why an author uses a specific literary technique. By layering the remedial with the sophisticated, students might be more inclined to continue to learn the remedial levels needed while seeing the connection between the remedial and the sophisticated. Another way to do remedial work is to work with students on scaffolding and developing metacognitive strategies. By thinking about the framework that we use to learn and looking more closely at "how we think about how we think," we can develop skills and strategies that challenge without becoming too basic. For example, by helping students isolate aspects of reading that are difficult and then asking them why, they can gain a greater understanding of themselves and a clearer sense of what they need to do to improve. While these techniques can be time consuming and require some dynamic planning and a solid understanding of the students' needs, the rewards are better prepared students who more consistently demonstrate their true potential in school.

Where do independent schools fit into how we work with students with dual exceptionalities? While we may boast of having a more formidable curriculum than most public schools, we do not have the kind of support that most public school systems have. In fact, many independent schools do not even have a teacher or administrator who coordinates services for students with learning disabilities. Yet while public schools have the staff and flexibility to support their students with dual exceptionalities, most do not have the rigorous curriculum and creative work loads that challenge a truly gifted student. As a result, while they would likely get the support they need, students with dual exceptionalities would likely not be pushed to discover their true potential.

Conversely, independent schools have the kind of demanding and accelerated curriculum that consistently attracts the best students. Independent schools have always been accessible for the affluent, but recently more middle income students have been making the move to independent schools for this very reason. With the increase in some schools' financial aid and the government's involvement with school vouchers, this makes the move that much easier. Yet are we better equipped to help students with dual exceptionalities? One advantage that independent schools, particularly boarding schools, have over our public school system is the notion that we can control large chunks of a student's time, thus creating opportunities that do not exist after 3:15 PM in the public sector. Two-hour mandatory study halls each night, with study halls during the day, and afternoon extra-help sessions create the kind of assistance from which most students with dual exceptionalities would benefit. Additionally, teachers who are also dormitory masters, coaches, and advisers can create a system where the cracks are rather small.

Are there downsides to independent schools? Absolutely. Independent school is cost prohibitive. Many teachers in independent schools have little formal education in teaching. Very few have any background in working with students with learning disabilities. This lack of background in learning disabilities and giftedness creates both a challenge and an opportunity. The challenge is to educate teachers in the concept of best practice and how to effectively work with students who are bright but have limitations. Since most teachers are masters of their subject, they are certainly knowledgeable of what the curriculum entails, yet many need help in learning the "craft" of teaching, specifically how to create learning experiences that engage everyone in their room without creating obstacles for the student with learning disabilities. This requires flexibility in the teaching faculty. It also creates the opportunity for teachers to expand their teaching repertoire and develop the ability to create this valuable learning experience. I attended a workshop on the seven intelligences and was amazed by the number of teachers who only taught to one or two. In my experience, teachers will give the extra support that these students need when they comprehend a rational reason for making changes.

Students with dual exceptionalities are not going away. In fact, with the advances in our ability to identify these students, their numbers are increasing. Thus, it makes sense that we serve them well, providing the kind of support they need to reach their potential. If we fail to do this, choosing instead to fall back on our past history of ignorance and denial, we run the risk of neglecting some of the most creative, gifted, and interesting students in our schools.

A COLLABORATIVE APPROACH TO MEETING THE NEEDS OF TWICE-EXCEPTIONAL STUDENTS

by Beverly Trail
Littleton Public Schools

Parents and educators in Littleton Public Schools recognized that there existed a unique population of students with bright inquisitive minds struggling to succeed in the regular classroom. These twice-exceptional students shared characteristics of both gifted students and students with learning disabilities. They had outstanding potential for learning and leadership. The learning disabilities of the twice-exceptional student often went undetected because the giftedness masked the disability. At other times, the disability masked the giftedness. Recognizing the students' special talents, identifying their learning difficulties, and providing services help twice-exceptional students to achieve their highest potential.

Supporters of gifted education in Littleton realized the need to initiate programming services for these twice-exceptional students, and began focusing district attention on this special population. The Littleton Association for Gifted and Talented Students provided a forum for prominent speakers in the field of gifted education to discuss issues related to underachievement. In 1996, the school board approved a charge from the LPS Gifted and Talented Advisory Council to investigate issues related to underachieving gifted students. The g/t facilitators, parents, and administrators began a three-year investigation of the needs of twice-exceptional students and what could be done to fulfill those needs. This investigation led to the development and implementation of programming options and strategies to meet the needs of underachieving gifted students.

Littleton used a collaborative approach to meet the needs of twice-exceptional students. The collaborative team identified the students' strengths, weaknesses, and interests. The team then developed a personal learning plan and implemented programming and teaching strategies. Intervention strategies were based on the unique needs of the individual student. A g/t facilitator, special education resource teacher, classroom teacher, parents, school psychologist, and other specialists comprised the collaborative team. Both special education and gifted education teachers supported classroom teachers. Programming services utilized existing staff in a collaborative effort. Case studies documented the characteristics, profiles, intervention strategies, and progress of each student.

Student Characteristics

Twice-exceptional students in Littleton had a wide range of interests and an impressive background of information on many subjects. They had a superior vocabulary and when interested articulated ideas and opinions beyond their years. Many enjoyed the challenge of solving difficult mathematical puzzles and demonstrated high-level problem-solving abilities. These twice-exceptional students were highly creative, curious, imaginative, and questioning. Although they had many of the characteristics of gifted students, they often appeared unmotivated and frequently failed to complete assignments. Classroom teachers wondered why these bright students were failing in school.

The strengths of the twice-exceptional case study students were accompanied by disabling weaknesses that negatively impacted their school performance. It was hard to understand why a verbally gifted student could not put his/her thoughts on paper, or a mathematically gifted student could not do the simpler math computations. Because the students had a broad background of knowledge and readily comprehended complex issues, it was easy to understand why teachers and parents mistakenly assumed they were unmotivated or lazy. These students also manifested characteristics of students with learning disabilities. Littleton's case study students had difficulty with written expression, lacked organizational and study skills, and were frustrated easily.

The discrepancy between the strengths and weaknesses puts this population at risk for failure and emotional problems (Baum, Owens, and Dixon, 1991; Beckley, 1998; Nielsen, Higgins, and Wilkinson, 1994; 1992; Silverman, 1993; Van Tassel-Baska, 1991). For the Littleton twice-exceptional student, the discrepancy between their abilities was significant. This discrepancy resulted in inconsistent academic performance, which was frustrating for teacher, parents, and the case study students. These students were very aware when they were not performing at a comparable level with classmates. Consequently, the twice-exceptional students perceived themselves as failures. They avoided school tasks, were frequently off-task, and often became behavior problems in the classroom. When working in their area of weakness, feelings of frustration along with a heightened sense of inefficacy sometimes resulted in aggressive behavior.

Student Profiles

The collaborative teams developed profiles of each case study student based on all available information. The school psychologists and resource teachers provided background information and results of comprehensive testing. A variety of assessments were used to identify strengths and areas of weakness for case study students, including psychological and achievement tests like the Wechsler Intelligence Scale for Children–Third Edition, the Woodcock-Johnson Revised, and the Wechsler Individual Achievement Test. Additional assessments measured specific skills in written language, auditory discrimination, skill mastery tests, and social inventories. As the collaborative team listed the strengths, weaknesses, and interests of each individual student, a number of similarities became apparent.

Scores on the Wechsler Intelligence Scale for Children showed significant discrepancy between the various subtests. The discrepancy between combined scores in both verbal and performance varied between students. One student had a thirty-three-point discrepancy between verbal and performance scores, while another student had only a five-point discrepancy. The discrepancy of five points between the verbal and performance scores appeared insignificant. For this student, however, significant discrepancies existed between the individual subtest scores within both the verbal and performance areas. His verbal subtest scores ranged from eighteen in vocabulary to a low in digit span where an accurate score could not be obtained because the student's frustration level was so high. Performance subtest scores ranged from an eighteen on object assembly to a nine in coding.

On average, case study students had a discrepancy between subtest scaled scores of eleven points, with an average high subtest score of eighteen and an average low subtest score of seven. Average scores were highest in the subtest of block design and lowest in the subtest of digit span. The block design subtest measured the student's ability to analyze and synthesize an abstract design. The digit span subtest measured short-term verbal memory of digits with no logical relationship to each other. Most case study students had difficulties with the coding subtest that requires perceptual organization, fine-motor dexterity, speed, accuracy, and ability to manipulate a pencil (Nicholson and Alcorn, 1994).

Profiles of Littleton case study students supported published research data. Researchers had found that twice-exceptional students were generally strong in abstract holistic tasks and much weaker in tasks involving sequencing and memorizing isolated facts (Baum, et al., 1991). Investigations by Schiff, Kaufman, and Kaufman (1981) concluded that gifted students with learning disabilities had above-average verbal comprehension and numerous creative talents.

They also had weaknesses in the cognitive area of sequencing, motor coordination activities, and emotional development. Waldron and Sapire (1990) found these students tended to depend on visual skills for word recognition and analysis, and they had weaknesses in auditory areas, such as sound discrimination and short-term memory. The students were able to conceptualize quickly, to see patterns and relationships readily, to reason abstractly, to generalize easily, and to enjoy the challenge of solving novel problems autonomously. They had difficulties with basic automatic skills such as graphomotor speed, sequencing, organization, and study skills (Barton and Starnes, 1989).

Littleton twice-exceptional students frequently failed to complete homework assignments. Incomplete assignments resulted in poor grades. When an assignment was personally interesting, the student would work very hard on the project. Even these assignments, however, were handed in late or never completed. Organization, time management, and procrastination were problem areas for all the students in the study. Frequently, completed homework was not an adequate representation of the student's depth of knowledge. Their homework often appeared sloppy and hastily thrown together. For many identified twice-exceptional students, writing was a slow, laborious process.

Procrastination and perfectionism often went hand in hand for case study students. They were highly sensitive to criticism and frequently commented on issues of fairness. These students were often very stubborn, opinionated, and argumentative. High expectations of parents, teachers, and the underachieving students themselves resulted in high levels of frustration for everyone involved. The perfectionist student felt they had to get everything right, and they put enormous pressure on themselves to be perfect. Procrastination served as an insurance policy for the perfectionist. The students put things off until the last minute then reasoned they could not be expected to do a perfect job if there was not enough time. For the perfectionist, fear of failure was so strong it could be very debilitating (Adderholdt-Elliott, 1987). One Littleton case study student was so afraid of failure that he was unable to function in the classroom. For this student the slightest hint of failure sent him into an uncontrollable tantrum.

Strategies for Twice-Exceptional Learners

The Littleton collaborative teams selected intervention and teaching strategies appropriate for their students. They developed a personal learning plan that would challenge the students in their areas of strength and help them compensate for areas of weaknesses. The g/t facilitators made sure the student was challenged and successful in their strength areas. Special education resource teachers monitored homework and worked with students in small groups to improve skills. Together, they helped the classroom teacher provide the structure and strategies twice-exceptional students needed to be successful. The team worked to make the classroom experience a successful one for the student by implementing these general strategies:

Focus attention on the development of the student's potential.

- Help students develop their strengths and bypass their disabilities.
- Provide open-ended assignments so students can use their strengths to demonstrate their true abilities.
- Encourage the use of higher-level thinking and problem-solving skills.
- Help students learn the skills necessary to become independent lifelong learners.
- Encourage students to take responsibility for their own learning.

Provide a nurturing environment that values individual differences.

- Honor and respect individual differences and learning styles.
- Avoid emphasis on competition and grades.
- Promote success as the ability to achieve realistic short-term goals.
- View mistakes as a valued part of learning.
- Help students maintain dignity and self-worth.

Teach so students can learn.

- Never teach an entire lesson in one modality; include multisensory and multi-modality approaches.
- Teach to complement students' learning styles.
- Modify worksheets and assignments when necessary.
- Teach to multiple intelligences instead of traditional academic intelligences.
- Relate new information to previously learned information.
- Group and regroup students in small clusters for learning so instruction can match student needs.

Be flexible and individualize the curriculum.

- Allow students to vary assignments and projects to utilize strengths when demonstrating knowledge.
- Differentiate the curriculum according to individual needs and learning styles of students.
- Use alternative methods of assessment that allow students to show what they have learned.

- Provide extra time for assignments and tests for students who process information slower.
- Provide multiple resources for learning and independent study.
- Use a flexible structure and encourage independence.

Remove barriers to learning and encourage compensation strategies.

- Find sources of information that are appropriate for students.
- Provide organizers to help students process and communicate information.
- Use technology to promote productivity.
- Offer a variety of options and opportunities for communicating ideas.
- Teach goal setting, implementation steps, and build a portfolio of successes.

Case Study Results

How did the collaboration of services impact the progress of case study students?

The students in the case studies made significant progress academically. A school psychologist reported the primary student "has been able to make gains that we have not seen in previous years!" The first-grade student improved to the extent that he met the objectives and no longer required special education services. The intermediate student "made significant progress in reading and writing. He is now a strong silent reader and writing improved when he was provided structure and when he uses the computer," according to the resource teacher. The middle school case study student "was on the A-B honor roll and was very proud of it," reported the resource teacher. She felt "the fact that he was recognized as truly g/t in math had influenced the rest of his academic achievement." He successfully completed an accelerated sixth-grade math class for gifted and talented students. According to the g/t facilitator, "recognition of abilities and structured follow-up by the special education resource teacher has produced an honor roll candidate."

The self-esteem of the case study students increased as they became more confident in their abilities and were more successful in school. A g/t facilitator commented, "the self-esteem of a middle school case study student has flourished this year as he made friends with other g/t students." Earning the respect and friendship of other g/t students has a positive effect on the student's self-esteem. Learning that making mistakes was a part of the learning process had enabled a primary student to begin making significant progress.

The case study students' behavior and attitude toward school improved, and these students became achievers. "He has taken ownership of his education and has made strides in his organization and willingness to follow educator's suggestions," reported a g/t facilitator. A classroom teacher said, "Their student was not throwing emotional tantrums anymore, but still showed signs of emotional instability. He was usually exempted from tests because he became so frustrated that he had an emotional breakdown. After interventions to help him deal with frustration, he actually took a class test and did pretty well."

How was the collaboration different from what may normally have happened for the students?

The collaboration of g/t facilitators and special education resource teachers supporting the classroom teachers was very effective. A school psychologist said, "We all shared ideas, gave each other support, brainstormed, and we let the student know that we were all in this together for him." A resource teacher "felt two people working for his best interest has helped." The collaboration allowed teachers and specialists to discuss a particular child and devise strategies that would be helpful for him.

The support was very important for classroom teachers who felt the educational and emotional needs of these students were more than one teacher could cope with in the regular classroom. "The support was of vital importance," according to a classroom teacher. She went on to say, "this student's problems were so diverse that any one person couldn't handle the load!" A resource teacher commented, "Due to the collaboration, I was provided new and different strategies to utilize with my student. It also helped me focus on his strengths instead of his weaknesses."

What was different because of the collaboration?

The collaboration allowed the district to utilize the expertise of the special education resource teacher, the g/t facilitator, school psychologist, and outside consultants to develop an effective plan. The comprehensive plan built on the student's strengths while providing the remediation and compensation strategies the student needed to be successful. "By learning about how our student responded during his g/t time, we discovered more about his strengths, what motivated him, and how best to help him deal with his frustration and impatience," commented a special education resource teacher. Each of the researchers provided services in his/her area of expertise to promote the effectiveness of the collaborative plan. Dr. Susan Baum and Dr. Mary Ruth Coleman visited the district several times during the study providing training for teachers and parents. "We have never consulted with experts outside the district, especially on such an intense level," said a school psychologist.

The teams shared the frustrations and successes. Reversing underachievement was extremely difficult, but members agreed that as a team they were effective. Assuming the responsibility individually would have been overwhelming. "Each of the team members was more likely to go to one another to share questions and successes, than to try to solve problems alone," said a school psychologist. Each encouraged the other in the beginning when progress was slow. Together they celebrated the smallest indications of positive change such as a smile, eye contact, or a thank you. They congratulated each other when it was evident they were making a difference. A resource teacher commented, "The classroom teacher expressed feeling supported by both special education and g/t teachers."

The collaborative plan developed by team members was comprehensive. The plans included strategies which celebrated the student's strengths, provided remediation and compensation strategies for areas of weakness, and strategies to deal with social/emotional concerns. No individual teacher or specialist had the time to implement the comprehensive plans. When team members worked together, it was possible to implement a comprehensive plan and reverse the underachievement. At the beginning of the study, team members were very frustrated by the lack of student progress. During this time, they wondered if the case study students would respond and if what they were doing would make a difference. For some case study students it took months of hard work before any progress was made. Even then, the progress was so small, they even wondered if it was progress. Little by little the improvements became more consistent and growth could be documented. The collaborative teams were encouraged by the progress of their students and were glad they had participated. At the conclusion of the case studies, these recommendations were developed to guide future collaborations:

Recommendations for future collaborations

- **Continue collaboration between special education and gifted education to meet the needs of twice-exceptional students.** The diverse needs of twice-exceptional students make it difficult for one educator to shoulder the burden. A collaboration of expertise between special education and gifted education is necessary and effective in meeting the educational needs of twice-exceptional students. As a team they can develop and implement a comprehensive plan to address the individual needs of students. The support team members can give each other really helps in the early stages when progress may be slow.

- **Identify twice-exceptional students as early as possible.** It is much easier to understand the impact of a disability on learning and to reverse underachievement before the influence of frustration and failure affects the student's self-esteem. The longer a student has been on a failure track, the more emotional problems have to be managed before educational progress can be made.

- **Acknowledge and nurture the strengths and passions of twice-exceptional students.** Once students are recognized by teachers and other students for accomplishments in their strength areas, they appear to be more willing to work on improving less proficient academic areas.

- **Provide opportunities for students to demonstrate knowledge through areas of strength.** Uneven academic skills make completing school tasks very frustrating for students. Teaching compensation strategies and remediating areas of weakness while providing opportunities for students to learn and to demonstrate their knowledge using their strengths helps twice-exceptional students achieve.

- **Support success through flexible teaching strategies.** Twice-exceptional students have varied learning styles. They are talented but have difficulty learning in the typical school setting. These students are often creative, nonsequential, and frequently spatial learners. They need flexible teaching strategies that allow choice, alternative assignments, and alternative assessments.

- **Promote positive self-esteem and integrate effective support as needed.** Many twice-exceptional students have difficulty relating to peers and teachers. In addition, there seems to be a parenting component related to underachievement. Parents need guidance so they can work collaboratively with the school to help their child succeed. In some instances, additional services in the area of counseling and family guidance might be extremely helpful.

The Future

The collaborative approach has proven to be successful in meeting the needs of twice-exceptional students. Determining the needs of this unique at-risk population of students and developing a collaborative model for providing intervention strategies has helped special education, gifted and talented, and the classroom teacher to provide appropriate programming services. Littleton Public Schools continue to use the collaborative team approach for twice-exceptional students and is expanding the collaborations to meet the needs of underachieving gifted students. The collaborative process allows the district to utilize the expertise of gifted education, special education, general education, and other support services to meet the needs of twice-exceptional students. In general, this approach improves the system's ability to meet the individual needs of underachieving gifted students. Individual case studies are important because they document the progress of each student and provides the district with a database of information that can be use to study the effectiveness of intervention strategies.

REFERENCES

Barton, J. M., and W. T. Starnes. 1989. Identifying distinguishing characteristics of gifted and talented/learning disabled students. *Roeper Review* 12, 23–29.

Baum, S., S. V. Owens, and J. Dixon. 1991. *To be Gifted and Learning Disabled.* Mansfield Center, Conn.: Creative Learning Press.

Baum, S. 1990. *Gifted but Learning Disabled: A Puzzling Paradox* (ERIC Digest #E479). Reston, Va.: Council for Exceptional Children. ERIC Document Reproduction Service No. ED 321 484.

Baum, S., L. J. Emerick, G. N. Herman, and J. Dixon. 1989. Identification, programs and enrichment strategies for gifted learning disabled youth. *Roeper Review* 12, 48–51.

Fox, L. H., L. Brody, and D. Tobin (eds.). 1983. *Learning Disabled Gifted Children: Identification and Programming.* Baltimore, Md.: Allyn & Bacon.

Gardner, H. 1983. *Frames of Mind: The Theory of Multiple Intelligences.* New York: Basic Books.

Nicholson, C. L., and C. L. Alcorn. 1994. *Educational Applications of the WISC-III: A Handbook of Interpretive Strategies and Remedial Recommendations.* Los Angeles: Western Psychological Services.

Nielsen, M. E., L. D. Higgins, and S. C. Wilkinson. 1994. Voices of experience: The world of the twice-exceptional. Paper presented at the Annual Meeting of The National Association for Gifted Children, November 11, 1994, Salt Lake City, UT.

Reis, S. M., T. W. Neu, and J. M. McGuire. 1995. *Talents in Two Places: Case Studies of High Ability Students with Learning Disabilities Who Have Achieved* (Research Monograph 95114). Storrs: The National Research Center on the Gifted and Talented, University of Connecticut.

Schwarz, J. 1992. *Another Door to Learning: True Stories of Learning Disabled Children and Adults, and Their Keys to Their Success.* New York: Crossroad Publishing Co.

Silverman, L. K. (ed.). 1993. Counseling the Gifted and Talented. Denver, Colo.: Love Publishers.

Van Tassel-Baska, J. 1991. Serving the disabled gifted through educational collaboration. *Journal for the Education of the Gifted* 14, 246–266.

Whitmore, J., and J. Maker. 1986. *Intellectual Giftedness among Disabled Persons.* Rockville, Md.: Aspen Press.

Winebrenner, S. 1996. *Teaching Kids with Learning Difficulties in the Regular Classroom.* Minneapolis, Minn.: Free Spirit Publishing Inc.

COMMUNICATING ACROSS CULTURES

by Christine Schulze
Concordia Language Villages

with Kiesa Kay

Deep in the woods of Minnesota, students immerse themselves in learning languages from around the world. The call of the loon mingles with the sounds of voices rising in the clear evening air. Whether swimming in the lake or singing by the campfire, students use the newly known language to communicate their most basic needs and their deepest dreams. Students who have difficulty learning language in the standard, one-hour-a-day classroom often find themselves fluent after a month at Concordia Language Villages, because there, they literally live in the language.

Some of the children return year after year, every summer, receiving their five-year World of Friendship pins or their ten-year Circle of Friends awards. Others go just one summer, but use the experience as a stepping-stone to language study abroad. The ones who return often say that what draws them back is that they can be who they really are in this language-learning setting. The students name themselves at the beginning of camp, choosing new names in the language that they will study. As they shed their English language materials at the door, they leave school clique identities behind them, too. Naming themselves begins the process of trying new things. Some of the students find particular talents that they had not previously discovered, new notions of who and what they can become.

Concordia College, a four-year liberal arts institution, sponsors Concordia Language Villages. Concordia offers language programs in French, Spanish, German, Norwegian, Chinese, Japanese, Swedish, Russian, Finnish, Danish, Korean, and English for young people aged seven to eighteen. There is a five-year age span within each village session. This age diversity allows younger students who have lived abroad or attend immersion schools to have more language fluency than older students, allowing for role modeling from below as well as from above. No age/grade lockstep exists at Concordia. Students attend for one, two, or four weeks in the summer, and the four-week course is the equivalent of one high school year of language study. The four-week sessions are accredited by the North Central Association of Schools and Colleges.

This unique language-learning setting works for many twice-exceptional students because they receive ongoing support in language for the entire experience. Whereas the one- and two-week sessions emphasize oral proficiency in a cultural immersion environment, the four-week sessions cover reading and writing skills, as well as speaking and listening. The four-week villagers receive grades for projects and participation, and they also produce portfolios to take back to their regular schools. At mid-session, the four-week participants trek into small towns to do their laundry, tiny towns where the most riveting event may be the weekly turtle race. Distractions from learning are few.

The staff to villager ratio is one to four, and 25 percent of the staff are native speakers of the language. This ratio not only offers support to the villagers new to the language, but also provides continual opportunities for students to observe language interactions between adults. These adults are fluent in the language and interact in everyday situations, in natural, casual communication. The staff consists of native speakers, college students, and young professionals fluent in the language. Since the program emphasizes content-based instruction, Concordia does not have only staff who are in the language-teaching profession or being trained for such, but also staff members from a multiplicity of academic backgrounds, such as environmentalists, journalists, dancers, and musicians. All lend their talents to create a dynamic and engaging curriculum for the participants.

In order to really learn something, it's vital to feel passionate about that learning. Concordia Language Villages offer authentic conversation in an authentic environment. Students change their American dollars into the village currency, such as Russian rubles or Japanese yen, and must use the language at the village bank or when buying cultural items at the village store. Three times daily they converse at meals, learning about new foods and dining customs. All the food is culturally authentic. For Spanish, French, and German, that means that the students eat foods from the many countries around the world where those languages are spoken.

Students, especially gifted and twice-exceptional students, often don't want to switch from class to class, refocusing attention on a new subject every fifty minutes. At Concordia, the learning of the language becomes a part of every daily activity. No artificial breaks mar the flow of the individual's learning process. Since there is no need to stop every fifty minutes, students can concentrate blocks of time on in-depth projects.

Instead of learning from textbooks, they learn from action and activity. The approach is friendly for kinesthetic and visual-spatial learners, as well as auditory sequential learners. Students who learn by doing will learn in this environment. The activities are all culturally authentic as well as fun and engaging in a recreational setting. For example, at the Korean village they may learn the martial art of tae kwon do; at the Russian village, they may paint Ukrainian-style eggs; at the Japanese village they may learn the customs of a tea ceremony; at the Finnish village they may learn new rules for baseball. In a traditional classroom, students may have to memorize a list of words. At Concordia, students have to use those words to keep score in a soccer game or learn the steps to a dance. By speaking the language to meet their own needs in daily activity, the students begin to own the concepts for themselves.

Each program creates community spirit through rituals particular to village life. Since singing facilitates language learning, there are songs or chants for mealtimes, flag raising or lowering, campfires, and cultural activities. These types of traditions reinforce language learning in fun and positive ways. Students who would never sing about their salad course in a traditional high school find themselves singing and laughing as the luncheon meal is served at Concordia, free to be joyful in a new language. Everybody starts on neutral ground, and friendships develop from there.

The founders of Concordia followed no prescribed paths, and could try anything, adjusting and adapting based on what worked with students. The mission of Concordia Language Villages is not only to teach language, but also to prepare young people for responsible citizenship in the global community. The cultural immersion blends with the language immersion in villages created to reflect the culture of place.

Some activities bring history into the present through simulations and role-plays. In an historical reenactment from the French Revolution, students take on the roles of the aristocracy and the peasants. They later discuss not only that revolution, but also other revolutions and areas of strife around the world today. When students in a Norwegian camp do a simulation of a refugee experience, they must leave their cabins in five minutes with only three things, and then try to get back, despite obstacles. They discuss what they chose, what they felt like, and what they want to provide to refugee children in their own communities once they leave Concordia. The students learn to respond creatively and critically to experiences that transcend national boundaries, a vital step in becoming a responsible, global citizen.

In a discrimination simulation at the German village, some students may feel discomfort or confusion. The staff links this situation to how learning another language allows students to reach people in other cultures more sensitively, more constructively. These lessons extend beyond simply acquiring language proficiency. The students are developing empathy for their neighbors in the global village. This experience may encourage them to be more open-minded and accepting of cultural differences, viewing them as opportunities for enrichment instead of reasons for alienation.

About 9,500 students attend Concordia camps every year, from all fifty of the United

States and twenty countries abroad. Abroad programs also are offered in France, Germany, Spain, Norway, and Japan. During the school year, Concordia Language Villages offers immersion weekends to classes in French, Spanish, German, and Japanese. These weekends take a thematic approach, such as Spanish Holidays Around the World, and all activities revolve around that theme. Concordia students live in these languages, learning to listen and to leap beyond cultural boundaries.

WHAT WE ARE LEARNING ABOUT EDUCATING STUDENTS "AT RISK"

by Lois E. Easton
Eagle Rock School
Estes Park, Colorado

In the past six years, staff members at the Eagle Rock School have learned a great deal about what keeps students in school and engaged in learning. One of our most important lessons is the value of smallness. Eagle Rock is purposefully small, and our students tell us that the small size of a school makes a big difference. With a maximum capacity of ninety-six students, each Eagle Rock student is known well by at least one adult. By "well," I mean that the adult knows how that student learns, what that student's personal issues are, and what's happening to that student on a daily, if not hourly, basis. Ted Sizer of Brown University calls this aspect of smallness "personalization."

Students report that there's no place to hide from learning in our small community. Our classrooms feature round seminar tables. There's no back of the classroom where a student can hide. Students and staff notice absences right away. Students sitting around the table quickly notice confusion in learning, and often are as eager to help as any teacher could be. Students cannot behave impolitely to each other and have either themselves or their actions remain anonymous.

"If I bumped into a student at my old high school, I didn't have to worry about apologizing too much," one Eagle Rock student said. "I knew I probably wouldn't see that student anytime soon."

No secrets scurry at Eagle Rock—the community is just too small to harbor them long, so students can't "get away with things" by hoping no one will notice. Being small enables all staff to be "sidewalk counselors." Walking around the campus, we greet everyone we meet with first name and some appropriate question or comment such as, "Did you talk to your grandmother last night? How is she?" or "You look a bit glum, Cedric. What's happening?" We take pleasure in these personal connections, and also can ascertain if the student needs to meet with one of our counselors.

Many decisions that are made in education result from the needs inherent in accommodating large numbers. Management decisions based on these large numbers sometimes seem to be counterproductive to what we know about how students learn. Tracking is partly a management decision, for example, and an effort to place students by ability. Unfortunately, even in tracked classes, the variance is wide, and in any class accommodating the differences among thirty-five students is nearly impossible. Eagle Rock students are not grouped by grade level. We have no "classes" of students such as freshman or seniors. Because the classes have around twelve students and two teachers (an instructor and an intern), we can make accommodations to help each student learn best. Sound educational practices prevail over management concerns.

So how does a huge school get small? Examples abound of huge schools getting smaller. Some shut down and reopen as small schools, sometimes within the former large school, occupying a floor or a wing. Others become schools within a school, sometimes called charters, academies, or houses. In both cases, students and staff usually choose which part of a formerly large school they want to join. I cringe whenever I hear administrators planning newer—and bigger—high schools. They may be more efficient and able to offer a cafeteria of educational opportunities, but they lose a lot by being so big—namely, the personal connections that many students need in order to take risks and succeed in learning.

Eagle Rock School and Professional Development Center is in its sixth year of operation. An initiative of the American Honda Education Corporation, Eagle Rock enrolls high-school-age students who have not succeeded in other educational settings. The school is year-round, residential, and full scholarship. The school serves as a laboratory school to the Professional Development Center, and educators from across the country visit to study what seems to keep young people in school, engaged, learning, graduating, and going on to worthwhile activities in their lives.

We have witnessed time and again the miracle that happens when a student formerly "written off" by a school or district blossoms as a learner. It's true that all students can learn something, but often, the conditions of school must change so that all students can learn optimally. What are these conditions? They are time, space, and opportunities to learn and demonstrate learning. These conditions usually are fixed, absolute. In most high schools, all freshmen need to learn knowledge in different subject areas over a nine-month period to be declared sophomores. We believe that it's the expectation that students learn sufficiently in each of the separate subject areas over nine months that leads to trouble. What's magical about nine months (not counting its old fit with an agrarian cycle and its new fit with family vacations)? Is nine months sufficient for learning mathematics, reading, social studies, and other bodies of knowledge for all kids? Of course not, yet old school timetables often cling to the calendar and don't pass those who fail to learn all or most of the bodies of knowledge within a specified time. Sometimes the students get labels or special classes. What if schools simply thought of time as an important variable in learning and expected that each student would take a different amount of time to learn?

At Eagle Rock we make time flexible in a number of ways. First, as mentioned earlier, students do not enter Eagle Rock as freshman, sophomores, juniors, or seniors; they are not expected to finish high school in four years or endure derision for their own pacing. Second, our curriculum is based on competencies, not seat time. Students enroll in classes to learn competencies they need to graduate. They do not get grades for classes; they either demonstrate proficiency by the end of the class or not. If they do, they receive credit for mastering that competency. If not, they have not failed; they are simply not ready—yet—to demonstrate proficiency. They will need to take a later class to learn more or differently and have another chance to demonstrate proficiency. For one student, it may take one class to demonstrate proficiency in a competency; for another, it may take four or five classes. Time is the variable.

Space also must be a variable. As most educators know, the school campus is not the only setting for acquiring knowledge. In fact, what students learn in school may very well be only a small part of what they learn during any given day. We respect what they discover in other locations and give students credit for learning outside school. A good example of this is what students learn on integrated service projects. When building a playground in a nearby town, for example, students learned mathematics—primarily geometry—as it applied to the construction problems they encountered, and they also found out about civics. In return for their labor on the playground, students received permission to interview citizens of the town, ranging from the mayor to the owner of the local fast-food restaurant that supplied them lunches at no cost. The end result of their interviews was to be a description of how a town works, and the resulting credit was to be in civics. The students composed a list of about twenty questions to ask citizens of this small town. Their first question was, "Why would you support the building of a playground?" The students understood that parents and youngsters could enjoy the playground, but they genuinely wondered why the retired couple down the street or the businessman who owned a bar on the corner would want it. The learning was meaningful, and it took place off campus.

Most integrated service-learning projects represent real learning to students. Students feel as if they are doing something real and important, as if they are making a contribution to greater society. They are being, as the poet Marge Piercy would say, "of use" as they learn, far different to them than just sitting in a classroom and listening to a lecture or reading a textbook. The learning they do around the service project seems more important, too, because usually it enables them to be successful on the project.

Another example of learning outside the classroom takes place on campus for us because we are a residential school, but it could take place in the form of chores or jobs in another day school such as a public school. Students at Eagle Rock have opportunities to work on KP (kitchen patrol) teams and to be crew leaders for these teams. A corollary for students in nonresidential schools might be required family chores or work responsibilities. Students receive credit for the work they do in KP, focusing on workplace skills and ethics. Teamwork, leadership, following directions, giving directions, and solving problems are among the skills that student learn on KP and might as easily learn doing chores or working after school. We seldom ask students what they learn when they're not at school. We might be surprised, even pleasantly so. Service learning provides an effective tool for applying formal education to real experience.

Many students have built up an image of schoolwork as worthless, without any direction or application to their lives. Off-campus or real work seems worthwhile and purposeful, while sitting in a classroom listening to a lecture or reading a textbook seems unconnected to their lives. "Real work," as Rose describes service learning, "is what counts. It has an effect. It is for a reason."

The third condition that must vary if we are to help all students learn has to do with learning styles and modalities and multiple intelligences. We believe the school should adjust learning and how students document learning so that all students can find their way through the curriculum to success. Our curriculum is not time-based; students do not get credit for seat time. It is based on competencies that we believe all students should master, based on the Colorado State Model Content Standards which are based on the standards for that national subject area devised by professional groups such as the National Council of Teachers of Mathematics. They do not get grades either. So, if they take one class and fail to demonstrate mastery of a competency, they are not given an "F" for the class, thus lowering the class rank or GPA. In fact, Eagle Rock has no class rank or GPAs. If they simply are not ready to demonstrate that competency, they may need more time or a different learning experience in order to help them learn and document mastery. Our classes are six weeks in length; chances are that another class, probably with a slightly different focus, will come along soon. Students who did not learn to master some concepts in geology on a class about the Southwestern desert might learn better when they take a class in the mountain environment. The former class may have required them to develop a portfolio, a medium that requires considerable writing. The latter class might have required students to teach elementary-age students from Denver area schools who visit Eagle Rock for a day to see the mountains firsthand and learn through games Eagle Rock students devise. This time, the student who wasn't ready to demonstrate proficiency in the first class may very well be ready to document it in the second class. This class, titled "Touch the Future," brings Eagle Rock students into a teaching role with elementary students. Both sets of students love this experience in the mountains.

Even more important in terms of individual differences in learning styles, modalities, or intelligences is the freedom students have in all of our classes to find their own meaning in what they are studying. Students essentially become researchers in most of our classes, picking the slant that means something to them. Within a class on revolutions, for example, one student may choose to study the Mexican Revolution, another the French Revolution, and a third the American Revolution. They will share the results of their research with each other so that all students have some knowledge of each of the revolutions but considerable knowledge about the nature of revolutions. You may ask at this point if we're not shortchanging students by not requiring them all to study the same thing. No one can know all there is to know, and we'd rather that students know some things well than all things slightly. And, we've found that, in going deep, students also go wide. Thus, in studying the American Revolution they learn about its forerunner, the French Revolution, and vice versa.

By offering students choices in the specific content they study, we're signaling to students that they can choose to learn the way they want. We open up the learning even more when we suggest a variety of ways students can go about their learning. Some students research on the Internet; others interview people who might have knowledge in the chosen subject; others read books and reference works; others watch videotapes or even popular movies; still others read fiction and poetry. And, finally, we give students a wide choice in terms of how they show us they've learned. Some write a paper; others prepare an oral presentation; some make a scrapbook; others paint a mural or put on a play.

Students whose preferences are not with written language cannot choose to avoid reading and writing altogether, since reading and writing competencies are among those we require for graduation. Similarly, students cannot avoid art, music, or drama at Eagle Rock. Nonetheless, when they're documenting their learning in social studies or science, they may choose a form of documentation that aligns with their learning styles, modalities, or preferences. Flexibility in what educators often perceive as givens or absolutes helps all students learn. Why not vary the time it takes to learn? Why not vary the space we use for learning? Why not vary the ways students go about learning . . . as well as the ways they show us they've learned?

Schools must operate according to a set of principles that are known and practiced by both students and staff on a daily basis. At Eagle Rock, it's more than a plaque that sits on the wall outside the principal's office. School principles are well-known and integral to the functioning of the school. Anyone who asks students and staff what the principles are and how they apply will get fulsome answers. Our set of principles is known as "8 + 5 = 10." As a former staff member said, "It may be bad math, but it's good education." We are guided by eight themes centering on individual integrity and citizenship. These lead to five expectations we have of all graduates. The themes and expectations merge to become ten commitments that all students promise to uphold when they come to Eagle Rock. Students new to Eagle Rock spend about an hour and a half a day for three weeks learning these concepts in depth. They find examples and non-examples of them, debate them, try to add or subtract from the formula, make collages, read stories and poems related to them, and, finally, teach them to others. We don't leave to chance that students thoroughly know and understand the principles that guide our life at Eagle Rock.

Veteran students conduct Gatherings (our first-of-the-morning community meetings) around elements in "8 + 5 = 10." Our near-graduates share their developing personal moral and ethical codes (one of the ten commitments) with the whole community as they near graduation. Instructors design classes that focus not only on the graduation requirements and the Colorado State Model Content Standards, but also on the principles that most apply to their classes. So, an American government class might focus on leadership for justice (one of the graduation expectations) as well as effective written and oral communication (also one of our expectations) and perhaps even something about stewardship of the planet if students look at local, state, and national policies related to the environment. When classes conclude, instructors report student learning in terms of competencies mastered as well as elements of "8 + 5 = 10" studied.

Our known and practiced principles have another use, too. They instruct us in how to live well with each other. The first commitment, "Live in respectful harmony with others," captures what it takes to live in a community. "Making healthy life choices" is another important commitment. These two commitments and others give us the rationale for behaviors that are necessary in any school. When we take disciplinary action, it is because students have broken their commitments. Other students often will "call" them on their violation, because all students share a vested interest in preserving the harmony of their community. When an infraction is more serious, such as with our nonnegotiables (no alcohol, no drugs, no tobacco, no sexual relations, no violence), our reference is the set of commitments students agreed to uphold. And, if students need to leave the campus because they have not or cannot uphold their commitment, everyone in the school—including the student who must live the consequence of behavior—understands.

What makes our principles so valuable, then, is that they are known and practiced on campus by everyone, staff and students alike. These reference points remain overt, not hidden. They don't compete with a separate and covert but real set of principles. They bind the community around some core beliefs. The more we teach at Eagle Rock, the more our students teach us about what works in learning and leadership.

ONGOING COMMUNICATION AND ACTIVE ACCELERATION

by Richard Beck, Journalism Teacher
Michelle Bird, Dean of Academics
John Cummings, Director of Admissions
Thomas Lovett, English Department Chair
Cynthia Stanton, Director of Special Services
St. Johnsbury Academy

Once twice-exceptional students enter a classroom community, several factors need to come together to ensure their success: the teacher needs to communicate early and often with parents, the teacher needs to communicate with the students' previous teachers, the teacher and student must establish a mentoring relationship, and the peer group needs to apply positive peer pressure toward high-level achievement.

The importance of early, open, ongoing, and honest communication between the parents and teacher cannot be overemphasized, especially if the student is new to the school. If the parents are not forthcoming about their children's learning difficulties (or perhaps unaware of the specific learning needs of their children), the students often experience a rocky start, stumbling over obstacles that an early parent-teacher conference could have avoided. In fact, we have found that the later in a student's career we identify learning difficulties, the less likely we are to be successful with that student. Too many failures, too many conflicts, and too little achievement have caused the student to resist taking risks or striving for academic excellence. Parents who are positive, cooperative, realistic, aware, and informed, have high expectations and no illusions regarding their children's learning, and meet with teachers early and often are the driving force behind student success.

When learning needs are identified early, teachers begin to strategize with parents, colleagues, and students and build mentoring relationships from the start. The students are more likely to take risks and strive for excellence, freed from the burdens of the negative school experiences of the past. The twice-exceptional student often displays exceptional verbal talent, leadership abilities, unflinching frankness, and a wonderful sense of humor when placed in this supportive environment. Resisting negative labels attached to them after classroom difficulties in earlier years, they bristle at the words "You can't do this," and strive to perform above previous expectations as long as they know teachers, parents, and their new peers are interested in both self-esteem and high achievement.

The teacher's colleagues can help suggest specific strategies to help encourage a particular student, and students do better when the demands, expectations, and rewards are consistent from teacher to teacher. At St. Johnsbury Academy, some particularly helpful means of communication, besides IEP meetings or informal conversations, have been student portfolios, department assessments, and student profiles. Colleagues also provide outlets for student frustrations; having established mentoring relationships earlier, students have a group of teachers who can offer advice or a listening ear, ultimately sending the student back to the current teacher with encouragement to make the mentoring work for them.

This mentoring relationship and the positive peer pressure of accelerated ability-level groupings are the two most obvious factors in determining twice-exceptional students' success. First, as mentor, the teacher is dedicated to providing "tough love" for the students: convincing them that they are capable of excellence, requiring one-on-one conferences regularly to encourage investment in high-quality work, challenging them to step beyond what is comfortable and familiar, and showing real emotion when students backslide or produce excellent work. The mentor's role is to persuade the students that they will achieve excellence, that it will take hard work and probably some emotional stresses, but that together as mentor and mentored, they can both experience great success. Our experience has been that this success subsequently breeds more success as students recognize the systems and strategies that are most helpful in their learning.

All students learn best when placed in classes in which they are taught at the appropriate level. This way, all students have the potential to experience success without being alienated by exasperating failures or numbing boredom. Our twice-exceptional students are particularly well-served by this policy, as they are placed in accelerated and sometimes advanced placement classes. They know they are in a group of people who are serious about academic achievement and who can and will challenge their glib or clownish comments (often used as a mask for lack of confidence). The classroom culture in accelerated classes is self-directed and mutually supportive. Classmates, often unaware of the twice-exceptional nature of students, will naturally be inclined to help them succeed so that the group can attain the excellence they desire. Accelerated-level students are tolerant of divergent thinking and learning styles and admire quality work when they see it. In lower-level groupings, these twice-exceptional students—because they are so bright—are able to spark disruption and gain a feeling of power by derailing class activities. These activities, presented and paced at a level below that of the exceptional students, gain their disdain, and the culture of the classroom in which academic work is not the primary value receives equal scorn. In mixed-ability classes, the positive peer pressure is diffused, there is no natural inclination to help the class meet high standards, and the twice-exceptional students often become troublemakers. If they try to rise above the norm, display divergent thinking, or take risks in order to excel, they often find themselves outcast.

The mentoring process for the twice-exceptional student starts during the admissions process. The admissions and special services staff work closely together to develop a strong working relationship with the student and the parent. During the interview process, we determine what the student/parent want and need in a school and for the student as an individual. We review how the Academy might meet the academic, social/emotional, and special needs of the student. This enables the parent/student to make an informed school choice. When talking about our admissions process, one parent expressed, "I felt there was a real desire to learn more about my son's needs." From the time her twice-exceptional son entered the Academy until he graduated, he was supported through his successes and his challenges.

This sense of belonging to a group of people who cares about academic excellence is the key to helping twice-exceptional students succeed. Actively involved and cooperative parents, mentoring teachers, and accelerated classmates, all working together to encourage, support, and challenge these students, provide a community of learners dedicated to high-quality performance. At St. Johnsbury Academy, we have found that it is in this kind of community that these students thrive, and that in other academic communities—where parents are not forthcoming, teachers do not form mentoring relationships, or classmates do not provide a serious academic culture—they often wither.

RESPONDING TO THE NEEDS OF TWICE-EXCEPTIONAL LEARNERS: A SCHOOL DISTRICT AND UNIVERSITY'S COLLABORATIVE APPROACH

by L. Dennis Higgins and M. Elizabeth Nielsen

There were times when I would sit at my desk and I would look out at the faces of the students in my twice-exceptional class and try to fathom what those kids will become. One of my students used to love to joke [that] he's going to become a homeless bum. Brilliant kid. Another student talked about becoming an aeronautical engineer. You look out at those kids and you just say My god! They are so important—what they have to offer is so important. . . . I look out there and I see the healers for our society. I see kids who, I hope and pray, become educators in some way. I see senators. . . . It's my prayer that we can continue to respond to the needs of these kids. (Interview with M. M., middle school teacher of twice-exceptional students, 1995)

The educational needs of gifted students with disabilities differ significantly from the needs of most students. Their academic, social, and emotional deficits often conflict with their remarkable gifts and talents, and this conflict places this population at-risk for failure and for emotional problems (Baum, Owen, and Dixon, 1991; Bireley, 1995; Coleman, 1992; Nielsen and Mortoroff-Albert; Silverman, 1989; Van Tassel-Baska; 1992). These twice-exceptional students clearly need unique academic programming; that is, they need access to services that address both their areas of strength and their deficit areas. One of the first descriptions of a special program for gifted students who simultaneously had a disability or who were experiencing serious school problems was the 1980 seminal work of J. R. Whitmore, *Giftedness, Conflict, and Underachievement*. During the twenty years since that publication, educators have continued to stress the need for special programs and interventions specifically designed to address the academic and social needs of this unique population (Baum, Owen, and Dixon, 1991; Bireley, 1995; Fox, Brody, and Tobin, 1983; Nielsen, et al., 1993, 1994; Schwarz, 1992; Silverman, 1989, 1993; Suter and Wolf, 1987; Van Tassel-Baska, 1991, 1992; Waldron, Saphrie, and Rosenblum, 1987). Few descriptions of school-based programs are available, which is a frightening indication that few comprehensive programs exist within public schools.

This chapter describes a large school district's (Albuquerque Public School System—APS) efforts to collaborate with a local university (University of New Mexico) in order to respond to the needs of twice-exceptional children and youth. This collaboration has led to comprehensive district-wide services and programs for twice-exceptional students at all grade levels and to the development of a graduate-level university special education course, *Teaching Twice-Exceptional Learners,* taken by more than 250 public school teachers.

School District Information

The Albuquerque New Mexico Public School system (APS) is a multicultural school district located in the southwestern section of the United States. The district, the 27th largest in the nation, covers an area larger than the state of Rhode Island. Enrollment exceeds 89,000 students. Approximately 11,000 students in the district receive special education service for some type of learning or communication disability; 1,400 have behavioral problems that need to be addressed through special education; and 3,700 receive special education services for their giftedness. The ethnic breakdown for the APS student population is as follows: approximately 43,000 (48.0 percent) of the students are Anglo-American; 37,000 (42.0 percent) are Hispanic-American; 4,500 (5.0 percent) are Native American; 3,000 (3.0 percent) are African-American; and 2,000 (2.0 percent) are Asian-American. Additionally, the dominant home language of 15 percent of the district's students is a language other than English.

An Historical Perspective of the School District and University Collaborative Response to Twice-Exceptional Learners

In 1985, the Albuquerque Public School District recognized that a unique group of students existed within its large special education population. This group consisted of students with disabilities who also had the characteristics of gifted students. The learning problems and academic difficulties of these twice-exceptional students tended to mask their gifts and talents, lower their self-esteem, and reduce the likelihood that they would be able to develop to their true ability or potential. The district developed a pilot program for a small group of these students. This program, consisting of a full-day, special class, was housed in one of the district's elementary schools and focused on addressing students' strengths while simultaneously addressing their academic weaknesses. By 1987, this pilot project expanded to two additional elementary school locations.

In 1990 the Albuquerque Public Schools and the special education department of the University of New Mexico (UNM) received federal funding to expand this service through a

Jacob K. Javits gifted and talented grant (Nielsen, 1989). This grant, titled the *Twice-Exceptional Child Project,* allowed the school district and the university collaboratively: (a) to develop a comprehensive identification model that resulted in the identification of over 250 elementary and middle school gifted students with learning disabilities as well as those with mild behavioral problems; (b) to expand the district-wide special classes for twice-exceptional learners to five additional elementary sites and to four middle school locations; (c) to provide 180 twice-exceptional students with gifted/special education services within self-contained classes; (d) to design and implement appropriate instructional strategies and curricula for twice-exceptional learners; and (e) to provide university training for teachers of these special-needs students.

In 1993 the Albuquerque Public School District and the University of New Mexico submitted and received a second Jacob K. Javits grant focused on twice-exceptional students (Nielsen, 1993). This three-year project (1993–1996), *Project Reach: Meeting the Needs of Twice-Exceptional Learners,* helped to establish service to twice-exceptional students at the high school level and extended the teacher training aspects through the development of video training tapes and the offering of yearly Summer Training Institutes to teacher-educators from across the United States (Higgins and Nielsen, 1991, 1992, 1993, 1994). Since 1996, the school district and the university continue to collaborate to meet the needs of twice-exceptional learners. The special classes for twice-exceptional students have become a permanent type of special education service. Beginning in fall 1999, the classes will be titled Venture Program classes (Albuquerque School District Gifted Task Force, 1999). The university course, *Teaching Twice-Exceptional Learners*, is offered every summer. Beginning in summer 1999, this course will be a required course for all APS teachers of the gifted. The remainder of this chapter provides an overview of lessons gleaned from the past decade of collaboration between the school district and the university.

Characteristics of Twice-Exceptional Learners

Since APS district-wide data on twice-exceptional students began to be collected in 1990, approximately 500 students have been so identified. Over half of these students have received service through the district's special classes for twice-exceptional students.

Sixty-five percent of the district's twice-exceptional students have an identified specific learning disability according to New Mexico's special education criteria (New Mexico State Department of Education, 1994). Ten percent have a serious emotional or behavioral disorder based on state criteria; 20 percent have more than one identified special education exceptionality; and the remaining 5 percent have other special education disabilities including language disorders, health impairments, and physical disabilities. Approximately 40 percent of the twice-exceptional students are culturally diverse. The majority of these ethnically diverse students are Hispanic (25 percent of the total twice-exceptional population). Thirteen percent of the twice-exceptional students are biracial, 3 percent are African-American, and 2 percent are Native American. These numbers parallel the ethnic diversity of the APS overall student population. Further, approximately half of the twice-exceptional students enrolled in the self-contained classes come from low-income families, based on family income information and eligibility for free/reduced lunches.

Twice-exceptional students have divergent strengths and weaknesses. Many are extremely curious, highly verbal, remarkably creative, and excellent critical thinkers. At the same time, these children frequently have great difficulty with reading and written language tasks, are frustrated by school, and have low self-esteem. Extensive reviews of the school records for about 250 twice-exceptional students within the Albuquerque Public School District found that school personnel as well as parents noted the following characteristics as being typical of this population.

Strengths

- superior vocabulary
- advanced ideas and opinions
- high levels of creativity and problem-solving ability
- extremely curious, imaginative, and questioning
- wide range of interests not related to school
- penetrating insight into complex issues
- specific talent or consuming interest area
- sophisticated sense of humor

Weaknesses

- poor social skills
- high sensitivity to criticism
- lack of organizational and study skills
- discrepant verbal and performance abilities

- poor performance in one or more academic areas
- difficulty in written self-expression
- stubborn, opinionated demeanor
- high impulsivity

In 1999, Dr. Elizabeth Nielsen, the principal investigator for the two funded Javits grants, assisted the Albuquerque Public Schools Gifted Task Force in the development of a matrix which details how the characteristics of twice-exceptional students are similar yet distinguished from the characteristics that traditionally have been attributed to gifted and talented learners. Analysis of test scores for twice-exceptional students identified by UNM/APS Project Reach demonstrates how closely these students parallel gifted students intellectually while paralleling learning-disabled students in terms of academic performance.

Identification of Twice-Exceptional Students

Twice-exceptional students within the Albuquerque Public School System (a) must have an identified disability according to New Mexico's statewide special education exceptionality criteria and (b) must meet the criteria for gifted and talented students. An adequate plan would include:

1. The student's present levels of performance including the impact of disability and of giftedness;
2. a summary of the student's needs based on disability and on giftedness;
3. the type(s) and degree (generally stated in terms of hours of service per day or per week) of educational service which the student will receive both for his/her disability and for his/her giftedness;
4. specific long-term goals and related short-term instructional objectives both for the student's areas of strength and areas of weakness; and
5. any specific modifications which will be made in the student's general education classes and in state/local testing situations to accommodate the student's disability.

Twice-exceptional students must have access to curricula that focus on the development of appropriate content-area competencies, critical and creative thinking skills, social and emotional competencies, and skills and compensatory strategies designed to enable them to overcome those barriers to learning that are related to their disabilities. After working with several hundred twice-exceptional students during the past decade, APS and project personnel are convinced that, in order to meet their full potential, the students must have access to all of these skills and competencies.

Twice-exceptional students, with their combination of strengths and disabilities, must be able to learn from teachers who are knowledgeable about special education and from teachers who are knowledgeable about gifted education. Both have much to offer these learners. Further, the Albuquerque Public School District and project personnel believe that twice-exceptional students who are unable to succeed in general education settings, in special education settings, in gifted education settings, or in any combination of these settings must have access to more intensive service where their unique needs can be addressed by a teacher who is extensively trained both in gifted education and in special education and where they have an opportunity to interact with other twice-exceptional students. The special twice-exceptional classes (i.e., Venture Programs) within the school district offer gifted students with disabilities access to such intensive service. The goal of the APS twice-exceptional classes is to assist students in the acquisition of those skills and technologies which they will need to eventually return to general education settings with support as needed from professionals in special education and in gifted education.

Before we consider the guiding principles behind the APS program, we should acknowledge that one important aspect of the overall program is experiential learning. Experiential learning activities utilize stress, perceived risk, physical challenges, and pleasurable experiences to provide an opportunity to evoke and deal with dynamic processes that emerge when the individual or group is stressed and forced to rely on self and others for basic safety and success. Learning from experiential activities occurs when a person engages in an activity, reflects upon the experience, abstracts useful insights from the analysis, and applies the knowledge to other areas of his or her life.

Within the twice-exceptional program, the experiential learning component consists of three core types of activities: (a) a series of group initiatives, (b) participation in a ropes course, and (c) a wilderness adventure. Initiatives are gamelike activities often designed so that success is achieved only when the whole group accomplishes a task or activity. Initiatives help to build group trust, communication, and teamwork. The ropes course is a series of high and low rope challenges, which students accomplish following a challenge-by-choice approach. Ropes course activities focus more on individual goal setting and achievement. For example, a high-rope challenge might be for a student to cross a web of ropes suspended twenty feet above the ground. Succeeding provides a sense of personal competence. The wilderness adventure consists of an overnight or weekend backpacking trip planned and organized by the students.

Guiding Principles for Services Provided within APS Twice-Exceptional Special Classes

More than a decade of collaborative work has led to the belief that three guiding principles are central to the successful education of twice-exceptional students.

PRINCIPLE 1: Twice-exceptional children and youth are at-promise.

Professionals who work with children and youth have become concerned by the growing personal, family, school, and societal problems which place students at-risk for school failure and sometime failure in life (Barr and Parrett, 1995; Dryfoos, 1990; Manning and Baruth, 1995; Means, Chelemer, and Knapp, 1991; Morgan, 1994; McWhirter, et al., 1993; Wang and Reynolds, 1995; Wood and Algozzie, 1994). While the national statistics support this concern, a focus on risk and failure can lead educators to a sense of hopelessness. The problems seem too large and pervasive. In opposition to this sense is the belief that children and youth are at-promise, and this latter philosophical stance provides direction for the twice-exceptional program. Rather than focusing on the risks faced by these students on a daily basis (e.g., academic failure, low feelings of self-worth, school drop out, limited career choices), the twice-exceptional program focuses on the remarkable giftedness and potential that reside within each of these students. It is the responsibility of the program to build resiliency skills within this population so that their promise can be fully realized. Resilient youth have the capacity to cope with the world around them no matter how severe the obstacles or disappointments they encounter or how adverse their life conditions (Barr and Parrett, 1995; Dugan and Coles, 1989; Garmezy, 1981; Hauser, et al., 1985; McCubbins and McCubbins, 1988; McWhirter, et al., 1993; Rutter, 1983; Werner, 1984; Werner and Smith, 1982).

PRINCIPLE 2: Twice-exceptional children and youth are intellectually diverse.

The intellectual discrepancies within the twice-exceptional population are extraordinary. Evaluation data for the program indicates that the average difference between twice-exceptional students' verbal ability (as measured by a standardized intelligence test) and their performance ability (as measured by a standardized intelligence test) is over 20 standard-score points. The mean difference between their intellectual potential and their mathematical performance (as measured by a standardized achievement test) is approximately 26 standard-score points, between their intellectual potential and their reading performance approximately 36 standard-score points, and between their intellectual potential and their written language performance approximately 42 points. With such remarkably high discrepancies between intellectual ability and academic performance, twice-exceptional students constitute a uniquely challenged population.

Examining average scores for this group fails to demonstrate the differences that exist between one twice-exceptional child and another. While many twice-exceptional students have serious reading difficulty and read well below their grade level, others are quite gifted in reading ability. Some of these students need to be accelerated in mathematics, while others struggle to learn the basic math facts and computational processes. The APS twice-exceptional program strives to recognize group and individual differences, to help students recognize their own personal differences in ability, and to celebrate those differences in a positive light.

PRINCIPLE 3: Twice-exceptional children and youth need to develop a positive view of self and to possess a positive future perspective.

Because of their history of academic failure, twice-exceptional students often develop feelings of low self-worth. Numerous theoretical papers and case studies of twice-exceptional learners discuss this self-esteem issue as it relates to twice-exceptional class.

These classes will vary in curricular content, because the curriculum must reflect the interests and strengths of the teacher to be optimally effective. For example, students in a class led by a teacher with journalistic skills create and publish a monthly school newspaper that includes interviews, photography, cartoons, letters to the editors, and articles of special interest. A teacher of another twice-exceptional middle school class has a strong background in science and computer technology. In his classroom, students approach the majority of their learning through more science-related issues such as environmental awareness or global change, with all work supported by the use of technologies. Finally, differences in the curriculum within specific twice-exceptional classes occur because of student differences. Because of the intellectual diversity among these students, the need for individualization within the classes is intense. Therefore, a group of students in one elementary class might be learning about the use of fractions while several other students in the same class are beginning to work in algebra. Many twice-exceptional students have unique areas of interest, which have become passion areas for them. A high school student who is reading at a fifth-grade level and who has an intense interest in auto mechanics will be more willing to struggle through reading an adult magazine about auto racing than to read a basic textbook. The teacher and students work together to develop interest-based units. All of the twice-exceptional classes build their curricular framework around three key approaches: (a) Gardner's theory of Multiple Intelligences, (b) Betts' Autonomous Learner Model for the gifted and talented, and (c) interdisciplinary thematic learning.

Multiple Intelligences

In *Frames of Mind: The Theory of Multiple Intelligences* (New York: Basic Books, 1983), Howard Gardner's conception of intelligence involves seven separate and somewhat independent intellectual domains (Armstrong, 1993; 1987; Gardner, 1983). The seven intelligences that Gardner describes are: (a) linguistic (verbal) intelligence, which includes verbal comprehension, understanding of semantics, strong vocabulary, and ability to express oneself in oral and written form; (b) logical-mathematical intelligence, which includes the ability to reason inductively and deductively as well as an understanding of mathematical and scientific concepts; (c) visual-spatial intelligence, which includes the ability to conceptualize and manipulate three-dimensional images and to see spatial relationships; (d) bodily-kinesthetic intelligence or the ability to learn, to reason, and to complete tasks by actively engaging the body; (e) musical intelligence, which includes sensitivity to rhythms, textures, pitch, and timbre as well as the ability to compose and perform musically; (f) interpersonal intelligence or the ability to understand others, their actions, and their motivations as well as the ability to respond to situations involving other people in a sensitive and productive manner; and (g) intrapersonal intelligence, which involves an understanding of self including awareness of one's strengths, weaknesses, emotions, and feelings.

This theory, which has roots in concepts discussed as far back as fifty years ago, validates the diverse and discrepant abilities of twice-exceptional learners. Students as well as teachers in the twice-exceptional classes learn about this theory and utilize it in the development and completion of units, activities, assignments, and products. Also, knowledge of individual students' both stronger and weaker intelligences allows the students and the teachers to develop more productive individualized education plans and is particularly helpful for creating successful accommodations and modifications within general education classes for specific twice-exceptional students.

Autonomous Learner Model

The Albuquerque Public School (APS) district, the *Twice-Exceptional Child Project*, and *Project Reach* believe that it is important for the various twice-exceptional classes across the school district to utilize a common curricular model. After careful examination of a wide variety of curricular models from the fields of gifted education, special education, and gifted education, Betts' Autonomous Learner Model was selected as the most comprehensive and appropriate model for the twice-exceptional classes (Betts, 1985, 1986; 1991; Betts and Neihart, 1988; see Appendix B). Central to that decision was the emphasis in Betts model given: (a) to the development of self-knowledge within students, (b) to addressing the social and emotional needs of learners, and (c) to developing autonomy and independence. All of these issues must be addressed when working with twice-exceptional children and youth, while striving to build resiliency within this population. Further, the Autonomous Learner Model is flexible enough to be effectively used at a variety of grade levels and across a number of years.

The Autonomous Learner Model is designed to address the needs of gifted and talented students using a curricular approach that encourages the development of those skills and abilities necessary in order for students to develop into autonomous learners, with the ability to be responsible for the development, implementation, and evaluation of their own learning (Betts, 1986). Five major components comprise this curricular model: (a) the Orientation Dimension, which includes understanding giftedness, personal development, and the responsibilities of program and school; (b) the Individual Development Dimension, which includes college and career development and organizational involvement; (c) the Enrichment Dimension, which includes explorations, investigations, and cultural activities; (d) the Seminar Dimension, which introduces knowledge in myriad forms such as futuristic or speculative, controversial general interest, pragmatic and advanced or specialized; and (e) the In-Depth Study Dimension, which involves mentorships, presentations, individual projects, group projects, and assessment (Betts, 1986).

Interdisciplinary Thematic Learning

Numerous educators in the field of gifted education have supported the use of integrated or interdisciplinary curriculum and recent educational reform efforts have voiced a similar support for interdisciplinary instruction for all students (Jacobs, 1989; Kersh, Nielsen, and Subotnik, 1987; Martinello and Cook, 1994; Van Tassel-Baska, 1994). Interdisciplinary learning is founded on the belief that students need the opportunity to investigate complex ideas and construct their own meaning for topics and content across a number of separate academic disciplines. According to Martinello and Cook (1994), "sound learning centers on the deep themes that underlie the content in the subject areas: principles, theories, and major generalizations. . . . This is best advanced through inquiry that formulates questions from the perspectives of many disciplines of study, organized around universal concepts and generalizations" (p. 4).

Twice-exceptional students have the ability to think globally and to more readily grasp the big picture rather than understand the smaller, separate pieces of knowledge. Therefore, the use of interdisciplinary curriculum and an interdisciplinary approach to instruction is a central tenet of the twice-exceptional classes. The Albuquerque Public School district's programs for twice-exceptional learners use the specific global themes in their district programs for gifted students. Interdisciplinary thematic curricular units for the classes are developed using unit-development guidelines established by Kersh, Nielsen, and Subotnik (1987) and Van Tassel (1992, 1994). The themes for the elementary schools are selected from the following concepts: change, choices, delicacy, development, diversity, investigation, patterns, and spaces. Middle school thematic options include: conflict, conformity, futures, human expression, perceptions, and relationships. High school thematic choices include: connections, decisions, power, social consciousness/justice, and technology.

Education Modifications Designed to Help Twice-Exceptional Students to Succeed

The school district maintains that twice-exceptional students should participate in those general education academic classes in which they can function successfully if appropriate curricular and instructional modifications are made. For example, if a twice-exceptional student can understand the concepts and principles within a general education social studies class, yet has difficulty with reading and written language, the student might be able to participate successfully in that social studies class if the teacher will make some basic changes. This approach to inclusion within general education requires careful collaboration between the twice-exceptional student's case manager or twice-exceptional classroom teacher and the student's general educators. The individual educational plans (IEPs) for twice-exceptional students must be developed carefully by a multidisciplinary team that includes teachers, an administrator, the student, and parents.

Teachers within the APS special classes for twice-exceptional students utilize a variety of instructional strategies, interventions, and methodologies to address the gifted needs of this population, to address their unique social and emotional needs, and to help them overcome those barriers to learning that occur because of their disabilities. Interventions include instructional strategies, social and emotional interventions, and strategies specifically designed to help students overcome personal barriers to learning.

Samples of General Education Modifications
for Twice-Exceptional Students

(adapted from E. Nielsen, *Educational Modifications and Accommodations for Twice-Exceptional Learners within General Education Settings,* 1993.)

1. Testing modifications
Example a: Divide the test into smaller sections, to be administered separately.
Example b: Orally read test items to the student.

2. Grading modifications
Example a: Do not penalize the student for handwriting problems, unless the assignment is a penmanship one.
Example b: Grade the student only for knowledge of specific content being taught and not for his/her ability to read the textbook.

3. Homework and assignment modifications
Example a: Allow the student more time to complete pencil/paper-type assignments.
Example b: Allow the student to use alternate (nontraditional) ways to present his/her knowledge and research (e.g., drawings, models, role-playing, demonstrations).

4. Textbook and worksheet modifications
Example a: Provide the student with tape recording of written materials.
Example b: Space math problems farther apart on the page.

5. Modification in how information is presented in class
Example a: Accompany oral directions with written directions (either on the blackboard or on paper) to which the student can later refer.
Example b: Use handouts, transparencies, maps, charts, and other types of visuals.

6. Modifications in how the student obtains information
Example a: Allow the student to tape-record lectures.
Example b: Provide the student with an outline of the lecture and refer to it.

7. Modifications in disciplinary interventions
Example a: Arrange a regular time to talk privately with the student regarding his/her behavior.
Example b: Avoid placing the student in negative behavior-inducing situations such as putting him/her under time pressures or in competition with other students.

8. Use of compensatory techniques/tools
Example a: Allow the student to access recorded books from the Recording for the Blind Services.
Example b: Allow the student to use graph paper to help organize writing and math work.

9. **Assistance from the special education resource room**

Example a: Let the student take general education tests within the special education classroom.

Example b: Have the special education teacher monitor the student's assignments.

Instructional Strategies and Interventions Designed to Address the Gifted Needs of Twice-Exceptional Learners

(Nielsen, *Gifted Educational Interventions for Twice-Exceptional Learners,* 1993).

- Teach twice-exceptional students to recognize, access, and use their gifts to bypass or compensate for their disabilities.
- Create a twice-exceptional learning environment that begins with gifted education, then adds special education and general education as appropriate.
- Enrich the curriculum of twice-exceptional learners through sophisticated materials and strategies such as simulations, Future Problem Solving Program, and Odyssey of the Mind (Gallagher and Gallagher, 1994).
- Expand the horizons of twice-exceptional students by engaging them in real-world, problem-based learning experiences.
- Help twice-exceptional learners to acquire the skills and strategies necessary to become creative, critical, and purposeful thinkers.
- Help twice-exceptional students acquire the skills which they will need to be come autonomous, self-directed partners in their own learning.
- Temper the pace of twice-exceptional students' learning according to their individual abilities (i.e., accelerate and remediate as needed).
- Modify the assignments and products of twice-exceptional learners so that their gifted abilities may be demonstrated.
- Channel twice-exceptional students learning through their passion areas.
- Encourage twice-exceptional students and those who work with them to accept and appreciate their remarkable gifts and talents.

Instructional Strategies and Interventions Designed to Address the Social and Emotional Needs of Twice-Exceptional Learners

(E. Nielsen, *Social and Emotional Educational Interventions for Twice-Exceptional Learners,* 1994).

- Create an emotionally safe learning environment for twice-exceptional children and youth where their ideas and feelings are accepted by teacher and peers.
- Provide a very consistent and predictable environment while helping twice-exceptional students learn to cope with change.
- Help twice-exceptional students to understand and embrace their gift(s) and their disability(ies).
- Provide twice-exceptional learners with role models who have successfully faced and overcome difficulties and disabilities.
- Directly teach social interaction skills, collaboration skills, peer pressure resistance, and negotiation skills.
- Regularly guide twice-exceptional students in group discussions which focus on emotional, stressful, personal, and global issues.
- Respect the high emotional vulnerability of twice-exceptional learners.
- Provide support to the families of twice-exceptional students by helping them connect with parents of similar students and/or with support groups.
- Assist twice-exceptional students and their families to face their fears about their future.
- Consistently monitor emotional responses to and interactions with these challenging students.

Instructional Strategies and Interventions Designed to Assist Twice-Exceptional Students to Overcome Their Individual Barriers to Learning

(E. Nielsen, *Educational Interventions for Twice-Exceptional Learners Designed to Overcome Barriers to Learning,* 1994.)

- Develop accommodations and modifications in general education and gifted education classes which will allow twice-exceptional students to be successful.
- Individualize specific content and development of skills while still allowing twice-exceptional learners to work in small and large groups for social skill development.
- Have twice-exceptional students access advanced literature through the use of tape-recorded books and other strategies while still teaching them basic reading and decoding skills.
- Have twice-exceptional students work with advanced mathematical and scientific concepts while still teaching them basic mathematical and computation skills.
- Incorporate multisensory and multimodal approaches into the instruction of twice-exceptional learners.
- Teach twice-exceptional students how to use specific learning strategies including the use of graphic organizers.
- Teach twice-exceptional students how to use specific organizational and study skills.
- Teach twice-exceptional students how to develop appropriate coping strategies.
- Provide twice-exceptional learners with access to compensatory techniques and tools including computers, spell checkers, calculators, and tape recorders.
- Be flexible with regard to the manner in which twice-exceptional obtain information.
- Modify the products, assignments, and time lines required of twice-exceptional students.
- Modify the tests, test-taking approaches, and assessment procedures for twice-exceptional learners.

REFERENCES

Armstrong, T. 1987. *In Their Own Way: Discovering and Encouraging Your Child's Personal Learning Style.* Los Angeles: Jeremy P. Tarcher, Inc.

———. 1993. *Seven Kinds of Smart: Identifying and Developing Your Many intelligences. New Problems, Adventure Games, Stunts and Trust Activities.* Dubuque, Iowa: Kendall/Hunt.

Rohnke, K. 1989a. *Cowstails and Cobras II: A Guide to Games, Initiatives, Ropes Courses, and Adventure Curriculum.* Dubuque, Iowa: Kendall/Hunt.

———. 1989b. *The Bottomless Bag.* Dubuque, Iowa: Kendall/Hunt.

Rutter, M. 1983. Stress, coping, and development: Some issues and some questions. In N. Garmez and M. Rutter (eds.), *Stress, Coping, and Development of Children.* New York: McGraw-Hill.

Scheiber, B., and J. Talpers. 1987. *Unlocking Potential: College and Other Choices for Learning Disabled People.* Bethesda, Md.: Adler and Adler.

Schmitt, A. 1994. *Brilliant Idiot: An Autobiography of a Dyslexic.* Intercourse, Penn.: Good Books.

Schoel, J., D. Prouty, and P. Radcliffe. *1988. Islands of Healing: A Guide to Adventure Based Counseling.* Hamilton, Mass.: Project Adventure.

Schwarz, J. 1992. *Another Door to Learning: True Stories of Learning Disabled Children and Adults, and Their Keys to Their Success.* New York: Crossroad Publishing Co.

Silverman, L. K. (ed.). 1993. *Counseling the Gifted and Talented.* Denver, Colo.: Love Publishers.

Silverman, L. K. 1989. Invisible gifts, invisible handicaps. *Roeper Review* 12, 37–42.

Smith, C. R. 1991. *Learning Disabilities: The Interaction of Learner, Task, and Setting* (2nd ed.). Boston: Allyn and Bacon.

Suter, D. P., and J. S. Wolf. 1987. Issues in the identification and programming of the gifted/learning disabled child. *Journal for the Education of the Gifted* 10, 227–238.

Tobin, D., and G. B. Schiffman. 1983. Computer technology for learning-disabled/gifted students. In L. H. Fox, L. Brody, and D. Tobin (eds.), *Learning-Disabled/Gifted Children: Identification and Programming.* Baltimore, Md.: University Park Press.

Tuttle, C. G., and G. A. Tuttle. 1995. *Challenging Voices: Writings by for, and about Individuals with Learning Disabilities.* Los Angeles: Lowell House Books.

Van Tassel-Baska, J. 1991. Serving the disabled gifted through educational collaboration. *Journal for the Education of the Gifted* 14, 246–266.

———. 1992. *Planning Effective Curriculum for Gifted Learners.* Denver, Colo.: Love Publishers.

———. 1994. *Comprehensive Curriculum for Gifted Learners* (2nd ed.). Boston: Allyn and Bacon.

Vogel, S. A., and P. B. Adelman, (eds.). 1993. *Success for College Students with Learning Disabilities.* New York: Springer-Verlag.

Wagner, M., R. D'Amico, C. Marder, L. Newman, and J. Blackorby. 1992. What happens next? Trends in postschool outcomes of youth with disabilities: The second comprehensive report from the National Longitudinal Transition Study of Special Education Students. Menlo Park: SRI International.

Waldron, K. A., D. G. Saphrie, and S. A. Rosenblum. 1987. Learning disabilities and giftedness: Identification based on self-concept, behavior, and academic patterns. *Journal of Learning Disabilities* 20, 422–428.

Wang, M. C., and M. C. Reynolds. 1995. *Making a Difference for Students at Risk.* Thousand Oaks, Calif.: Corwin Press.

Werner, E. E. 1984. Resilient children. *Young Children* 40, 68–72.

Werner, E. E., and R. S. Smith. 1982. *Vulnerable, but Invincible: A Longitudinal Study of Resilient Children and Youth.* New York: McGraw-Hill.

Whitmore, J. R. 1980. *Giftedness, Conflict, and Underachievement.* Boston: Allyn and Bacon.

Wilkinson, S. C., K. W. Webb, L. D. Higgins, and M. E. Nielsen. 1993. College bound or college blocked? Paper presented at the Annual Meeting of the Council for Exceptional Children Division on Career Development and Transition, November 16, 1993, Albuquerque, NM.

Wood, K. D., and B. Algozzie. 1994. *Teaching Reading to High-Risk Learners.* Boston: Allyn and Bacon.

FINDING GOLD:
THE GOLD PROGRAM FOR GIFTED
LEARNING DISABLED ADOLESCENTS

by Corinne Bees
Prince of Wales School

The GOLD program addresses the needs of gifted, learning disabled students at the secondary school level. Although gifted students with learning disabilities have multiple learning needs, they rarely qualify for multiple services (Brody and Mills, 1997). The GOLD program is a successful, unique, multiple service that goes beyond the traditional resource room. Aspects of this model, including the program description and data from more than fifty teens, could be useful for addressing the difficulties that gifted and learning disabled adolescents encounter.

The GOLD Program

The GOLD program began in September 1989 in Vancouver, British Columbia, with funding for one teacher, three-quarter time, to provide support for fifteen students grades eight to ten. Before 1989, existing services for students with learning disabilities had a strong emphasis on modification and remediation, but did not address the gifted potential of the twice-exceptional population. The program now includes one additional full-time support staff and serves twenty students grades eight to twelve, and these students have a high level of learning potential and needs. The author continues as the teacher of this program. Prince of Wales School, the secondary school that contains the GOLD program, resides in a middle- to upper-middle-class urban neighborhood. Historically, because of the school's academic nature and the lack of special programs within the school, the grades eleven and twelve student population did not include students with complicated learning disabilities or high-risk behavior problems. Students with such problems often transferred to other secondary schools or were discouraged from taking senior academic courses. Others went to private schools where they could receive attention for their disabilities. As experience with GOLD students increases, teachers at Prince of Wales have become more flexible, as they understand, enjoy, and accept this stimulating population.

Entrance Criteria and Process

Entrance criteria for the GOLD program have been adapted and refined as experience with the program increases. Elementary school counselors send applications to the GOLD screening committee. The screening committee identifies gifted potential and learning disabilities, reviews psychological assessments such as the Wechsler Intelligence Scale for Children—Revised (WISCR) or Stanford Binet IQ tests, and considers academic assessment data. An IQ score or a partial IQ score in the superior or very superior range indicates gifted potential. Discrepancies between IQ potential, as opposed to achievement and academic assessment scores, indicate a learning disability.

Brody and Mills (1997) raise several controversial issues regarding the identification process, and thus the GOLD program criteria avoid rigid cutoffs. Assessment includes teacher and counselor referral and personal interviews with the potential student. The GOLD program has accepted a student whose gifted potential was recognized by his teacher, but whose IQ tests were average. Sometimes discrepancies in test scores can signal the existence of a learning disability for a gifted student. Brody and Mills (1997) conclude, "Trying to find one defining pattern or set of scores to identify all gifted students with learning disabilities is probably futile." Students whose primary difficulties were emotional fragility or attention deficit hyperactivity disorder (ADHD) rather than learning disabilities also have been accepted into the GOLD program. These diagnoses are not always obvious during screening and may be masked by an apparent learning disability, but they become known once the GOLD staff is familiar with the student.

In the last four years, the GOLD screening committee has excluded students whose learning disabilities and/or behavior problems are so severe that they cannot write a complete sentence or do simple arithmetic problems. These students benefit more from a program focusing on students with severe learning disabilities.

The GOLD program requires a specialized staff dedicated to this unusual population. The program has one teacher with a master's degree in special education, including courses in gifted education, and one support staff. Both work three-quarter time within the GOLD program. Unofficial support personnel include peer counselors and volunteers. One-to-one support for each student, at least part of the time, is an essential ingredient of this program.

The GOLD program model is as flexible as possible responding to the individual needs of the students, but also takes restrictions of the school into account. The current model ensures that each GOLD student has at least one GOLD class (three hours per week) as part of an eight-class timetable. Each GOLD class, which contains six to eight students, provides time for the

GOLD curriculum, discussions, and subject support. The class can become a haven, where students find social support as well as organizational assistance. Grade eight students all have GOLD English 8 for extra support during their first year of high school. In addition, several GOLD students have more than one GOLD class. This extra class can accommodate a student who is taking a course by correspondence, a student who needs an extra support block, or a student who is completing an academic course under the supervision of the GOLD teacher. GOLD students have earned academic credit for English 10, Math 9, and modified Science 10 by completing the work with the GOLD staff. The GOLD teacher receives support from math and science teachers to provide outlines and tests. Students have received additional GOLD support for many reasons: severe learning disabilities (particularly in math), student-subject teacher personality conflict, or the need for more emotional support. Although math is often difficult for GOLD students, currently two GOLD students have enrolled in enriched Math 9. Other than their GOLD classes, most GOLD students integrate fully into regular classes.

Approximately fifty students have enrolled in the program over eight years, forty-six of them boys. Most of them feel angry and anxious, not uncommon emotions for this population. Brody and Mills (1997) state, "The social and emotional consequences of having exceptional abilities and learning disabilities when one or both of the conditions is unrecognized, can be pervasive and quite debilitating." The GOLD program has had several students who take ADHD medication, or antidepressant medication. Many students have had school phobia problems (previously missing at least three months of school). Three students have been in adolescent psychiatric hospitals. Three students have attended secondary schools for gifted students, but did not complete the program or were unsuccessful.

The most common learning disabilities are in the areas of visual-motor processing speed, reading speed, and spelling. Even though a student's visual-motor processing speed may not be below average, the frustration of being gifted with only an average processing speed results in severe written output problems for some GOLD students. This discrepancy seems to particularly plague them when writing out math problems. Other common problems include organizational difficulties and a disinclination to pay attention to deadlines.

The GOLD Program

The GOLD program provides a meaningful school connection for these students. GOLD students feel motivated not only by an enriched curriculum or acceptance of their difficulties, but also by finding meaningful connections.

Many of the GOLD students experience anxiety. "The learning disabled/gifted child is seldom referred for psychological assessment because of a skill deficiency but rather for the psychological manifestations of distress" (Senf, 1983). Thus, optimism, humor, and encouragement for the staff are vital components. A GOLD graduate recently commented that the author could talk all she wanted to the staff of the school about learning disabilities but nobody would really understand the pain that is experienced every minute the student spent in the school building. Giving students the chance to laugh and relax can lighten these feelings. We tell jokes, act silly, and try and look at the humorous, lighter side of situations without taking away from the seriousness of the students' concerns.

Reward and celebration are essential. When a student describes an achievement, when a persistently tardy student arrives on time, or for any other important reason, we bring out licorice to share with everyone. Licorice seems to have quietly become a symbol of success. We recognize that for the majority of our students success has become a far greater motivating factor than failure because they already feel like failures. "Self-efficacy results mainly from success experiences and reciprocally motivates better performance"(Baum and Owen, 1988). Other extrinsic rewards exist. For instance, with several students we have instituted point systems to encourage work output, better organization, or nondisruptive behavior. The reward has nearly always been excused time from school. When students bring their homework agenda books, checks are given and these checks can be cashed in for rewards. In the hustle and bustle of a busy school atmosphere, the GOLD class becomes a place where students can celebrate achievements that might be overlooked in the traditional setting.

Trust and a nonjudgmental atmosphere characterize the GOLD environment. "Trust and acceptance must be accomplished between teacher and students before students build those qualities into classroom relationships" (Kendig, 1988). Problems and issues always receive open discussion, and mutual respect characterizes that discussion. The staff tries not to contact parents or administrators without student involvement, and we do not criticize a student for being off task or failing. We simply hear the students, present our viewpoints, and help them be aware of their choices. We discourage sarcasm, competition, the word "should," and put-downs. Negative peer pressure has become an important topic of our discussions. We comment to students who infringe on this policy, and often ask them to leave the room for a short period. In turn, we expect students to comment on staff's infringement of the rules. We do not have rigid behavior restrictions, but our room must be seen as a safe place for each of our students. Establishing trust is the cornerstone in helping students decrease their defenses, take risks and overcome their difficulties.

Problems frequently are discussed with a group of GOLD students rather than with a single student, either at lunch or during one of our class meeting times. The GOLD staff will ask students' permission before we have a meeting. Open discussions become opportunities to teach alternatives to anger or avoidance. We stress recognizing hurt but using critical thinking skills, negotiation, and compromise as alternatives. Peers offer reasonable suggestions, which adds to the cohesiveness and trust level.

We encourage student empowerment and self-advocacy. The GOLD staff has learned that allowing students to make choices, rather than allowing their parents or staff to make choices for them, helps to keep them in school and to dispel some anxiety. Staff and parents can offer suggestions, but in most cases it is crucial that students make their own decisions even if they appear wrong. This decision-making process is especially important if trust has not been established in the group. Empowering students in the decision-making process itself can matter more than the outcome of any decision.

Several organizational aspects of the GOLD program distinguish it in relationship to the school as a whole. For at least part of their schedule, the GOLD students are grouped homogeneously with other intellectual peers who also have learning disabilities. They begin to recognize that they as individuals are not alone, that they are not stupid or lazy, and that there are other bright students who are like them. The opportunity to make friends with others in this group matters a great deal. "Programs for the gifted and learning disabled help these students gain support from others who have seemingly contradictory strengths and weaknesses"(Brody and Mills, 1997).

GOLD students are integrated into mainstream classes for most subjects. Students have commented that this combination of mainstream and GOLD programs has been a strength for the program. The GOLD teacher interacts with administration each year to organize a schedule for each GOLD student that will have the best teacher-student match possible.

Administration and staff flexibility have resulted in several GOLD students having adjusted timetables that reflect the amount of time they are able to attend school. For example, a few students are allowed partial timetables, and some students are waived from physical education requirements. The GOLD teacher has discretion in allowing extra studies in the GOLD room, allowing a student to come late one morning, or allowing a student to miss a class last period in the afternoon.

The GOLD classroom is a welcome place for students as much as staff. The room, which has windows facing south, contains tables, carrels, five computers, a laptop, a stereo, tape recorders, a telephone, and a microwave along with subject support material. The classroom is open to GOLD students most of the time. Some of the students do not feel comfortable roaming the school at break and lunchtime. The GOLD room offers respite from the hustle and bustle of the regular school setting. Students have limited use of the phone, the microwave, computers for word processing and research, and the use of one computer for games at lunch and breaks. Some students use the room to store their books instead of using a locker. A student who recently graduated commented that her haven was the GOLD room, for here she could talk about what was important intellectually. Students needn't conform to peer pressure or be part of adolescent gossip.

The GOLD staff is committed to a high level of personal involvement. Many of our students relate to adults more than to their peers, so staff strives to be available to listen and empathize. The staff often spends lunch hours or break times talking to students or helping them with subject work.

The GOLD class frequently starts with a discussion that occasionally takes the entire class time. Following discussion, students work individually or in small groups. They may choose not to do any of their own work during the GOLD class, but they are not allowed to interrupt the working space of others.

The structuring of an individual student's work in the GOLD class is based on that student's individual education plan (IEP) as required by the Ministry of Education. When planning the IEP, students' psychological and academic assessments as well as past difficulties are discussed so that causal factors for the learning problems and/or lack of achievement receive attention. The IEP is written personally with each student. Goals, objectives, strategies and adaptations specific to that student are included to deal with past difficulties and achieve current wishes. Students state their opinions of their assessments in an attempt to verify results, talk about causes, and make the IEP relevant. The parent and counselor receive copies of the IEP.

The IEP contains a commitment of time and strategies for work on any or all of the following: difficult subjects, completion of a correspondence course, a deficit area such as spelling, mechanics in writing or decoding, or keyboarding skills. Work on a strategy for word pronunciation seems to have been the final notch in the key that unlocked reading for one of our grade nine students. This brilliant person who learned best from television and movies has become a voracious reader.

In the past, the GOLD staff has insisted that the IEP contain time devoted to learning word processing skills. In almost all cases, our insistence on learning word-processing skills has been accepted by our students and has proven valuable to them. Increasingly, students arrive from elementary school with basic keyboard skills, so less emphasis is needed in this area.

The staff has found that use of computers aids not only in written work, but also in helping students focus on their work. Many of our students appear to be bodily kinesthetic learners (Lazear, 1991). For these students, and students who are ADHD, using computers seems to require that extra bit of muscle involvement that helps keep their minds focused on work.

Adaptations are also part of the IEP. Adaptations are allowances given to compensate for learning disabilities. They are not changes to the prescribed learning outcome. The most common adaptations used by GOLD students are extra time, use of a computer and spell checker, and use of a tape recorder. Extra time is allowed for students who use a computer, who have processing speed difficulties, or who have visual motor speed difficulties. The Provincial Ministry of Education allows adaptations for Grade 12 Provincial Exams if they have been in place for the last two years of secondary school and if they are validated by assessment. The adaptation form is completed with each student and then given to appropriate teachers. In most cases, we have no difficulty obtaining these adaptations. As more GOLD students take senior courses, more teachers of these courses have come to accept, or at least go along with, the requested adaptations. Resistant students, as well, see others benefit from these opportunities, and will begin to take advantage of these rights.

The GOLD Curriculum

The GOLD curriculum, taught during the discussion part of each GOLD class, includes skills in self-awareness, communication, critical thinking, advocacy, anger management, learning strategies, and discussions on values and ethics. It is important that GOLD students be aware of and learn to articulate their own learning profiles. While in the GOLD program, students complete achievement tests, the Myers Briggs Type Indicator (1977), and Multiple Intelligences (1993) questionnaires. These assessments are discussed with each student. The discussion framework includes all aspects of learning to discuss the individual's strengths and weaknesses. Students are regularly asked the question, "How did you learn that?" Research on learning disabilities, gifted learning disabilities, case studies such as "A Case Study: Marcia" (Whitmore and Maker, 1985), and videos on these topics are included in the GOLD curriculum. Use of videos to initiate discussions about learning disabilities has often led to disclosures of past difficulties. One student told how the learning assistance teacher in elementary school pounded the table in frustration because the student just couldn't learn how to say words she had placed on flash cards. A window has often opened during these discussions, and students have been prepared to confront issues, rather than continue to avoid or deny difficulties.

Assertiveness and self-advocacy are taught through discussion and role-play, and students are encouraged to be their own advocates. By advocating for himself, a GOLD student, who is a Shakespeare expert, was allowed to make a video rather than participate in class work on *The Merchant of Venice*. Students need to use their self-advocacy and assertiveness skills to be an effective part of this process. At the same time, we accept that self-advocacy is not always possible given the variety of teacher and student styles, and we act as strong advocates for our students. On behalf of students, the staff might ask for flexibility in such areas as attendance, behavior parameters, alternate assignments, and adaptations. At least one student has commented that our advocacy was the most important part of this program.

Strategies to deal with anger, panic attacks, unproductive work habits, and ineffective studying are included topics. Currently, we are discussing memory, what strengths or deficits each student's memory includes, mnemonic devices, and how these relate to learning styles. We relate strategies to learning styles and talk about positive rather than negative compensating strategies. How to deal with panic attacks was included in one student's IEP.

We also include time for discussions on values and ethical issues. This time is often the only opportunity in school for these students to express themselves and hear others in return. Our students thrive during these discussions and have commented on their importance.

Help is always available for a GOLD student having difficulty in any subject. The staff helps students with organization such as keeping track of homework, finding compatible tutors for difficult subjects, and teaching appropriate learning strategies. The staff has regular contact with subject teachers and are aware of what goes on in many of the students' non-GOLD classes. After-school study sessions are common.

GOLD English

"It is students whose talents and disabilities overlap and are both in academic areas who are most likely to be misunderstood, under-served, and in need of special services" (Brody and Mills, 1997). The GOLD program includes English for any new student at the Grade eight or nine level. This opportunity for the staff to have more contact with these new young students allows the English program to be enriched as well as adapted for particular individual needs. Some students have written output difficulties but high reading comprehension abilities, while others have written output difficulties with severe reading disabilities. These combinations need to be accommodated, and the teacher needs to learn about these students as individual learners in order to achieve success. The author currently teaches English 8-9 to eight students.

The enriched curriculum varies depending on the needs and interests of the students, but the purpose is to challenge these gifted students and yet accommodate their difficulties. Students choose their own themes much of the time, and projects allow students to explore their own interests and make presentations using their strengths. Thus, students experience the learning process as something that they initiate and own, rather than as something they must do to conform or comply. One student wrote a computer program for a book report. Students who have never given an oral report in elementary school have anxiously accomplished this task in this small setting, and other students have been allowed to prepare written reports rather than make oral presentations. Students use computers for nearly all written work. This model encourages students to advocate for flexibility in assignments in other classes.

Historical and Continuing Difficulties

Inflexibility of school regulations, emotional difficulties of students, unsupportive attitudes of teachers or parents, and the lack of appropriate structure of the GOLD program have been some of the difficulties along the way. Additionally, for the GOLD staff, dilemmas regarding the best way to help particular students are always present.

At times, the school would not provide an unusual timetable for a GOLD student. As students on partial timetables have managed to make it through rough years, administrators have become aware of the benefits of flexibility.

Anxiety, depression, and school phobia have been roadblocks for students. Anxiety can lead to denial of problems and enduring avoidance. School phobia, with accompanying illness, can lead to so many absences that the goal of passing grades seems unachievable. We have overcome school phobia twice but only since the program has added support staff who can provide more individual contact. Depression in at least two situations has been too severe for us to counteract.

ADHD, perfectionism, and severe learning disabilities are some of the difficulties impeding success for the GOLD students. The academic demands of Prince of Wales curriculum and the behavior requirements in many classrooms make accommodating the needs of ADHD gifted and learning disabled adolescents almost impossible. As well, there appears to be little support other than medication for ADHD adolescents.

Students can become discouraged when attitudes and teaching practices make it difficult for them to succeed. Adults in their educational environments have made statements like: "All these students need is a kick in the pants." "He is just lazy." "Reading speed problems are an indication of a reading comprehension deficit problem and therefore an indication of low intelligence." "What if I gave all my students extra time?" These comments demonstrate a lack of knowledge of the most basic needs of twice-exceptional students. Fortunately, these attitudes continue to evolve as teachers learn more about the way their twice-exceptional students think.

Difficulties with parents have included unstructured home life, parental expectations of the student that interfere with school attendance, and parental inability to share power with the school so that, no matter how successful the student is at school, success is not reinforced at home. In very rare cases, there may be an apparent need in a family for the student to continue to have problems. So far, we have not been very successful in counteracting these parental attitudes. In one case, a student who was finally overcoming school phobia and written output problems was pulled from the program by his parents. In many cases, these parents also decline family counseling.

In the early years, several problems hampered the GOLD program. The foremost problem was lack of support staff. As well, expectations of students were not high enough, students selected were often inappropriate, and GOLD classes needed more structure. As the staff has become more sure of themselves and familiar with the students, the program has gained the necessary structure. The goals and objectives addressed in the IEP are an excellent way for students to remain aware of what they need to do to be successful. An ongoing cause of stress for staff is the many dilemmas we face. A chart developed by the author contrasts characteristics of gifted learning disabled students (Whitmore, 1980), from the author's personal experience, with how these characteristics can be perceived by the jaundiced eye. It is often difficult to avoid seeing some of these characteristics with a jaundiced eye and then acting from this inappropriate vision.

TYPICAL BEHAVIOR CHARACTERISTICS OF THE GIFTED/LD

CHARACTERISTIC	THE "JAUNDICED" EYE
Perfectionist	Lazy
Fear and feelings of failure	
Idealist	
Highly sensitive	Self-indulgent
Problems with social skills	Immature
Socially isolated	Snob, depressed
Low self-esteem	Helpless
Hyperactive, distractible	No control
Inattentive	Doesn't care
Fails to complete assignments	
Psychomotor inefficiency	Sloppy, doesn't care
Frustrated	Overemotional
Need for control	
Excessively critical of self and others	Unpleasant
Rebellious against drill and excessive repetition	Spoiled
Different learning style	
Disparaging of work required	Arrogant, stubborn
Become an expert in one area and dominate discussions in this area	Show-off
Deny learning disability	Defensive
Teacher dependent	Hard to get along with
Bored	Daydreamer
Ethical	Self-righteous, intolerant

As well, the GOLD staff must be constantly conscious of the need to encourage independence and intrinsic motivation in the students, and to avoid learned helplessness, but we must balance this with our determination to find a way to help these students be happier and be successful.

Grade nine, ages fourteen and fifteen, seems to be a crucial year for GOLD students. Three students have moved to private schools in the middle of grade nine, and three students have dropped out of school. As far as the author is aware, the latter three have never returned successfully to any school.

Anxiety, a common characteristic of the GOLD students, is not fully addressed in this program. Some GOLD students who remain tracked with their peers for their senior years in the traditional structured school environment experience an almost unbearable amount of stress. This stress can be eased by allowing the students to proceed at their own level and pace, advancing to college-level learning where appropriate, or taking more time to complete coursework when necessary. A lunch-hour support group can soothe students at all levels, and the GOLD program utilized this approach until funding cuts halted that aspect of the program.

Identification and understanding of gifted learning disabled students at the elementary school level has improved in the last three years, as the Vancouver school district has hired a part-time support teacher for this population. Consequently, many of the current GOLD students were identified early and have not had to endure seven years of elementary education with no understanding of their difficulties.

The GOLD program does not include mentors and work experience at this time. Limited amounts of student time and energy are the primary reasons, and many students are able to find their own mentors. We currently encourage two GOLD students to gain work experience in the computer field, but again, this might consume too much of the limited time and energy that they have, and interfere with their ability to be successful in school.

Final Comment

The atmosphere in the GOLD room, although sometimes stressful and full of complaints about the oppressive system, is more often invigorating, full of ideas, and exhilarating to both students and staff. It provides a safe haven, and a place where students can express their enthusiasm for learning without experiencing derision from less academically interested students. During a recent English class, as the author read a passage from Dickens, a GOLD student, unable to contain himself, jumped up and exclaimed, "I just love this. This is what I love."

REFERENCES

Baum, S., and S. Owen. 1988. High ability/learning disabled students: How are they different? *Gifted Child Quarterly* 32(3): 321–323.

Brody, L. E., and C. Mills. 1997. Gifted children with learning disabilities: A review of the Issues, *Journal of Learning Disabilities* 30(3): 282–286.

Canadian Achievement Tests, 2nd Edition. 1991. Canadian Test Centre Inc., Markham, Ontario.

Consulting Psychologists Press, Inc., 577 College Ave., Palo Alto, CA 94306. Copyright 1976, 1977 by Isabel Briggs Myers. Copyright 1943, 1944, 1957 by Katherine C. Briggs and Isabel Briggs Myers.

Gates, A. and W. H. MacGinitie. 1965. Gates-MacGinitie Reading Tests, Teachers College, Columbia University.

Kendig, K. 1988. Practical techniques for dealing with underachievement and self-concept. *The Gifted Child Quarterly* 11(3): 7–9.

Lazear, D. 1991. *Seven Ways of Teaching: The Artistry of Teaching with Multiple Intelligences,* Palatine, Ill.: Skylight Publishing.

Senf, G. M. 1983. The nature and identification of learning disabilities and their relationship to the gifted child. In L. Fox, L. Brody and D. Tobin.

Thorndike, R. L., E. P. Hagen, and J. Sattler. 1986. *Stanford-Binet Intelligence Scale: 4th Edition,* Chicago: Riverside.

Wechsler, D. 1974. Wechsler Intelligence Scale for Children—revised. New York: Psychological Corporation.

Whitmore, J. R. 1980. *Giftedness, Conflict and Underachievement.* Boston, MA.: Allyn and Bacon.

Whitmore, J. R., and C. J. Maker. 1985. *Intellectual Giftedness in Disabled Persons.* Rockville, Md.: Aspen Publications.

COLLEGE PLANNING FOR GIFTED STUDENTS
WITH LEARNING DISABILITIES

by Sandra Berger
Council for Exceptional Children

The decision to send a child with learning disabilities to college (regardless of giftedness) is not one to be taken lightly. For an individual with deficits in social, study, and organizational skills, the decision looms large. Support systems meticulously worked out in high school cannot follow the student to college. Parent advocacy must be replaced by self-advocacy. Academic learning must be pursued while the student develops a medley of independent living skills, seeks friends, and separates from home and family. The student who is thinking of college must be made aware of all these difficulties and understand that the choice to attend or not to attend is his or her own.

Once the student decides to pursue attending a college, the personal (Who am I?) and college (Who are they and what will they expect of me, etc.?) evaluations begin. Discussions also begin with guidance counselors and college advisers. There are college fairs to attend, guides and directories to review, visits to be made, and applications to be completed.

For a student with learning disabilities, the basic college-planning steps and schedules resemble those for a more typical student, but the student and his parents must expand upon the basics and focus on specific, unique issues. For example:

- They must learn to distinguish schools that merely accept students with learning disabilities as a condition of continuing federal support from those that actively encourage their enrollment by providing specialized programs.
- They must investigate the school's support to determine whether it is unstructured (provided as needed) or structured (records on the student are maintained and progress is monitored).

As the list of college criteria is assembled, the student and parents must be honest about their perceptions of the student's needs. Basics such as distance from home and available transportation for home visits, single-sex education or coeducation, size of student body, and academic standing must be expanded to include issues such as the following:

- Is there evidence of an organized program? Is there evidence of a full-time staff in the program, as well as a full-time director to monitor activities?
- Is there evidence of special considerations for students, such as allowing tape recorders in the classroom, untimed tests, writing laboratories, tutors in every subject area, and allowing extended time for graduation?
- Is there evidence of successful career placements of students in their chosen fields following graduation?

As with any college search, the list will narrow to five to seven good candidates. The schools must then be contacted, interviews arranged, and family visits planned. Campus tours and the opportunity to sit in on classes must be given particular attention. The student personally judges the level of difficulty of the instruction, observes the interaction of other students, and gains for himself or herself a sense of the relationship between the students and the faculty.

The admissions interview may not answer all the questions regarding programs designed for these students. If this is so, the student and his or her parents must seek out and meet with a member of the learning disabilities program staff. A list of questions based on family concerns and perhaps stimulated by a review of the college directories and guides or discussions with high school guidance personnel should be prepared prior to the visit. Questions might include the following:

- What type of support is available for students with disabilities?
- Does a full-time professional staff monitor the program?
- Has the program been evaluated, and if so, by whom?
- Are there any concerns for the program's future?
- Who counsels students during registration, orientation, and course selection?
- Which courses provide tutoring?
- What kind of tutoring is available, and who does it—peers or staff?
- Is tutoring automatic, or must the student request assistance?
- How well do faculty members accept students with learning disabilities?
- May students take a lighter load?
- Are courses in study skills or writing skills offered?
- Have counselors who work with these students received special training?
- How do students on campus spend their free time? Are there programs that will interest and accommodate them?

- May students take more time to graduate?
- Whom can parents contact if they have concerns during the academic year?

Dilemma constantly stymies the adolescent's progress toward adulthood. Decisions and choices must often be based on fragmentary knowledge and perceptions or distorted recollections. The dilemma faced by students, most particularly gifted students with learning disabilities, stems from their desire to demonstrate independence from parents, counselors, teachers, and tutors, and the equally strong desire to maintain the respect and support of those same parents, counselors, teachers, and tutors. Students frequently wish to make the decisions that will frame their future, even while sensing that they may not be realistic or ultimately doable.

College and career planning for gifted students with disabilities is practicable, but it requires extraordinary participation, cooperation, and patience. The following suggestions may help those who guide gifted students with learning disabilities:

1. Many students are not identified because they can mask a learning disability and achieve at what seems like a normal or average rate. In fact, it is only because they are gifted that they can accomplish this. Comprehensive testing should be recommended for any student having difficulty, particularly in fifth or sixth grade. Results may be more accurate if the student is tested in the environment in which he or she is expected to perform.

2. To assist gifted students with learning disabilities we must focus on their strengths rather than their learning weaknesses (Vail, 1987).

3. Students should be informed that there are several forms of the SAT and many other standardized tests. Students may request to take an untimed version of the SAT. For more information, contact SAT Services for Students with Disabilities, P.O. Box 6226, Princeton, NJ 08541-6226, http://www.collegeboard.org or ETS http://www.ets.org/prog03.html.

4. Students who might have difficulty completing a written or typed college application should investigate *MacApply, College Link,* or other computerized methods of completing a college application.

NATIONAL CLEARINGHOUSES

The following agencies provide information and resources to parents, teachers, counselors, and others who are interested in the special needs of gifted students with disabilities.

THE ERIC CLEARINGHOUSE ON DISABILITIES AND GIFTED EDUCATION (ERIC EC), The Council for Exceptional Children, 1920 Association Drive, Reston, VA 22091, 800-328-0272. E-mail: ericec@cec.sped.org. URL: http://ericec.org.

ERIC is a national information system on education, with the world's largest database of education-related documents, journal citations, and other print materials. As one of sixteen ERIC clearinghouses nationwide, ERIC EC gathers, selects, and abstracts the best of the professional literature on disabilities and gifted education. The ERIC EC Web site includes a comprehensive array of reading material and links to other resources.

HEATH Resource Center, the National Clearinghouse on Postsecondary Education for Individuals with Disabilities, http://www.acenet.edu/Programs/HEATH/home.html.

Provides information on educational support services, policies, procedures, adaptations, and opportunities on American campuses, vocational-technical schools, adult education programs, independent living centers, transition, and other training entities after high school for individuals with disabilities.

National Information Center for Children and Youth with Disabilities (NICHCY), http://www.nichcy.org.

An information and referral center that provides information on disabilities and disability-related issues. The focus is on education and children and youth, ages birth to twenty-two years.

INTERNET SITES WITH INFORMATION ON GIFTEDNESS AND DISABILITIES ERIC EC: http://ericec.org

LD Online: http://www.ldonline.org
The Mining Company (Special Education Section): http://specialed.miningco.com

CONCLUSION:

IF NOT YOU, WHO?

by Kiesa Kay

If a child with an IQ that's one in a million has a disability that's one in a thousand, how likely is it that she will have others in a class who learn the same way that she does? Shall we ignore that child's learning needs because it's not a majority concern? Statistics from the Children's Defense Fund show that one in twelve children have some kind of disability, and gifted children are among the upper 2 percent of the learning population. Although they may find one another on the Internet, few of these children will find learners like themselves in a classroom setting. Individualization in education is essential if these children are going to meet their highest potential. Teacher education rarely requires extensive knowledge of giftedness or special education needs, yet these teachers work with students who have these needs in every working day. The time has come to consider each learner as an individual, not as part of a mixed-ability group.

Many answers exist to the question of how to reach and teach twice-exceptional learners, how to inspire them and help them achieve their dreams. The home-schooling parents have the individualization that helps inspire real learning in areas of interest. The private schools, boarding and day, often have academic rigor to challenge and interest students. The public schools have legal obligations through federal law to serve students with disabilities, and have created a few innovative programs. Still, without the law to enforce fairness, the student's needs might rely entirely on the knowledge and sensitivity of an administrator.

At the time of this writing, no federal mandate exists to support the learning needs of gifted students. When one administrator looked at our child's 504 plan, he deleted those things that pertained to giftedness needs, telling us that he would do the legal minimum for our child. Most administrators have vision and insight, however, and do not share this man's lack of regard for gifted children.

Twice-exceptional students are like other experts, in that they can do some things with stellar grace, and other things with difficulty. Once they escape from the confines of a linear school system, they may become quite adept and successful in the world—if the system itself has not destroyed their self-confidence. They will flourish in environments that allow the development of their strengths. When giftedness combines with other learning differences, children in traditional, left-brained settings may find themselves feeling very alone. Sensitivity to these special needs seems to be the first step.

Teaching these children requires more than a single methodology or theory. Overall improvement of teaching strategies, and required classes in giftedness and in special education for all teachers could benefit these students. Mentors to provide one-to-one attention and real caring would help. Rewarding creativity as well as obedience would help. Most of all, these students cannot learn effectively in the fifty-minute classes that constitute so many middle school and high school learning situations. They need thematic continuity among classes, rhyme and reason to their days. These students cannot think their best about math for an hour, then switch to English, then switch to government, et cetera. They need connected strategies that link the subjects along a contiguous continuum. At the same time, creating flexible scheduling for students can be very challenging to school staff.

Many of the true creative geniuses have not been generalists. Instead, they have specialized in a single subject area, with great results. Perhaps we need to encourage our children to specialize, to allow time and space for their own particular interests to flower. An ideal situation would allow at least three afternoons a week for the child to study what that child wants to know. As an adult, I feel cheated if I do not have time in every week to discover something new in areas that interest me. My children deserve no less. When my children begin new projects of their own, there is no question of whether they'll complete their work. They become enthralled, looking up material on the Internet, asking to go to the library, eschewing television and other pursuits in order to pursue their quests for real knowledge. They falter when the work assigned to them has no meaning or validity in their own lives. They are not worksheet children, ready to regurgitate facts to get a good grade. They are disinclined to waste their own time that way. Grades mean little to them, and learning is all. Some children are born with a purpose, a brilliant light, a mission that they can sense from an early age. They have the intelligence to learn what they need to know. It is up to us to find a way for them to express that intelligence, to discover that cognitive ability, to encourage the blossoming of these minds. We can connect them to resources across the globe, and show them areas of knowledge heretofore inaccessible.

An ideal program would have individualization of all subject areas. Certainly, history would be taught, but not for an hour a day or less. Instead, the student could immerse himself or herself in a history project, spending hours at a time learning more and more in detail and depth about a subject. Mathematics needs to be taught on a daily basis, due to the nature of that learning, but the other subjects should be taught for an afternoon or a morning at a time, two or three times a week, more like college classes. Self-initiated learning would be encouraged by teachers, and time would be set aside for individual exploration of things that matter to the children. We need to stop interrupting these students just as they begin to become enthralled with learning.

There will be gaps at first, but not for long. We're talking about children who can read a book in a day and remember every word of it—but not comprehend more than 10 percent of a lecture. We're talking about children who can absorb every spoken word they hear, but take a month to read a novel. The pace of most classes is excruciatingly slow for some of them, and they tune out, bored beyond words. Sometimes they meet a challenge and tune out then, too, because it's become a habit by high school. Sometimes they genuinely do not know how to learn new material, how to study, because they've never encountered anything challenging in a classroom setting.

Small class size with cognitive peers would help support these students. No teacher should have to try to teach twenty-five to thirty students for one hour in six different groups in a single day! No student should have to try to fight for learning time! These students need time to absorb and consider ideas, apart from timed tests or dull worksheets. They need real, long-term projects that engage their creative imaginations. They need time. We need to teach the students, not the curriculum. Instead of having a set curriculum and expecting every student to jump as high as possible to meet it, perhaps we could consider each student, and ask what that student can learn, and how, and in what time period. Learning belongs within a meaningful context.

Take, for example, poetry. Students who meet poetry in a classroom setting sometimes consider it a tawdry thing, forced upon them by unrelentingly monotonous teachers who ask them to slice and dice a set of words. These same students delight in the street poetry of their musical favorites. A path exists between the street poets and a true appreciation of poetry across time, but students condemned to cutting poetry into syllabic bits for analysis probably will not find that path with ease. Appreciation must precede effective analysis.

Thus, appreciation of our twice-exceptional learners must come before we analyze how to work with them. Celebrating their differences can help them appreciate themselves. We hover on the edge of creating a new system of individualized education, where these learners can flourish.

Who bears the ultimate responsibility for identifying and meeting the needs of twice-exceptional students? Who is responsible for making sure that these children have the accommodations that they need in order to achieve their highest potential? At what point will the confusion come to a screeching, shuddering halt?

Federal law asserts that all students have the right to a free, appropriate public education. It doesn't say that students have a right to an optimal education. The 504 law and the Individuals with Disabilities in Education Act both indicate that the schools must create learning plans for students with special needs, but no federal law exists to protect the rights of students who have giftedness. The Office for Civil Rights, which oversees the implementation of Section 504 law, has no teeth, no power to penalize those districts that ignore the law. It takes vast need, deep pockets, and time to pursue any kind of legal recourse for discrimination against these students. The preferred course of action would be early identification and consistent accommodations.

Who will discover the uniquely gifted students and help them find learning pathways that work? Parents are the most accurate identifiers of giftedness in their own children, with an accuracy rate about 75 percent. Teachers, in contrast, hover at about 25 percent for accurate identification of gifted children. Administrators lack the interpersonal time with students in learning situations that could lead to identification of twice-exceptionality, and researchers often deal with students as research subjects.

Most teachers lack the training in special education and giftedness that would help them make the early identification, but they have the interpersonal time and opportunity to assess these children. Standardized achievement tests might give some inkling of special needs, if anybody takes time to analyze them on an individual basis. The private schools and some charter schools need not concern themselves with traditional teacher certification standards, so subject experts teach classes. For the twice-exceptional student, it's a mixed blessing. The subject expert will possess the enthusiasm and depth of knowledge that gives flight to the student's own interests, but often will not know much about teaching strategies for diverse learning styles.

Even at schools for gifted children, no assurance of identification exists. The schools that require pretesting usually choose who enters, so a student with a strong desire for admittance might strive to conceal a disability in hopes of attaining a position at the school of choice. At a recent conference on gifted education, a teacher asked what she was supposed to do when the administrators told her not to spend the school's money on testing—and yet the child in front of her clearly had educational issues that interfered with the learning process. Her moral obligation would be to refer that child for testing—but too many referrals, too much money spent, would incur the wrath of her budget-conscious bosses.

Parents frequently initiate testing, either through advocacy at a school or through independent means. Then, they're in a conundrum—unable to go into the school and absolutely ensure that those test results have some influence on the curriculum and accommodations for their children, and unwilling to ignore the significance of those results to the children's lives. Parents may have the ability to pursue identification, but only home-schooling parents have the ability to ensure implementation.

Disabilities take diverse shapes, and students themselves often try to blend into the crowd, preferring a safe anonymity to the pressure of being different. If a student strives to hide a disability, at what point is the school responsible for ferreting that information from the student? How can a school serve the imperceptible? Twice-exceptional students are exceptionally good at unintentional concealment of their own learning extremes. Teenagers, especially, want to fit somewhere. In the quest for social acceptance, vast learning time dissolves.

"My kid beat up your honor student," reads one obnoxious bumper sticker. It's all too true. As an acquaintance told me, "We didn't have gifted kids when I was growing up. We just had smart kids who got beat up a lot." Gifted children too often are scapegoats, with no federal protections for a cognitively appropriate education. It does not benefit a student in the immediate social strata of a school system to be too different, too smart, or too much in need of support. Sometimes students will object strenuously to being identified as twice-exceptional, because they fear that the labeling will hurt their future chances of success in admission to college or even high school. The resistance to labeling results in a lack of information about what might work to reach and teach these students.

Once identification occurs, who is responsible for finding the teaching strategies that will fit the unique learning styles of these students? Is it up to administrators to insist upon the use of these strategies, to provide resources to their teachers? What do teachers do if an administrator represses and repels their own progressive efforts, refusing access to conferences and training due to a hard look at the financial costs? Some schools are led by insightful administrators who realize the needs of these students, and encourage their teachers to keep learning and sharing. Many parents end up buying books and giving them to teachers, who also download information from the Internet for themselves. At the same time, not all twice-exceptional children come from resourceful families. Sometimes the teacher is the first to notice the signs, and then that teacher has to determine how to explore possibilities with parents without alienating them.

After years—literally, years—of effort, one mother active in school events said, "I wasted all that time, and it made no difference." At some point, as a parent, I decided that I could not tolerate even one more meeting in which an administrator or teacher degraded or criticized my child. I could not stand to explain my child's unique constellation of needs even one more time, not to anybody.

In a parents' group, I clutched a book that mattered to me and declared, "See? It's right in here. Here's research that says my child exists."

As a parent, I simply did not have an educational background in the issues that became daily facts of my life when these children were born. I did not plan to become knowledgeable about twice-exceptionality as a research subject. It quickly became apparent, though, that an understanding of these issues was essential if I was to become a strong advocate for my children. ADD looks suspiciously like spacey sleepiness to the uneducated observer. Sensory integration looks like sloppy handwriting and slouching. The negative conceptualizations had to be stricken from my realm of thought before I could overcome my own intense denial.

What are our responsibilities to these children, and to ourselves? I had this fantasy that when the children reached school age, my time would become my own during the days when they went to school. I had no idea about the tearful, worksheet-riddled nights, the utter lack of family time during the weekdays, the hours that I would spend trying to negotiate with a school district that simply did not serve twice-exceptional students in any meaningful way.

As a parent, it is too easy to complain about what's not there. For a time, I thought that the teachers and administrators owed it to my children to obey the laws, but now I know that even that much obligation cannot taken for granted by my family.

The poet Essex Hemphill said that "A starving man creates sustenance from whatever is available." My family began to create sustenance from the sparse resources in our immediate environment, and soon the resources seemed to multiply beneath our fingertips. In the meantime, my children grew older day by day. While five years may seem like a short span of time for the implementation of effective school policies, five years is a very large percentage of a twelve-year school experience for a child. My family could not wait. We tried the geographical solution, moving to where the resources were said to be more plentiful for gifted children, hoping against hope that the twice-exceptionality issues would be understood there.

The answer exists in a blended, strong, relentless effort by the entire team of teachers, administrators, and family members, solidly grounded in understanding of research literature. I know what an appropriate program would contain. Program implementation would have to be as strong and sure as philosophical certitude.

We need to create places where truly creative thinkers can thrive without remorse for being who they are. An ideal program would be individualized to suit the needs of each student, and every student would receive testing on the WISC-III and the Stanford Binet LM—or Stanford Binet V, when it comes available. Every teacher would receive training in recognizing giftedness, and in disabilities of every type. Differentiating the curriculum would be a given, making sure that each student has materials at his or her own cognitive level and pace. Every student would receive support above criticism, in a one to three criticism/support ratio. Children would be grouped by ability and interest, encouraged to develop their dreams, their hopes, their plans. Every summer, they'd go to a language learning or academic camp and to the athletic camp of their choice.

And it would be close to home—very close to home. Boarding schools work for some students, but other families really need to stay together. Many boarding schools have a subculture of violence, especially among freshman boys, that makes them an inappropriate choice for gifted or sensitive children. Some of the high schools, both public and private, have a thriving drug trade in Ritalin now. Children who legitimately obtain the drug can sell it to classmates for $5 to $20 a pill, especially during finals time. In the boarding schools, dorm masters can't be everywhere all the time, and they're frequently teachers who teach a full class schedule every day. Those teachers sleep at night. Anybody with teens knows that many teens don't sleep much at night. Saturdays are particularly dangerous to freshmen, as the teachers cherish a few afternoon hours to themselves. Sometimes there's hazing. At one school quite recently, freshman boys were challenged to run to a flagpole in very little clothing, and the older boys yanked down their underwear. It might seem funny, but to a sensitive teen, it's not fun. Adolescents often lack the readiness to thrive alone. Parental attention remains a vital part of the student's whole education.

So we need schools that provide mentorship, kindness, adult guidance, academic excellence, and individualization. Emotional supports and peer supports mean as much to these students as computer competence and good test scores.

Intense distress and family stress can result when a child doesn't have a good match with a school. Home schooling has been chosen by many twice-exceptional students who later become successful, as has placement in programs geared to mitigate negative effects of disability. Sometimes, even schools for gifted children don't have room for children with other special needs, or for highly or profoundly gifted learners.

Gifted children have intensity, a powerful ability to focus, and often a heightened awareness of justice, morality, and emotions. The gifted child accused of "exaggerating" very well may be a child with more sensitivity to certain stimuli than the other children have. Just because s/he perceives the world differently does not mean that s/he is wrong. Perhaps that old stereotype of the absentminded professor has its roots in twice exceptionality.

I think that the keys to educating these students remain individualization and mentorship. Group-think does not work with these students. They need groups, for social support and emotional development, but not all the time. Some of them get overwhelmed with too much group interaction, but have no time during the school day to be alone with their own thoughts.

The advent of the Internet offers some wondrous potential that did not exist twenty years ago. With basic keyboard competence, a student can find papers from experts on virtually any subject of interest. I think that an educational program for twice-exceptional learners would include extended hours for reflection, detailed assignments with possibilities for creative responses, and extensive use of Internet exploration during school time. Everybody cares about something, and these passions can form the basis for deeper learning. At least a quarter of a student's school day should be spent in independent research on topics of personal interest, so that the student can learn to initiate and answer questions that matter to the self. The end product of the research matters, to give evidence of that research process and to heighten the sense of accomplishment.

With all of the worksheets and homework chosen by other people, time for one's own thoughts, plans, and dreams can drain away. Every student should be allowed the right to time for daydreaming and for considering personal projects. Resentment builds when adults control all of the thinking time.

I recently observed a classroom full of gifted children, ranging in age from eight to twelve. They were moderately, highly, and profoundly gifted, and even though there were only ten of them together, that teacher had her hands full. Some children didn't understand an assignment, and others had completed it with relative ease. Even though all of the children had intellectual ability beyond the norm, they had different areas of strength. It's not enough to put gifted children with a competent teacher, without differentiation of instruction for every child in the class. Nonetheless, it's better than an undifferentiated mixed ability class of thirty. When all the students start with the same knowledge base, there's no need for differentiation—but it's rare that all students begin with the same background. Differentiation can allow expression of learning for several learning styles. Plus, many twice-exceptional students would do well to study one subject in great depth, searching for myriad avenues to understanding rather than bouncing from one unrelated topic to the next every hour. Why not give students concentrated, intensive learning times for a single subject? Instead of having an hour of math, an hour of science, an hour of social studies, and an hour of language—why not study only two subjects a day, in depth? Support their assignments, stay nearby to keep them on-task, and let them work. Even the brightest students often need direction.

Once a student shows a profound interest in a subject area, that student should be paired with a mentor who has higher-level knowledge of the subject itself. Mentors can meet with their students in small groups of three to five, organizing a group project with room for creativity. We can find these mentors among parents, teachers, administrators, college professors, community activists, and businesspeople. To keep them, we can pay them. Too often, mentoring programs fail because the mentors are expected to work for free, in a volunteer capacity, while other teachers get paid for their time.

Many of these students need praise the way other students need oxygen—daily, regularly, constantly, for the things that they do that genuinely are helpful, workable, and progressive. They will work so hard if somebody shows an interest in them as thinking, feeling people. They will redouble their efforts when they receive support for their work.

When my son was little, he came home one day and told me, "Momma, you need to say more good words to me. You can say, 'Good work,' and 'You're a good player.' Now, you try it, Momma."

So I did.

These students also don't learn much in disconnected fifty-minute spans of time, and not all of them adapt well to an early morning schedule. They should be allowed the same flexibility that many college students receive, with class choices that include ninety-minute options, and even two-hour evening classes. Sometimes I wonder, why not let them play midnight basketball, attend school in the evenings and afternoons, and sleep or go to appointments in the mornings? Why can't we subvert the dominant paradigm? If a student despises morning classes, then that student's classes can begin at 10:30 A.M. The late-rising teachers can teach the late-rising students, or there can be some overlap. I think that school should be a three-quarter-time adventure throughout the year, instead of full-time work for nine months with three months of summer vacation. The other quarter of time is for independent learning projects. Especially with twice-exceptional students, it's important to keep those learning processes and time management strategies going for twelve months a year, not nine.

Mutual respect among all the people who work with twice-exceptional learners will lead to positive solutions that work. Parents bring their knowledge of their children, from birth to the present time, a longitudinal resource of immeasurable benefit. Children bring their knowledge of themselves. Teachers offer educational strategies, and administrators tend to consider the group as well as the individual's needs. With a strong foundation in current research, we can emerge with new hope for the most creative learners in our schools. These students need all of us.

BIBLIOGRAPHY FOR *UNIQUELY GIFTED: IDENTIFYING AND MEETING THE NEEDS OF TWICE-EXCEPTIONAL STUDENTS*

The following books are particularly useful in identifying and meeting the needs of twice-exceptional students, and individuals who have contributed essays to the book wrote many of them.

Ayres, Jean. *Sensory Integration and the Child.* Los Angeles: Western Psychological Services, 1979.

> This book has been the classic work in the field of sensory integration for twenty years. Although it's written with some professional terms that can be a bit problematic for the general reader, Ayres provides precise terminology and exemplification of the fundamentals of the field.

Baum, Susan, John Dixon, and Steve V. Owen. *To Be Gifted and Learning Disabled: From Identification to Practical Intervention Strategies.* Mansfield Center, Conn.: Creative Learning Press, 1991.

> The practical intervention strategies offered here can facilitate heightened learning without increasing frustration. Charts and graphs make this book accessible and useful to teachers.

Betts, George T., and Jolene K. Kercher. *Autonomous Learner Model: Optimizing Ability.* Greeley, Colo.: ALPS Publishing, 1999.

> The authors originally created the Autonomous Learner Model for gifted and talented students, and this five-dimensional model has been expanded for use by all learners in several settings. Th e model is designed to meet cognitive, emotional, and social needs of the student as a whole person.

Berger, Sandra. *College Planning for Gifted Students.* Reston, Va: Council for Exceptional Children, 1994.

> In addition to her excellent work for the Council for Exceptional Children, Sandra Berger has written a book that guides students through the quagmires of applications, essays, and dreams. Her well-reasoned approach reduces the mystery of college planning for high school students.

Clarke, Jean Illsley, and Connie Dawson. *Growing Up Again: Parenting Ourselves, Parenting Our Children.* New York: Harper and Row, 1989.

> After reading dozens of books on parenting, it is safe to say that this one is the very best of the best. By identifying characteristics of marshmallow parenting, constructive criticism, and more, the authors offer a guideline that emphasizes a positive, healing approach. The feelings chart and nurturing buttons are gems.

Crosier, Louis M. *Casualties of Privilege: Essays on Prep Schools' Hidden Culture.* Washington, D.C.: Avocus Publishing, 1991.

> This book gives startling insights into prep schools. In addition to demonstrating some troubles, the book goes that additional step to offer solutions.

Crosier, Louis M. *Healthy Schools, Healthy Choices: The Residential Curriculum.* Washington, D.C.: Avocus Publishing, 1992.

> This book is the sequel to *Casualties of Privilege*, and offers thoughtful consideration into how to create healthy experiences for students within boarding schools.

Damasio, Antonio R. *Descartes' Error: Emotion, Reason, and the Human Brain.* New York: Avon Books, 1994.

> This book draws upon the interwoven nature of emotions and rational thought. It's an accessible, well-written book on neurobiology.

Davis, Ronald D., with Eldon M. Braun. *The Gift of Dyslexia: Why Some of the Smartest People Can't Read . . . and How They Can Learn.* New York: Perigee Books, 1994.

> After a poignant and personal beginning, this book plunges into some strategies that really help people with dyslexia and dysgraphia learn to read and write with greater ease. This book takes a positive approach.

Delisle, James. *Guiding the Social and Emotional Needs of Gifted Youth.* New York: Longman Publishing Group, 1992.

> Children need access to educational materials at their own cognitive levels, and they also need a sense of place, and friends. James Delisle offers advice on how to empower youths to find their own way toward social and emotional development.

Ford-Harris, Donna. *Reversing Underachievement Among Gifted Black Youths: Promising Policies and Programs.* Teachers College Press, 1996.

> Donna Ford-Harris encourages making gifted programs accessible to African-American youths, identifying those youths, and incorporating aspects of African-American culture and heritage into the curriculum in order to retain students without making them feel split at the root.

Freed, Jeffrey, and Laurie Parsons. *Right-Brained Children in a Left-Brained World.* New York: Simon & Schuster, 1997.

> This book has become one of the most popular ones to share at conferences and on-line discussion groups. Jeffrey Freed and Laurie Parsons turn traditional strategies topsy-turvy to emphasize the strengths of right-brained thinkers. By the end of this book, any reader would be perceiving the assets as the biggest part of this kind of difference.

Gardner, Howard. *Extraordinary Minds.* New York: Basic Books, 1997.

> This short, easy-to-read book delineates the development of some great thinkers, illustrating commonalties among extraordinary minds.

Gardner, Howard. *Frames of Mind: The Theory of Multiple Intelligences.* New York: Basic Books. Tenth anniversary edition, 1993.

> This book has become a classic among educators who wish to explore new learning styles.

Gross, Miraca U.M. *Exceptionally Gifted Children.* New York: Routledge, 1993.

> Miraca Gross originally studied twelve profoundly gifted children to determine what set them apart from other students. The results may astound readers.

Guyer, Barbara. *The Pretenders: Gifted People Who Have Difficulty Learning.* Homewood, Ill.: High Tide Press, 1995.

> Barbara Guyer is a parent of a twice-exceptional daughter, as well as a professional in the field. In this book, she explores tough choices and meaningful moments.

Handler, Lowell. *Twitch and Shout.* New York: E.P. Dutton, 1998.

> This photographer has written an autobiographical book about what it's like to live with Tourette's syndrome.

Hartmann, Thom. *ADD Success Stories.* Grass Valley, Calif.: Underwood Books, 1995.

———. *Attention Deficit Disorder: A Different Perception.* Grass Valley, Calif.: Underwood Books, 1997.

———. *Healing ADD.* Grass Valley, Calif.: Underwood Books, 1998.

> All of Thom Hartmann's books explore the benefits and helpful strategies for people with ADD. He explains that people with ADD are like hunters, in a world dominated now by farmers. They need the quick responses, the attuned attitude, that would help them to flourish in environments where fast decisions may mean survival.

Hollingworth, Leta Stetter. *Children Above 180 IQ.* North Stratford, N.H.: Ayer Company Publishers, Inc. Reprint of 1942 ed. 1997.

> This brilliant book covers concepts and characteristics of genius, and asks the important question: "How shall a democracy educate the most educable?" Profoundly gifted children are underrepresented in available educational literature, and this book can become a starting point for considering the educational needs of this significant population.

Jamison, Kay Redfield. *An Unquiet Mind.* New York: Random House, 1995.

> This professor of psychiatry writes from her own professional experience and life experience as a brilliant woman with manic-depressive illness.

Kearney, Cassidy, and Kevin Kearney. *Accidental Genius.* Murfreesboro, Tenn.: Woodshed Press, 1995.

> The Kearney family has two profoundly gifted children, Maeghan and Michael. This book explores their journey through the labyrinth of educational possibilities for their intellectually accelerated son.

Kerr, Barbara A. *Smart Girls Two: A New Psychology of Girls, Women, and Giftedness.* Dayton, Ohio: Ohio Psychology Press, 1994.

> Thorns or shells? Barbara Kerr explains what it takes to protect creativity and brilliance as a woman in the world. She knows the obstacles, and she's not afraid to tell how women jump those obstacles in order to survive and thrive.

Kranowitz, Carol. *The Out-of-Sync Child: Recognizing and Coping with Sensory Integration Dysfunction.* New York: Skylight Press, 1998.

> Carol Kranowitz knows movement. In this book, she discusses sensory integration dysfunction, using examples and details to enhance reader understanding.

Lee, Christopher, and Rosemary Jackson. *Faking It: A Look into the Mind of a Creative Learner.* Portsmouth, N.H.: Boynton/Cook Publishers, 1992.

> Christopher Lee didn't know that he could learn to read until he reached college. This book tells his story.

Ratey, John. *The User's Guide to the Brain.* New York: Pantheon Books, 2000.

> John Ratey draws upon the most recent findings in brain research in this book. He discusses the brain in many aspects, and the implications of guidance from the brain.

Ratey, John, and Edward Hallowell. *Answers to Distraction.* New York: Simon and Schuster, 1996.

> If your child has ADD, this book and its section on a HOPE educator could change your family's life for the better. It is a companion book to *Driven to Distraction.*

———. *Driven to Distraction: Recognizing and Coping with Attention Deficit Disorder from Childhood through Adulthood.* New York: Simon & Schuster, 1995.

> Many books have been written on ADD at this point, and this one was the first one that my family read. It offers insight without harsh judgments.

Ratey, John, and Catherine Johnson. *Shadow Syndromes: The Mild Forms of Major Mental Disorders that Sabotage Us.* New York: Bantam Books, 1997.

> This deep, well-reasoned exploration of mild forms of disorders takes a humane view of different ways of thinking, and how to cope.

Reis, Sally. *Curriculum Compacting: The Complete Guide to Modifying.* Mansfield Center, Conn.: Creative Learning Press, 1992.

Reis, Sally, and Renzulli, Joseph. *Secondary Triad Model: A Practical Plan for Implementing Gifted Programs at the Junior and Senior High School Levels.* Mansfield Center, Conn.: Creative Learning Press, 1985.

> Sally Reis does not want children to be bored in classrooms. She believes in compacting, and her work is seminal to the understanding of how gifted programs can develop.

Schopler, Eric, and Gary B. Mesibov, eds. *High-Functioning Individuals with Autism: Current Issues in Autism.* New York: Plenum Press, 1992.

> This book contains a moving poem and essay by Jim Sinclair, founder of Autism Network International. It is part of a series on autism, and it takes a positive view of the potential and hopes of high-functioning individuals.

Silverman, Linda Kreger. *Counseling the Gifted and Talented.* Denver, Colo.: Love Publishing Co., 1993.

> This collection of essays touches upon the entire spectrum of counseling issues for gifted and talented students. It was named one of the top ten books in gifted studies by *The Roeper Review.*

Spitzer, Robert L., Miriam Givvon, Andrew E. Skodol, Janet B.W. Williams, and Michael B. First. *DSM-IV Case Book: A Learning Companion to the Diagnostic and Statistical Manual of Mental Disorders, 4th Ed.* Washington, D.C.: American Psychiatric Press, Inc., 1994.

If a child is diagnosed with a disorder, it helps a lot to know what the psychiatric jargon means. This bulky book offers specific case studies, indexed by type, and readers may get a sampling of what the disorders look like.

Winebrenner, Susan. *Teaching Kids with Learning Difficulties in the Regular Classroom.* Minneapolis, Minn.: Free Spirit Publishing, 1996.

This book delineates a number of specific learning difficulties and discusses how the classroom teacher can modify assignments to suit the needs of learners. The hands-on suggestions and the practical possibilities not only offer immediate answers, but also spark creative thought.

———. *Teaching Gifted Kids in the Regular Classroom.* Minneapolis, Minn.: Free Spirit Publishing, 1992. Susan Winebrenner teaches teachers how to teach, and these books contain some of her strongest strategies. They also are available on videotape. Her seminars are wonderful, full of strategies that can be put to immediate use. As a bonus, the videotape also contains an excellent "Super Sentences" workbook to help teachers differentiate class assignments. Her work can be extremely beneficial for the teacher in the mixed-ability grouping classroom.

Winner, Ellen. *Gifted Children: Myths and Realities.* New York: Basic Books, 1996.

Ellen Winner confronts the gap between ability and achievement among gifted students, and notes case studies to show how schools dumb down the most gifted children. She discusses child-centered homes and other aspects of gifted development.

APPENDIX A: INTERNET RESOURCES FOR EXPANDING OPTIONS IN THE CLASSROOM

by Sandra Berger

Resources on Giftedness and Disability

- DO-IT Program

  http://weber.u.washington.edu/~doit/

  A Web site for people with disabilities who successfully pursue academics and careers. Includes programs to promote the use of technology to maximize the independence, productivity, and participation of people with disabilities.

- The ERIC Clearinghouse on Disabilities and Gifted Education

  http://ericec.org/gifted/gt-menu.htm

- LD-online

  http://www.ldonline.org

- GT-SPECIAL, a listserv for discussing issues related to raising "twice-special" kids (gifted/special needs such as ADD, LD, other special needs)

  Subscription address: lyris@gtworld.org

  Post messages to: gt-special@gtworld.org

WWW Search Engines and Directories

- AltaVista—http://www.altavista.com
- Dogpile—http://www.dogpile.com
- Excite—http://www.excite.com
- Infoseek—http://www.infoseek.com
- Magellan—http://www.mckinley.com
- Webcrawler—http://WWW.WebCrawler.com
- Yahoo (a searchable directory)—http://www.yahoo.com
- And more . . . a variety of others can be seen at: http://cuiwww.unige.ch/meta-index.html OR http://infopeople.berkeley.edu:8000/src/srctools.html

Indexes, Subject Guides, and Libraries

Subject guides are developed by individuals who maintain coverage of specific subjects, adding a level of human filtering between resources and the user.

- American Library Association (search engine for subject area resources)
  http://www.ala.org
- Argus Clearinghouse
  http://www.clearinghouse.net/
- Federal Resources for Educational Excellence (FREE). Makes hundreds of Internet-based agencies across the U.S. Federal government easier to find. Includes a searchable subject index.
  http://www.ed.gov/free
- Iconnect Curriculum Resources
  http://www.ala.org/ICONN/socialst.html
- InfoMINE—Scholarly Resources on the 'Net (NEW!)
  http://lib-www.ucr.edu/
- W3 Virtual Library
  http://www.w3.org/

ERIC CLEARINGHOUSES

- **The ERIC Clearinghouse on Disabilities and Gifted Education**
  Gifted Education—http://ericec.org/gifted/gt-menu.htm
  Links to other resources include the National Research Center on Gifted/Talented and University-Based Gifted Centers and Talent Search Programs that provide summer programs and other services

AskERIC

A free question-answering and education reference and referral service about teaching and learning, educational administration, or education technology. E-mail your education question to: askeric@ericir.syr.edu

http://ericir.syr.edu/ithome/askeric.htm

- Search the ERIC Database
  http://ericae.net/search.htm
- ERIC Virtual Reference Desk, established to connect the K–12 community to digital reference experts in all fields.
  http://www.vrd.org/
- Gateway to Educational Materials. A new one-stop educational resource that provides information, lesson plans, and activities pertaining to all K–12 subjects.
  http://gem.syr.edu/

Useful Sites for Administrators and Policy Makers

- Staff development
  http://www.ties.k12.mn.us
  http://www.freenet.msp.mn.us
- Internet School Policies—Bellingham Public Schools
  http://www.bham.wednet.edu/policies.htm
- Funding Opportunities (E-rate)
  U.S. Department of Education Technology Initiatives
  http://www.ed.gov/Technology/
- National Center for Technology Planning
  http://www.nctp.com
- Network of Regional Technology in Education Consortia was established to help states, local educational agencies, teachers, school library and media personnel, administrators, and other education entities successfully integrate technologies into kindergarten through twelfth grade (K–12) classrooms, library media centers, and other educational settings, including adult literacy centers.
  http://rtec.org/ (a very busy site)
- Resources for Policy-makers
  http://www.ael.org/rcl/policy/

Useful Sites for Educators

- Awesome Library—K–12 Education Directory—NEW!
  http://www.neat-schoolhouse.org/awesome.html
- Busy Teachers' WebSite (includes interactive projects)
  http://www.ceismc.gatech.edu/BusyT
- Chronicle of Higher Education
  http://chronicle.merit.edu
- Classroom Connect
  http://www.classroom.net
- Library of Congress
  http://www.loc.gov
- Putnam County (NY) BOCES State Standards (twelve sets of state standards) http://www.putwest.boces.org/standards.html
- Smithsonian
  http://www.si.edu
  http://educate.si.edu (lesson plans)

- Teacher's Edition Online
  http://www.teachnet.com
- Teachers Helping Teachers
  http://www.pacificnet.net/~mandel//
- Teachers.Net
  http://www.teachers.net
- The Well Connected Educator™—online publishing center and forum for the K–12 community to read, write, and talk about educational technology.
  http://www.gsh.org/wce/
- WWW 4Teachers (South Central Regional Technology in Education Consortium) http://www.4teachers.org/home/index.shtml

Useful Sites for Parents

- A Comprehensive List of Distance Learning Sites
  http://online.parkland.cc.il.us/ramage/
- CyberSchool
  http://www.cyberschool.k12.or.us
  The Eugene, Oregon, public schools offers this virtual high school. Students can enroll from any geographic location.
- A Guide to E-mail-Based Volunteer Programs Designed to Help Students Master Challenging Mathematics, Science, and Technology http://www.ed.gov/pubs/emath/
- America Links Up: A Kids Online Teach-In—a public awareness and education campaign sponsored by a broad-based coalition of nonprofits, education groups, and corporations concerned with providing children with a safe and rewarding experience online. Buried in this Web site is information on Internet filter software.
  http://www.americalinksup.org
- American Library Association Parents page
  http://www.ala.org/parentspage/greatsites
- The Comprehensive Distance Education List of Resources
  http://online.parkland.cc.il.us/ramage
- Distance Education Clearinghouse
  http://www.uwex.edu/disted/home.html
- The Gifted and Talented Students Education Act of 1998
  http://www.cec.sped.org/pp/4127.htm
- The Learning Odyssey (a full Internet-based K-9 curriculum)
  http://www.tlo.net/

- National Parent Information Network (ERIC Clearinghouse)
  http://npin.org/
- Technology Inventory: A Catalog of Tools that Support Parents' Ability to Choose Online Content Appropriate for their Children. Site includes Cyberspace 911.
  http://www.research.att.com/projects/tech4kids/

Interesting Places for Kids

- Exploratorium: The museum of science, art, and human perception
  http://www.exploratorium.edu/
- FDA Kids Homepage
  http://www.fda.gov/oc/opacom/kids/
- KidsConnect, a question-answering, help and referral service to K-12 students on the Internet
  http://www.ala.org/ICONN/kidsconn.html
- Kids Web
  http://www.npac.syr.edu/textbook/kidsweb
- Kids Tools for Searching the Internet
  http://www.rcls.org/ksearch.htm
- The Smithsonian
  http://www.si.edu
- White House for Kids
  http://www.whitehouse.gov/WH/kids/html/kidshome.html
- Yahooligans: A Web Guide for Kids
  http://www.yahooligans.com/

Academic Disciplines

Arts

- Art Lesson Plans—Kentucky Educational Television
  http://www.ket.org/Education/CC/ArtOnAir/LessonPlans.html
- The Getty Education Institute for the Arts
  http://www.artsednet.getty.edu/ArtsEdNet/home.html
- Ferris University Museums, Galleries, Exhibits, and Festivals. Includes links to lots of museums, including *The Museum of Dirt.*
  http://http://www.ferris.edu/weblinks/arts/museums/

Ask the Expert

The Internet has lots of Web sites that respond to questions on science, although finding them can be quite a daunting task. There is a list at
http://www.halcyon.com/sciclub/kidquest.html

Computer Science

- USA Computing Olympiad
  http://usaco.uwp.edu
- The Computer Museum offers 170 interactive exhibits, including *The Virtual Fishtank* and the *Walk-Through Computer*. A good site for safety guidelines and Internet filters.
  http://www.tcm.org/

Humanities—Literature

Full-text e-texts

- ALEX
  http://sunsite.berkeley.edu/alex/ (NEW!)
- Project Gutenberg
  http://www.promo.net/pg/
- Carrie (a full-text electronic library)
  http://kuhttp.cc.ukans.edu/carrie/carrie_main.html
- The Complete Works of Shakespeare
  http://the-tech.mit.edu/Shakespeare/works.html
- Random Elizabethan Curse Generator
  http://www.tower.org/insult/

Children's Literature and Writing

- Children's Literature Web Guide
  http://www.ucalgary.ca/~dkbrown/
- Cyberkids
  http://www.cyberkids.com/
- Database of Award-Winning Children's Literature—NEW!
  http://www2.wcoil.com/~ellcrbcc/childlit.html
- Inkspot—a resource for writers
  http://www.inkspot.com/

Student Publishing

- Houghton Mifflin—A long list of links to student publishing sites
  http://www.eduplace.com/rdg/links/rdg_2.html

Mathematics (many of the science URLs include mathematics)

- The Math Forum
  http://forum.swarthmore.edu/
- Mega-Mathematics!
  http://www.c3.lanl.gov/mega-math/
- E-Math: A Guide to E-Mail-Based Volunteer Programs Designed to Help Students Master Challenging Mathematics, Science, and Technology (new URL)
  http://www.ed.gov/pubs/emath

Science

In science, more than any other discipline, technology can enhance the learning experience by providing cost-effective enrichment that would not be possible using other strategies.

- Amazing Space Web-Based Activities (NEW)
  http://oposite.stsci.edu/pubinfo/amazing-space.html
- Carolina Biological Supply Company Web site includes an interview with John Glenn, a re-play of the launch, and minute-by-minute coverage from NASA.
- Cool Science for Curious Kids (sponsored by The Howard Hughes Medical Institute) http://www.hhmi.org/coolscience/
- Eisenhower National Clearinghouse
  http://www.enc.org
- Explorer (a collection of educational resources for K–12 science and mathematics education)
  http://explorer.scrtec.org/explorer/
- The Mad Scientist Network
  http://www.madsci.org/ (New URL)
- Mathematics, Science, and Technology
  http://tiger.coe.missouri.edu/mathsci.html
- The Museum of Dirt
  http://www.planet.com/dirtweb/dirt.html
- NASA
  http://spacelink.msfc.nasa.gov/index.html
  http://mpfwww.jpl.nasa.gov (Mars Missions)

- Netfrog Title Page
  Directions and pictures of actual frog dissection. Virtual practice before the real thing.
  http://teach.virginia.edu/go/frog (new URL)
- The Science Learning Network (SLN)
  http://www.sln.org/index.html
- The Science Education Network—Young Scientist Program
  http://medicine.wustl.edu/~ysp/
- U. S. Geological Survey
  http://www.usgs.gov/education/

Social Studies/History

- History/Social Studies Web Site for K–12 Teachers (easy access to all major subtopics)
  http://www.execpc.com/~dboals/boals.html
- Kids Web—Social Studies. Under the categories of geography, government, and history are links to some of the most useful and interesting sources located on the Internet for K–12 social-cial studies curriculum. Worth browsing through lynx.
  http://www.npac.syr.edu/textbook/kidsweb
- National Council for the Social Studies
  http://www.ncss.org/
  http://www.ncss.org/links/links.html (lesson plans)
- The Oregon Trail
  http://www.isu.edu/~trinmich/Oregontrail.html
- MayaQuest (new URL)
  http://mayaquest.classroom.com/
- Mapmaking. The Mathematics of Cartography provides overviews of maps, map history, and the mathematical concepts behind maps. Solve some mathematically-oriented map problems, learn about different careers in cartography, and find links to map-related resources on the Web.
  http://math.rice.edu/~lanius/pres/map/
- USGS: Educational resources for cartography, geography, and related disciplines includes lesson plans and teacher's guide for grades K–3, 4–8, and 7–12.
  http://mapping.usgs.gov/www.html/1educate.html

Miscellaneous

- Bibliography on Evaluating Internet Resources
  http://refserver.lib.vt.edu/libinst/critTHINK.HTM
- The Center for Critical Thinking
  http://www.sonoma.edu/cthink/ (a busy site)

- Thinking Critically about Discipline-Based World Wide Web Resources
  http://www.library.ucla.edu/libraries/college/instruct/web/discp.htm
- Thinkquest
  http://io.advanced.org/thinkquest/

Web Sites with Information about Accessibility

- Accessibility Web Site:
  http://www.ed.gov/offices/OSERS/techpack.html
  This is an extensive document discussing computer accessibility for students with disabilities. It raises and answers a number of important questions about how to help students with disabilities and what is required to meet federal laws.

- Bobby. Bobby is a Web-based public service offered by CAST that analyzes Web pages for their accessibility to people with disabilities as well as their compatibility with various browsers.
  http://www.cast.org/bobby/
- Center for Communicative and Cognitive Disabilities
  Researches computer technology and special education resources for students with disabilities.
  http://www.uwo.ca/cccd
- DREAMMS for Kids
  http://www.dreamms.org
  Practical articles about new products, services, and events on assistive technology.

Obtaining Help

- IBASICS. An online course sponsored by the American Library Association.
  http://www.ala.org
- Newbie.NET Cyber Course.
  http://www.newbie.net/CyberCourse/
  A training site on the Web, especially for new Internet users ("newbies").
- Roadmap and Other Resources by Patrick Crispen.
  http://netsquirrel.com/index.html

Web Sites with Information about Evaluating Web Sites

Curriculum Connections: Integrating Internet Resources into the Curriculum
http://www.ala.org/ICONN/curricu2.html
These pages (from the American Association of School Librarians, a division of the American Library Association) provide information on rating Web sites. An evaluation form is included.

Evaluating Internet-Based Information

http://lme.mankato.msus.edu/class/629/cred.html

This page was prepared as part of a course on "Internet and the School Library Media Program" at Mankato State University. The page contains questions to ask when evaluating a Web site.

Evaluating Web Resources

http://www.science.widener.edu/~withers/webeval.htm

These pages are part of a module for teaching evaluation skills for Web resources that is used at Widener University's Wolfgram Memorial Library. Lists of questions to ask when evaluating Web pages are provided for five types of sites (advocacy, business, news, informational, and personal). The questions are grouped under five criteria: (1) authority; (2) accuracy; (3) objectivity; (4) currency; and (5) coverage.

Kathy Schrock's Guide for Educators: Critical Evaluation Surveys

by Kathleen Schrock (1997).

http://discoveryschool.com/schrockguide/eval.html

These pages contain links to Web sites related to Web site evaluation, and evaluation survey forms to be used at the elementary, middle, and secondary levels. An evaluation form is included.

Library Selection Criteria for WWW Resources

by Carolyn Caywood (1996). Originally appeared in *Public Libraries,* May/June 1996.

http://www6.pilot.infi.net/~carolyn/criteria.html

This page provides criteria for evaluating a Web site that are related to access, design, and content. The page also lists some additional references.

National School Network Site Evaluation

http://nsn.bbn.com/webeval/form1.htm

This site includes a feedback form for educators to provide comments on the educational value and design qualities of education Web sites. An evaluation form is included.

Thinking Critically about World Wide Web Resources

by Esther Grassian (1997). Los Angeles: UCLA College Library.

http://www.library.ucla.edu/libraries/college/instruct/web/critical.htm

This page presents criteria for evaluating Web sites in four areas: (1) content; (2) source and timeliness; (3) structure (i.e., organization and design); and (4) other.

WWW CyberGuide Ratings for Content Evaluation.

by Karen McLachlan (1996).

http://www.cyberbee.com/guide1.html

This worksheet, compiled by a high school media specialist, provides a checklist of items for evaluating a Web site. Categories are: (1) speed; (2) first impression; (3) ease of navigation; (4) use of graphics, sound, and videos; (5) content; (6) currency; and (7) availability of further information.

Note: **The Internet is a dynamic place, and changes take place rapidly and without warning. The Web sites listed above were checked recently. If a URL cannot be found, try again later. Hint: try truncating the URL by deleting part of the address on the far right side until you reach the domain name. For example, the URL http://www.lib.ncsu.edu/staff/morgan/alex/ might be truncated to http://www.lib.ncsu.edu/.**

© Sandra L. Berger

APPENDIX B: THE AUTONOMOUS LEARNER MODEL

by George T. Betts and Jolene K. Kercher

Introduction

Models of teaching which meet the diversified needs of all learners vary in form and substance. Some models may be applied to pull-out or resource settings, while others provide opportunities in the regular classroom. Furthermore, teachers are continuously faced with designing activities that are appropriate for different levels of ability and learning.

Additionally, although it is generally accepted that intellectually gifted, creatively gifted, and talented children are all in need of special help in developing their gifted potential (Feldhusen and Treffinger, 1980), these ideas are often ignored. Programs addressing not only the needs of all learners but, specifically, the needs of the gifted and talented, have not been extensively developed.

On closer examination, the major goals of gifted programs are to help gifted and talented learners realize their full career potential and to experience a sense of personal fulfillment or self-actualization in maturity (Feldhusen and Treffinger, 1980). Clark (1983) states that gifted youngsters learn early in life that their ideas and interests are quite different from their chronological peers. Once they are able to be together, they will begin to develop their potential for self-actualization. As a result, it is important to examine models for teaching that adapt easily to providing learning situations that address these considerations.

The Autonomous Learner Model

The Autonomous Learner Model (ALM) for the Gifted and Talented was developed specifically to meet the diversified cognitive, emotional, and social needs of learners. Originating at Arvada West High School in Arvada, Colorado, it is now successfully implemented in kindergarten through high school with the gifted and talented as well as *all* learners in the regular classrooms. Emphasis is placed on meeting the individualized needs of learners through the use of activities in the five major dimensions of the model:

- Orientation
- Individual Development
- Enrichment
- Seminars
- In-Depth Study

The **Orientation Dimension** of the model provides learners, teachers, administrators, and parents the opportunity to develop a foundation of the concepts of giftedness, talent, intelligence, creativity, and the development of potential. Learners discover more about themselves, their abilities, and what the program has to offer. Activities are presented to give learners an opportunity to work together as a group, to learn more about group process and interaction, and to learn more about the other people in the program.

During the Orientation Dimension, a series of inservices are presented for educators, parents, and involved community resource people. Again, emphasis is placed on the opportunities possible for learners, the responsibilities for learners and involved personnel, and information is given regarding the overall format of the Autonomous Learner Model.

The **Individual Development Dimension** of the model provides learners with the opportunity to develop the cognitive, emotional, social and physical skills, concepts, and attitudes necessary for lifelong learning. In other words, learners become autonomous in their learning.

Areas within this dimension include opportunities for the inter/intrapersonal development of the learner, the appropriate learning skills for lifelong learning, and the area of technology. Also, learners will participate in college and career involvement, the development of organizational skills and the importance of productivity skills, which are almost always used when information is presented in a variety of ways.

The **Enrichment Dimension** of the Autonomous Learner Model was developed to provide learners with opportunities to explore content that is usually not part of the everyday curriculum. There are two types of differentiation in this dimension. The first is the differentiation that is made to the regular curriculum by the teacher, and the second type is differentiated by the learner. Since most content in the schools is prescribed, the Autonomous Learner Model differentiated approach frees the teacher and the learners to go beyond the usual content, which may be surface learning for the learner or may already be known. The highest level of learning is manifested when a learner has the freedom to select and to pursue content or topics in their own style.

The **Seminar Dimension** of the model is designed to give learners in groups of three to five opportunities to research a topic, present it as a seminar to the rest of the class and other interested people, and to assess it by criteria selected and developed by the learners. A seminar is essential because it provides learners the chance to move from the role of a student to the role of a *learner*. If students are to become learners, they must have the opportunity for independent individual and group learning, which means having a structure that allows and promotes the developments of new knowledge for the individuals.

The **In-Depth Study Dimension** of the Autonomous Learner Model empowers learners to pursue areas of interest through the development of a long-term small group or individual in-depth study. The learners determine what will be learned, how it will be learned, how it will be presented, what facilitation will be necessary, what the final product will be and how the entire learning process will be assessed. In-depth studies are usually continued for a long period of time. Plans are developed by learners, in cooperation with the teacher/facilitator, content specialist, and mentors. The plans are then implemented and completed by the learners with presentations being made at appropriate times until the completion of the project. A final presentation and assessment is given to all who are involved and interested.

Philosophy

As the needs of learners are being met, they will develop into autonomous learners with the abilities to be responsible for the development, implementation, and assessment of their own learning.

When learners are involved in autonomous learning programming, they have the opportunity to pursue their own interests to whatever depth they wish. Becoming an autonomous learner is a difficult task, one which requires new orientations to learning and new development of skills, concepts, and attitudes which are necessary for continued learning.

As a result of investigations dictated by this philosophy, the Autonomous Learner Model was begun. The overall goal of the model is to provide learners with many different options to enable them to become independent, self-directed learners. In other words, by the time students graduate from high school, they should be autonomous learners (Betts and Knapp, 1981).

Today the Autonomous Learning Model is not only used with gifted and talented learners, but with *all* learners. It has proven to be effective in developing lifelong learning for all students. Although the Autonomous Learner Model was developed at the high school level, it has been modified and is presently used in grades K–12. The model is now being used throughout the United States and in Canada, Taiwan, Singapore, Australia, and New Zealand.

At the elementary level, the model is incorporated into the regular classroom for all learners and at the same time, an advanced Autonomous Learner Model is used with identified gifted and talented learners in pull-out or resource room programs. Within the middle school, the junior high school, and the high school, the Autonomous Learner Model is usually presented to learners as an elective course which, hopefully, will be offered for more than one year. The model has also been incorporated into the curriculum of most courses, including social studies, language arts, and science.

Basic Principles

The Autonomous Learner Model is based on basic principles that resulted from information gleaned from consultation with nationally recognized leaders, reviews of the literature on teaching and learning, the educational training of the teachers, and the experiences of learners, teachers, administrators, and parents working together to build a new approach which would meet the diversified needs of learners. The basic principles of the Autonomous Learner Model include:

- Emphasis is placed on the cognitive, emotional, social, and physical development of the individual.
- Self-esteem is encouraged and facilitated.
- Social skills are developed and enhanced.
- The regular classroom is the central support of programming.

- Pull-out/resource programs and special courses are necessary for total development.
- Curriculum is differentiated by the teacher(s).
- Curriculum is differentiated by the learner.
- Curriculum is based on the interests and passions of the learner.
- Learners are involved in guided open-ended learning experiences.
- Responsibility for learning is placed on the learner.
- Students need experiences which allow them to become lifelong learners.
- Teachers are facilitators of the learning process, as well as dispensers of knowledge.
- Learning is integrated and cross-disciplinary.
- Learners develop a broader foundation of basic skills.

THE AUTONOMOUS LEARNER MODEL

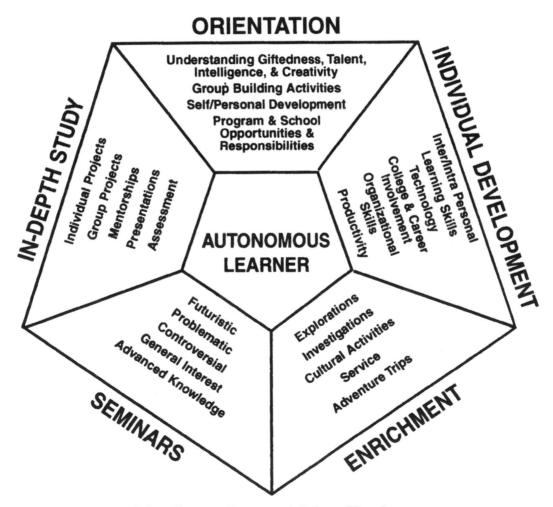

© by George Betts and Jolene Kercher

- Higher-level, critical, and creative thinking skills are integrated, reinforced, and demonstrated in the learning process.
- Learners develop appropriate questioning techniques.
- Varied and divergent responses are sought from the learners.
- Content topics are broad based, with emphasis on major themes, problems, issues, and ideas.
- Time and space restrictions for schools are removed for in-depth learning.
- Learners develop new and unique products.
- Learners use varied resources in the development of in-depth studies.
- Cultural activities and enrichment provide new and unique growth experiences.
- Seminars and in-depth studies are essential components of the learning process.
- Mentorships provide adult role-modeling, active support, and individual instruction and facilitation.
- Completions and presentations of in-depth studies are integral in the learning process.
- Assessment of self-development and of learner-created products is necessary and worthwhile.
- Changes within the model are continuous as new knowledge is added.
- *This list of basic principles is complete now but not for the future.*

Standards

The standards of the Autonomous Learner Model are fundamental to the program and underlie the basic principles for optimizing ability.

- Develop more positive self-concepts.
- Comprehend own abilities in relationship to self and society.
- Develop skills to interact effectively with peers, siblings, parents, and other adults.
- Increase knowledge in a variety of areas.
- Develop critical and creative thinking skills.
- Develop decision-making and problem-solving skills.
- Integrate activities which facilitate the cognitive, emotional, social, and physical development of the individual.
- Develop individual passion area(s) of learning.
- Demonstrate responsibility for own learning in and out of the school setting.
- Ultimately become responsible, creative, independent, lifelong learners.

These standards are necessarily broad. We do not want to define them more specifically because that is the task of each learner and each facilitator.

@1999 reprinted with permission from *Autonomous Learner Model: Optimizing Ability*

CONTRIBUTORS

Harriet Austin, Ph.D., a zoologist and educator, taught at the University of Wyoming before she began de-schooling her three sons. She devotes her time to research into preventative possibilities for juvenile diabetes and to teaching her children at home.

Amy Talbert Bailey, M.A., has more than twenty years of experience teaching English to academically gifted students, twice-exceptional students, and students with learning disabilities. She was a Mellon Fellow at the University of North Carolina at Chapel Hill and piloted the Fast Forward English program (college courses offered to high school seniors) for the University of North Carolina at Greensboro.

Richard Beck teaches journalism at St. Johnsbury Academy in Vermont.

George T. Betts, Ed.D., is professor of special education in the area of gifted and talented education and the director of the Center for the Education of the Gifted and Talented at the University of Northern Colorado in Greeley, Colorado. He is a former high school teacher of the gifted and cofounder of the Autonomous Learner Model of the Gifted and Talented. George is also a national and international consultant in the field of gifted education.

Michelle Bird is the dean of academics at St. Johnsbury Academy in Vermont.

Corinne Bees, M.Ed., is a special education department head at Prince of Wales Secondary in Vancouver. She has a master's in special education with a focus on learning disabilities, and founded the GOLD program for adolescents who are gifted and have learning disabilities.

Sandra Berger, M.Ed., is the author and editor of *College Planning for Gifted Students,* 2nd ed. She is the gifted education information specialist at the Council for Exceptional Children, ERIC Clearinghouse on Disabilities and Gifted Education. She writes a regular column on technology for *Understanding Our Gifted.*

Daphne Pereles Bowers, M.Ed., is the twice-exceptional resource teacher and a learning disabilities specialist for Cherry Creek School District in Englewood, Colorado. She also has taught middle school English and theater, a self-contained behavior disorder classroom, and more. She was the director of education at a psychiatric hospital for two years before beginning her work at Cherry Creek.

Diane Cooper, Ph.D., is the headmaster of St. Edward's School, a coed, college preparatory school in Vero Beach, Florida. She earned her M.Ed. in English and secondary education from the University of North Texas and holds a doctorate in private school administration from the University of San Francisco. She may be reached via e-mail at dcooper@steds.org.

Beth Crothers organizes home-schooling for her twice-exceptional son. She also originated the informative Britesparks Web site, at www.britesparks.com. Her e-mail address is beth@britesparks.com.

John Cummings is director of admissions at St. Johnsbury Academy in Vermont.

Ameli Cyr is a student and an avid horseback rider. Her artwork has appeared in *Rocky Mountain Horse Connection.*

Benjamin Cyr is a high school student whose writing has been published in *The Chicago Tribune KidNews, Dragon Tales, Highly Gifted Children, Why Not?* and more. He is at work on a forthcoming book of poetry titled *Relentless: Poems from the Edge of Childhood.* His e-mail address is benjamincyr@hotmail.com.

Ronald Davis, author of *The Gift of Dyslexia,* was labeled ineducably mentally retarded as a child. Despite his inability to read, he became an engineer in the aerospace industry, a successful businessman, and a sculptor. Tests showed an IQ of 169 when he was twenty-seven, but he didn't learn to read until age thirty-eight, when he discovered the root causes of his own dyslexia. Training and services using Davis Dyslexia Correction® are now available throughout the world through Davis Dyslexia Association. His e-mail address is RonDavis@dyslexia.com.

Lois Easton works for the Eagle Rock School, a coeducational boarding school sponsored by the Honda Corporation, located in Estes Park, Colorado. Her e-mail address is leaston@psd.k12.co.us.

Jeffrey Freed, M.A.T., a therapist and consultant in Evergreen, Colorado, wrote *Right-Brained Children in a Left-Brained World* with Laurie Parsons. As an educational therapist and consultant, he works exclusively with ADD and gifted children.

Howard Gardner, Ph.D., has written extensively on multiple intelligence theory. His books include *Frames of Mind, Extraordinary Minds,* and many more. He is professor of education and codirector of Project Zero at Harvard University.

Barbara Priddy Guyer, Ph.D., is a parent/professional and the author of the landmark book, *The Pretenders.*

Thom Hartmann, Ph.D., formerly worked as executive director of a residential treatment facility for children and adolescents, and is the father of a child diagnosed with ADD. He has written many books, including *Healing ADD: Simple Exercises that Will Change Your Daily Life, ADD Success Stories,* and *ADD: A Different Perception.* He can be reached via e-mail at ThomHartmann@cs.com.

L. Dennis Higgins, Ed.D., teaches twice-exceptional children for the Albuquerque Public Schools in Albuquerque, New Mexico. He is also an adjunct professor in the College of Education at the University of New

Mexico. He served as the project coordinator for the Twice-Exceptional Child Project, a collaborative project between the University of New Mexico and the Albuquerque Public Schools.

Rebecca Hutchins, O.D., F.C.O.V.D., is a behavioral and developmental optometrist in Boulder and Niwot, Colorado.

Kiesa Kay, B.S.J., M.A., wrote *Thunder Is the Mountain's Voice.* She is the mother of two creative, highly gifted children. She may be reached at kiesakay@email.msn.com.

Kevin Kearney, the father of two profoundly gifted children, cowrote *Accidental Genius* with his wife, Cassidy Kearney.

Jolene Knapp Kercher is cocreator of the Autonomous Learner Model. She coordinated a high school gifted and talented program for twenty-three years, was named 1994 CAGT Teacher of the Year, and serves as a consultant and presenter. She currently acts as a gifted and talented resource teacher for Jefferson County Public Schools (Colorado).

Judith Giencke Kimball, Ph.D., OTR/L, FAOTA, is a professor and founding chair of the department of occupational therapy at the University of New England. Her e-mail address is JKimball@mailbox.une.edu.

Carol Stock Kranowitz, M.A., is the author of *The Out-of-Sync Child: Recognizing and Coping with Sensory Integration Disorder* and *101 Activities for Kids in Tight Spaces.* She has taught classes in music, movement, and drama since 1976. Her e-mail address is ckranowitz@aol.com.

Thomas Lovett is the chairperson of the department of English at St. Johnsbury Academy in Vermont.

Abigail Marshall has a degree in applied behavioral sciences and is the parent of two highly gifted children. Her older child is dyslexic and excels in math and computer graphic arts. She manages the *Dyslexia, the Gift* Web site at http://www.dyslexia.com/. Her e-mail address is abigail@dyslexia.com.

Stewart Matthiesen is an eighteen-year-old college senior at Whitman College in Walla Walla, Washington. He is obtaining a double major in astrophysics and English. After graduating, he plans to join the Peace Corps and later continue his education. Stewart can be reached by e-mail at lynx@olympus.net

Marea Nemeth-Taylor, Ph.D., works with twice-exceptional children daily as an educational pathologist. Her e-mail address is mareat@magna.com.au.

M. Elizabeth Nielsen, Ph.D., was a principal researcher on Project REACH, a collaborative project between the University of New Mexico and Albuquerque Public Schools. She is a professor at the University of New Mexico.

Margi Nowak, Ph.D., is a cultural anthropologist and author of several works on liminal people in society (e.g., refugees and persons with disabilities). These include *Tibetan Refugees: Youth and the New Generation of Meaning,* published by Rutgers University Press. Dr. Nowak also served as the founding editor of *Connections,* the newsletter of the Washington State Tourette Syndrome Association.

Laurie Parsons, formerly an award-winning radio reporter, currently is executive producer for three of Denver's top AM news-talk stations. She cowrote *Right-Brained Children in a Left-Brained World* with Jeffrey Freed.

John J. Ratey, M.D., is the coauthor of *Driven to Distraction, Answers to Distraction,* and *Shadow Syndromes: The Mild Forms of Major Mental Disorders that Sabotage Us.* He works as assistant professor of psychiatry at Harvard Medical School and executive director of research at Medfield State Hospital in Massachusetts.

Sally M. Reis, Ph.D., is a professor at the University of Connecticut. She cowrote *The Schoolwide Enrichment Model: A Comprehensive Plan for Educational Excellence; The Complete Triad Trainer's Inservice Manual; Secondary Triad Model: A Practical Plan for Implementing Gifted Education at the Junior and Senior High School Levels;* and *Triad Reader,* with Joseph Renzulli. She is the president of the National Association for Gifted and Talented. Her e-mail address is reis@uconn.edu.

Marlo Payne Rice, M.S., assists families as the director of the Center for Education Enrichment, 2885 Aurora Ave., Boulder, Colorado. Her e-mail address is smrice@mindspring.com.

Michael Rios is an independent computer consultant and the father of three highly asynchronous children. He is a volunteer counselor for parents with highly asynchronous children and has conducted extensive research in the field. He can be reached at mikerios@juno.com.

Deborah Robson, M.F.A., is a professional writer and the mother of a brilliant, twice-exceptional daughter. Her e-mail address is DRRobson@compuserve.com.

Christine Schulze, J. D., works as the executive director of the Concordia Language Villages. She can be reached via e-mail at clv@cord.edu.

Ken Seeley, Ph.D., who has done extensive research into giftedness and underachievement, is the executive director of the Colorado Foundation for Families and Children.

Linda Kreger Silverman, Ph.D., recently received the Lifetime Achievement Award from the Colorado Association for Gifted and Talented. She is the director of the Gifted Development Center in Denver, and she edited *Counseling the Gifted and Talented.* She may be reached via e-mail at gifted@gifteddevelopment.com.

Jim Sinclair founded Autism Network International, an e-mail exchange for individuals who have autism. He has been a guest lecturer at numerous conferences and a featured guest on television programs. He bases his work in Syracuse, New York. The ANI Web site address is http://www.ani.ac, and Jim Sinclair may be reached at http://members.xoom.com/JimSinclair.

Lee Singer continually advocates for gifted children through the Internet, conferences, and community activism.

Cynthia Stanton teaches and counsels students at St. Johnsbury Academy, a Blue Ribbon School of Excellence in Vermont. Her e-mail address is cstanton@stj.k12.vt.us.

Beverly Trail, M.A., is a G/T facilitator and twice-exceptional consultant for Littleton Public Schools. She has nineteen years' experience in gifted education teaching gifted students and facilitating gifted programs. Beverly is treasurer of the Colorado Association for Gifted and Talented Executive Council and the proud parent of two gifted children. Her e-mail address is btrail@lps.k12.co.us.

Meredith Warshaw is the co-list owner of the GT-Special e-mail list for families with gifted/special needs children, and the mother of an eight-year-old son who is many-times special. Her e-mail is mwarshaw@alum.mit.edu.

Susan Winebrenner, M.A., leads teacher-training workshops throughout the country. She has twenty years of experience as a teacher of gifted children. Her books include *Teaching Gifted Kids in the Regular Classroom* and *Teaching Kids with Learning Difficulties in the Regular Classroom.*

Ellen Winner, Ph.D., is a professor of psychology at Boston College and senior research associate at Harvard Project Zero. She is the author of *Invented Worlds: The Psychology of the Arts; The Point of Words: Children's Understanding of Metaphor and Irony;* and *Gifted Children: Myths and Realities.*

Tristram Dodge Wood, M.Ed., is the director of academic support at The Peddie School in Hightstown, New Jersey. His e-mail address is TWOOD@peddie.org.

PERMISSIONS

This book began as a guest-editing project for *Highly Gifted Children,* the publication of the Hollingworth Center for Highly Gifted Children. Consequently, initial versions of some selections first appeared in the Fall 1998 issue, Vol. 12, No. 2, guest-edited by Kiesa Kay: "Asynchrony and Mental Health: A Model for Understanding the Relationship," by Marlo Payne Rice; "The Two-Edged Sword of Compensation," by Linda Kreger Silverman; "Scholastic Gardens: A Look at My Educational Experience," by Benjamin Cyr; "Dyslexia and the Seeds of Genius," by Ronald D. Davis and Abigail Marshall; "A Profile of a Twice-Exceptional Program: A Personal Journey," by Dr. Dennis Higgins; and "Special Ed or Gifted? It May Be Hard to Tell," by Susan Winebrenner. The writers created and modified the articles for the dual purposes of the book and the newsletter at the request of Kiesa Kay. We would like to thank the Hollingworth Center for Gifted Children for initiating interest in this project. The Hollingworth Center can be reached at 827 Central Avenue #282, Dover, NH 03920-2506, or by telephone at 207/665-3767.

Margi Nowak's article was adapted from its original form, on the Web site for New Horizons for Learning Center at 2128 38th Avenue E., Seattle, WA 98112, http://www.newhorizons.org. Thom Hartmann's essay was published initially in *Attention Deficit Disorder: A Different Perception,* by Underwood Books of Grass Valley, California. Howard Gardner's chapter is from *Extraordinary Minds,* copyright © 1997 by Howard Gardner, reprinted by permission of Basic Books, a division of Perseus Books, L.L.C. Ellen Winner's essay was from *Gifted Children: Myths and Realities,* copyright © 1996 by Ellen Winner, reprinted by permission of Basic Books, a member of Perseus Books, L.L.C. Sandra Berger's "Gifted Students with Learning Disabilities" was adapted from *College Planning for Gifted Students,* second edition revised (1998) by Sandra L. Berger, Reston, Va.: The Council for Exceptional Children, and adapted with permission. John J. Ratey's "The Social Brain" was adapted with permission from his work on his forthcoming book, *The User's Guide to the Brain,* Pantheon Books, April 2000. Michael Rios's article also will appear in *Understanding Our Gifted,* a national magazine for parents and educators of gifted youths.

Errata for *Uniquely Gifted*

Below please find a corrected Table of Contents with pagination.

The title page should read "Uniquely Gifted: Identifying and Meeting the Needs of the Twice-Exceptional Student" edited by Kiesa Kay.

In addition, we advise our readers that they may write to Avocus Publishing if they would like expanded bibliographies for: "Responding to the Needs of Twice-Exceptional Learners: A School District and University's Collaborative Approach" by M. Elizabeth Nielsen and L. Dennis Higgins, and "When Individuals With High IQ Experience Sensory Integration Or Sensory Systems Modulation Problems" by Judith Giencke Kimball.

We apologize for the inconvenience and hope that you enjoy the book.